The handbook of project-based management

THE HENLEY MANAGEMENT SERIES

Series Adviser: Professor Bernard Taylor

Also available in the McGraw-Hill Henley Management Series:

MANAGING INFORMATION
Information systems for today's general manager
A V Knight and D J Silk   ISBN 0-07-707086-0

THE NEW GENERAL MANAGER
Confronting the key challenge of today's organization
Paul Thorne   ISBN 0-07-707083-6

THE COMPETITIVE ORGANIZATION
Managing for organizational excellence
Gordon Pearson   ISBN 0-07-707480-7

TOTAL CAREER MANAGEMENT
Strategies for creating management careers
Frances A Clark   ISBN 0-07-707558-7

CREATING THE GLOBAL COMPANY
Successful internationalization
Colin Coulson-Thomas   ISBN 0-07-707599-4

Details of these and other titles in the series are available from:

The Product Manager, Professional Books, McGraw-Hill Book Company
Europe, Shoppenhangers Road, Maidenhead, Berkshire SL6 2QL
Telephone 0628 23432   Fax 0628 770224

The handbook of project-based management

Improving the processes for achieving strategic objectives

J. Rodney Turner

McGRAW-HILL BOOK COMPANY

London · New York · St Louis · San Francisco · Auckland
Bogotá · Caracas · Hamburg · Lisbon · Madrid · Mexico
Milan · Montreal · New Delhi · Panama · Paris · San Juan
São Paulo · Singapore · Sydney · Tokyo · Toronto

Published by
McGRAW-HILL Book Company Europe
Shoppenhangers Road, Maidenhead, Berkshire SL6 2QL, England
Telephone 0628 23432
Fax 0628 770224

British Library Cataloguing in Publication Data
Turner, J. Rodney
    Handbook of Project-based Management:
    Improving the Processes for Achieving
    Strategic Objectives. – (Henley
    Management Series)
    I. Title   II. Series
658

ISBN 0-07-707656-7

Library of Congress Cataloging-in-Publication Data
Turner, J. Rodney (John Rodney)
    The handbook of project-based management: improving the
    processes for achieving strategic objectives / J. Rodney Turner.
        p.   cm.—(The Henley management series)
    Includes bibliographical references and index.
    ISBN 0-07-707656-7
    1. Industrial project management.   I. Title.   II. Series.
HD69.P75T85   1993
658.4′04—dc20   92-23429

234 CUP 9543

Typeset by BookEns Ltd, Baldock, Herts.
and printed and bound in Great Britain at the University Press, Cambridge

To Edward:
who was conceived and born at the same time as the
material on which this book is based

Contents

Foreword

Books about project management give a static impression, a feeling that the book proposes to encapsulate a fund of knowledge and experience, a body of knowledge, which can be absorbed to give the capability of managing a project effectively.

After reading these books, I am usually disappointed – not because useful information and insights are not given – but because expectations are not realizable in practice. Dr Turner's handbook gives at once a touch of realism. It is about new approaches to general management based on projects. It is about managing change – a very challenging and dynamic endeavour. It is about managing that change through *projects*, the emerging idea that widens the scope of project management.

Project management has developed quite markedly over the last 20 years, from a systems-oriented methodology, through 'goal orientation', to project-based management. From a topic in which computers were pre-eminent, to one in which people, interpersonal and inter-group relationships predominate.

There has been a broadening of the definition of projects, and a broadening of the scope of project management. Management by projects, the theme of the INTERNET World Congress in Vienna in 1990, was a signpost to the new directions in which project management was moving.

Dr Turner's book, *The Handbook of Project-Based Management*, catches the tide of development trends. It is current, relevant and timely.

I was pleased to see that the single point contact – the emphasis on the project manager – is maintained. Having gone through the mistaken phase myself of believing that systems would, in the end, make the role of the project manager redundant, I support the unified theory, which Turner quotes from Exodus 20.3 'Thou shalt have no other gods before me', indicating that the reality of the matrix organization has been anticipated, but the prime authority always remained with the Great Project Manager in the Sky.

That seems an appropriate point for me to admit a small regret that male chauvinism prevails yet again. The skills in the management of change in the modern world are by no means confined to the male. There should be more female project managers. Their success in computer systems development and new project development has been well proven.

Quality is given a welcome and effective treatment. This is an area requiring great care and attention, and is a high risk area for a project manager, as quality issues almost always involve cost and time effects.

I find the concept of 'zero defects' difficult, partly because one person's defect may be acceptable to others, and partly because 'customer requirements' are not fixed, nor easily defined. Sufficient to remember that 'The best is the enemy of the good'. Nevertheless, the section on quality includes the salient issues and will be found very useful.

The sections on management procedures come towards the end of the book, in Part 5, and this is the right emphasis for the 1990s. This implies the view, which I support strongly, that if one gets the issues in Parts 2, 3, and 4 wrong, the best systems in the world will not work. If the issues in Parts 2, 3, and 4 are right, the Part 5 matters will not constitute a problem in themselves.

I was particularly pleased to read the section on international projects in Part 6, and the inclusion of cultural factors researched by G. Hofstede. This is required reading by everyone involved in international projects and change projects across cultural boundaries – very relevant in today's changing world.

The book includes a fund of information across the whole spectrum of contemporary project management as applied to the management of change. The material is presented without pedantry or oversimplification, yet in a form that makes it easily assimilated. It is readable page after page, holding the interest – a rare quality for a book with this depth and breadth of information, which could so easily have become superficial or academic. Key issues, checklists, and practical comments are readily found on any topic for reference.

The book has much for anyone engaged in the management of change and management of projects. It will help experienced project managers to understand more fully what they often do by instinct, and hence improve their performance.

Aspiring project managers, on the other hand, will be helped to understand the basics of the subject – and most importantly – to get the priorities right.

It will be valuable, too, for all involved in the provision of project management services; in the vital areas of planning and scheduling, cost control, cost engineering, materials management, contracts management and so many others, helping them to understand the role of the project manager, and advising on how to improve the quality of the information and of the service which they supply.

The book will be on my bookshelf and is required reading for all involved and interested in the management of change and the emerging concepts for effective management in the nineties.

Eric Gabriel
Consultant Project Manager
Vice-President, Association of Project Managers

Preface

The first book in the Henley Management Series (Paul Thorne, *The New General Manager*, McGraw-Hill, 1989) identified the rapid, structural changes taking place within modern organizations, and how this is leading to a new brand of general manager. This rapid change has been brought about by an explosion in the rate of change of technology and communication, and the access of managers to information. The second book in the series (Tony Knight and David Silk, *Managing Information*, McGraw-Hill, 1990) explained the key role of information to business success.

Both of these books identified a parallel development, driven by the rapid change in modern organizations: project-based management has become the new general management. The bureaucratic organization, introduced in the nineteenth century to provide efficiency through permanence, can no longer respond to the competitive environment of the 1990s. Organizations must now be flexible to respond quickly and effectively to changing circumstance, and this requires that new general managers are able to manage change through projects. This will involve them in:

- the management of a portfolio of projects, through a team of project managers working for them
- the management of individual projects, as project managers, through teams of people who do not normally respond directly to them
- the management of the interface between these projects, the rest of the organization, and the external environment.

This change is not limited to a few, small organizations. British Telecom has identified that half its operations are project based. Translate this to the economy as a whole, and the annual spend on projects in the United Kingdom is £250 billion, and this consumes 27 million man-years of effort.

The management of projects has therefore become a skill that general managers require in their portfolio of skills alongside more traditional disciplines, such as accounting and finance, marketing and strategic management. This book aims to provide a comprehensive guide to the discipline for general managers, and will enable them to:

- define projects required to achieve their business objectives
- manage the work and organization required to achieve them

- achieve their objectives to the required specification, and at a time and price that make the investment worth while
- undertake the work of different stages of a project
- ensure timely and effective completion of the project
- understand their role as managers of the project in building and maintaining the team
- compare the application of project management in different circumstances.

It describes a structured approach to the management of projects, and is illustrated throughout by reference to real examples of projects with which the author has been associated. It is designed to be read through to provide an overview of the approach, or to be referred to as a handbook to give specific advice on how to manage certain aspects of projects, and the tools and techniques to use. The overall model of the approach (Figure 2.5, page 29), together with the contents page, should help readers to find their way around the book, and to dip into specific chapters. The book is intended for busy managers, as well as for more formal study by students on programmes leading to an MBA or an MSc in a project-related subject.

Part One defines projects, and introduces the structured approach to project management described in the book. Part Two deals with the context of projects. It defines projects, describes why companies undertake them and the impact they have on the organization, and explains how to adopt strategies for successful projects. Part Three describes the first set of methods of the approach: the objectives of project management, i.e. how to define the projects required to achieve business objectives, and how to manage the scope of work required, the project organization to deliver them, the constraints of quality, cost and time, and the risk inherent in projects. Part Four describes a second set of methods of the approach: the management processes required to undertake projects. It follows the project management life cycle and shows how the objectives are managed at each stage. Part Five introduces further tools and techniques covering specific management systems and procedures, including project administration, the use of computer systems, and the role and skills of the project manager. Part Six concludes the book by describing some specific applications of the management of projects. It covers projects from different stages of the product life cycle, various industries and sectors, different sizes of project, and projects involving international collaboration.

The ideas expressed in this book are those of the author and his contributors. They do not necessarily represent the views of Henley Management College or its agents.

Acknowledgements

The content of this book is based largely on my experience as a project manager and consultant. I am grateful to the organization that provided my experience, including my employers (ICI, Coopers & Lybrand, Henley Management College), and those whom I have advised as a consultant. Through Henley, I have had contact with many practising project managers and organizations such as the Engineering Construction Industry Training Board and the Association of Project Managers, all of whom have provided insights. My clients I cannot mention, both because they are too many and because I need to preserve their confidence. However, I should like to thank Steve Kenny for the pleasure of working on his projects, and for providing the model on which the running case study in this book is based. (Although the case study is based on a project on which I worked, the company in which it is set is totally fictitious.)

I also wish to thank the people mentioned below, who contributed distance learning material – through course material or through articles written jointly – for courses at Henley Management College: John Dingle (Oxford College of Petroleum Studies); Lynn Thurloway, Frances Clark, Alex Lord, Mahen Tampoe, Debbie Carlton, Susan Foreman and Padma Nathan (Henley Management College); Peter Morris (Bovis and Templeton College, Oxford); Julie Hartley (University of Central England); Alan Oliver (SD-Scicon); Simon Bissel (British Aerospace); Bob Thomas (W.S. Atkins); Morten Fangel (Management Consultant); Nick Aked and Roger Sharp (Coopers & Lybrand Deloitte); Paddy Lewis and Martin Samphire (Nichols Associates); Richard Morreale (Life Cycle Management Systems); Janice Light and Gordon Edge (Scientific Generics Ltd); David Topping (Peter Brett Associates); Steven Kirk (Brown & Root Vickers); Anne French (Farnborough College); and Svein Arne Jessen (The Norwegian School of Management). Their contributions have, with acknowledgement, been incorporated to a greater or lesser extent into corresponding chapters in this book.

I should like to thank all the people who have given support and advice while I have been writing the text, and in particular Kate Allen the editor and the reviewers whom McGraw-Hill asked to peruse early proposals and manuscripts. Their comments and advice have been very valuable.

As great as the contribution of all these people has been, it is small compared to that of Kristoffer Grude, Tor Haug and Erling Andersen. Their book, *Goal Directed Project Management*, the English edition of which I wrote, provided the embryonic structure and approach of this book. However, their contribution has gone further: a section of Chapter 3 is derived from a paper I wrote jointly with Tor, and I have spent many hours with Kristoffer sharing his experience and philosophy of project management.* To acknowledge the direct contribution of these authors would require repeated statements in Chapters 2, 4, 5, 6, 7, 14 and 18. To acknowledge their indirect contribution would require statements on almost every page.

Finally, I would like to thank the following people who have contributed to this book in their own way: Beverley, my wife, who gave me the space to work on my projects; John Logan, who provided the opportunity to develop the material of my previous book into the present structure; and David Birchall, since without my liaison with Henley I would not have had the oppportunity to develop the material or approach.

* Mr Grude and Mr Haug are partners with Coopers & Lybrand Management Consultants in Oslo. They were founding partners of PSO, which merged with Coopers & Lybrand in 1984. Previously Mr Grude was managing director of Data Logic, software consultants in Oslo, and Mr Haug was organizational development manager with Norsk Folk Insurance Company. Professor Andersen was until 1991 Dean of the College of Computer Sciences in Oslo. He is a visiting professor at the Norwegian School of Management.

PART ONE
INTRODUCTION

1
Projects and their management

1.1 Managing change through projects

Projects touch all our lives, in working and social environments. However, since the Industrial Revolution, most managers have not been directly involved in the management of projects. Bureaucracies have been viewed as providing an efficient, stable and certain environment in which to conduct business.[1] Change was mistrusted. Managing change was limited to specialist, usually technical, functions within the organization, and its introduction was carefully controlled.

That has now changed. Change is endemic, brought on by an explosion in the development of technology and communications. Rather than being the preferred style of management, bureaucracies are viewed as restricting an organization's ability to respond to change and thereby to maintain a competitive edge.

The last 30 years characterized this changing emphasis. The 1960s were years of mass production. Manufacturing companies strove to increase output, and production methods and systems were introduced to facilitate that process. High production rates were achieved, but at the expense of quality. During the 1970s, in an attempt to differentiate themselves, companies strove for quality. By imposing uniformity, and by restricting their product range, managers could achieve quality while maintaining high production. In the 1980s, the emphasis shifted to variety. Customers now wanted their purchases to be different from those of their neighbours. No two Granadas coming off the production line were the same, and non-smokers would rather have a coin-tray in place of the ash-tray. Companies introduced flexible manufacturing systems to provide variety, while maintaining quality and high production. Now, in the 1990s, customers want novelty. No one buying a new product wants last year's model. Product development times and market windows are shrinking, requiring new products to be introduced quickly and effectively. Organizations must adopt flexible structures to respond to the changing environment.

In this new environment, all managers – either by themselves, or through teams of people working for them – must manage change through projects. Project-based management has become the new general management through which organizations respond to change to develop and exploit markets ahead of their competitors,[2,3] and hence project management is a skill that all managers need in their portfolio, alongside more traditional disciplines. This book provides the general manager with a structured approach to the management of projects.

Let us start by defining projects, explaining the essential features they have that demand a management approach different from the routine work of an organization, and considering what the elements of that approach might be. In Chapter 2 the structured approach to the management of projects – which forms the basis of this book – will be introduced.

1.2 What are projects?

Projects come in many guises. There are traditional major projects from heavy engineering industries such as shipbuilding, aerospace, construction and energy. These are significant endeavours involving large, dedicated teams, and often requiring the collaboration of several sponsoring organizations. On the other hand, the projects with which most of us are involved are smaller. Typically, projects at work are smaller: engineering or construction projects to build new facilities; maintenance of existing facilities; implementation of new technologies or computer systems; research, development and product launches; or management development or training programmes. Social environment projects include: moving house; organizing an event in the community; or going on holiday. From the very largest, to the very smallest, what is the essential feature that differentiates projects from other activities?

Definitions

The simplest definition of a project is 'something which has a beginning and an end'.[4] This definition is a useful start, but needs qualification. First, many projects do not have a measurable beginning; they crystallize over a period. Secondly, the daily production in a baked bean factory can be said to meet this definition. However, when repeated day after day, it is not a project. Finally, there is a sense that there must be more to projects. Several other definitions have been attempted:

a human endeavour which creates change; is limited in time and scope; has mixed goals and objectives; involves a variety of resources; and is unique[5];

a complex effort to achieve a specific objective within a schedule and budget target, which typically cuts across organizational lines, is unique, and is usually not repetitive within the organization[6];

a one-time, unique endeavour by people to do something that has not been done that way before.[7]

Initially, I was amused by the tautology of the third definition, but we shall shortly see that this comes closest to capturing the essence of projects. The above definitions have several common threads. They mention:

– complex endeavours to do work which creates change
– mixed objectives, especially constraints of quality, cost and time
– the involvement of people often from throughout the organization
– uniqueness.

However, when we ask why this is different from routine operations, we find it is only the fourth of these that is different.

Projects vs operations

I once worked worked with a company, in the food industry, who were offended by these definitions of projects:

1. Operations create change, and of two types: the processing of raw beans and ingredients into cooked and canned baked beans is change; and operations continually enhance their performance through a process called *Habitual Incremental Improvement* (HII).
2. Operations are subject to mixed objectives and conflicting priorities, particularly time constraints, production targets, budgets and quality control.
3. Operations involve a variety of resources, usually under one manager's command, but often from across the organization.
4. However, operations are not unique: they exist to perform repetitive tasks.

The one parameter by which projects differ from operations is the level of uniqueness. Human endeavours range from totally repetitive to totally unique. At one extreme is the production of baked beans; at the other is the construction of the Thames Barrier. In between lie endeavours such as shipbuilding, space shuttle launches, and the development of new recipes for canned food. Looking at the two extremes, we see what difference the one parameter of uniqueness creates (Table 1.1).

Table 1.1 Projects vs operations

Projects	Operations
Unique	Repetitive
Finite	Eternal
Revolutionary change	Evolutionary change
Disequilibrium	Equilibrium
Unbalanced objectives	Balanced objectives
Transient resources	Stable resources
Flexibility	Stability
Effectiveness	Efficiency
Goals	Roles
Risk and uncertainty	Experience

1. Projects are unique; operations are repetitive.
2. Projects therefore exist for a limited period; operations create a lasting, stable environment (the first definition above becomes a necessary, but not sufficient, condition for a project).
3. Projects therefore bring about revolutionary improvements; operations improve by evolution.
4. To bring about revolutionary change, projects must create a state of disequilibrium; operations evolve always in equilibrium.
5. To create disequilibrium, project managers deliberately set out to disrupt the status quo (by unbalancing opposing forces); the operations manager's purpose is to maintain equilibrium by balancing conflicting requirements.
6. Being finite, projects use transient (novel) teams of people, whereas operations build stable (permanent) teams.

The above features create four major cultural differences:

1. The operations environment is stable, whereas the project environment is flexible. This is the requirement of the new competitive age.
2. Operations, through HII, become increasingly more efficient, whereas in a project, having no precedent, the team must look to be effective in achieving its objectives. A project can be efficient at delivering the wrong things; that is not effective.
3. In operations, people fulfil roles defined by precedent, and so can lose sight of their objectives. Project teams must be goal oriented, which may require individuals to fulfil several roles.

4. Projects carry considerable risk. Having no previous experience, we are uncertain whether we can achieve our targets. In operations, because we have previous experience, we are more certain that we shall continue to deliver targets we have achieved often in the past. Projects are risk management; operations are status-quo management.

Table 1.1 defines a project. Many themes of the definitions above appear. However,if projects carry considerable risk, why do we undertake them? The answer to this question exposes a shortcoming in Table 1.1 which needs to be resolved before proposing a complete definition of a project.

1.3 Why have projects?

Table 1.1 focuses on the work of both projects and operations, and thereby implies that the work is done for its own sake. That is not the case. The work is done to produce a product, and that product is expected to deliver some benefit or purpose. In the case of a project that purpose may be:

- a business purpose, for example to increase profitability, efficiency, turnover or employment;
- a social purpose, for example to achieve relaxation or enjoyment, or to raise funds for a worthy cause;
- a humanitarian purpose, for example to provide disaster relief.

We undertake projects because we cannot produce, or achieve the benefit, by doing routine things, and the expected benefits from doing the project outweigh the risks. It is common for people to say that projects are successful if the work is completed within constraints of quality, cost and time. The final assessment is more complex than this simple statement implies.[8] However, whether or not the project achieves its purpose is far more important, because achieving beneficial change is the primary reason a project is undertaken. On the other hand, the change only has a value at a certain time and price, and so achieving it on time, and within the budget, will affect the assessment. We shall return to the assessment of the success of projects, and strategies for reducing risk and uncertainty in Chapter 5.

1.4 Definition of a project

To be complete, the definition of a project should therefore reflect this successful achievement of the purpose. The approach to the management of projects derived in this book is based upon the following definition of a project (Figure 1.1):

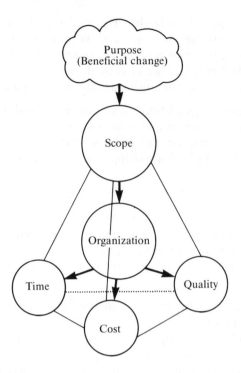

Figure 1.1 The five objectives of projects

>an endeavour in which human, material and financial resources are organized
>in a novel way, to undertake a unique scope of work, of given specification,
>within constraints of cost and time, so as to achieve beneficial change defined
>by quantitative and qualitative objectives.

Delete 'in a novel way', and replace 'unique' with 'repetitive', and this
definition might apply to operations. Hence, the essential features of a
project are that it is a unique piece of work, undertaken using a novel
organization to deliver beneficial change. These features imply that projects
carry considerable uncertainty and risk, that a key role for project managers
is integration of the novel organization, and that they are finite in duration.

Projects, facilities, and products

There is an important point implied in the above discussion: that is, the
difference between a project, the facility it delivers, and the product produced by the facility (Figure 1.2).

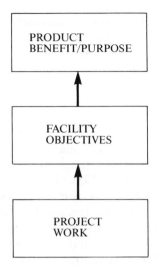

Figure 1.2   Projects, facilities and products

Products are what the organization is in business to make or sell, as stated in its mission. They may be manufactured goods or services. The products generate revenues and therefore deliver the purpose or benefit of the project.

Facilities are required to produce the products. Facilities may be factories and equipment, product designs, computer systems, distribution networks, management processes, or organized groups of people. A facility is the product that a project delivers; it is defined by the quantitative and qualitative objectives of the project, and its completion marks the end of the project.

Projects are undertaken by organizations in order to deliver, construct, maintain or renew facilities. They are the vehicles, consisting of a scope of work and a project organization, required to deliver facilities.

We should also remember that *routine operations* are required to operate the facility, after the completion of the project, to produce the product.

1.5 What is project management?

The first, direct, answer to this question is that it is the process by which a project is completed successfully. A second is to consider whether this can be developed into a structured management approach. In answering the direct question, there are two views:

- the traditional view defines project management in terms of a body of knowledge of tools and techniques;
- the alternative view proposed here defines project management in terms of the management processes required to undertake a project as defined in the previous section.

The body of knowledge

Project management, as a modern management discipline, is about 40 years old. Its beginnings are sometimes measured from the Atlas Project in the United States, starting in 1953.[9] In those 40 years, a considerable body of knowledge has built up of effective tools and techniques.[10,11] However, there is little formal guidance of how and when to apply them, because the body of knowledge is only just forming into a structured approach. There exists within the body of knowledge two methodologies, the *critical path method* (CPM) and the *cost specification* (C/SPEC).

1. CPM was developed independently in the chemical, shipbuilding and power generation industries in the 1950s. It focuses on a single objective, managing time, using critical path networks (Chapter 10). The CPM methodology is sometimes called CPA (critical path analysis) or PERT (programme evaluation and review technique), although strictly the latter should only apply when the network is also used to track progress.
2. C/SPEC (or cost/schedule control system criteria (C/SCSC)) was developed by the US defence industry.[12] It focuses on three objectives: managing scope, organization and cost. Scope is managed through a structured definition of the work called a *work breakdown structure* (WBS); see Chapter 6), and organization through an *organization breakdown structure* (OBS; see Chapter 7). The two-dimensional matrix formed by the WBS×OBS at any level is called a *linear responsibility chart* (Chapter 7). Cost is managed through a *cost breakdown structure* (CBS) and the three-dimensional matrix formed by the WBS ×OBS×CBS is called the *cost control cube* (Chapter 9).

This view produces an undue focus on the work, and completing it within time, cost and quality. The work is done for its own sake.

The alternative view

The alternative view defines project management as the process by which a project, defined above, is completed successfully; that is, it achieves its business purpose. There are three dimensions to this process:

- the project objectives
- the management processes to achieve the objectives
- the levels at which the processes are applied.

The first dimension addresses the word *project*, the second the word *management*, and the third links *project* and *management* together, and links the project to the outside world.

THE PROJECT OBJECTIVES

The definition of a project given above implies that the delivery of the project's purpose requires the management of five project objectives (Figure 1.1), not just one or three:

- managing scope
- managing organization
- managing quality
- managing cost
- managing time.

Since each objective contains an element of risk, a sixth, managing risk, can be added. However, throughout this book, that is assumed to be an inherent part of the five objectives above.

The traditional approach focuses on the last objectives (Figure 1.3). The management of projects is a compromise by which quality, cost and time are traded against each other to achieve the optimum outcome. The objection that this ignores the work is countered by saying it is part of the specification. The term *performance* is sometimes used to cover scope and quality. The objection that quality should not be compromised, especially

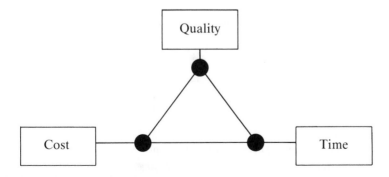

Figure 1.3   The time/cost/quality triangle

in a total quality environment, cannot be countered. (Even though quality is commonly mentioned as one of three key measures of project success, its management is hardly ever covered.) The North American Project Management Institute introduced a fourth objective,[10] managing scope (Figure 1.4). This overcomes the objections; scope can be traded separately. However, it implies that quality is divorced from cost, and scope from time. The pyramid in Figure 1.1 overcomes this and shows how organization integrates all four. Now the compromise can be made in any face of the pyramid, or plane through it. It is more common to compromise scope against time and cost than against quality, accepting less on time and budget rather than nothing at all. Alternatively, a level of performance between scope and quality can be chosen, and that can be traded against time and cost.

Figure 1.1 also shows that two of the objectives – scope and organization – are mandatory. Without the scope there is no project; without the organization it cannot be implemented. The other three – quality, cost and time – though desirable, are optional. They are soft constraints. To be of value,

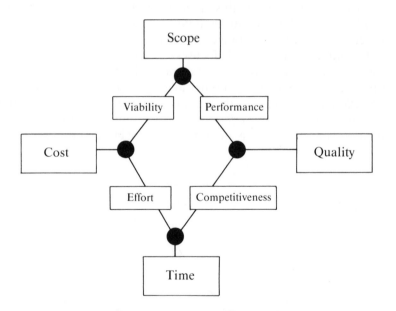

Figure 1.4   The scope/quality/cost/time diamond

Source: Reproduced from *The Revised Project Management Body of Knowledge*, published by the Project Management Institute, PO Box 43, Drexel Hill, PA 19026, a worldwide organization for advancing the state-of-the-art of project management.

the benefit must be of certain specification, be obtained for a certain cost, and by a certain time. However, these constraints can be traded against the scope, as described above. This is contrary to the common view, implied by the earliest definition of a project, that time is the overriding objective. It is interesting to consider why project managers may have this heavy focus on time. It might be

– that the systems for controlling time (networks) are the most advanced;
– that project managers have greater control over time than cost or quality;
– that time is the most visible objective;
– inherent in the make-up of people who make good project managers.

THE MANAGEMENT PROCESSES

To achieve each objective requires the use of management processes that address the unique and transient nature of projects. There are two views on management processes:

1. *The problem-solving cycle* addresses the uncertainty, viewing the project's purpose as a problem, and applies standard management processes for problem solving. There are various ways of expressing this. A classic approach[13] uses four basic steps: plan; organize; implement; control.
2. *The project management life cycle* addresses the transience of projects directly. Having a beginning and an end, projects go through several stages of development. There are many versions of the life cycle.[14] The simplest has four basic stages: germination; growth; maturity; death.

THE FUNDAMENTAL LEVELS

A project has three fundamental levels at which each objective is managed[14]:

– *Level 1*: the integrative level
– *Level 2*: the strategic level
– *Level 3*: the tactical level.

For *scope management* the project is integrated into the business at level 1, by defining how the project's purpose meets the business's objectives. At level 2, a strategy for achieving the purpose is derived, and at level 3 a tactical plan is developed for achieving each element of the strategic plan. These three levels can be evolved to lower levels, and form the basis of the WBS, mentioned above. However, if you are to focus on the purpose of the project, and the quantitative and qualitative objectives that will deliver that purpose, then it is more appropriate to focus not on the work, but on the results or deliverables produced by that work. We should therefore talk about a *results breakdown structure* or *product breakdown structure*. In fact, you will see in Chapter 6 that at higher levels (levels 1 and 2), the plans tend to be results oriented, whereas at lower levels (level 3 and below) they are more work oriented.

For *organization*, level 1 of management integrates the project into its context, level 2 translates corporate objectives into project strategies, and level 3 implements the strategies. These three levels form the basis of the OBS, mentioned above.

For *quality*, *cost* and *time*, parallel hierarchies exist.

The three levels therefore provide horizontal integration, linking the project objectives with each other and with the management processes. They also create vertical integration, linking the project with its context at the top level and with the tools and techniques used to implement the processes at the bottom level.

A structured approach

The direct answer therefore views project management as the management of five project objectives through three fundamental levels. The next chapter shows how this can be used to create a structured approach to the management of projects as a modern management discipline. The approach used in this book merges the CPM and C/SPEC methodologies, together with a third, *total quality management* (TQM), to provide an approach which uses the body of knowledge to manage all five of the project objectives (Figure 1.5).

1.6 Summary

1. A project:
   - is a *unique* scope of work
   - is undertaken using a *novel* organization
   - achieves *beneficial* change.
2. A project therefore:
   - carries considerable uncertainty and *risk*
   - requires the *integration* of the novel organization
   - is subject to *constraints* of time, cost and quality.
3. A project delivers a facility;
   which is operated to produce a product;
   which in turn generates the benefit.
4. Project management is the process by which a project is brought to a successful conclusion.

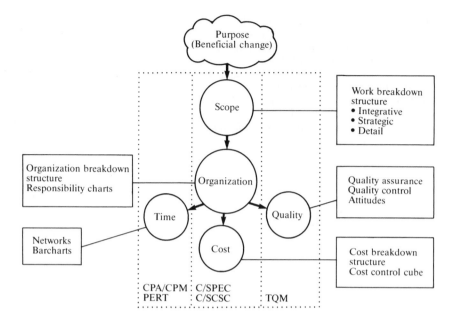

Figure 1.5   A structured approach to project management

5. Project management has three dimensions:
   - the *objectives*: scope, organization, quality, cost, time
   - the *management processes*: plan, organize, implement, control
   - the *levels*: integrative, strategic, tactical.

References

1. Weber, Max, *Wirtschaft und Gesellschaft*, Mohr, 1956.
2. Sharad, D., 'Management by projects: an ideological breakthrough', *Project Management Journal*, **17** (1), 61–3, 1986.
3. Gareis, R. (ed.), *The Handbook of Management by Projects*, Manz, 1990.
4. Barnes, M., in *Have Project, Will Manage*, BBC2, 1989.
5. Andersen, E. S., Grude, K. V., Haug, T., and Turner, J. R., *Goal Directed Project Management*, Kogan Page, 1987.
6. Cleland, D. I. and King W. R., *Systems Analysis and Project Management*, McGraw-Hill, 1983.
7. Smith, B., 'Project concepts', in *Effective Project Administration*, Institution of Mechanical Engineers, 1985.
8. Morris, P. W. G. and Hough, G. H., *The Anatomy of Major Projects: A study of the reality of project management*, Wiley, 1987.
9. Morris, P. W. G., *The Management of Projects: Lessons from the last fifty years*, Thomas Telford (to appear).

10. Wideman, R. M., 'The framework', in *The Revised Project Management Body of Knowledge*, Project Management Institute, 1987.
11. Cleland, D. I. and King, W. R. (eds), *The Project Management Handbook*, Van Nostrand Reinhold, 1988.
12. DOD, 'Work break-down structures for defence material items', *Military Standard 881a*, Department of Defenses, Washington, 1975.
13. Fayol, H., *General and Industrial Management*, Pitman, 1949.
14. Morris, P. W. G., 'Interface management: an organisational theory approach to project management', *Project Management Quarterly*, **10** (2), June 1979.

2
A structured approach to managing projects

2.1 Introduction

In the first chapter, I defined a project and gave an overview of project management. I shall now explain the structured approach to the management of projects followed throughout this book. In doing that, I shall introduce concepts described more fully later, and provide an overall summary that readers can use to find their way around the book, and hence use it as a handbook of project-based management.

The management of projects is a process by which beneficial change is defined and implemented. The structured approach to this process is derived from two assumptions. The first is that a project is

> an endeavour in which human, material and financial resources are organized in a novel way, to undertake a unique scope of work, of given specification, within constraints of cost and time, so as to deliver beneficial change defined by quantitative and qualitative objectives.

The second is that the approach, like a project itself, has three fundamental levels (Table 2.1). Over the next three sections I shall summarize the three levels, and indicate how they are described in Parts Two to Five of the book. In the last two sections of this chapter I shall introduce models of the approach and relate them to the structure of the book.

Table 2.1 Hierarchical approach to the management of projects, and how the levels relate to the parts of this book

Level	Function	Question	Elements	Part
1	Premises	Why?	Purpose, context and principles	Two
2	Strategy	What?	Methods: objectives, processes, levels	Three/Four
3	Tactics	How?	Tools and techniques	Five

2.2 The premises

Let us start by defining the basic premises of the approach: its purpose, context and principles.

Purpose

The purpose is given by the definition: to deliver beneficial change, by undertaking a unique scope of work using a novel organization. The change will have value only if it meets certain quality standards and is achieved within a certain cost and time. Because the organization is novel and the work is done over a limited time, its management is transient. Similarly, because the work is unique, it involves a level of risk. Because, it can cost more to eliminate this risk than the potential damage it might cause, it is more effective to manage it than to eliminate it. Project management, therefore, becomes the management of risk.

Context

A project is not an island; the work is not done for its own sake, although traditional approaches to project management often treat it as such. The project exists within a context. I should say that, throughout this book, I differentiate between the project's environment and its context.

- The *environment* is a physical concept. It is the neighbourhood in which the facility is built.
- The *context* is an abstract concept, but includes the environment. It is the complete economic, human social and ecosystem in which the project exists.

The context has three primary elements, as detailed below.

PROJECTS AND CORPORATE STRATEGY

If work is not undertaken for its own sake, then some organization wants the result, and that means it fulfils some future strategic objective within that parent organization. The beneficial change of projects is therefore driven by corporate strategy.

THE PARTIES INVOLVED

There are several parties involved in a project:

- the parent organization (the owner of the facility), represented by the sponsor

- the users, who will operate the facility on behalf of the owner to achieve the benefit, represented by the champion
- the supporters, who will supply the resources (human, material and financial) to undertake the work to build the facility, directed by the project manager and integrators
- the stakeholders, who are affected by the project, either by the work or by the operation of the facility, but are not otherwise involved.

STRATEGIC MANAGEMENT OF PROJECTS

The management of the project within its context requires the adoption of a strategic management approach, which comprises several elements:

- the attitudes of the parties involved, from top management down
- the purpose and objectives of the project
- the vehicle or approach for managing the project
- the management of the context of the project
- the resources to undertake the project.

Principles

This strategic management of projects defines five principles of good management which are essential to the structured approach adopted:

- manage through a structured breakdown: the management system is built around a structured breakdown of the facility delivered by the project into intermediate products or results
- focus on results: what to achieve, not how to do it; the deliverables, not the work for its own sake
- balance the results between different areas of technology; and between technology and people, systems and organizational changes
- organize a contract between all the parties involved, defining their roles, responsibilities and working relationships
- adopt a clear and simple management approach.

The three chapters of Part Two describe the three elements of the context, respectively, and Chapter 5 concludes by expanding on the five principles.

2.3 The methods

There are three dimensions to the methods:

1. The project management objectives
2. The management processes
3. The levels of the project.

The project management objectives

The five objectives of project management were introduced in Chapter 1: scope, organization, quality, cost and time (Figure 1.1). The ordering of the five objectives is deliberate. We start by defining the scope from the project's stated purpose and the facility required, and then derive the organization. That may be sufficient to undertake the project. If not, we state the specification, or quality, required, and estimate the cost of producing it. Finally, we calculate how long the project will take and compare that to the time available. We also assess the level of risk inherent in the five objectives. At any step during this process we may return to an earlier step, to trade one objective off against another, especially in the light of any identified risks.

Part Three of the book covers the management of the five objectives, the management of risk, and other special techniques, including the balancing of the objectives and their management at all levels of the project.

The management processes

The second dimension of the methods describes the management processes by which each objective is achieved. There are three complementary views:

- the classical view
- the problem-solving cycle
- the project management life cycle.

THE CLASSICAL VIEW

This view, proposed by Henri Fayol,[1] Figure 2.1, addresses the integration of the novel organization. It has five basic management functions – four direct and one integrative:

- planning the work to be done
- organizing the resources to do it
- implementing by assigning work to people
- controlling progress to achieve the plan or replanning if necessary
- leading the team of people involved.

THE PROBLEM-SOLVING CYCLE

This part of the process views the project's purpose as a problem, and applies structured methods for problem solving to its management. Figure 2.2 illustrates a ten-step cycle, and Table 2.2 describes the management

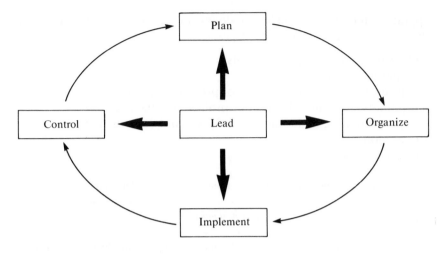

Figure 2.1   Five functions of management

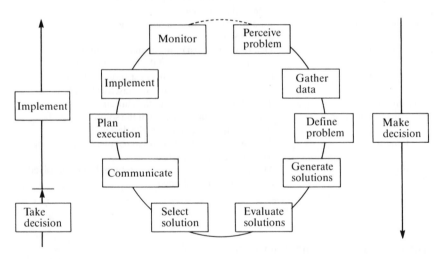

Figure 2.2   Ten-step problem-solving cycle

processes derived from it. Some of the steps mirror the direct functions above. People divide these ten steps into three major stages: decision making (steps 1 to 5); decision taking (step 6); and execution (steps 7 to 10).

The World Bank defines a seven-stage approach, which follows the problem-solving cycle quite closely. It places heavy emphasis on appraisal and selection and less on design and execution, perhaps reflecting the bank's concerns. The seven stages are:

- identification of project concepts
- preparation of data
- appraisal of data and selection of project solution
- negotiation and mobilization of project organization
- implementation, including detail design and construction
- operation
- post-project review.

Table 2.2   Management processes derived from the problem-solving cycle

Step	Management process
Perceive the problem	Identify that there is an opportunity for providing benefit to the organization
Gather data	Collect information relating to the opportunity
Define the problem	Determine what the value of the opportunity and potential benefits are
Generate solutions	Identify several ways of delivering the opportunity and achieving the benefits
Evaluate solutions	Determine the cost of implementing solutions, the likelihood of success and the levels of benefit
Select a solution	Choose the solution giving best value for money, accounting for all factors, and baseline the plan
Communicate	Tell all parties involved of the chosen solution
Plan implementation	Complete a detailed design of the solution, plan the implementation, and freeze the design
Implement	Authorize work, assign tasks to people, undertake the work and control progress
Monitor	Monitor results to ensure the problem has been solved and the benefits obtained

THE PROJECT MANAGEMENT LIFE CYCLE

This view addresses the transience of projects. The emphasis of project managers and the way they apply the management processes changes as the project progresses through its various stages. There are many views of the life cycle, with varying numbers of stages. Table 2.3 shows the management processes derived from a four-stage cycle. In the past I used the word 'birth' in place of 'germination'. However, the former implies that projects have a precise start after a fixed period of gestation. The analogy of the seed is better. It can exist for a long time (the average period is put

Table 2.3   Four-stage view of the project management life cycle

Stage	Name	Management objectives
Germination	Proposal and initiation	– project definition – scope and business objectives – functional design – feasibility – initial estimates to ±30% – go/no go decision
Growth	Design and appraisal	– systems design for sanction – planning and resourcing – sanction estimates to ±10% – baseline – sanction
Maturity	Execution and control	– education and communication – detail planning and design – control estimate to ±5% – work allocation – progress monitoring – forecasting completion – control and recovery
Death	Finalization and close-out	– completion of work – use of product – achievement of benefits – disbanding/rewarding the team – audit and review – historical records

at 50 years or more for major projects) and only germinate when conditions are favourable. Growth will subsequently only continue if conditions remain favourable.

Again you will see words repeated between Tables 2.2 and 2.3; the problem-solving cycle is essentially a life cycle with ten stages. Figure 2.3 is adapted from a version of the life cycle used by British Telecom for managing internal projects. Furthermore, it is possible to view each stage of the life cycle as a problem to be solved, or a small project. The management processes are then repeated at each stage, as illustrated in Figure 2.4, with implementation of one stage leading to the next.

People tend to jump from perceiving a problem to choosing a solution, or worse, to implementing a solution. Similarly, they go straight to the execution stage of a project, without first determining whether the proposal is worth while or how it is to be achieved. If you choose a solution without

PROPOSAL AND INITIATION			DESIGN AND APPRAISAL			EXECUTION AND CONTROL			FINALIZATION AND CLOSE-OUT
Perceive problem	Gather data	Define problem	Generate solutions	Evaluate solutions	Select solution	Communicate	Plan execution	Implement	Monitor
			Plan	Organize		Implement		Control	

Figure 2.3 Relating the three views of the life cycle

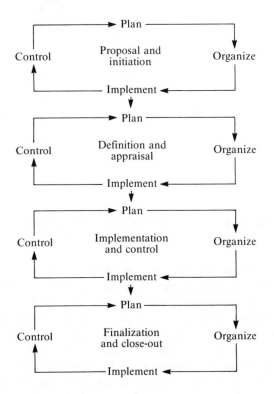

Figure 2.4 Repeating the processes at each stage

going through the decision-making process, you will find your solution cures the symptoms, but does not get to the cause of the problem: like a teenager applying a cleansing gel to spots without first diagnosing they have measles. Similarly, if you develop a plan for your project, through to commissioning, without first determining whether your proposal is feasible and what is to be achieved, your plan will deal in generalities only. The management processes provide a structured approach to the project to achieve the best result.

The management processes by which a project is undertaken is the subject of Part Four. This follows the four-stage life cycle (Table 2.3), illustrating how the five objectives are managed at each stage. In the process, further tools and techniques are introduced. In Chapter 16 and Part Six, I introduce other versions of the life cycle from different types of project. Example 16.4 contains a five-stage cycle for information systems projects. Figure 16.4 is a seven-stage cycle for contract management. Chapter 19, describes several cycles which place the project within a life cycle for the facility or the product it produces. Chapter 20 describes cycles for engineering design, engineering construction and information systems projects, and Section 20.4 traces the development of the last of these from early two-stage cycles to multi-stage spiral models. This last cycle should also find application to organizational development and R&D projects.

I have presented here views of the project management life cycle, and used the word *stage* as a step in that life cycle, with distinct management processes. Throughout the book, I differentiate between *stages* and *phases*. The latter is an element in the WBS, in which the work can be identified as taking place in a certain period of time, especially when the facility is extended through a number of steps. Phase One of Docklands Light Railway was from the City to Canary Wharf and Phase Two is from there to Stratford. Stage One is Feasibility, Two is Design, and Three Execution. The stages may be repeated for each phase.

Sometimes phases are given names of stages in the management life cycle. For example software development projects can follow a highly structured life cycle (Chapter 20). When taken to extremes, this approach can delay projects, because when a package of work is identified as being associated with a unique time window, the work of that package is only done in that window. Furthermore, if work of one package is planned as the previous one finishes, work with a long lead time may be left until it inevitably delays the project. The other disadvantage of this approach is that plans become totally generic and do not address the needs of the particular project at hand. Developing a plan with work-package names which address the unique features of the current project helps the project team to focus on its particular requirements.

The levels of the project

There are three fundamental levels to the approach, which link the system objectives with the management processes and the project with its context at the top and the people doing the work at the bottom:

THE INTEGRATIVE LEVEL

The purpose is stated, and the facility required to deliver it is defined through quantitative and qualitative objectives. Areas of work and categories of resource required to undertake them are defined, and basic parameters or constraints determined for time scales, costs, benefits and performance specification. Any risks and assumptions are stated. The *Project Definition Report* (Chapters 6 and 13) is a tool used to record this information. A *functional design* of the facility is developed. This defines the basic features or processing steps of the facility required. For a chemical plant or computer program this will be a *flow chart* showing inputs and outputs from each major processing element. For a training programme it will be the definition of the major elements of the programme, and the learning objectives of each.

THE STRATEGIC OR ADMINISTRATIVE LEVEL

Intermediate goals or milestones required to achieve the objectives are defined. Each milestone is the end result of a package of work. The responsibility of organizational units, functions and disciplines for work packages is defined. Work packages are scheduled in the project, and budgets developed. At this level the manager aims to create a stable plan which remains fixed throughout the project. This provides a framework for the management strategy, and allows changes to be contained within the third level. Responsibilities are assigned to organizational units. The *milestone plan* (Chapter 6) and *responsibility chart* (Chapter 7) are tools used for this purpose. A *systems design* of the facility is developed. This shows what each of the major processing elements does to deliver its outputs, and includes a design of the processing units within each element. For a chemical plant, the systems design is based on a *piping and instrumentation diagram*, and includes specifications of all the pieces of equipment. For a computer program, it describes what each subroutine within the program achieves, how each handles the data and the hardware architecture. For a training programme, it will break each element into sessions, and describe the format and learning objectives of each session.

THE TACTICAL OR OPERATIONAL LEVEL

The activities required to achieve each milestone are defined, together with the responsibilities of named people or resource types against the activities. Changes are made at this level within the framework provided at the strategic level. The *activity schedule* (Chapters 6 and 14) and *responsibility chart* are tools used for this purpose. A *detail design* of the facility is developed. This provides enough information to the project team to make parts of the facility, and assemble them into a working whole which meets the purpose of the project. For a chemical plant, this includes piping layout and individual equipment drawings. For a computer program, it includes the design of data formats, the definition of how each subroutine achieves its objectives, and the detail specification of the hardware. For a training programme, it will include the script and slides of lectures, structure of exercises, and perhaps details of testing procedures.

2.4 The tools and techniques

In order to implement the methods, we chose tools and techniques from the Project Management Body of Knowledge.[2,3,4] Some of the principle tools and techniques are (Figures 1.5 and 2.5 and Table 2.4):

1. *For managing scope*: work or product breakdown structure (WBS or PBS). Because this is the primary objective, WBS is the backbone of project management; the root for many project control systems. Other tools include configuration management, change control and data management.
2. *For managing organization*: organization breakdown structure and linear responsibility charts. Others include materials management, drawing registers, and aspects of commercial, financial and legal management, and of project leadership.
3. *For managing quality*: quality assurance, quality control, and change control. Others are less well developed for project management than for operations management, but may include total quality, Taguchi methods and just-in-time.
4. *For managing cost*: cost breakdown structure, and cost control cube. Others include parametric techniques for estimating costs, and variance methods for forecasting cost to completion.
5. *For managing time*: critical path networks (mathematical tools for calculating schedules and time to completion) and Gantt charts (visual tools for communicating schedules to the organization).
6. Associated with all five objectives are work lists for communicating the plan to the organization, and for gathering progress data.

Table 2.4 The tools and techniques of the approach

Method	Techniques	Tools	Chapter
Managing scope	Product breakdown	Milestone plans	6
	Work breakdown	Activity schedules	6
	Configuration management		16
	Data management	PMIS	16, 17
Organization	Organization breakdown	Responsibility charts	7
	Organization development		4
Quality	Quality assurance/control	Quality plans	8
	Quality management	Procedures manuals/audits	16
	Analysis	TQM techniques	8
Cost	Cost control cube		9
	Estimating techniques		9
	Earned value		9
Time	PERT/CPA	Networks/bar charts	10
Risk	Risk management		11
General	Balancing objectives	Triangle	12
	Nesting plans		12
	Rolling wave planning		12
	Baselining		12
Start-up	Start-up workshop	Definition report	13
Feasibility	Launch workshop	Definition report	13
Definition	Definition workshop	Definition report	13
Implementing		Work-to lists	14
Control		Turn-around documents	14
		S-curves	14
Close-out		Checklists	15

2.5 Project management models

Several models of project management can be derived from the above summary.

The first (Figure 2.5) integrates the three dimensions of the approach, and indicates the structure of Parts Three and Four. The five objectives are shown as vertical columns, with the level of definition evolved down through three levels. This process is primarily undertaken during the definition of the project. During execution, the detail definition is integrated, and work assigned to resources (human, material and financial). As work is

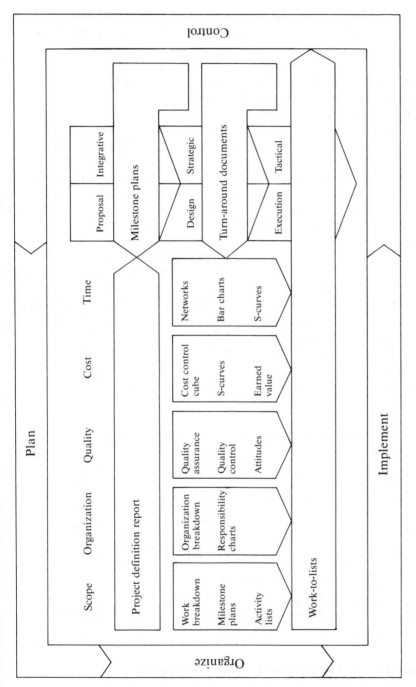

Figure 2.5 An integrated model of project management

done, progress is controlled bottom-up, between the tactical and strategic levels on one time scale, and between the strategic and integrative levels on another (longer) time scale. It is appropriate to describe the methods and the tools and techniques for managing each of the system objectives first, and then to show how these are integrated at each stage of the project life cycle to manage a project in practice.

The second (Figure 2.6) illustrates a message to be met throughout this book: the management of projects requires the negotiation of formal or informal contracts between the parties involved. Project planning is a process of negotiation. At the management level (the integrative and strategic levels) a contract is made between the owner and the project team (Section 4.2). The definition of scope, as represented by the milestone plan, shows what the project team will deliver to the owner, both as the facility produced at the end, and intermediate products throughout the project. The definition of the organization shows the support the owner will give the project team to let them deliver those results. Like all contracts, this one between owner and contractor must be agreed through bipartite discussions, not by one party imposing its will on the other by developing the plans unilaterally. At the detail (tactical) level the project team agree how they will work together to deliver the results for which they have accepted responsibility. This contract must also be agreed through discussion, and not by a member trying to impose his or her will unilaterally. (This is not a recipe for anarchy, because as part of the contract the team will accept the leadership of one of their number. If they do

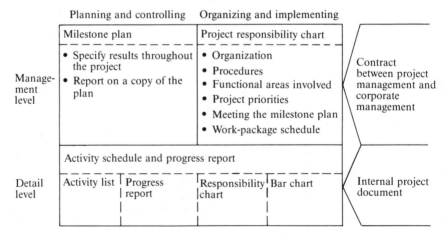

Figure 2.6 A contractual model of project management

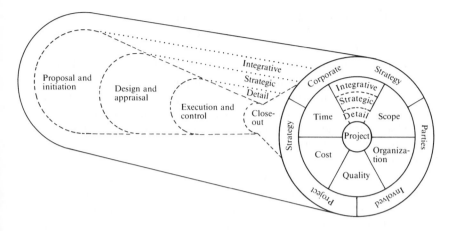

Figure 2.7 The project system

not accept that leadership they cannot be on the team. However, the team members will be more willing to accept the contract if they have been involved in the agreement of its terms.)

The final model is the project system (Figure 2.7). At the centre is a project, which exists within a context with three elements: the purpose; the parties involved; and the strategies for managing projects. Driving the system, and linking the project to its context is the approach, the management of projects. This approach has the three dimensions, the objectives, the management processes, and the levels.

2.6 Structure of the book

The structure of this book is linked to this last model. Part Two deals with the context; Parts Three, Four and Five with the approach; and Part Six with the projects, central to the system.

Part Two describes the context of the project, why the approach is necessary. Level 1 links the project and its management to its context. The purpose of the project is the benefit, or competitive edge, it is to deliver. In Chapter 3 I shall describe how the business planning process identifies a need for projects, and how they are selected. The parties involved include the owner (or sponsor), the users and their champion, the manager, the team and the integrators, and the stakeholders. They have two important relationships with each other: the commercial relationships and the human relationships. I shall discuss the latter in Chapter 4; the former are outside the scope of this book. The strategies for implementation include how the project is to be judged successful, and the management approaches that will be adopted accordingly. These strategies are explained in Chapter 5.

Part Three explains the first set of methods, what is achieved to satisfy the need, and associated tools and techniques. Chapters 6 to 10 explain the methods of managing each of the five objectives, scope, organization, quality, cost and time respectively; Chapter 11 deals with managing the risk which permeates the five objectives; and Chapter 12 introduces special techniques for balancing and integrating the five objectives at the three levels of the project.

Part Four describes the second set of methods – the management processes through which the approach, its methods and tools and techniques are used to undertake projects. Chapter 13 explains the process of project start-up and definition; Chapter 14 the execution of the work and its control; and Chapter 15 the termination of the project.

Part Five identifies further tools and techniques, specific procedures and systems used in the management of projects. Chapter 16 deals with project administration; Chapter 17 with the use of computer systems in the management of projects; and Chapter 18 with project teams and the role and skills of the project manager.

Part Six describes some applications of management of projects, to show what the approach means in practice. Chapter 19 covers projects arising at different stages of the product life cycle; Chapter 20 covers projects from various industries and sectors; Chapter 21 deals with projects of different sizes; and Chapter 22 discusses projects involving international collaboration.

2.7 Summary

1. Project management has three levels:
    - *why*: the purpose, context and principles of the approach
    - *what*: the methods of the approach
    - *how*: the tools and techniques of the approach.
2. The purpose is to deliver beneficial change successfully.
3. The context has three elements:
    - projects and corporate strategy
    - the parties involved
    - the strategic management of projects.
4. The approach is based on five principles of good management:
    - manage through a structured work breakdown
    - focus on results
    - balance results

- organize a contract between parties involved
- keep it simple.
5. The methods are the three dimensions of project management:
   - the five project objectives
   - the management processes
   - the three levels.
6. There are three views of the management processes:
   - the *classical approach*: plan, organize, implement, control
   - the *decision-making cycle*: make the decision, take the decision, implement the decision
   - the *life cycle*: germination, growth, maturity, death.

References

1. Fayol, H., *General and Industrial Management*, Pitman, 1949.
2. Andersen, E. S., Grude, K. V., Haug, T. and Turner, J. R., *Goal Directed Project Management*, Kogan Page, 1987.
3. Cleland, D. I. and King, W. R. (eds), *The Project Management Handbook*, Van Nostrand Reinhold, 1988.
4. PMI, *The Revised Project Management Body of Knowledge*, Project Management Institute, 1987.

PART TWO
THE CONTEXT OF PROJECTS

3
Projects for implementing corporate strategy

3.1 Introduction

A project, as defined in Chapter 1, contains two essential features, the task is unique and the method of achieving it is novel, and this implies a further inherent feature:

Projects carry considerable uncertainty and risk.

Because projects are unique, we cannot be sure that our plans and estimates are correct. In fact, it is shown in Chapter 9 that, in the planning process, we reach a point at which the cost of further planning is more than the value of the data we obtain. It is better to manage the latent risk than to plan any further. If projects carry considerable uncertainty and risk, *why do organizations undertake them?* The answer addresses the first element of the project's context: the purpose of projects. Organizations undertake projects when they can achieve their business objectives more effectively than by doing routine things; when the potential benefits outweigh the risks. Projects may be the most effective medium, and sometimes the only medium, for managing change in an organization.[1] Managers might then consider that if their company is successful now, could it not remain successful by maintaining the *status quo*? The short answer is that it cannot, if it is to maintain its competitive advantage. Porter[2,3] shows how companies cannot remain static in the modern environment. The competition are changing the way they do their business, so if an organization fails to adapt, it will lose its markets. All projects should therefore arise from a need to fulfil specific strategic objectives and achieve competitive advantage. This is true whether they are business projects, government

37

infrastructure or defence projects, humanitarian projects, or private and social projects.

The role of general managers is to identify and select projects within their areas of responsibility which:

- are aimed at achieving the organization's mission;
- are aimed at achieving corporate objectives and strategy;
- deliver timely benefits which justify the expense.

Unfortunately, this is often not the case. Projects are initiated at junior levels of management for what seem compelling reasons, which perhaps match the previous direction of the company but are now contrary to the development of the business (see Example 3.1).

I worked with a company in the computer industry running a series of project launch workshops in the Research and Development Department. One project was to develop an accountancy package, which a salesman had suggested as a result of several requests. However, this was at a time when the senior management of the company were trying to focus on software more oriented towards the requirements of managers (such as estates management and manufacturing planning) rather than functionally oriented packages. When we came to assign resources, the only person available was the project manager, and the project quickly died.

Example 3.1 A project not aligned with corporate strategy

In this chapter, I shall describe the role of projects in corporate strategy, review the business planning process, and consider how that can lead to continuing routine operations and new projects. The chapter concludes with a review of methods of selecting projects. How the manager defines a project required to achieve specific objectives is covered under 'Managing scope' in Chapter 6.

3.2 The business planning process

There are four essential steps in the business planning process:

- Define the mission of the business
- Set long-term objectives for achieving the mission
- Develop strategies for achieving the objectives
- Develop tactical plans for achieving each element of strategy.

These steps are often illustrated as a pyramid or hierarchy (Figure 3.1).

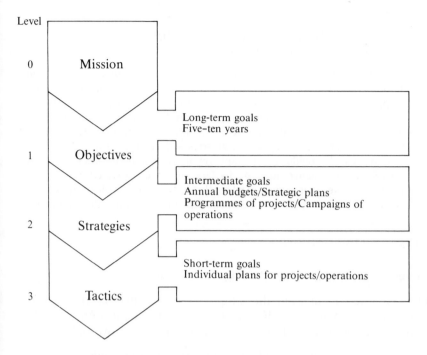

Figure 3.1 The hierarchy of the business planning process

Define the mission of the business

The *mission* is the axiom which initiates the business planning process. It is a statement of the reason for the organization's existence; its purpose for being in business. It may be a statement as simple as: *to make profit for the shareholders*. However, it is more common to include statements on:

– the type of products
– the positioning of the products in the marketplace
– the relationship with the employees
– other hygiene factors
– relationships with other stakeholders, especially local communities.

A 'mission statement' is given in Example 3.2.

TRIMAGI COMMUNICATIONS BV
MISSION STATEMENT

TriMagi Communications is in business to supply visual, voice and data communication networks based on its leading edge in glass fibre and laser technology. It will supply two-way cable television services to domestic and educational customers, data communication networks to these and commercial customers, and telecommunication services through its cable and data networks. It will be the first choice provider in the European countries within which it operates.

The company will provide secure employment to its staff, at rates of pay competitive with similar organizations. All its services will be provided in a way that has no impact on the environment. Above all, TriMagi Communications will supply its shareholders with a secure investment which increases in value annually.

Example 3.2 Mission statement

Set long-term objectives for achieving the mission

Having defined the mission, the company sets objectives for the next five to ten years (or longer) to deliver it. These are statements of the position the organization will reach in the relevant time scale, covering:

- the types and ranges of products, and turnover from each
- return on sales and assets
- type, number, skills and remuneration of employees
- environmental impact
- social and community activities
- growth of dividends.

A set of objectives is given in Example 3.3.

TRIMAGI COMMUNICATIONS BV
OBJECTIVES

From its current domination of the market in the Benelux countries, TriMagi Communications will establish operating subsidiaries in the following regions:

Year 1: France
Year 3: Germany; British Isles
Year 5: Iberian Peninsula; Italy; Austria; Switzerland
Year 7: Scandinavia; Baltic States . . .

Each new subsidiary will break even within two years, with a turnover of at least 100 million ECU, and from there will achieve a growth of 50 per cent per annum for the next three years. By the fifth year it will have achieved a return on assets of

20 per cent, and will contribute 10 per cent of turnover to the parent company to fund further product development.

Each subsidiary will employ operating personnel, and sufficient technical staff to install and maintain the networks. They may maintain a small marketing effort to develop local opportunities for using the network. These local opportunities will contribute at least 15 per cent of turnover.

The parent company will employ technical staff to maintain the company's leading technical edge, and to develop new products and opportunities for using the networks. New products and opportunities will enable established subsidiaries to maintain a growth of at least 20 per cent over and above that available from increased market, or increased market share, beyond their initial five years.

Example 3.3 A corporate objectives statement

Develop strategies for achieving the objectives

Having set objectives, the organization can then develop *strategic plans* for achieving the objectives. These can take several forms. The forms will sometimes be given different names; however, I prefer to view them as different versions of the same thing.

ANNUAL BUDGETS

These show, year by year, how the business will develop towards the position envisaged in the long-term objectives. The budgets for the current year and the year immediately following are the plans to which the business is presently working. Budgets for future years will become increasingly more speculative, and will be revised annually. For example, each of TriMagi's subsidiaries would have annual budgets for capital expenditure, income and revenue costs.

SUBSIDIARY GOALS AND MILESTONES AGAINST EACH OBJECTIVE

The annual budgets show where the business is expected at each year-end against the objectives. These can be summarized into a plan against each objective, showing intermediate milestones for achieving each one. These are sometimes called the *goals* of the business, and may be drawn as one or more *milestone plans*[4] for the development of the objectives.

CAMPAIGNS OR PROGRAMMES FOR FUNCTIONS, OPERATIONS OR PROJECTS

The annual budgets will set, or be based on, campaigns or programmes for individual departments or functions within the organization. These may be campaigns for continuing operations or programmes for new projects. The business-planning process is iterative, and so these programmes are developed in parallel with the annual budgets, by a process of negotiation and compromise. Furthermore, there may be several iterations between levels before the plan is agreed. However, all but the first of the programmes below tend to be set within constraints of the annual budgets. The first sets the basis from which the budgets and goals are derived. The particular types of campaign or programme are:

Programmes of corporate planning or marketing

These describe the evolution of the technologies, products or markets of the business. The corporate planning programme tends to deal with the time scale of the objectives. The term *strategies* is sometimes reserved for the corporate planning programme, because that sets the basis for deriving the goals and annual budgets. The marketing campaign is of shorter duration, and deals more with the balance between products, pricing, distribution channels and promotional campaigns to achieve the annual budgets.

There are several tools for deriving the corporate planning or marketing programmes. For example the *Ansoff Matrix*[5] (Figure 3.2) proposes that an organization has four basic strategies:

- service existing products and markets, but plan for market growth
- sell existing products to new markets for growth
- sell new products to existing markets for growth
- attempt to move into totally new territory.

The choice of whether to maintain existing products or markets, or to develop new ones may be based on a *SWOT* analysis – a review of the organization's Strengths, Weaknesses, Opportunities and Threats. Porter[2,3] describes several, more sophisticated, corporate planning techniques.

Campaigns for existing operations

When a business decides to maintain its existing products, markets or cash cows, this will define a campaign for existing operations. This may be for production, or sales, or services.

Programmes for new projects

However, when this analysis suggests that the business should adopt new products, markets or technologies, or should undertake some other

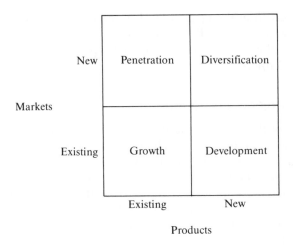

Figure 3.2   Ansoff matrix

improvement to its existing operations, then that requires a programme of projects to develop or introduce them. The projects will deliver new facilities, in the form of product designs, factories or technologies to produce them, computer systems to manage their production, or new organization structures with trained staff and managers to undertake the production.

Example 3.4 describes the options facing TriMagi.

The objectives which TriMagi has set indicate that it will maintain its existing operation in the Benelux countries. It will fund further growth using the income from those operations to expand into new markets, then achieve further growth as each new market becomes established. Initially, it will sell existing products in the new markets, but as these products become established new products will be developed. It will also try to use those new products in its old markets, where possible, to achieve further growth. The objectives also imply that the operation in the Benelux countries will split into an operating company, and a parent company undertaking new product development.

Example 3.4   The strategic options facing TriMagi

Develop tactical plans for achieving each element of strategy

The plans for individual campaigns or programmes, or for functions, operations or projects form the tactical level of the business plan. They describe how the organization will achieve each element in its strategic plans. These tactical plans may be marketing plans, production plans, or milestone plans for projects.

3.3 The role of projects and operations

I have just shown how the business-planning process can identify a need for routine operations and projects. These then become the media through which organizations achieve competitive advantage. Either they do more of the same, though always striving to improve efficiency through habitual increment improvement (HII), or they do new things with novel organizations – that is, projects. Until the 1980s, the former dominated. However, with the development of more sophisticated corporate planning techniques,[2,3] and with the explosion of technical innovation and communication, the latter is beginning to dominate. Thus project-based management is becoming the way in which organizations fulfil their business plans.[1]

Just like the business as a whole, each operation and project has three levels of planning (Figure 3.3): the integrative level, the strategic level, and the tactical level.

There may be lower, more detailed levels of planning. For particularly large projects, there can be up to seven levels of work breakdown, and we shall return to this concept in Chapter 6.

Integrative level

This defines the purpose of the campaign or programme, as defined by the corporate objectives, and the objectives it must achieve in order to satisfy the annual budgets.

1. For *sales and marketing* this will be objectives for turnover expected from each product, and budgets for distribution, promotion and over-heads for the sales department.
2. For *operations* this will be production targets, and budgets for cost of sales.
3. For *projects* this will be a definition of what the project is to produce, the specification, and constraints of time and cost.

Strategic level

This defines subsidiary objectives that each function must achieve in order to satisfy its overall objectives.

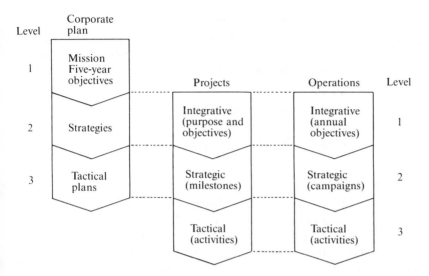

Figure 3.3   The project and operations hierarchy (product breakdown structure)

1. For *sales and marketing* this may be individual campaigns for selected products, product launches, advertising campaigns, or testing of new outlets (each of which may result in a project).
2. For *production* this will be targets for each product, or for efficiency improvements.
3. For *projects* this will be a milestone plan or work-package plan for the project.

Tactical level

This defines the detail of how the work to achieve each of the subsidiary objectives is to be undertaken.

3.4 Selecting projects[6]

The business-planning process will identify a number of possible projects. Usually, there will be insufficient resources (in the form of money, people and materials) to fund them all, and so the organization must assign priorities to selected projects that are most beneficial. There are several quantitative and qualitative techniques for making this selection. It is not my intention to give a detailed description of them here – that is more appropriate for a book on management accounting or project financing – but it is worth while giving a brief introduction to some of the concepts that will be met later. I shall focus on four issues:

1. Prioritizing projects
2. Investment appraisal and the planning gap
3. Accounting for risk in quantitative methods
4. Managerial judgement.

Prioritizing projects

The selection of projects should be driven 'top-down' from the business plans. Projects should only be adopted which are aimed at achieving the organization's objectives, and should only be adopted if there are adequate resources to allow those projects to be delivered in a timely and efficient manner. Projects must compete for resources with operations and other projects, existing and new. Because the business-planning process is iterative, it should be confirmed in the annual budgets that there are adequate resources to undertake all the new projects envisaged. (There may also be a level of contingency for projects arising during the year which prove imperative.) Unfortunately, this is often not the case.

1. Projects can arise at a low level in the organization, and, although they may be 'good' projects, they are not aimed at achieving the corporate mission, and so are starved of resources. Example 3.1 describes one such case. One of the R&D staff in the company asked me: 'What if the project is right?' Even if it is right, it will be starved of resources unless a champion can be found to make it central to the organization's business plan.
2. Projects, even some arising at a high level, that are not adopted as part of a structured business-planning process are not given priority alongside other projects or existing operations. The result, again, is that sufficient resources are not allocated to undertake them (see Example 3.5).

Both of these conditions lead to an inefficient and ineffective use of resources. People waste time – which could be better spent elsewhere – working on projects that are never completed. Techniques for managing projects in this multi-project environment, and for assigning priorities, are described in Chapters 16 and 21.

I worked in a company in the food industry, where no projects were given priority. In one factory, three *core* projects were consuming 30 per cent of the factory manager's time. If individuals are working Monday to Friday on their operational duties, they are working Saturday and Sunday morning on their project work. We were able to identify a hundred projects in total. Because no priorities had been set, individuals were assigning their own priority, with the result that no projects were being achieved.

Example 3.5 Assigning priority to projects

Investment appraisal and the planning gap

An organization undertakes projects because the planning process identifies a difference between what it would like future revenues to be, and what it predicts they will be if the *status quo* is maintained. This difference is called the *planning gap* (Figure 3.4(a)). Projects are expected to fill this gap. They do not ideally for two reasons: first, almost all projects have negative cash flow initially, while the facility delivered by the project is being constructed; secondly, after the facility is commissioned, the income usually reaches a maximum and then tails off (Figure 3.4(b)).

Most techniques for appraising projects assess whether the predicted cash outflow during the life of the project is justified by the predicted inflow after the facility is commissioned. The cash flows appraised should be the difference between those that would be obtained with the project, and those that would be obtained if the *status quo* were maintained. This may not necessarily be the same as the direct cost of the project and the income generated. The project may reduce income from existing products, or enhance them, and it may also save maintenance or other costs that would otherwise be incurred.

When appraising a project it is also common to apply a *discount factor* to the cash flows. This is a nominal interest rate, or return on investment, that is deducted from future cash flows. The effect is to give greater weighting to money in early years than money in later years. Income must overall be greater than expenditure, and quick early returns are of greater value than increasing cash flow into the future.

The approach is to assess cash flows against certain quantitative criteria, using given norms for the business. Several investment criteria are used to judge the value of the cash flows, and they all give different weightings to different projects.

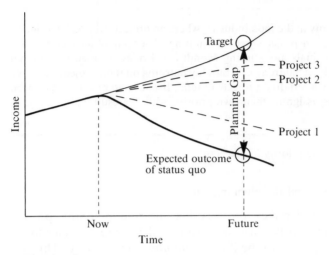

(a) The planning gap

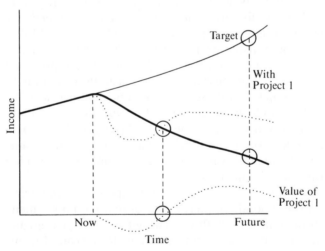

(b) The value of a project

Figure 3.4 Differential cash flows

1. The *net present value* (NPV) is the total of all the discounted cash flows, out and in, over the expected life of the project and its product.
2. The *internal rate of return* (IRR) is the discount rate which gives zero NPV over the life of the project and its product.
3. The *pay-back period* is the time the product takes to pay for the project: the time to give zero NPV at the chosen discount rate.
4. The *productivity index* is a measure of the difference between the IRR and the chosen discount rate.

Accounting for risk in quantitative methods

In quantitative approaches such as this, there are two common methods of accounting for perceived risk, and its predicted impact.

– making some allowance in the figures calculated;
– calculating a range of possible outcomes, and the chance of each.

An allowance for risk can be made in one of three ways: by reducing the predicted income, by increasing the expected cost, or by increasing the discount factor, or required IRR. The allowances that are made will depend on the impact of the risk, its chance of occurring and the strategic importance of the project.

A range of possible outcomes for the project can be calculated if we can estimate the impact of elements of risk, the factors that may adversely affect the project. If there is only a single element, we try to determine the worst case, the best case, the most likely outcome and the probability of each of these occurring. The investment criteria can be assessed for each outcome. With a few elements of risk, this can be repeated for each element. A simple model is built up, in which the project has a small number of possible outcomes, each of which is assessed as before.[7] Where there are multiple elements of risk, a *Monte Carlo* analysis is performed. A comprehensive model is made of the project, with ranges put on each element of risk. The criteria are then calculated many times; 100, 500 or 1000 is common. Each time they are calculated, a random value is chosen for each element of risk, within the range of possible values, to give a range of possible outcomes for the project, together with the likelihood of each occurring. In this way, the chance of the project's meeting its investment criteria is determined. The project can then be accepted or rejected as before, depending on its strategic importance.

A word of caution is necessary. The more elements of risk incorporated into the model, the more difficult it is to determine those that are primarily contributing to the variability of the output. It is then more difficult to determine where to put management effort to reduce the risk, should the project be adopted. A simple model, based on a work breakdown structure, provides more management information for assessing and controlling risk. (Risk management is described in Chapter 11.)

Managerial judgement

We have just discussed quantitative models for selecting projects. Often, however, the final selection rests not on the outcome of these models, but on the 'gut feel' of the managers making the judgement, and there are many qualitative or heuristic elements to the decision that cannot be quantified. While the quantitative model forms only a small part of the overall decision, the heuristic elements include:

- moral considerations
- the reputation of the organization
- the impact on existing businesses
- the view of the shareholders
- the impact on the hygiene factors in the mission statement
- the impact on the environment
- public opinion.

When shown, through quantitative data alone, that his pet project would not work, the chairman of one of the UK's top 30 companies is reputed to have said:

> Don't confuse me with the facts, tell me how it can be made to work!

3.5 Summary

1. Projects should only be undertaken which:
   - deliver the parent organization's mission
   - are aimed at achieving corporate objectives
   - deliver timely benefits which justify the expense.
2. There are four levels to the business planning process:
   - the mission
   - the strategic objectives
   - the strategic plans
   -the tactical plans.
3. The strategic plans will suggest an organization should:
   - continue with existing operations, improving efficiency through habitual incremental improvement

- undertake projects, either to introduce new operations, or to deliver bespoke products.
4. In selecting projects:
   - priorities must be assigned to projects so that there are adequate resources to undertake those selected
   - they must meet agreed investment criteria
   - allowance must be made for risk
   - final selection is based on managerial judgement, taking account of both quantitative and qualitative criteria.

Notes and references

1. Gareis, R. (ed.), *The Handbook of Management by Projects*, Manz, 1990.
2. Porter, M. E., *Competitive Strategy*, Free Press, 1980.
3. Porter, M. E., *Competitive Advantage*, Free Press, 1985.
4. Andersen, E. S., Grude, K. V., Haug, T. and Turner, J. R., *Goal Directed Project Management*, Kogan Page, 1987.
5. Ansoff, H. I., 'Strategies for diversification', *Harvard Business Review*, 113–24, May 1957.
6. Section 3.4 contains ideas contributed by John Dingle, who was previously a project manager in the oil and gas industry and is now a consultant and lecturer at the College of Petroleum Studies, Oxford.
7. Cooper, D. F. and Chapman, C. B., *Risk Analysis for Large Projects*, Wiley, 1987.

4
Projects and the parent organization

4.1 Introduction

The second inherent feature of projects is that their management requires the integration of various parties into novel organizations. The primary party is the parent company, the one funding the project as part of its strategic development. Others are internal and external to the owner organization. Not all parties share the owner's stated, or overt, objectives for the project; they have their own covert objectives. Although the project is subsidiary to the parent organization, it usually has an impact on it, for two reasons. First, the project is undertaken to introduce change, because the organization recognizes it cannot achieve its objectives by doing routine things. This change may be technical, to produce physical facilities, or cultural, to change the structure of the organization, its people and systems. These cultural changes are the source of many of the covert objectives mentioned above, and the manager must recognize and manage them. Using the methods of *organizational development* can aid this process. Secondly, the processes required to manage through projects may be foreign to an organization that normally does routine things, and so the mere act of undertaking a project can have an impact.

In this chapter, I shall consider the parties involved in a project, and the impact of projects and project management on the parent organization. I shall also describe how to implement project-based management where it does not already exist.

4.2 The parties involved

The owner/contractor model

It is common to talk about the project team as a single group of people, all with the same objectives. This is not the case. A simple model proposes at least two groups involved in each project: the owner and the contractor (Figure 4.1).

The *owner* is the group (or individual) who will own and operate the facility. They define the requirements, provide the finance (money) to undertake the project and deliver the facility, and will benefit from its products. Their objectives are to achieve the optimum product at the best price.

The *contractor* is the group (or individual) who consume the finance to provide resources (people, materials), to deliver the facility. They define the work required to achieve the objectives and deliver the results to the owner. They achieve their reward from doing the work, and, unless they are also eventual users, cease to be involved when the project is finished. Their objectives are to maximize their profit, while satisfying the client (owner).

Even with this simple model, the two groups involved have conflicting objectives: the owner wants best price, the contractor wants maximum profit. On a project like the Channel Tunnel, where owner and contractor are different organizations (see Table 4.1), these conflicting objectives are clear; that is the basis of the contract between them. When a project takes place within a single organization, the people involved often still adopt these two positions, although in this case *maximum profit* is usually from non-financial sources. This can cause a conflict of interest, especially where users have both an owner and a contractor role.

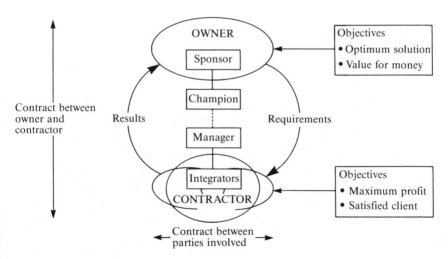

Figure 4.1   The owner/contractor model

Figure 4.1 shows four further roles associated with the model:

1. The *sponsor* is the person (or group) who makes the finance available to buy the project's products. The sponsor has the same objectives as the owner (see Table 4.1).
2. The *champion* is a senior user representative, who convinces the sponsor that this project should have priority for support ahead of others. The champion usually wants the best product, but is only concerned about price in that this project must gain priority ahead of others.
3. The *manager* is the person (or group) responsible for planning, organizing, implementing and controlling the work so that the facility is delivered to specification, under budget, and on time. The manager has the same objectives as the contractor.
4. The *integrators* are responsible for ensuring that transient teams of people are able to work together effectively for the duration of the project. They usually have the same objectives as the contractor, but often view the project manager as an owner's representative.

The champion, project manager and senior user representatives will often form a *steering committee*. The project manager, integrators, and often the champion, may form a *project management team*. On engineering projects the integrators are often called *project engineers*. Other terms include *project leader*, *assistant project manager* and *work-package manager*.

Figure 4.1 provides a simple view of the parties involved. In reality there are many other groups, including:

- *users*: the group who will operate the facility on behalf of the owner. They may or may not include the owner. Their objective is usually to obtain the best (not optimum) product, at any price. They will only be concerned about price if the owner is part of the group, or if they, like the champion, need to get priority for their project ahead of others.
- *supporters*: groups who provide goods or services to the owner and contractor, so that they may undertake the work to construct the facility. They may include subcontractors, suppliers, financiers, insurers, government and users as resource providers. Their objectives are usually the same as the contractor, except, being one step removed, they will be more concerned about satisfying the manager than the owner.

– *stakeholders*: all the people or groups whose lives or environment are affected by the project, but who receive no direct benefit from it. These can include the project team's families, people made redundant by the changes introduced, people who buy the product produced by the facility, and the local community (sometimes called NIMBYs – not in my back yard).

Table 4.1   The parties involved in the Channel Tunnel project

Role	Position	Group
Owner		Eurotunnel; its shareholders
Users	Operator	Eurotunnel
	Provider of services	British Rail and SNCF
Manager		Trans Manche Link
Supporters	Financiers	Banks world-wide
	Subcontractors	Partners in TML consortium
	Project auditors	W. S. Atkins
	Suppliers, include	British Rail and SNCF
Stakeholders	Buyers	Travelling public, hauliers
	Competitors	Cross-Channel ferries
	Communities	London, Kent, Pas de Calais

Overt vs covert objectives

A theme running through this discussion is that the parties involved have different objectives. A standard mnemonic on how to judge project success is that it is completed on time, to cost, and to specification – but who judges: the owner, champion, users, manager, stakeholders? (We shall return to the question of success in the next chapter.) Individuals will judge a project to be successful if it meets their personal objectives. These may not be the same as the stated, *overt*, objectives, and the time, cost and quality constraints imposed. Individual's personal objectives are their *hidden agenda*, or *covert objectives*. Typically they may be:

– project managers aiming to enhance their careers
– operations managers wishing to maintain the *status quo*
– managers hoping to widen their sphere of influence
– managers planning to reduce head count
– people wishing to protect their jobs
– people generally being resistant to change.

I was involved with a project where the user representative on the project team would probably be made redundant if the project was successful. He had been appointed by the 'champion', the general manager of the department, because the project was likely to make a large proportion of his department redundant, reducing the size of his empire. The project was not successful; and in fact came to an abrupt halt when we held a Project Definition Workshop (see Chapter 13). It was impossible to maintain the pretence. However, two years later it was overtaken by a larger project which merged several subsidiary companies into a larger unit. The general manager lost his job.

Example 4..1 Covert objectives

Sometimes these covert objectives support the overt objectives. Often the two sets are in conflict. That will cloud individuals' judgements about the success of the project, and, more importantly, reduce their motivation towards successful completion. This is especially true for users or stakeholders who stand to lose (see Example 4.1). The manager must attempt to identify the covert objectives; to reinforce those that are in unison with the overt objectives and reduce those that are in conflict. This is part of the skill of managing the change within the parent organization.

4.3 Changing the parent organization[1]

Technical vs cultural change

The change introduced by a project will be of two types:

1. *Technical change*, i.e. change to the technology or physical environment of the organization. This may be as a result of:

   - engineering work: civil, mechanical, electrical, chemical, etc.
   - IT work: hardware, software, networks, etc.

2. *Cultural change*, i.e. change to the culture of the organization itself. This may involve changes to:

   - the people of the organization: their skills, values and knowledge
   - the management processes and systems: the ways of working
   - the structure of the organization.

There are projects which result in purely technical change, and others in purely cultural change. However, the vast majority result in a mixture (Figure 4.2). The term 'PSO projects' (people, systems and organization) was coined to describe these projects.[2] In Figure 4.2, I describe building a

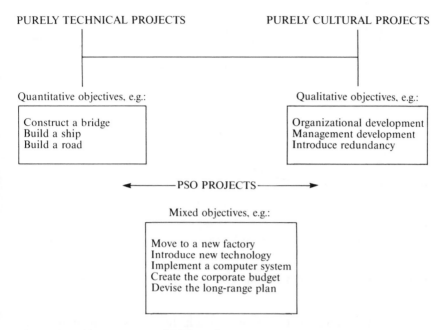

PURELY TECHNICAL PROJECTS   PURELY CULTURAL PROJECTS

Quantitative objectives, e.g.:   Qualitative objectives, e.g.:

Construct a bridge   Organizational development
Build a ship   Management development
Build a road   Introduce redundancy

◄———————PSO PROJECTS———————►

Mixed objectives, e.g.:

Move to a new factory
Introduce new technology
Implement a computer system
Create the corporate budget
Devise the long-range plan

Figure 4.2 The spectrum of PSO projects

road as a purely technical project. However, the people of Hampshire
and Kent may not agree that extending the M3 and building the rail link
from the Channel Tunnel to the centre of London, respectively, are
purely technical projects. Even projects which at first sight appear purely
technical often involve a mixture of technical and cultural work. In these
two cases it is the cultural work which caused the greatest delay, and this
is common on all projects (see Figure 4.3). Cultural changes are more difficult and more time consuming than technical changes. As the latter can
be described in concrete terms and is quantifiable, it is therefore easy to
plan and implement. Cultural work, however, can only be described in
abstract terms and requires people to change, which they may resist.

I used to doubt Figure 4.3. The Channel Tunnel I thought to be a
purely technical project which has taken 200 years. I wondered whether
what was plotted was a quantum of change, and with major projects the
complexity was magnified. However, when you compare the Channel
Tunnel to the recently constructed CERN nuclear accelerator near
Geneva a different picture emerges. The former is three 20-mile holes
through chalk, which crosses the French/English border once and
involves road and rail technology. The latter is a 60-mile hole through

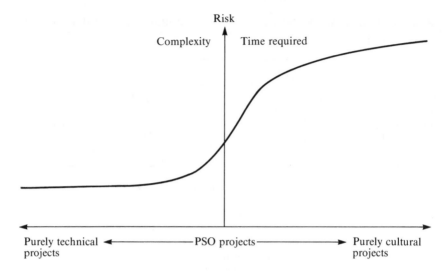

Figure 4.3   Complexity of managing PSO projects

granite, which crosses the Swiss/French border several times and involves technology at the boundary of particle physics. The former has taken 200 years; the latter was completed on time and to budget in about four years. The nuclear accelerator is clearly the technically more difficult project; the Channel Tunnel the culturally more difficult, involving English–French cooperation, a scar on the Kent landscape, parliamentary bills, creating Eurotunnel plc, and collaboration of different cultures. Because technical work is quantifiable, our attention tends to run down the curve in Figure 4.3 to the technical end of the spectrum. However, we ignore the cultural work at our peril.

Organizational development: managing the cultural change

Managers of projects therefore need both technical and people management skills. It is the people affected by the change (the users and stakeholders) who ultimately determine its success or failure, and it is the cultural change which has the greatest impact on them. It is often said that people resist change; it is more true to say they resist having change imposed on them. If they are involved in the change process, they may accept it more readily. Increasingly, managers are adopting the techniques of *organizational development* as an effective aid to the management of change. Organizational development has its origins in the behavioural sciences, but the project manager can benefit from the practical application of its principles. It involves the planning and managing of change in a manner which emphasizes the involvement of people in all aspects of the change process. The project manager, as change agent, achieves this by:

- planning the change effectively
- recognizing the causes of conflict and resistance to change
- overcoming the resistance by building motivation and commitment to the planned change.

Planning the change

Once it is decided to make a change, the project manager needs to plan its integration into daily operations. This means designing the technical change, and defining strategies to enable people in the organization to accept the proposed changes and internalize the cultural element. To plan adequately, the change manager must set clear goals and expectations, both to give the project implementation some form of structure and to give guidelines of events to the people in the organization. The use of a plan that is developed at a detailed level only will not help this process. If there are no milestones, it will be hard to carry through implementation, and difficult to get people to accept the project and its objectives. It is therefore essential to develop the plan through a *breakdown structure*, which balances the technical and cultural elements, and shows how they deliver the overall purpose of the project (see Chapter 6).

Planning from a people perspective means reviewing the present systems and structures, and then overlaying options that are likely to achieve the project objectives. This will highlight the gap between present practices and future needs, and this is the gap the project manager must close. As part of this process, the manager should consider possible reactions from all groups likely to be affected. Ideally representatives from each affected party should be involved in discussions at the project-planning stage. It is important that the project manager remembers that although plans should always be made, unknown variables or changes in circumstances may require revisions to the plans, and hence allowances to enable flexibility should be incorporated.

Conflict and resistance to change

These can come from the people affected by the change, or from the culture of the organization itself.

THE PEOPLE AFFECTED

The fear of how planned changes may affect individuals or groups, underlies much of the resistance. We see below how much of this can be avoided by communicating with people, and involving them in the change process. To do this we need to be able to identify the fears and concerns, which may include:

- fear that working relationships may change, upsetting both formal and informal relationships
- fear that the nature of work may change, requiring the learning of new, very different skills
- fear of job loss
- fear of loss of control or autonomy over one's own, or others', work.

Conflict is also likely when people:

- are not consulted or told what is going on
- do not understand or agree with the changes being made
- do not see or understanding the benefits the changes may bring
- have different perceptions of what changes are needed, or whether they are needed at all
- have not internalized previous changes fully, or such changes have not been implemented properly
- are fed up with constant change
- are just set in their ways.

THE ORGANIZATIONAL CULTURE

This in itself can create a resistance to change, by creating an inertia to its introduction.[3] When I worked as a management consultant, I often found that this was the cause of the greatest resistance to proposed changes by the individuals within the organization. Culture influences every facet of the organization, including management styles, attitudes, goals, standards, dress and adaptability to change. This can be true not only for the organization as a whole, but for the subcultures that exist at department or group level. The effect of culture must be considered throughout the project.

Overcoming the resistance

The principles of organizational development suggest many ways to help overcome the conflict and resistance to change:

EFFECTIVE COMMUNICATION

This is central to the successful management of change. This means talking to, and persuading, the right people to take action or accept the proposed changes. However, it is important to remember that communication also means listening and using information received. Project managers should use both the formal and informal communication systems (especially face to face). They should constantly *walk the patch* to break down barriers and mistrust caused by remoteness, build up working relationships with people at all levels, and attempt to instil confidence in those affected by the change.

Organizational structure can also affect communication systems and the change process. Many large companies have tall, stratified hierarchies, with complex communication channels. This may lead to information being filtered out, distorted or lost. Formal, centralized structures tend to be less flexible, particularly to change, than flatter organizations. However, even in the latter, communication flows can be distorted or broken. This is most likely to occur when people who are used to working on their own feel they may lose personal autonomy and control through proposed changes.

PARTICIPATION

Implicit within the notion of organizational development is the need for people to participate fully in the change process. For this to be effective, the manager should ensure that the need for change is fully explained and understood, and that the objectives and benefit of the project to specific groups and to the organization as a whole are fully understood. The benefit of allowing people to participate is that it helps them to feel they have some control over their work and the change process. If they understand the project's objectives, and see that those objectives may be of benefit, they are more likely to contribute positively to the project's success. This is part of the process of negotiation (see Figure 2.6).

TRAINING AND DEVELOPMENT

Training aims to provide people with specific skills to do a job. Development is a continuous process, which aims to identify and fulfil the long-term potential of individuals and to focus this potential onto the organization's objectives, thereby enhancing the performance of both. While training (especially when new technology or different systems are introduced) is a natural response to change, many companies ignore the long-term development of their employees. However, there are advantages from implementing programmes that address this need. Development of employees, especially managers, contributes to overall commitment to common goals and processes. Development programmes can also help motivate staff and gain their acceptance of both change and specific training needs implicit in the change process. Employee development further improves internal communication and participation, which underpins the success of many projects. (A training programme and the initiation of a development programme are themselves projects.)

TEAM DEVELOPMENT

The project manager should encourage people to work together in teams, and to interact with others in the organization. This is not just confined to the project team, but should cover all departments and groups involved in the change. The project manager needs to be aware that subcultures and different goals may exist in each group, and that these may open up the opportunity for potential conflict, as each tries to protect its position. If this occurs, it is to the detriment of the project and the organization as a whole. One of the most effective ways to stimulate team development and intergroup cooperation is to encourage people to communicate frankly with each other. This can help them understand each other's perspective, and may help develop mutual goals which override individual interests, contributing to the project's overall success.

LEADERSHIP

It may seem that, by allowing people to participate in the planning and management of change, the project manager relinquishes responsibility and leadership. The opposite is true. Managing projects in this style requires clear leadership, direction and vision from the manager, so that people understand what is expected of them. Leadership means knowing when to delegate downwards and across functions, and when not to. It may also be necessary for the project manager to act as arbiter to resolve conflict. We shall return to the project manager as leader in Chapter 18.

COMMITMENT FROM THE TOP

If the application of organizational development practices to the management of projects is to be effective, the project manager must have the backing and commitment of top management. This is because the use of this approach requires long-term planning and dedication at all levels of the organization, and because the project manager must have, and must be seen to have, the authority and autonomy to design and implement development programmes. However, top management must feel confident in the project manager. They must also feel able to delegate authority for the process to the project manager. Hence, the project manager needs to involve them fully in all aspects of the project, and keep them informed by regular progress reports.

4.4 Introducing project-based management[4,5]

I have described how organizations undertake projects to implement change, and have shown how the techniques of organizational development can be used to facilitate this process. However, the very act of undertaking projects introduces change. An organization that has traditionally done routine work needs to adapt considerably to accept the different culture of projects. This can occur in one of two ways: in a hybrid environment, in which projects and operations sit alongside each other; or in a project environment, in which all the organization's work is managed through projects. In the hybrid environment, the organization undertakes a few, isolated projects to introduce specific changes into the operations environment. This creates an interface between operations and projects, which requires careful management. This was the situation in the food factory mentioned in Example 3.5, and will be the situation in TriMagi's operating companies, Example 3.4. The project environment has traditionally been used by engineering contractors and consultancies, but is now being adopted, at least in part, by organizations such as British Telecom, which has recognized that 50 per cent of its operations are project based. It will also be the approach used in TriMagi's head office for product development.

In this section and the next, I discuss these two environments, starting with the project-based organization. The reason is that by understanding the developments associated with the adoption of management by projects in that environment, the cultural difference across the project/operations interface in the hybrid environment can be easily explained.

Developments associated with project-based management

When an organization changes from a functional line structure to a project-based structure, it needs to change its management structure, its management systems and procedures for running the business, and the working lives of the people employed. Many people (managers and workers) are uncomfortable with the impact these developments have on the working environment, creating further resistance to change.

ORGANIZATION

Most organizations doing routine work have management structures based on functional hierarchies. This is the case in the process industries, production manufacturing, and most of the public sector. This structure can be very efficient for repetitive tasks. It is also possible to manage projects through a functional hierarchy, but it tends to be inflexible, so it is common to adopt more flexible structures for the management of projects. These include matrix structures, in which individuals have dual lines of reporting to functional (and transient) task managers, or approaches based on core/peripheral workers, or even structures based entirely on transient teams, which form and reform for each new task.[6]

SYSTEMS

With task teams, companies may adopt flatter management hierarchies, with communication by-passing the centre (Figure 4.4). Decisions can be

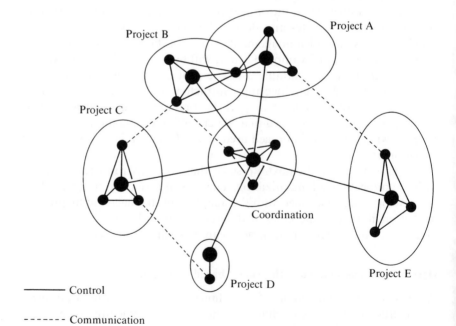

Figure 4.4 Flatter management hierarchies for project-based management

made within teams, or by communication directly between teams, without involving senior management.[7] This is sometimes called a 'galaxy' or 'cluster' approach.

PEOPLE

With rapidly changing technology, and the use of transient teams, there has also been a shift from the employment of clerical and manual workers, to entrepreneurial, knowledge workers. These knowledge workers no longer need to be permanent employees of the organization, but can be employed on a freelance basis, directly into the transient teams as they form and reform. They may also use modern technology to work from home.[8,9]

Table 4.2 The developments associated with project-based management and their impact on organization, systems and people

New developments	Impact areas		
	Organization	*Systems*	*People*
Organization: Matrix structure, task hierarchy	Inefficient and ineffective use of resources	No permanent expertise or new systems	Dual reporting, lack of career structure
Systems: Flat hierarchies, with devolved decisions	Lack of overall cooordination	Managers lack formal controls	Lack of career opportunity
People: Freelance and knowledge workers	Lack of strong culture and identity	Difficult to track and motivate	Unfulfilled development and career needs

The impact of project-based management

The impact of these developments on the organization, its systems and people is not always welcome (Table 4.2).

ORGANIZATION

A purely tasked-based structure can also be inflexible. Without a functional hierarchy, it is difficult to share resources between projects to reflect changing demands. In addition, organizations employing freelance workers may lose corporate culture and identity.

SYSTEMS

Companies with a purely tasked-based structure cannot develop expertise without a functional hierarchy in which to store experience and expertise as teams form and reform.[10] Task groups are usually not interested in developing the management systems of the organization, only their project-related part of it, being unwilling to carry the additional overhead. With the distributed decision making, managers may feel they lack control. They may need to make greater use of informal networks and information systems to monitor and control the projects.[11]

PEOPLE

Many people are uncomfortable with the uncertainty created by dual reporting and diffused decision making. They try to impose structures which suit them, but are at odds with corporate strategy. In particular, people in a matrix organization are subject to divided loyalty between two superiors. Often, the functional manager receives the subordinate's loyalty, as they conduct the annual appraisal.[6,12] People may not have a conventional career structure within this new environment. This is the case for both freelance and permanent staff: the former because they do not belong to the company; the latter because flatter hierarchies create less promotion opportunities, and because without a functional hierarchy there is no defined route. Maslow[13] suggests that people work for social and developmental reasons. These needs are unlikely to be satisfied for freelance workers working from home, or for transient teams members.

Historical lessons

There are historical lessons which indicate how this impact can be resolved, and turned to the organization's benefit. An early statement on matrix management appears in Exodus 20:3:

> Thou shalt have no other gods before me.

Clearly it is believed that people could not cope with the uncertainty of dual reporting; but at that time the priests were also the rulers. That was not the case by the time of the Roman empire, when church and state in

Israel were separate. When he and his followers were accused of challenging the imperial authority (Matthews 22.21), Christ said:

> Render therefore unto Caesar the things which are Caesar's; and unto God the things that are God's.

However, early Christians gave their primary allegiance to God. It was not until church and state were later merged under the Emperor Constantine that people were able to give their loyalty to both without conflict. Throughout most of European history the most stable government has been achieved where church and state are merged. Machiavelli[14] devotes a chapter to this. In the Holy Roman Empire this was achieved by the kaiser being crowned by the pope, in the Vatican by the pope himself being head of state, and in England by the king declaring himself head of the church. Since Henry VIII did that, only three kings have lost their crown, Charles I, James II and Edward VIII. All three lost their position as head of the church, the last two by their own making.

Historically, matrix management has worked best when a person's two managers, priest (functional head) and governor (project head), are seen to be ultimately responsible to the same authority and to be working to the same common goals. Individuals can then fulfil their needs by satisfying both managers together. This historical review probably contains few surprising messages for managers of projects:

- the management style preferred by most people is a line hierarchy
- some endeavours may have both secular and non-secular requirements, and matrix management may then be the most effective style
- functional (permanent) and task (temporary) managers must then be seen to be working to the same corporate goals

Successfully implementing management by projects

This approach may resolve some of the issues identified above.

ORGANIZATION

The optimum style for management by projects may be matrix management. This may overcome the inflexibility associated with both functional and task hierarchies. The task hierarchy focuses on achieving goals, while the functional hierarchy allows sharing of resources between tasks, and focuses on developing expertise, management systems and provides people with a career structure. However, senior management must ensure that task and functional managers are seen to be working to the same corporate objectives, to resolve the uncertainty created by dual reporting. This can be achieved by cascading the corporate strategy to lower management levels through a clearly defined structure of objectives, a product breakdown structure (Chapter 6).

SYSTEMS

By clearly defining the corporate strategy through a cascade of subsidiary objectives, senior management can delegate decision-making processes to task teams. They monitor achievement of the objectives, and pay close attention to decision making where results deviate from requirements. People can also identify their career opportunities through the corporate strategy, rather than a top heavy functional hierarchy.

PEOPLE

The corporate strategy and retained functional hierarchy may also provide the focus for developing corporate culture and identity. It remains only for senior management to satisfy the developmental needs of freelance, knowledge workers.

4.5 Creating a culture for project management[15]

The transition from functional organization to project organization just described as PSO project involving a single transition. The cultural problems arising can be overcome by adopting a matrix organization in which functional and task managers are seen to be committed to the same corporate mission. In a hybrid organization, the interface between projects and operations exists permanently. Operations managers replace functional managers, but the same message applies; they and the project managers must be seen to be working to the same strategic objectives. Both have a responsibility to ensure that project staff know what is required of them to deliver the organization's development objectives, and that the staff do not suffer a conflict of loyalty due to unclear priorities. This dual relationship is illustrated in the *Projectivity Model*[16] (Figure 4.5). (The word 'projectivity' is used to represent an organization's ability to achieve its development objectives through projects.)

Responsibilities of operations managers

The responsibility of operations managers is to ensure that the organization delivers adequate resources to enable selected projects to take place.

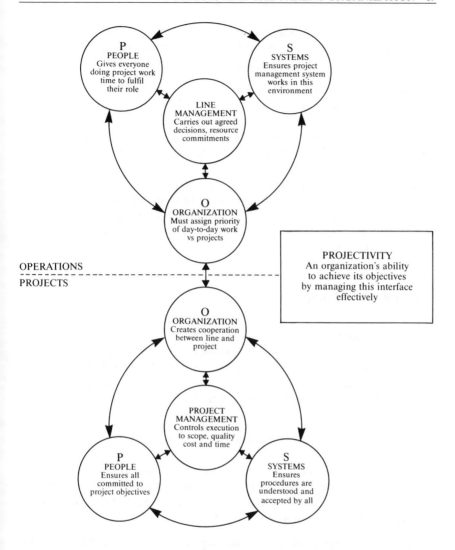

Figure 4.5   The projectivity model for cooperation between operations managers and project managers across the projects/operations interface

Once priorities have been assigned, the operations managers must ensure they are adhered to. This primarily means a commitment to taking professional decisions for which they are responsible, and supplying the resources required by the project, at the time agreed in advance. They must support projects by ensuring that:

- staff are given time to meet their project goals
- project systems are understood in the operations environment
- the project has priority alongside the daily operations.

Operations managers must be aware of their commitments to enable the project to take place, and achieve its objectives. Symptoms of a lack of commitment are: agreements are forgotten, meetings are not attended, there is a lack of interest in the project by the management team, or failure becomes a self-fulfilling prophecy because the line managers give the project inadequate support. Operations managers make their commitment by agreeing a contract with the project (Figure 2.6). The project contracts to deliver development objectives of benefit to the operations managers, and in return they promise to provide resources and support. The benefit may merely be to enable them to fulfil their role more effectively, but that is consistent with what was said above.

Responsibilities of project managers

The responsibility of project managers is to manage the achievement of results. This means planning the scope of work required, organizing by assigning roles and responsibilities to the parties involved, implementing by assigning tasks to resources, and controlling by monitoring progress and taking timely, corrective action to achieve the development objectives. In particular, to manage the interface with operations effectively, project managers must:

- ensure that all participants understand and are committed to the project's goals
- ensure that the project's systems and documents are understood by all
- create cooperation between project and operations by communicating project plans in a form in which they and their consequences are understood and accepted.

Symptoms of inadequate project management are described in Section 5.3. To fulfil their responsibility, project managers must play their part in the negotiations leading to the contract between project and organization. In particular, the requests for resources must be based on sound data, so the commitments made by the other side are realistic. Furthermore, the managers would do well to follow the principles of organizational development given in Section 4.3. Undertaking an education programme to ensure that all staff understand the consequences of the project, and ensuring that project reports concentrate on the achievement of future results, and do not dwell on past mistakes, are particularly valuable.

4.6 Implementing project-based management[15]

Implementing the management of change through projects, whether within a project-based or hybrid environment, is a PSO project, with a heavy cultural element, and should be implemented as a project as part of the corporate development programme. The managing director or other senior manager should manage this project. There are six key steps, which build on the ideas of this and the previous chapters:

1. *Assign priority to development work*: the first requirement is to assign priority to the organization's development programme, and the projects it contains (Section 3.4).
2. *Make a contract between operations and project managers*: the second requirement is for operations managers to commit resources to projects. This is achieved by negotiating a contract at the strategic level of the project hierarchy (Figure 2.6).
3. *Formalize the resource requirements*: the resource requirements are formalized at the next level, where work is allocated to specified resources. Plans are made to release personnel to the project on the due date, against the contract made at the higher level.
4. *Give visibility to the plans*: for the setting of priorities, making of the contract and allocation of resources to be effective, it is vital that plans and progress reports are clearly visible. People can then see clearly what is required of them, and make alternative arrangements in response to changing circumstance. Visibility is achieved by:
   - adopting single page reporting at each level of the project hierarchy, or work breakdown structure
   - expressing the documents in a language understood by all involved, and avoiding the use of jargon.
5. *Adopt a company wide approach to project management*: cooperation is further enhanced if the organization uses a company wide approach to project management, at least at the integrative and strategic levels. All people then understand the project plans, and projects are compared on a common basis when assigning priorities. This is especially true where projects cross international or other cultural boundaries.
6. *Educate all personnel in its use*: training is an important element of the organizational development approach, and this applies to the implementation of project management. Educating people means not only training them in project management techniques, but also making them aware of the strategic importance of project management in the organization's development programme. This should be repeated periodically to continue to raise the organization's efficacy at achieving its development objectives through projects; that is, its projectivity.

4.7 Summary

1. The parties involved in a project include:
   - *the owner*: the organization whose strategic plan creates the need for the project
   - *the sponsor*: the person or group who authorize expenditure on the project
   - *the users*: the people who will operate the facility on behalf of the owner
   - *the champion*: a senior user who campaigns for the project
   - *the contractor*: the group which designs and builds the facility for the owner
   - *the project manager*: the person or group who plans, organizes, implements and controls the work of the contractor to deliver the facility within constraints of time, cost and quality
   - *the supporters*: parties who provide goods and services to the work of the project
   - *the integrators*: people who coordinate the work of the supporters for the manager.
2. The parties involved have two sets of objectives:
   - *overt objectives*: the stated objectives derived from the owner's strategic plan
   - *covert objectives*: personal objectives which may conflict with the overt ones.
3. The work of the project is of two types: *technical* work and *cultural* work.
4. The cultural work is easily ignored, yet is more difficult to manage. It can be managed using the techniques of organizational development. The following can help to overcome the resistance to change:
   - communication
   - participation
   - training and development
   - management by objectives
   - team development and leadership
   - commitment from senior management.
5. The change to a project-based organization has associated cultural changes. The most effective management structure may be a matrix organization, but this requires both functional and task managers to be seen to be working to the same corporate mission.
6. In a hybrid environment operations managers must ensure that
   - staff are given time to meet project goals
   - project systems are understood in the operations environment

- projects are given priority alongside daily operations;
and project managers must ensure that
- all participants are committed to project goals
- project management systems are understood by all
- cooperation exists between projects and operations.
7. Implementing management by projects is a PSO project with six steps:
- assign priority to the organization's development work
- make a contract between project and operations managers
- formalize the resource requirements
- adopt clear and simple documentation
- adopt a company wide approach to project management
- educate all personnel involved in projects in its use.

Notes and references

1. Section 4.3 incorporates material written by Lynn Thurloway, who was previously a manager in a recruitment agency, responsible for over 200 temporary workers, and is now an ESRC Teaching Fellow at the College.
2. Andersen, E. S., Grude, K. V., Haug, T. and Turner, J. R., *Goal Directed Project Management*, Kogan Page, 1987.
3. Elmes, M. and Wileman, D., 'Organizational culture and project leader effectiveness', *Project Management Journal*, **19** (4), 55–63, 1988.
4. Section 4.4 incorporates material from a paper written jointly with Dr Frances Clark and Dr Alex Lord (Turner, Clark and Lord, 1990). Dr Clark is an assistant director of Company Programmes at Henley Management College, and works in the areas of organizational development, total quality and the use of information technology. Previously she has worked in training and consultancy in the public and private sectors, working for, among others, the Greater London Council and Coopers & Lybrand. Dr Lord is an ESRC Teaching Fellow at the College, and works in the area of project leadership.
5. Turner, J. R., Clark, F. A. and Lord, M. A., 'The impact of management by projects on the organisation, systems and people of companies in the industrial sector', in *The Handbook of Management by Projects* (ed. R. Gareis), Manz, 1990.
6. Davis, S. M. and Lawrence, P. R., *Matrix Management*, Addison-Wesley, 1977.
7. Doujak, A., Haslauer, H., Madl, M. and Rattay, G., 'The role of the top manager in project orientated companies', in *Proceedings of the 13th INTERNET International Expert Seminar* (ed. R. Gareis), INTERNET, 1989.
8. Handy, C., *The Future of Work: A guide to changing society*, Blackwell, 1988.
9. Drucker, P., *The New Realities*, Heinemann, 1989.
10. Allen, T. J., 'Organisation structure, information technology, and R&D productivity', *IEEE Transactions of Engineering Management*, **33** (4), 212–17, 1986.
11. Dawson, P. and McLoughlin, I., 'Computer technology and the redefinition of supervision', *Journal of Management Studies*, **23** (1), 116–32, 1986.
12. Knight, K. (ed.), *Matrix Management*, Gower Press, 1977.

13. Maslow, A. H., *Motivation and Personality*, Harper & Row, 1954.
14. Machiavelli, N., *The Prince*, 1514; reprinted, Penguin, 1961.
15. Sections 4.5 and 4.6 incorporate material from a paper written jointly with Tor Haug (Haug and Turner, 1989). Mr Haug is a partner in the Norwegian firm of Coopers & Lybrand management consultancy. He has been involved in the management of projects for nearly 20 years, previously as a change manager in a Norwegian insurance company.
16. Haug, T. and Turner, J. R., 'Projectivity: creating an environment for increasing productivity and effectiveness in project work', in *Proceedings of the 13th INTERNET International Expert Seminar* (ed. R. Gareis), INTERNET, 1989.

5
Strategic management of projects

5.1 Introduction[1,2]

I now turn to the third element of the project's context: the strategies for successful implementation. The way one approaches a project determines largely how successful it will be. We have known for generations that time spent planning a project is time well spent, yet we consistently spend too little in a project's early stages, failing to consider adequately the range of issues that will subsequently cause problems. I have often heard the complaint: 'We do not seem to have time to plan the work adequately, but we seem to have time to do it twice.'

Managers of projects need to think better and at an early stage about what will influence the success of their project, and to manage all the internal, external and strategic factors that will deliver that success. A model for the strategic management of projects will assist them in this task. A strategy can be defined as:

> a vehicle for the successful attainment of one's objectives, taking account of the constraints of the environment within which one is operating, and the resources available.

There are five essential parts to this definition, which address all the inherent features of projects and their management introduced in Chapters 1 and 2:

- success
- objectives
- the vehicle
- the environment
- the resources.

However, before we can develop the model for the strategic management of projects, we need to know how we shall assess projects as being successful, and what threats and pitfalls there are to achieving that success. The next two sections will deal with these two issues. I shall then describe a model for the strategic management of projects, and discuss the five principles of good project management followed in this book.

5.2 Judging project success

The standard mnemonic for judging success of a project is to say the work should be completed *on time*, *within budget*, and *to specification*. These three constraints figure strongly in many of the definitions of a project given in Section 1.2. However, this measure of success focuses solely on the work of the project, and views it primarily from the point of view of the contractor. It is also sometimes quite subjective (Example 5.1).

In the early 1980s, I worked as an engineer on four ammonia plants in the northeast. Every six months we closed a plant for biennial refit. Over a period of four weeks we did 100 000 man-hours of work. We planned the overhauls to within four hours, but were usually about two days late. However, we were *only* two days late. We pulled all the stops and managed our way through all the problems to deliver the project within two days of target. On one overhaul we coasted in four hours early and felt we had failed. If we had been given a tighter target we could have really proved ourselves and achieved a shorter duration!!! The plant overhaul did not satisfy our need to prove ourselves as managers.

Example 5.1 Completing projects on time

A project is undertaken to deliver a facility, which in turn produces a product. The owner is primarily interested in the benefit the product brings, although to be of value it has to be available within a certain time and for a certain price, and meet certain quality standards. Time, cost and quality are constraints that affect the owner's judgement, but are not the primary concern. The contractor, on the other hand, wants to complete the project on time, within budget (in order to make a profit), and to specification so that the owner will accept the facility and pay for the work. The actual people involved in the project may also have a host of covert objectives which will cloud their judgement, regardless of the outcomes above (cf. Section 4.2). Morris and Hough[3] reviewed performance on eight major projects from the 1960s, 1970s and 1980s, and derived four criteria for success: the project delivers its functionality; it is on time, to cost, to quality; it is profitable for the contractor; and, if necessary, it is terminated early. They judged their eight case studies against these, and found again that subjective perceptions can cloud the judgement. In particular:

- the *Fulmar Oil Field* in the North Sea was late, but extremely profitable for the owner, so was judged to be successful
- the *Thames Barrier* was late and overspent, and was quite badly managed in its early stages, but is a tourist attraction and made a profit for most of the contractors, so is now judged a success
- *Concorde* was late and overspent, but was a technical success, gave France an aerospace industry, and contributed to Britain's entry to the EC, so is judged to be successful
- *Heysham II Nuclear Power Station* was well managed, and nearly on time and budget, but the judgement is clouded by the rest of Britain's nuclear power programme, and the public's perception of the nuclear industry, so it is judged to be unsuccessful.

These projects were major infrastructure projects. The benefits were social good, not financial return. They therefore only say that the project should achieve its functionality, not that it should provide benefit. Developing the concepts of the last two chapters, I would propose a more extensive list for judging success:

- It achieves its stated business purpose.
- It provides satisfactory benefit to the owner.
- It satisfies the needs of the owner, users and stakeholders.
- It meets its prestated objectives to produce the facility.
- The facility is produced to specification, within budget and on time.
- The project satisfies the needs of the project team and supporters.

There are several interesting points. First, most of the criteria are subjective; only time and cost are objective. Secondly, the judgement is affected by the assessor's covert objectives. Thirdly, the measures are not necessarily compatible, so the judgement depends on a complex balance. However, the measures are not mutually exclusive, so it is possible to satisfy them together, but you must start with that objective, and through the strategy for implementation negotiate the balance. You cannot force them to be compatible at the end of the project. Finally, the measures are not judged simultaneously. The first two can only be judged after the facility has been commissioned, and the product obtained, which, sometimes, is many years after completion of the project. The Thames Barrier is awaiting the first major flood, and the public image of Concorde has improved with time. The next three are judged on completion of the project, as the facility is commissioned, and the last occurs throughout the project.

5.3 Pitfalls

This view of a success is the basis for the strategy for implementation (see Section 5.4). However, let us first describe some pitfalls that can threaten successful implementation. Pitfalls are not risks in the work itself (see Chapter 11) but are management mistakes made by project managers. They can occur in the way the project is established, or the way it is planned, organized, implemented or controlled. Many of the following pitfalls were observed by Grude[4] from his experience as managing director of a firm of software engineers.

Pitfalls in establishing the project

These are pitfalls in the way the project is set up within the parent organization, and include:

- project plans not aligned with business plans
- procedures for managing projects not defined
- project priorities not communicated to the parties involved
- no shared vision.

PROJECT PLANS ALIGNED WITH BUSINESS PLANS

Projects are undertaken to fulfil a purpose, usually to achieve business benefit, and satisfying that purpose is the ultimate measure of success. Therefore, the project plans must be derived from the business plans. The accountancy package at the computer company described in Example 3.1 is an example of what can happen if they are not. This pitfall often arises by starting with detail planning, and is the one pitfall that will usually cause a project to fail.

PROCEDURES FOR MANAGING PROJECTS DEFINED

Projects use transient teams to undertake novel assignments. The teams must come together quickly in order to undertake the task successfully. That will not happen if they spend time at the start defining the management processes to be used. Having a company-wide approach to project management can help knit project teams. (Procedures are described in Chapter 16 and team formation in Chapter 18.)

PROJECT PRIORITIES COMMUNICATED TO PARTIES INVOLVED

In Example 3.5, I described what can happen when priorities are not communicated. People assign their own, usually different, priorities with the result that there is no coordination and no work is done.

This can be a powerful motivator and a way of building commitment to the project and its objectives. We saw in Section 4.4 how it is essential to stable government, and to effective project management.

Pitfalls in planning

These are pitfalls in the way the time and cost schedules are calculated, and how the work is defined and communicated to the project team. They include:

- planning on a single level
- using cumbersome, unfriendly tools
- discouraging creativity
- estimating unrealistically.

HIERARCHICAL PLANNING

This is how we ensure the work delivers the required benefit. The usual pitfall is to plan at a detailed level only; computer software unfortunately encourages this. Sometimes work is planned only at a very high level, and there is no coordination. The following Chinese proverb illustrates that in almost every area of human endeavour work is planned on many levels. Projects should be no different.

A journey of a thousand miles begins with a single step. (Mao Tse-Tung)

On a journey there are at least two levels of planning between the end objective and the single steps: the milestones (towns and villages) and the route map (roads). The former is the strategic plan, comprising intermediate goals or products, and the latter the tactical plan. At the milestone level, we try to hold our plan constant, providing key, fixed points for measuring progress towards our objective. The road map we also try to keep fixed. However, there are two ways we can build in flexibility. If we find the route blocked, we can make a detour, but still aim to reach the next milestone. The detour is occasionally better than our originally proposed route, but changes are contained at a low level. We can also adopt *rolling-wave planning*; that is, we do not need to define the route between the last two towns until we reach the penultimate town, and sometimes we cannot get the necessary information until we arrive at that point. We only need to estimate the distance between the towns to plan the time and cost of the journey. The single steps are planned as we progress.

USING FRIENDLY TOOLS

The complexity of project planning tools has grown over the last 30 years due to the increasing power of software. However, at best, complex plans achieve nothing; at worst, they confuse the situation (see Example 5.2). The plans and progress reports should be cascaded through WBS (Section 12.3). This can help build the vision for the project.

A delegate on a project management course at Henley Management College said that he had three people on his project who spent all day every day developing plans on a well known PC-based package, and he got no useful information out. His total project team consisted of about 20 people, and so 15 per cent of them were contributing nothing!!!

Example 5.2 Cumbersome, unfriendly tools

One reason why detail planning tools have developed is they were used so successfully on the Polaris Project in the USA in the 1950s. There is no doubt that PERT (the program evaluation and review technique), which was first developed on the project, was a powerful analytical tool that helped identify and eliminate risk, and so removed two years from an eight-year schedule. The project manager was also a very charismatic man, and he used the technique to help build the vision for the project.[5] However, the following quotation illustrates a covert use of the technique:

> These procedures were valuable in selling the importance of the mission. More importantly, the PERT charts and the rest of the *gibberish* let us build a fence to keep the rest of the Navy out and get across the message that we were the top managers.[6]

Complex plans were deliberately used to confuse outsiders getting too closely involved in the project, and thereby protecting the project team from interference. This is a valid use of complex plans, but you also need to maintain the simple plans, or you will also confuse yourself.

ENCOURAGE CREATIVITY

In the modern environment it is impossible for a project manager to be a technical expert in all areas of a project. Yet it is not uncommon to see project managers dictating to technical experts through the plan, telling them how to do their jobs. This can demotivate them, and isolate them from the project. What the project manager should do is delegate elements of the strategic plan to the experts, state the milestones for which they are responsible, by when and at what cost, but allow them to determine the best method of achieving that. In this way they can retain their integrity, while meeting the project's goals.

ESTIMATE REALISTICALLY

There are several causes of unrealistic estimates. It is common when preparing estimates to believe that the owner may not accept them and, therefore, reduce them. Inevitably the work turns out as originally estimated, resulting in perceived failure. Secondly, there may be inadequate historical data to estimate the work accurately, in which case the risk must be identified and an appropriate contingency added. Thirdly, people have different abilities. You must plan for the people you have, not for some unobtainable ideal. Finally, it is sometimes assumed that project personnel are able to do 260 days (2080 man-hours) of work in a year. A person working full time on a project is available much less than that. Lost time is caused by holidays, bank holidays, sickness, training, group meetings, etc. When planning, this lost time must be accounted for (see Sections 7.5 and 10.3).

Pitfalls in organizing and implementing

The pitfalls in building the project organization and assigning work to people include:

- lack of cooperation
- resource providers uncommitted
- resources unavailable when required
- unclear management responsibility
- poor communication
- technical management rather than project management.

ACHIEVING COOPERATION

It is not uncommon on projects to wonder if you all work for the same organization, as covert objectives get in the way of the overt objectives. Cooperation is achieved in two ways: by building a clear vision for the project; and by negotiating agreement to the plans (cf. Chapter 4).

GAINING COMMITMENT OF RESOURCE PROVIDERS

Project managers often use resources on secondment from other managers. The latter will not willingly release their resources if they are not committed to the project. That commitment can be won in ways already described.

ENSURING AVAILABILITY OF RESOURCES

It is not adequate to just send the resource providers a plan and expect their people to be available at some point in the future. Even if they are committed to the project, you must ensure that they understand the requirements of the plan. This is helped by using a simple plan, by discussing the requirements of the plan with the resource providers, and by negotiating their release. They must also plan to release their resources at the required time.

DEFINING MANAGEMENT RESPONSIBILITY

When defining roles on projects, it is common to consider only those people who do work, e.g. cutting metal or writing code. However, people have other roles that consume time or can delay the project. These tend to be management roles, especially those that cause delay. These roles include taking decisions, managing information and managing progress.

MANAGING COMMUNICATION

Surprisingly, poor communication on projects is often caused by too much rather than too little. Communication out of a project is often achieved by sending every piece of information to everyone involved. People soon learn that only a few documents are relevant to them, so all go directly into the waste-bin. The project manager must define those who need the information, so that when people receive something they know they ought to read it. If some other person wishes to be included in the circulation of information, then that can be negotiated. Similarly, committees are often used for communication into a project. Once invited, people tend to stay on the committee, even if they are no longer required. Committees grow organically. Worse still, it is those people who have least to contribute who do most of the talking at meetings, as they talk to justify their presence. Channels of communication into a project must be clearly defined and limited, and any additions discussed and negotiated.

TECHNICAL VERSUS PROJECT MANAGEMENT

One reason why construction of the Thames Barrier was poorly managed in the early stages was there was no integrative project management. The 'project managers' were primarily technical managers, with responsibility for managing the design. There was little coordination of the work in the modern sense of project management. It is still common to hear design managers refer to themselves as project managers, especially in the software and building industries. In the latter, architects take responsibility for project management, and yet they are primarily designers. Often, these 'project managers' are not good at delegating work. They believe, often quite rightly, they can do the work better than anyone else, and so surround themselves with idle people while they work themselves into an early grave. It is my view that an industry has truly matured in the management of projects when it stops calling design managers 'project managers' and stops using design engineers as such.

Pitfalls in control

Finally pitfalls in monitoring and controlling progress include:

- the project members do not understand the purpose of control
- the plans and progress reports are not integrated
- the review process is not formalized
- the project manager has responsibility but no authority.

These pitfalls are illustrated by a small project I was asked to audit (see Example 5.3).

I once audited a project where the manager felt he had lost control, but was not sure why. The project was to develop a trade exhibition, held in Birmingham, in December of one year. There were 15 syndicates of four companies collaborating in this exhibition. Work started in July. Each syndicate prepared its own material, and then came together at a test site in September, moving to Birmingham in late November. The project manager was a contractor. In July he had a meeting with the representative of each syndicate, showed his plan, and said if a syndicate had any problems with the plan, let him know. Those were his first and second mistakes: he dictated to the experts by telling them his plan instead of developing a plan with them; and no comment was interpreted as agreement. The project manager then held weekly meetings attended by the representatives at which they gave verbal progress reports. Each person spoke for about 15 minutes, resulting in a four-hour meeting; but the project had been set up in such a way that they were not interested in what each other was saying. Each meeting therefore consumed

64 man-hours to no effect. At each meeting the representatives usually reported that everything was going to plan. I was called in mid-September because, in spite of that, materials were not arriving at the test site at the due time. The manager wondered what was going on. What had happened was that after the first meeting most of the syndicates had ignored the project manager's plan and worked to their own. When they said things were going according to plan, they meant their own plan, but the project manager assumed they meant his, and the two bore no relation.

Example 5.3 Pitfalls in control

UNDERSTANDING THE PURPOSE OF CONTROL

The purpose of control is not to hold meetings or talk about progress. The purpose is to monitor progress, to compare progress to the plan, and to take necessary action to achieve the project's goals. This may mean continuing to follow the existing plan, revising the plan, or revising the goals.

MONITORING PROGRESS AGAINST THE PLAN

Control will only be effective if there is a common basis for control, which means a common plan. This is achieved most effectively by reporting progress on a copy of the plan.

EFFECTIVE REVIEW MEETINGS

In order to be effective, review meetings must be formalized, which means three things: controlled attendance; fixed criteria for reporting; and fixed intervals. Discussing progress at the coffee machine may be part of good leadership and team building, but is not part of good control. At the other extreme, large meetings where most people are not interested in what others are saying waste time. Meetings must be formalized, with people invited because they have something to contribute. Holding review meetings at two or more levels of the planning hierarchy can aid this. (The manager in Example 5.3 should have had weekly meetings with the representatives individually, and less frequent meetings with the whole group to discuss common issues.) The meetings must have a fixed agenda, which means reporting against fixed criteria, including the plan. Without a structure people will report progress in a way that is most favourable to themselves. Finally, people sometimes hold meetings only when they have something to discuss. By then it is usually not possible to avoid the problems for which the meeting was called, but only to limit the damage. Meetings must be held at fixed intervals, although the frequency may vary depending on the risk, and the point in the project life cycle.

RESPONSIBILITY WITHOUT AUTHORITY

This is an impossible position for any manager. The manager in Example 5.3 had no direct authority over the syndicates, and was not able to use other sources, including that obtained by negotiating agreements. Without authority for control, the manager cannot take action to achieve the project's goals.

5.4 Strategies for success[1,7]

I shall now describe a model for the strategic management of projects (Figure 5.1) which incorporates the five elements of strategy introduced in Section 5.1.

1. The attitudes represent people's approach to and perception of the success of the project.
2. The definition describes its objectives.

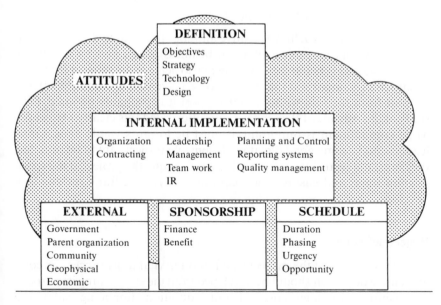

Figure 5.1 The project strategy model

3. The internal implementation is the vehicle.
4. The external factors are the environment.
5. The sponsorship and schedule define the available resources.

This strategic model mirrors the project system (cf. Figure 2.7). The definition describes the project, at the heart of the system; the internal implementation addresses project management, a vehicle linking the project to its context and drives the system; and the three elements in the base address the project's context: sponsorship represents the project in corporate strategy, the benefit the sponsor expects to receive from the project and the financial support they are willing to give in return; the external factors represent the external parties involved, including parent organization; and the schedule is the strategy for implementation. It is appropriate that the strategic model for managing implementation addresses all the elements of the system.

Attitudes

This is the first and most important element. The chances of success are substantially diminished unless:

- there is a major commitment to making the project a success
- the motivation of everyone working on the project is high
- attitudes are supportive and positive.

I have shown that to achieve positive attitudes it is vital to develop a clear mission, by linking project plans to business plans, and by functional and task managers being seen to cooperate to achieve the same objectives. It is particularly important that the project receive visible commitment and support from the top; without that support it is probably doomed. (The study of the Advanced Passenger Train[3] illustrated this clearly.) However, while commitment is important, it must be towards viable ends. Great leaders can become great dictators. If sensible projects are to be initiated, they must not be insulated from criticism. Critique the project at the specification stage, and ensure that it continues to receive frank reviews as it develops.

Project definition

The development of the project's definition is vital to its success. A comprehensive definition should be developed from the start, stating its purpose, ownership, technology, cost, schedule, duration, financing, sales and marketing, and resource requirements. If this is not done, key issues essential to the viability of the project may be omitted or given inadequate attention, resulting in poor performance later on. Through the project definition, the vision for the project is created, the purpose of the project is defined, the project plans are aligned with the business plans and the basis of cooperation agreed. This is achieved by:

- setting the project's objectives
- defining the scope through a strategic, or milestone, plan
- setting the functional strategies and assessing technical risk
- carefully managing the design process
- managing resources and the context.

SETTING OBJECTIVES

Little can be done until clear, unambiguous objectives have been set for the project. I have shown how a project's success can be compromised by objectives that are unclear, do not mesh with longer term strategies, and are not clearly communicated and agreed.

DEFINING THE SCOPE

Scope definition, and cost, time and performance criteria are intimately related. If they are unrealistic, expectations for the project will not be met, and it will be said to 'fail'. The strategic plan for attaining the project's objectives must also be developed in a comprehensive manner from the start. If the project objectives change, the scope definition and investment criteria must be reconsidered.

SETTING FUNCTIONAL STRATEGIES

The setting of a project's functional strategies must be handled with great care, and requires the determination of the design, the technology to be used, the method of its implementation and eventual operation best suited to achieving the objectives. The design standards selected will affect the difficulty of construction and eventual operation of the plant. Technical risk in particular needs to be assessed. Many studies have shown that technical problems can have a huge impact on the likelihood of project overrun.[3]

MANAGING THE DESIGN PROCESS

No design is ever complete; technology is always progressing. A key challenge is to achieve a balance between meeting the schedule and making the design that bit better. Central to modern project management is the orderly progression of the design and its technical basis through a sequence of review stages. At each stage, the level of detail is refined, with strict control of technical interfaces and changes (through 'configuration management', see Section 16.3). Changes can result in extensive rework, as people on other parts of the project may have based their assumptions on the agreed design. You should therefore aim to achieve a progressive design freeze as soon as possible. This is usually feasible in traditional engineering projects, but I show in Chapter 8 that an early design freeze may conflict with meeting the customer's requirements, especially in organizational development, high technology and information systems projects. In setting up projects, care should be taken to appraise technical risk, prove new technologies, and validate the project design, before freezing the design and moving into implementation. The management of the design process is described in Chapter 13, and its application on engineering design and information technology projects in Chapter 20.

RESOURCES AND CONTEXT

It is no good defining what you want to achieve if you do not have the right number of good, committed people, sufficient money, adequate infrastructure, etc. In fact, getting adequate resources, managing them well and ensuring that the context is supportive are at the heart of successful strategic management, yet are rarely addressed by the literature on strategy. I shall cover resources under both the project's internal organization and its external context.

Strategies for the internal organization

Areas addressed during organization of the project should include:

- organization
- people issues
- planning and control systems.

ORGANIZATION

There are two organizational issues, both of which must be considered from the earliest stages of project definition:

- the relevant management structure: project–matrix–functional
- the extent of owner involvement.

Management structure

A project structure is expensive on resources (cf. Section 4.4). Many projects begin and end with a functional line structure, but change to a matrix during implementation.[6] In addition, implementing a matrix takes time, and effort must be put into developing the appropriate organizational climate. Assistance from organization behaviour may be considered in adopting a matrix organization. (The issues in selecting a structure are described in Section 7.4.)

Extent of owner involvement

The issue is the extent to which the owner does not possess the necessary skills to undertake the work, but has a legal or moral responsibility for assuring that it is done to a satisfactory standard. The first constraint is the most common. In building and civil engineering industries, because of the nature of the demand, owners rarely have sufficient resources in-house to accomplish the project. Outside resources, principally designers, contractors and suppliers, are brought in. The owners focus more on running their businesses. Yet some owner involvement is usually necessary, for if no project management expertise is maintained in-house then active, directive decision making of the kind that is generally necessary will not be available. However, if operators who are not really in the implementation business get too heavily involved, there is a danger that the owner's staff may tinker with design and construction decisions at the expense of effective implementation. This is a common complaint of contractors in the defence industry, and when I worked for ICI in the early 1980s we recognized the consequence of our doing it. The solution to this dilemma is not easy. What is right will be right for a given mix of project characteristics, organizations and personalities. The key, ultimately, is for owner-operators to concentrate on predetermined milestone review points, to schedule these properly and to review the project comprehensively as it passes across each of them. Milestone scheduling by owners is now much more accepted as appropriate than the more detailed scheduling of the past.

PEOPLE ISSUES

Projects usually demand extraordinary effort from the people working on them (often for modest financial reward, and with the ultimate prospect of working oneself out of a job). I showed in Chapter 4 how significant institutional resistance must be overcome if the many factors listed are to be achieved. This puts enormous demands on the personal qualities of all those working on the project, from senior management through the professional teams to artisans. The implementation of the initial stages of a project may require considerable leadership and championing. Beware, though, of unchecked champions and leaders: of the hype and overoptimism that too often surrounds projects in their early stages. The sponsors must be responsible for providing the objective check on the feasibility of the project. The sponsors might be considered as those people providing the business case, and the resources, for the project. Evidently they ought to be convinced of the merits of the project on as objective a basis as possible. The project champion, however, is by definition someone who is promoting the project: pushing it, and hence being less objective than the sponsors.

We should recognize the importance of team working, of handling the conflicts which arise on projects positively, and of good communications. Consideration should be given to formal start-up sessions at the beginning of a team's work (mixing planning with team building), as stated in Chapter 13.[8] The composition of the team should be looked at from a social as well as a technical viewpoint: people play social roles on teams, and these will be required to vary as the project evolves (see Chapter 18).

PLANNING AND CONTROL SYSTEMS

Plans should be prepared by those technically responsible for their work, and integrated by the Project Support Office (Chapter 16). Initial planning should be at a broad, *systems* level with detail only being provided where essential, and in general on a *rolling-wave* basis (Chapters 6 and 12). Similarly, cost estimates should be prepared by *work breakdown* element, detail being provided as appropriate (Chapter 9). Cost control should be in terms of physical progress, and not in terms of invoiced value (Chapter 14). Cost should be related to finance, and be assembled into forecast out-turn cost, related both to the forecast actual construction price and to the actual product sales price. All changes to the proposed project baseline, proposed as well as actual, should be monitored extremely carefully. Implementation of systems and procedures should be planned carefully so that all those working on the project understand them properly. Start-up meetings should develop the systems procedures in outline, and begin substantive planning while simultaneously 'building' the project team (Parts Four and Five).

Strategies for the project's context

The strategies for handling the project's context must address:

- the external influences
- financing the project
- scheduling the project.

EXTERNAL INFLUENCES

An analysis of causes of project overruns, shows that external factors are a principal cause. Several may be identified, but the project's political context, its relationship with the local community, the general environment, and the project's location and the geophysical conditions in which it is set are particularly important. It may be asked how much management can influence such external factors. Often its ability to influence them directly is limited, but some influence can often be exerted, if only to provide some protective action or contingency.

Most projects raise political issues, and hence require political support. These issues must be considered from the outset. People working on a project must be attuned to political issues and be ready to manage them. To be successful, project managers must manage upwards and outwards, as well as downwards and inwards. The project manager should court the politicians and influential managers, helping allies by providing information needed to champion their programme. Adversaries should be coopted, not ignored.

The stakeholders, especially the local community, are an important external influence. The management of change must take account of this influence, and so techniques such as the Environmental Impact Analysis (EIA) procedure have now been adopted. This process shows how substantive dialogue can help reduce potential opposition. The value of the EIA process is that it allows consultation and dialogue between developers, the community, regulators and others, and yet forces time to be spent at the 'front end' in examining options and ensuring that the project appears viable. Thus, the likelihood of community opposition and of unforeseen external shocks arising is diminished. Furthermore, in forcing project developers to spend time planning, the EIA process emphasizes precisely that project stage which traditionally was rushed, in spite of the obvious dangers.

FINANCING THE PROJECT

Raising the finance required for the Channel Tunnel 1986/87 illustrates well how finance interacts with the elements of project strategy. Raising the £7.5 billion required certain technical work to be done, planning approvals to be obtained, contracts to be signed, political uncertainties to be removed, etc. Since the project raised most of its funding externally, a significant amount of bootstrapping was required: tasks could only be accomplished if some money was already raised, and so on. Actions had to be taken by a certain time or the money would run out. Further, a key parameter of the project's viability was the likelihood of its slippage during construction. A slippage of three to six months meant not just increased financing charges but the lost revenue of a summer season of tourist traffic. Thus, the Channel Tunnel also demonstrates the significance of managing a project's schedule and of how its timing interrelates with its other dimensions.

SCHEDULING THE PROJECT

Determining the overall timing of the endeavour is crucial to calculating the risks and dynamics of implementation and management. How much time one has available for each of the basic stages of the project, together with the amount and difficulty of the work to be accomplished in those phases, heavily influences the nature of the task to be managed. Therefore, in specifying the project, the manager should ensure that the right amount of time is spent within the overall duration. Milestone scheduling of the projects at the earliest stage is crucial. It is important that none of the development stages of the project be rushed or glossed over (a fault that has caused many project catastrophes in the past).

A degree of urgency should be built into a project, but too much may create instability. The manager should avoid beginning implementation before technology development and testing are complete. This situation is known as *concurrency*. (Concurrency is sometimes employed quite deliberately to get a project completed under exceptionally urgent conditions, but it often brings major problems in redesign and reworking.) Concurrency is now increasingly synonymous with *fast track*; that is, building before design is complete. If faced with this, be under no illusion as to the risk. Analyse the risk rigorously, work element by work element, milestone by milestone. The term 'fast build' is now being used to distinguish a different form of design and construction overlap: that where the concept, or scheme, design is completed but the work packages are priced, programmed and built sequentially, within the overall design parameters, with strict change (configuration) control being exercised throughout. With the use of fast build, the design is secure and the risks are much less.

5.5 Principles of good project management

The remainder of this book focuses on two elements of this strategy model: the definition of the project and its implementation. These correspond to the inner two circles of the project management system in Figure 2.7. The book develops the structured approach to the management of change through projects. It shows how to define the project to achieve a business purpose, both in terms of the facility to be produced and the work to be done, and then how to plan, organize, implement and control the work required to produce the facility. It also describes the leadership role of the project manager. The management of the external factors is beyond the scope of this book, and will only be considered as far as those factors impact on the definition and implementation of the project.

In order to avoid the pitfalls described above the approach is based on five principles of good project management. An approach built on these five principles will also satisfy the requirements of the model for the strategic management of projects. The five principles are:

1. Manage through a structured breakdown of the facility.
2. Focus on results: *what* to achieve, not *how* to achieve it.
3. Balance results through the work breakdown, between areas of technology and people, systems and organization.
4. Organize a contract between all the parties involved, by defining their roles, responsibilities and working relationships.
5. Adopt a clear and simple reporting structure.

Manage through a structured breakdown of the facility

Ultimately a project is successful if it provides benefit and achieves its purpose (see Section 5.2). Hence, the definition of the purpose and benefit must be the starting point for project definition. The facility required to deliver the purpose is defined through quantitative and qualitative objectives. Then, top-down, through a *product* or *work breakdown structure* (WBS), we define the scope of work required, and impose constraints of time, cost and quality. Through the three fundamental levels of work breakdown – the integrative, strategic and tactical levels – the project team members can see how their work contributes to the overall mission of the project. Most of the other control systems are built around the WBS, so this technique is the backbone of project management. A common pitfall is to start with a detailed definition of the work, and through an 'amalgamate-up' process try to match that to the perceived objectives.[9] This pitfall arises because people have an undue focus on time and the work for its own sake, and misuse the critical path method.

Focus on results

Elements of work in the breakdown structure are defined by the results they deliver, often called their *deliverables*. These are the intermediate products of the facility. There are two reasons for focusing on results:

1. *It gives a more stable plan* The work required to reach a result can change as the project develops and new information becomes available, whereas the objectives and intermediate products will remain fixed if the project definition does not change.
2. *It gives a better control of the scope of work* Work is done because it delivers a result that builds towards the project's objectives, not for its own sake, or because it is contained in the plan.

To illustrate the difference between results and work, the first two results in my day are 'when I am awake' and 'when my hunger is satisfied'. The first is not 'when the alarm clock rings'. If I forget to set it or if I am in a hotel, I may never reach that, but I can wake in other ways. If I define my plan by the result, I can continue no matter how I wake; but if I define it by the method of achieving it, the plan collapses if I use a different approach. Similarly, the second result is not 'when I have had a full English breakfast'. I may want a full English breakfast or a cup of coffee, depending on what I had the night before; but I shall be in the best position to decide that at the breakfast table, not some time before. I can decide what work I need to do to achieve the result when I have all the information, not do work because my plan tells me to do it.

If the work is defined in terms of results, the term 'product breakdown structure' (PBS) may be more appropriate than 'work breakdown structure' (WBS); in manufacturing terms it is the *bill of materials* for the facility. The term PBS is used on information systems projects[10] and WBS on engineering projects.[9] There is an important conceptual difference between the two, and this principle implies that the former is preferred. However, I shall defer to majority usage, and from here on use WBS to refer to both.

Balance results through the work breakdown

The plan at the strategic level can be used to ensure that proper emphasis is given to all areas of the project, and to ensure that the levels of ambition for different areas of technical work – and for changes to people, systems and organization – are consistent, balanced and appropriate to the project's purpose. I showed in Chapter 4 how the team's attention can focus on technical work. A balance must be achieved through the strategic plan.

Organize a contract by defining roles and responsibilities

The project organization defines the type, level and role of resources against work elements at each level of the WBS. Defining roles means not just work roles, but management responsibility and communication channels. In particular, one person should be responsible for managing progress of each element in the WBS. This is a principle known as *single point responsibility*. Together the definitions of work and organization form a contract between project and corporate management, trading what the project will deliver against the support the owner will give in return (Figure 2.6). Project managers must agree both the work and organization with the operational line managers and resource providers through a process of discussion to gain their cooperation.

Adopt a clear and simple reporting structure

Project management is difficult, and is not made any simpler by adopting complex planning and reporting methods. This is especially true when trying to gain the commitment of transient teams of resources, or of the users and stakeholders, as discussed in Chapter 4. It is therefore important to represent the plan and report progress between each level of the work breakdown and project organization on a single sheet. This provides a clear, simple vision for the project. On a single sheet, people are able to see their contribution and how it fits into the project at a higher level. This helps to build their commitment to the project's objectives, and to the work required.

5.6 Summary

1. The strategy for successful management of projects ensures that:
   - there exists an attitude for success
   - the objectives by which success is measured are defined
   - there is a vehicle for achieving the objectives
   - the environment is supportive
   - adequate and appropriate resources are available.
2. The criteria for judging success of a project are:
   - it achieves its stated business purpose
   - it provides satisfactory benefit to the owner
   - it satisfies the needs of the owner, users and stakeholders
   - it meets its prestated objectives to produce the facility
   - the facility is produced to quality, cost and time
   - the project satisfies the project team and supporters.

3. Pitfalls in establishing the project include:
   - project plans are not aligned with the business plans
   - procedures for managing the project are not defined
   - project priorities are not communicated
   - there is no shared vision.
4. Pitfalls in planning the project include:
   - using cumbersome, unfriendly tools
   - discouraging creativity
   - estimating unrealistically.
5. Pitfalls in organizing the project include:
   - lack of cooperation
   - resource providers uncommitted
   - resources unavailable when required
   - unclear management responsibility
   - poor communication
   - technical management rather than project management.
6. Pitfalls in controlling the project include:
   - the project members do not understand the purpose of control
   - the plans and progress reports are not integrated
   - the review process is not formalized
   - the project manager has responsibility but no authority.
7. The correct attitudes for success require:
   - a major commitment to success
   - the support of top management.
8. Strategies for project definition cover:
   - setting the project's objectives
   - defining the scope through a strategic, or milestone, plan
   - setting functional strategies, and assessing technical risk
   - carefully managing the design process
   - managing resources and the context.
9. Strategies for internal organization cover:
   - organization
   - people issues
   - planning and control systems.
10. Strategies for the project's context cover:
    - the influences of the context
    - the financing of the project
    - the scheduling of the project.
11. The approach to project management followed in this book is based on five principles of good management:
    - manage through a structured work breakdown
    - focus on results

- balance results
- organize a contract between parties involved
- keep it simple.

Notes and references

1. Sections 5.1 and 5.4 incorporate material written by Dr Peter Morris, and drawn from his forthcoming book (Morris, 1992). Dr Morris is director of special projects at Bovis. Previously he was executive director of the Major Projects Association. He is an Associate Fellow of Templeton College, Oxford, and a member of the Engineering subfaculty of the University. His career in project management spans 20 years.
2. Morris, P. W. G., *The Management of Projects: Lessons from the last fifty years*, Thomas Telford (to appear).
3. Morris, P. W. G. and Hough, G. H., *The Anatomy of Major Projects: A study of the reality of project management*, Wiley, 1987.
4. Andersen, E. S., Grude, K. V., Haug, T. and Turner, J. R., *Goal Directed Project Management*, Kogan Page, 1987.
5. Deal, T. E. and Kennedy, A. A., *Corporate Cultures: The rites and rituals of corporate life*, Addison-Welsey, 1986.
6. Morris, P. W. G., 'Interface management: an organisational theory approach to project management', *Project Management Quarterly*, **10** (2), June 1979.
7. Section 5.4 also incorporates ideas contributed by John Dingle.
8. Fangel, M. (ed.), *The Handbook of Project Start-up: How to launch projects effectively*, INTERNET, 1987.
9. Kerzner, H., 'Pricing out the work', in *The Project Management Handbook* (eds D. I. Cleland and W. R. King), Van Nostrand Reinhold, 1988.
10. CCTA, *PRINCE*, NCC Blackwell, 1991.

PART THREE
MANAGING THE
PROJECT
OBJECTIVES

6
Managing scope

6.1 Introduction

In this part, I shall describe methods, tools and techniques for managing the five project objectives: scope; organization; quality; cost; and time. I shall start with scope, and the next four chapters will deal with the other four objectives. I shall then describe the management of the risk inherent in them, and end this part by identifying several special techniques used to manage all five objectives and to achieve a balance between them.

It is through the process of managing the project's scope that the owner's requirements are converted first into the definition of a facility to produce the expected benefit and then into a statement of the work required to construct and commission that facility, and that the work identified is brought to a successful conclusion. This is the *raison d'être* of project management, and so scope management is the principal project objective. The other four are enabling objectives or constraints.

In this chapter, I shall describe the methods, tools and techniques used to manage scope. I shall start by defining scope management, recalling principles of good management which relate to it, and recalling its processes. I shall then describe the use of work breakdown structure. In the next three sections, I shall explain how the work of the project is defined at the three fundamental levels of breakdown: how to define the facility required to achieve the owner's purpose and the broad areas of work required to construct that facility; how to break the facility into intermediate products, or milestones, in each of the areas of work; and how to specify the work, as activities or tasks, required to produce the intermediate products. I shall close the chapter by illustrating the concepts with several case studies.

6.2 Purpose, principles and processes of scope management

The purpose of scope management can be defined as: *ensuring that enough, but only enough, work is undertaken to deliver the project's purpose successfully*. There are three key elements to this definition:

- an adequate, or sufficient, amount of work is done
- unnecessary work is not done
- the work that is done delivers the stated business purpose.

I shall show that in order to achieve this purpose, scope management needs to satisfy all but the fourth of the principles of good management introduced in Section 5.5. To achieve this purpose, there are, as with each of the system objectives, four basic steps to managing scope (Table 2.3):

1. Develop the concept through the project's objectives.
2. Define the scope through the work breakdown structure.
3. Authorize and execute the work, and monitor and control progress.
4. Commission the facility to produce the product, and obtain benefit.

The main emphasis is at the start of this process, as mistakes made there can never be corrected. The next is at the end, to ensure that the project has been worth while. The remainder of this chapter deals with the first two steps. The other two are covered in Chapters 14 and 15. I shall start by describing the use of a work breakdown structure.

6.3 Work breakdown structure

Work breakdown is a technique by which *the work of a project is divided and subdivided for management and control purposes.* Rather than breaking the work of the project into a low level of detail in a single step, it is devolved through increasing levels of detail. A work breakdown structure (WBS) is developed by breaking the facility into intermediate or subproducts. The work required to produce each subproduct and the work required to assemble and commission the facility from the subproducts is identified. I previously described three fundamental levels

Table 6.1 Typical work breakdown structure

Work element	Deliverable	Duration
Programme	Corporate strategy	5–10 years
Project	Specified change	9–18 months
Areas of work	Intermediate products	6–18 months
Work package	Milestone	1–3 months
Activity	Measurable result	1–3 weeks
Task	–	days
Item	–	hours
Step	–	–

of breakdown: integrated, strategic and detail. However, a WBS can be developed to many more levels, and seven have been used on large engineering projects. Table 6.1 shows a typical structure, with several levels of work elements, associated deliverables, and possible relative durations. This structure shows the project as part of a much larger *programme* of work, required to deliver the company's five- or ten-year objectives.

There is no universal agreement on the terms to be used for the work elements and their deliverables. There is one supplier of project management software which uses the sequence project–phase–activity–task in one of its products and project–phase–task–activity in another.

Advantages of work breakdown

There are several reasons for using work breakdown:

- It provides better control of work definition.
- It allows work to be delegated in coherent packages.
- It allows work to be defined at an appropriate level for estimating and control for the current stage.
- It allows risk to be contained within the WBS.

BETTER CONTROL

The use of a work breakdown satisfies the first three principles of good management listed in Section 5.5. One of the pitfalls in planning is to develop the work definition at a single, detailed level. Developing the work definition in a structured way ensures better results. Further, defining work through its deliverables ensures that, as the project progresses, only work that is necessary to produce the facility is done, not work that was envisaged some months previously but is no longer required. Hence, the plan also becomes more stable. The work required can change in changing circumstances, but only certain results build towards the required end objective. This is clearly the case in research and development projects, where the process of doing the project defines the work to be done. However, it can also be true of engineering, construction, information technology and organizational development projects. For example, the construction of an aeroplane and a submarine involve similar activities:

- the fabrication of metal into a cylindrical pressure vessel
- internal outfitting to support life in a hostile environment
- the fitting of propulsion equipment.

On a detailed level the work appears the same. However, one set of intermediate products leads to an Airbus, and another set to a submarine. The high levels of the structure can also be used to balance areas of work on a project. By developing the definition at a detail level only there is a risk that we give undue emphasis to one area only. This may be technical work over cultural work (Section 4.3), or it may be our own area of expertise at the expense of another. On Heysham II Nuclear Power Station, the computer systems required to operate the plant were not given sufficient emphasis in the plan, swamped by the amount of engineering work, and would have delayed the commissioning of the station several months, if it were not for another technical problem. A small amount of work could have kept a multi-billion pound investment lying idle.

COHERENT DELEGATION

The parcelling of a work in a breakdown structure is natural, because it is aimed at achieving a product. Responsibility can then be assigned to individual parties for each product. In fact, they can be left to identify the actual work required, and in this way experts retain their integrity, while being set measurable targets. Sometimes this can be the only way to control progress on a research project, as the work itself is unknown, only the measurable, intermediate results. If work is defined at a detail level and amalgamated into packages, then they may not actually be natural packages of work, and project managers can appear to be telling people more technically skilled than themselves how to do the work.

LEVELS OF ESTIMATING AND CONTROL

The lowest level of work breakdown appropriate for estimating and control depends on several factors:

- the size, type and duration of the project
- the purpose for which the estimates will be used
- the current stage in the project management life cycle
- the requirement for effective control.

I find on projects of a year's duration that activities of two weeks' duration are the lowest appropriate level for planning and control. There is a law of diminishing returns which makes it inefficient to plan and estimate at lower levels, except in areas of high risk.

Lowest level of work breakdown

If the activity level is the lowest level of estimating and control, it is also the lowest level of breakdown for central planning. However, team leaders may assign work to people at the task level, and individuals may plan their own time at the item level. The lowest level does depend on the size of the project. On the four-week overhaul of ammonia plants, the lowest level of planning was activities of two to four hours. On the other hand I worked briefly on a project of seven years' duration, on which people were planning items of four hour's duration six months in advance. The plans were meaningless.

Lowest level of estimating

Because of inherent uncertainties, only a certain level of accuracy can be expected. It is pointless to plan in greater detail. The people on the seven-year project thought that planning at lower levels improved the overall accuracy. Unfortunately, this is not the case. There is a mathematical theorem called the binomial theorem which states that the percentage error of the part, as a ratio of the percentage error of the whole, is inversely proportional to the square root of the size:

$$\frac{\pm e\%}{\pm E\%} = \sqrt{\frac{S}{s}}$$

We might expect to finish a year long project, $S = 52$ weeks, to within a month, $E = \pm 10$ per cent. Therefore, on an activity of two weeks' duration, we need to be accurate to within one week, $e = \pm 50$ per cent. On a task of two days' duration, we need to be accurate to within two days, $e = \pm 110$ per cent. The accuracy on items is even more meaningless.

Planning in greater detail also requires more effort in estimating. The binomial theorem implies that to double the accuracy of the estimate requires four times as much planning effort, and this has been measured in the petrochemical industry.[1] Therefore, at early stages of the project, you want very coarse estimates, obtained by planning at high levels of work breakdown, with lower levels developed only as the project is shown to be viable at the high levels. You also reach a point at about $E = \pm 5$ per cent accuracy, at which it costs more to estimate than the value of the data you are getting. This sets a limit on the lowest worthwhile level of work breakdown for estimating purposes. I shall return to this concept in Chapter 9.

Lowest level of control

Similar arguments apply to the level at which the project is controlled:

controlling at a lower level can mean more time is spent in control than doing work; controlling at a higher level means slippages can get out of hand before they are recognized. The appropriate size of activity for control is the same as the frequency of control meetings. If meetings are once a fortnight, activities should, on average, be a fortnight long. Then, at each review an activity is either not started, finished, or half finished – three simple states. If activities are very much shorter, it will be difficult to determine what is critical for completion. If they are very much longer, then the percentage completion will be reported as the elapsed time divided by the original duration while that is less than 1, and 99 per cent while it is greater until the activity is actually finished.

CONTAINMENT OF RISK

I qualified the remarks above by saying that planning and estimating did not apply in areas of high risk. In fact there is no need to take the WBS down to a consistent level. The lowest level of WBS may vary according to the level of risk: in areas of low risk you may stop as high as the work-package level; in areas of high risk you may continue to a very low level of WBS. The lowest level of WBS may depend on:

– the uncertainty introduced by the risk
– the need to contain the risk.

Figure 6.1 illustrates a project in which all risk is thought to be in work-package A, activity A3 within that, and task A3A within that. At the task

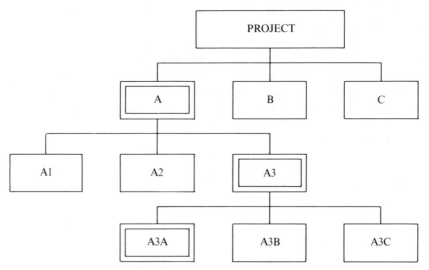

Figure 6.1 Containment of risk in the work breakdown structure

level, the uncertainty introduced by the risk, ±100 per cent, is less than the estimating error, ±150 per cent, and since the task is only of two days' duration, the maximum impact it can have on the project's duration is two days.

6.4 Defining projects

Project definition initiates the project and therefore relates the work of the project to the owner's business objectives. To achieve this, it is necessary to state the owner's requirements, to identify the facility expected to satisfy them, and to identify the work required to construct the facility.

Owner's requirements

The following three requirements should be defined:

- the purpose
- the scope
- the objectives.

THE PURPOSE

This is a statement of the business need to be achieved by the project, as described throughout Part Two. It may be a problem to be solved, an opportunity to be exploited, a benefit to be obtained, or the elimination of an inefficiency, but will be derived from the strategic objectives of the parent organization (Chapter 3). The statement of the purpose should be clear and precise, and should contain both quantitative and qualitative measures. Once the project is underway, it will become the 'mission' of all those involved in the project, both as project team members and as resource providers. It can be a powerful motivating force if it is seen to be worth while and beneficial to the business, and can help to build cooperation. Of course it can be a powerful demotivator if it is seen to conflict with individuals' self-interests (Example 4.2).

THE SCOPE

This is an initial, high-level description of the way in which the purpose will be satisfied. If the purpose is viewed as a problem to be solved, the scope will identify possible solutions, and the one selected for further work (the fourth, fifth and sixth steps in Figure 2.2). The statement of scope includes two things:

- the work that falls within the remit of the project, and is required to solve the problem and achieve the benefits
- the work that falls outside the remit of the project.

The inclusions will later be made redundant by the intitial stages of work breakdown. However, it is important to include them in the statement of project definition. They form the key steps in the problem-solving process, which indicate the thought processes of the people drawing up the definition, showing how they reached their conclusions. The exclusions can arise either because the work is not required to achieve the benefits (although it would be nice to have), or because it is being handled elsewhere. The owner does not have a limitless pot of gold, and so a boundary must be set on the work to be done. Sometimes the potential benefit must be reduced to match the available funds. Also, when a project is taking place as part of a larger programme, it may share work with other projects. It can then be more efficient to have one project handle all the joint work. This is especially true when projects create a need for redeployment or redundancy. One project may then delegate the work to the other. For whatever reason, the exclusions must be clearly stated, so that they are understood by people joining the project later.

THE OBJECTIVES

These are quantitative and qualitative measures by which completion of the project will be judged. In effect they identify the facility to be produced by the project. If the facility is an engineering construction (e.g. factory, dam, or chemical plant), then the objectives may be, for example:

> . . . when the facility has been constructed, the supporting establishment is in place, the facility has been commissioned, and is operating to a certain percentage of capacity.

A similar statement can apply to a computer system, management development programme, or organizational change. You will notice that this statement implies that it has been shown that the facility is able to achieve some of the benefits. People are usually quite happy with this for a factory, but less so for a computer system or organizational change process. In the latter cases, the project is over once the system is commissioned, and the project team have no responsibility for ensuring that it works properly!!! In Section 5.2 it was stated that it is not always possible to set the project's benefits as the objectives, as they may not be achieved until some time after the end of the project, and the facility has been commissioned. However, it is important that the objectives are likely to deliver the benefits, and that the project team address the question of how they are to be attained. Furthermore, the objectives should:

- address all the work within the scope of the project
- not address work outside the scope of the project
- begin to set parameters for managing quality, cost and time.

You will see now why it is important to record the scope of the project.

Initiating work breakdown

The statement of the objectives completes the project definition. It is now possible to define *areas of work*, which begins the process of work breakdown. Each area of work delivers one of the project's objectives, linking the integrative level (level 1) to the strategic level (level 2). The areas of work may form subprojects, as in Table 6.1. In Chapter 13, I describe the *Project Definition Report*. The statement of purpose, scope and objectives appears in an early section, and sets the scene for the project. The areas of work appear in the section on work breakdown. Again it is important that the areas of work cover all the objectives, but no more.

Standard documentation

Some companies use standard forms for defining purpose, scope, objectives and areas of work. They can serve a useful purpose in enforcing discipline in project proposal. However, I prefer a standard document, produced on a word processor. That gives greater flexibility, and can be built into the Project Definition Report later. Whichever is chosen, the document should be no more than two or three pages long.

Case study

The concepts can be illustrated by a case study. This is based on a real example but is adapted to illustrate the points. A project brief is given in Example 6.1, followed by a statement of purpose, scope, objectives and areas of work. These would be sections 3, 4 and part of 5 of the contents of a Project Definition Report (Chapter 13) and are written as such. The model is developed as new concepts are introduced.

The objectives here could have focused more on the facility produced, as shown in Example 6.2. Which you choose would depend on your personal preferences. I prefer the version in the full answer because it already gives equal balance to all areas of the project, whereas the alternative gives primary importance to the estates work. In the actual project, writing the operating procedures for the new offices was the critical work, while the project team focused on the location of the offices.

The definition of the project contains a statement of the expected time scale: five months to the commissioning of the first offices and nine months to completion of the project. At this stage these are targets. People familiar with the technology should be able to say whether they are realistic, but the precise time scale would only be determined as the project plan is developed to lower levels. However, I am a great believer in being *goal directed*, aiming to achieve this target and scheduling the work appropriately, rather than allowing rather theoretical mathematics in the form of a network to impose a longer duration. Tight time scales can often be achieved with management effort. Similarly, there is already enough information for experts to begin to develop initial estimates of capital cost and revenue for the project.

TRIMAGI COMMUNICATIONS BV PROJECT DEFINITION REPORT

Rationalization of the Customer Repair and Maintenance Offices

3 Background

With its expansion in Europe, TriMagi Communications intends to rationalize its Customer Repair and Maintenance Offices, CRMOs, in the Benelux countries, starting in its home base in Holland.

There are currently 18 CRMOs in the region. Each office is dedicated to an area within the region. An area office receives all calls from customers within the area reporting faults. The fault is diagnosed either electronically from within the office, or by sending an engineer to the customer's premises. Once diagnosed the fault is logged with the field staff within the office, and repaired in rotation. Each area office must cope with its own peaks and troughs in demand. This means that the incoming telephone lines may be engaged when a customer first calls, and it can take up to two days to diagnose the fault.

To improve customer services the company plans to rationalize the CRMO organization within the region, with three objectives:

- never have engaged call receipt lines within office hours
- achieve an average time of two hours from call receipt to arrival of the engineer at the customer's premises
- create a more flexible structure able to cope with future growth both in the region and throughout Europe, and the move to 'enquiry desks', dealing with all customer contacts.

This improvement can be achieved by changing the CRMO structure using new technology recently developed by the company's R&D department. In the new structure there will be three call receipt offices, two diagnostic offices and four field offices servicing the entire region. It would be possible to have just one office for 'call receipt' and 'diagnosis', but that would expose the service to technical failure.

Incoming calls would be switched to a free line in one of the call receipt offices. It will be logged automatically, and passed on to a diagnostic office. The diagnostic office will try to diagnose the fault electronically, which should be possible in 90 per cent of cases. The diagnostic offices are also able to discover faults before the customer notices them. The diagnostic offices will pass the faults to the field offices to repair the faults, and diagnose the remaining 10 per cent.

The field offices will be nominally assigned to an area within the region, but will share cases to balance their workload.

4 Project definition

PURPOSE

The purpose of the project is to rationalize the CRMO organization:

(a) to improve customer service so that:
– all customers calling the receipt offices obtain a free line
– all calls are answered within 10 seconds
– the average time from call receipt to arrival of an engineer on site is two hours;
(b) to improve productivity and flexibility so that:
– the costs are justified through productivity improvements
– the call receipt offices can be made part of a unified 'enquiry desk'
– but there are no redundancies so that all productivity improvements are achieved through natural wastage, redeployment or growth.

SCOPE

The work of the project includes:

– changing from the existing structure of 18 area offices to three call receipt offices, two diagnostic offices and four field offices
– investigating which of two new CRMO networking technologies is appropriate for the new structure, and to implement the chosen technology
– refurbishing the nine new offices to current standards
– training and redeploying staff to meet the needs of the operation of the new CRMOs
– installing hardware to connect the CRMOs to the new customer information system (CIS), and to implement a statistical package to analyse fault data.

The work of the project excludes any staff who are surplus to requirements within the CRMO structure; they will be passed to central personnel for redeployment on other expansion projects. Also, with the implementation of the new customer information system, the call receipt offices may, within the next two years, be incorporated into unified 'enquiry desks' dealing with all customer contacts. However, it will not be the project team's responsibility to achieve that integration.

OBJECTIVES

The objectives of the CRMO Rationalization Project are:

- to install the CRMO facilities in nine offices (three call receipt offices, two diagnostic offices and four field offices) within nine months
- to select and implement appropriate networking technology and statistical MIS to achieve the required customer service levels
- to design and implement appropriate operating systems and procedures to achieve the required customer service levels and productivity improvements
- to train and redeploy staff to fill new positions, and vacate old positions
- to manage the work to achieve timely and effective completion with the first offices operational within five months and the work complete within nine.

5 Work structure

AREAS OF WORK

In order to achieve the project's objectives, the following areas of work are required:

A   *Accommodation*   Refurbish new offices, install hardware and furniture. (There is only one floor area available in the region large enough to take the first call receipt and fault diagnosis offices. The remaining eight offices must be housed in existing CRMO space.)

T   *Technology*   Decide on networking technology to be used, implement statistical MIS, implement networking technology in new offices.

O   *Organization*   Communicate all changes to the staff involved, define the operation of the new CRMOs, train and redeploy staff to fill new positions.

P   *Project*   Plan the project, organize the resources, obtain financial approval.

The last is required to allow for the actual management of the project, and will deliver the last of the objectives listed above.

MILESTONE PLAN

....

....

Example 6.1 Project definition for the case study project

OBJECTIVES

The CRMO Rationalization Project will be completed when the CRMO facilities have been installed and are operational in nine offices (three call receipt offices, two diagnostic offices and four field offices) with:

- appropriate networking technology and supporting statistical MIS required to achieve the stated customer service levels
- appropriate operating systems and procedures required to achieve the customer service levels and productivity improvements
- appropriate numbers of trained staff, and no surplus staff
- the first offices operational within five months and the work complete within nine months.

Example 6.2 Alternative objectives for the case study

6.5 Planning at a strategic level: milestone plans

Having defined the project, we are in a position to develop the work breakdown structure to the second level, the *strategic level*. In this section, I shall describe the requirements for planning at this level, and then introduce a tool, the *milestone plan*,[2] which satisfies these requirements.

Requirements for planning at the strategic level

At the second level of work breakdown, the project manager sets the basic strategy for the project. The plan at this level:

- shows how the intermediate products, or deliverables, build towards the final objectives of the project
- sets a stable framework, fixed goal-posts, for the project team, and thereby provides a common vision
- controls devolution of the management of the scope to other parties.

I described above how similar activities are involved in the manufacture of an Airbus or submarine, yet one set of intermediate products delivers an aircraft, another a submarine. It is at the second level of the work breakdown that we set the strategy, showing how the intermediate products build towards the facility to be delivered by this project. Because only one set of intermediate products delivers the required final objective of this project, the plan at this level can be made stable. This can be a powerful motivating tool, giving the project team a common vision.

To build a common vision, the plan should be represented on one page. It then presents a clear picture of the strategy for the project. It is through this single page, the milestone plan, that the project manager communicates the overall strategy of the project upwards to the project sponsor and champion, and downwards to the project team. This was the fifth principle of good project management introduced in Section 5.5. It is also at this level that focusing on the deliverables can help delegate work to subproject teams. A team accepts responsibility for the delivery on an intermediate product, and plans its own work to deliver that milestone independently of other project members. They know that they must achieve their milestone by a certain date to enable the project to proceed, but they are able to work without interference. We have seen how this can allow professional people to retain their integrity when working for a project manager from a different discipline.

Milestone planning

It is common, when developing the plan at the second level, to define the packages of work first and then define the deliverable that results from each work package. However, for the reasons above, I suggest that you define the deliverables or milestones first, in the form of a milestone plan. The packages of work which result in each milestone are derived later. The milestone plan is a strategic plan or framework for a project, defined in terms of intermediate products or results to be achieved. It shows the logical sequence of the conditions or states a project must pass through to achieve the final objectives, describing what is to be achieved at each state, not how the state is to be achieved.

Figure 6.2 illustrates the milestone plan, with the circles representing the milestones and the lines joining them representing the logical dependency between them. Hence, the milestone plan represents a logical network for the project.

We shall return to networks in Chapter 10, where two types of networks are described: a precedence network and an activity-on-arrow network. In a *precedence network* the work is represented by the nodes or boxes of the network. These are joined by arrows representing the logical dependency between the work. In an *activity-on-arrow network* the work is represented by the arrow. The nodes are events in time, and the logic is represented by the way the arrows join at the nodes. The milestone plan is a precedence network. The circles in Figure 6.2 represent the packages of work, defined by the results they deliver. The arrows show that one package follows another, and are known as *end-to-end dependencies*: the end of one package (milestone) is dependent on the end of a previous one. They say nothing about the start of the work: one package can start before a previous one has finished. This allows greater flexibility in scheduling the work.

Result paths or areas of work

In Figure 6.2, the milestones are grouped into vertical columns representing the areas of work; these vertical columns have been called the *result paths*. One of the principles of scope management is: *Balance the changes and level of ambition through the work breakdown structure.* I suggested that

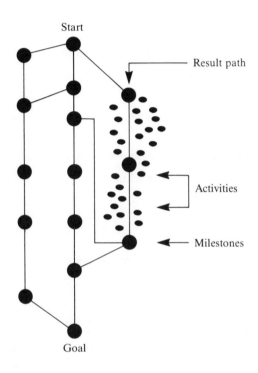

Figure 6.2   The milestone plan

the WBS should be used to ensure that equal emphasis is given to work in different areas. The result paths give visual representation to this. By inspecting the result paths you can ask yourself one of two questions, as illustrated in Example 6.3:

- Have all the areas of work been covered, or has something been left out? In particular, have the cultural changes been addressed?
- Is equal emphasis given to all the areas of work, or has unnecessary focus been given to one area?

I did some work with a research establishment where they were installing a larger computer to store the empirical data from a particularly large experiment they were conducting. They previously had a DEC minicomputer and were changing to an IBM mainframe. I helped them plan the project to make the change. The plan had three result paths:

- hardware and software
- the database
- the establishment.

Down the first path there were a large number of milestones:

- hardware and software selected
- hardware installed
- operating system loaded
- database software loaded
- system tested.

There were a similar number of milestones in the third path:

- computer room ready to receive machine
- furniture obtained
- operating procedures written
- operators recruited
- operators trained.

There were only two milestones in the central path:

- data transferred
- system commissioned.

Without prompting from me, the two people working with me on the development plan said, 'Hold on! The purpose of this project is not to obtain new hardware and software, and not to create a new establishment. It is because the data has got too large for the old machine. We ought to be giving greater emphasis to the database.' They therefore inserted two more milestones in the centre column: one dealt with data cleanse, i.e. removing incorrect, incomplete or redundant data; the other dealt with restructuring the database to meet future, rather than historical, requirements. Some people say that these two milestones may have made the rest redundant!!!

Example 6.3 Balancing objectives through the result paths

Selecting milestones

A good milestone plan:

- is understandable to everyone
- is controllable, both quantitatively and qualitatively

- focuses on necessary decisions
- is logical, with decisions and work packages in the right order
- gives an overview at the right level.

UNDERSTANDABLE

The milestone plan is a tool to build cooperation and commitment. It must therefore be understood by all those involved in the project. This requires the milestone descriptions to be written in English, not in technical jargon that is only understandable to a few.

CONTROLLABLE

The plan is also a tool for control, and so the descriptions must be precise, so that you can determine when they have been achieved. Technical milestones can be given a quantitative measure: e.g. 'when the new machine tool is operating at design capacity'. Other milestones must be given a qualitative description, with some measure of quality written in. For example, it is not adequate to say: 'when a report is written'. Two lines on the back of an envelope can satisfy that. The report must:

- meet certain requirements
- satisfy a steering committee
- allow a decision to be made.

DECISIONS

The milestones represent conditions en route to the final objective. Often the interesting condition is not the production of a design or a report. That is not the purpose of doing the work. It is the taking of a decision, based on the design or report, to allow more work to proceed. That is the required deliverable, and is controllable.

LOGICAL

The milestone plan is a logical plan. It contains a network which shows the strategy for building through the intermediate products to achieve the final objective.

SINGLE-PAGE OVERVIEW

The objective is to produce a plan, on a single page, which clearly communicates the project strategy. This is only achieved if the number of milestones and areas of work are limited. I find the ideal number of milestones to be somewhere between 15 and 25. With fewer the plan does not give a useful structure, and with more it becomes confusing. Similarly, I recommend two, three or four result paths. Setting limits on the number of milestones determines the size of the work packages, rather than allowing the size of work packages to determine the number of milestones. On small projects this will be the only level of planning. On large projects it will be the first of several.

Standard form for the milestone plan

In Figure 6.2, the milestone plan is drawn down the page, whereas it is common to draw a network across the page. The reason is simple. I suggest that a form should be used for the milestone plan as (Figure 6.3), with three columns:

MILESTONE PLAN		Company:
		Project description:
Planned date:		Milestone:

Figure 6.3 Blank milestone plan form

- the central one contains a drawing of the network
- the right-hand one contains descriptions of the milestones (which in themselves describe the packages of work)
- the left-hand column contains the milestone dates, once the work has been scheduled (see Chapter 10).

The right-hand column gives adequate space in which to write a full description of the milestone, whereas if you draw the network across the page, your writing must be very small to fit the description of the work package into the box or onto the arrow. It may be considered heretical to draw the network down the page, but it does allow the network and a full description of the work to be portrayed on a single page, as required. Figure 6.4 is a milestone plan for the CRMO Rationalization Project, showing the use of the form.

MILESTONE PLAN

Company: TRIMAGI COMMUNICATIONS BV

Project description: RATIONALIZATION OF THE CUSTOMER REPAIR AND MAINTENANCE ORGANIZATION (CRMO)

Planned date:	Project P	Operations O	Accommodation A	Technology T	Milestone:
	P1				P1: When the project definition is complete, including benefit criteria milestone plan and responsibility charts.
		O1		T1	O1: When a plan for communicating the changes to the CRM Organization has been agreed. T1: When the technical solution, including appropriate networking and switching technology has been designed and agreed.
		O2			O2: When the operational procedures for the CRM offices has been agreed.
		O3		T2	O3: When the job design and management design is complete and agreed. T2: When the functional specification for the supporting management information system (MIS) has been agreed.
		O4			O4: When the allocation of staff to the new offices, and recruitment and redeployment requirements, have been defined and agreed.
			A1	T3	A1 and T3: When the estates plan and roll-out strategy has been defined and agreed / When the technical roll-out strategy has been defined and agreed.
	P2				P2: When the budget for implementation has been determined, and (provisional) financial authority obtained.
		O5	A2		O5: When the management changes for sites 1 and 2 are in place (first call receipt and first diagnostic centres). A2: When sites 1 and 2 are available.
		O6		T4	O6: When a minimum number of staff have been recruited and redeployed and their training is complete. T4: When the system is ready for service in sites 1 and 2.
			A3	T5	A3: When sites 1 and 2 are ready for occupation. T5: When the MIS system has been delivered.
		O7			O7: When sites 1 and 2 are operational and procedures implemented.
	P3				P3: When a successful intermediate review has been conducted and the roll-out plans revised and agreed.
			A4		A4: When the last site is operational with the procedures fully implemented.
	P4				P4: When it has been shown through a post-implementation audit that the criteria has been met.

Figure 6.4 Milestone plan for the CRMO Rationalization Project

Developing the milestone plan

Ideally, the milestone plan should be developed in a *launch workshop* (Chapter 13), with selected key managers and project personnel present. Developing the plan in a group session builds greater commitment than if the project manager developed the plan personally and tried to impose it on the team. However, to be effective the workshop should not have more than about six people present. The process I recommend for developing the plan has six steps:

1. Start by agreeing the final milestone, the end of the project. The Project Definition Report should help this.
2. Generate ideas for milestones. Brainstorm them on to flip charts.
3. Review the milestones. Some will be part of another milestone. Some will be activities, but will generate ideas for new milestones. As you rationalize the list, record your decisions, especially where you have decided that a milestone is part of a larger one.
4. Experiment with result paths. Draw them on a flip chart or white board. Write the milestones on 'Post-It' notes and stick them on the

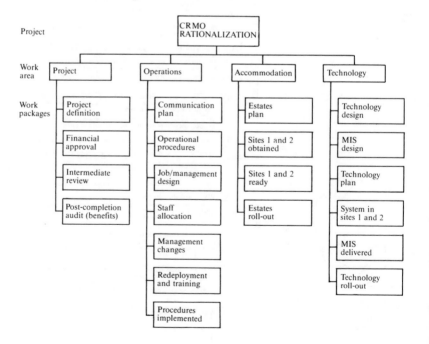

Figure 6.5   Work breakdown structure for the CRMO Rationalization Project

paths in the order they occur down the path. Experiment with different paths, and review them as suggested above. Note that this may change the definition of the areas of work.

5. Draw the logical dependencies, starting with the final objective and working backwards. This may cause you to review the definition of milestones, add new milestones, merge milestones, or change the definition of the result paths.

6. Make a final drawing of the plan.

Work breakdown structure

The milestone plan, as shown in Figure 6.4, is a tool used to communicate the project strategy to the parties involved. It represents both the work and its logical relationship. However, we should not lose sight of the fact that we are developing level 2 of the WBS. Figure 6.5 shows the WBS tree, to that level for the CRMO Rationalization Project. It is this representation of the work, coupled with the logic in the milestone plan, which may be used to derive the more formal precedence network (Figure 6.6) when scheduling the project.

6.6 Planning at lower levels

The plan at level 2, the milestone plan, is part of the WBS and will therefore be supported by plans at lower levels. These will include:

- activity plans
- work-package scope statements
- subsidiary milestone plans.

Activity plans

These detail the work packages which lead to the milestones. They describe the work at the next level of work breakdown, level 3. Following the principle of single-page reporting, the number of activities making up a work package should be limited to 15 to 20. I usually find 6 to 10 a useful number. This again determines the size of activities. Figure 6.7 is an activity plan for milestone P1 in the CRMO Rationalization Project.

There are some project management methodologies which recommend that a full definition of all the activities required by the project be derived before any work is done.[3] People who misuse networking systems, creating the activity definition without the supporting WBS, are forced into this. However, most modern approaches to project management recommend what is called a *rolling-wave* approach to activity planning.[4]

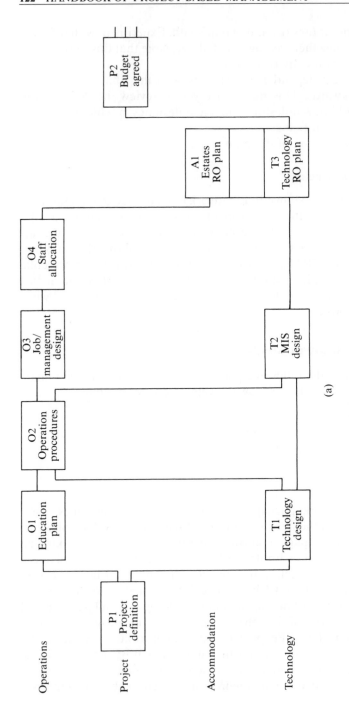

(a)

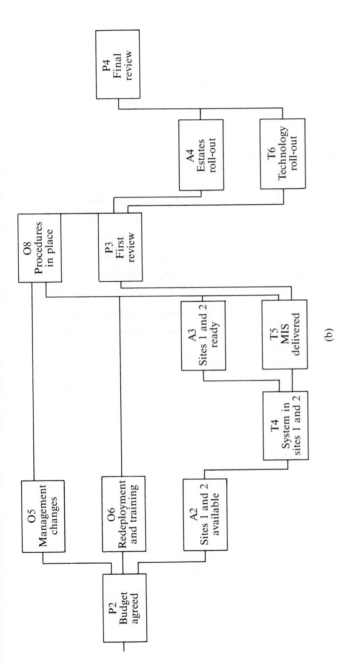

(b)

Figure 6.6   Precedence network for the CRMO Rationalization Project

																		No.	Activity/Task Name:

ACTIVITY SCHEDULE

Project:	Milestone No./Name:
CRMO RATIONALIZATION	P1: PROJECT DEFINITION

Work Cont. H/D/W

Period: 199X Week Number	Issue/Date: A/2 Jan	Approved by: JRT

4	5	6	7	8	9	10	No.	Activity/Task Name:
								Produce project proposal
								Hold project definition workshop
								Define required benefits
								Draft project definition report
								Hold project launch workshop
								Finalize milestone plan
								Finalize responsibility chart
								Prepare estimates – time
								Prepare estimates – cost
								Prepare estimates – revenue
								Assess project viability
								Assess risks
								Finalize project definition report
								Mobilize team

Figure 6.7   Activity plan for milestone P1 in the CRMO Rationalization Project

Fully detailed activity plans are only derived and maintained for those work packages that are current or about to start. The detailing of later work packages is left until necessary, so that as much current information as possible is used to derive the activities. Some computer-based networking packages will support this approach by allowing the nesting of networks. There are several reasons for this approach:

1. You wait until you know you are likely to do the work before expending the effort on detail planning. I spoke above of increasing the accuracy of the estimates during subsequent stages of the project management life cycle by spending increasing time on planning and design. To prepare estimates at project initiation stage you should estimate at the work-package level, and not prepare the activity definition. Some people find this uncomfortable, but I have worked in organizations that have prepared quite detailed designs and estimates for projects, only to find the projects totally uneconomic.
2. You prepare detailed activity plans when you have maximum information. If you prepare a detailed plan for a year-long project at the start, the only thing you can guarantee is that you will be wrong. You will have excluded items that should be included, and included items that should be excluded. It is better to prepare the detailed activity definition when you have gathered information about the best way to achieve the milestones. This is especially true on development projects, where the work in the early stages will determine the work in the later stages. You will know what the later milestones are, if you are to reach your final objective, but you will not know how they are to be achieved. Furthermore, there is no point in trying to guess, because it serves no purpose and wastes time.
3. You can delegate the definition of activities to reach a milestone to the teams who will be undertaking the work, as described before.

Detailed activity planning is discussed further in Chapter 14.

Work-package scope statements

Although the detailed activity planning is done on a rolling-wave basis, it is necessary to prepare some definition of the scope of each work package at an earlier stage. There are several reasons for this:

1. It is necessary to prepare some form of estimate of work content and duration for early, high-level estimating and scheduling. This should be based on some substance, even if it is only an approximate statement of the most likely outcome.

TRIMAGI COMMUNICATIONS BV
WORK-PACKAGE SCOPE STATEMENTS

MILESTONE	P1: when the project plans have been prepared and resources assigned to the project.
SCOPE	The work package requires the preparation of high-level plans and estimates to be prepared, to enable resource budgets to be prepared and their availability agreed.
AREAS OF WORK	Identify key managers
	Hold launch workshop
	Finalize milestone plan
	Finalize project responsibility chart
	Estimate resource requirements and durations
	Schedule resource requirements
	Discuss requirements with managers
	Plan and agree their availability.

Example 6.4 Work-package scope statement

MILESTONE PLAN

Company: NORTHERN ELECTRONICS

Project description: EVE COMPILER DESIGN

Planned date	Quality (T)	Computer Development (C)	External (E)	Documentation (D)	Milestone
06 Jun	T1				T1: When the team has agreed the plan and the procedures to be used to check the quality of the product. Milestone includes the order of intermediate builds.
20 Jun		C0			C0: Project start. Assume there is a rebuilt subset front end with most of the subset functionality. This is assumed stable enough as a basis for design.
27 Jun			E1		E1: When the requirement document and product-definition has been approved by the technical planning committee.
18 Jul	T2				T2: When the build procedures operate.
29 Aug	T3				T3: When test procedures operate, and have been used to check the grammar in the compiler against the ACVC tests.
29 Aug				D1	D1: When the user interfaces are defined and agreed. This includes only the language independent parts.
07 Nov		C1			C1: When the team agrees that the data structure definitions are adequate for further work (i.e. 'complete').
28 Nov		C2			C2: When the design of the modules is 'complete', i.e. adequate to write the case. Agreement is reached by reviews.
12 Dec	T4				T4: When the specification for all external modifications have been accepted by the relevant teams to do the job (debugger, linker and scheduler teams).
12 Dec				D2	D2: When the manual craft for the user interface has been written and reviewed.
31 Dec		C3			C3: End of Phase One.
01 Jan		C4			C4: Phase Two.

Figure 6.8 Milestone plan for developing a compiler language

2. Work packages may include activities with a long lead time. These must be recognized and started in time.
3. While preparing the milestone plan you may not include one milestone, assuming it to be part of another. This must be recorded.

These requirements can be satisfied by preparing work-package scope statements. These will be akin to the definition of scope and areas of work for the project as a whole, but on a smaller scale. The milestone name, remember, defines the purpose and objectives of the work package. Example 6.4 contains a sample work-package scope statement for milestone P1 in the CRMO Rationalization Project.

Subsidiary milestone plan

Sometimes there is a milestone in the plan which requires a particularly large amount of work of long duration. You may want to define intermediate milestones as control points through that work, but there may be

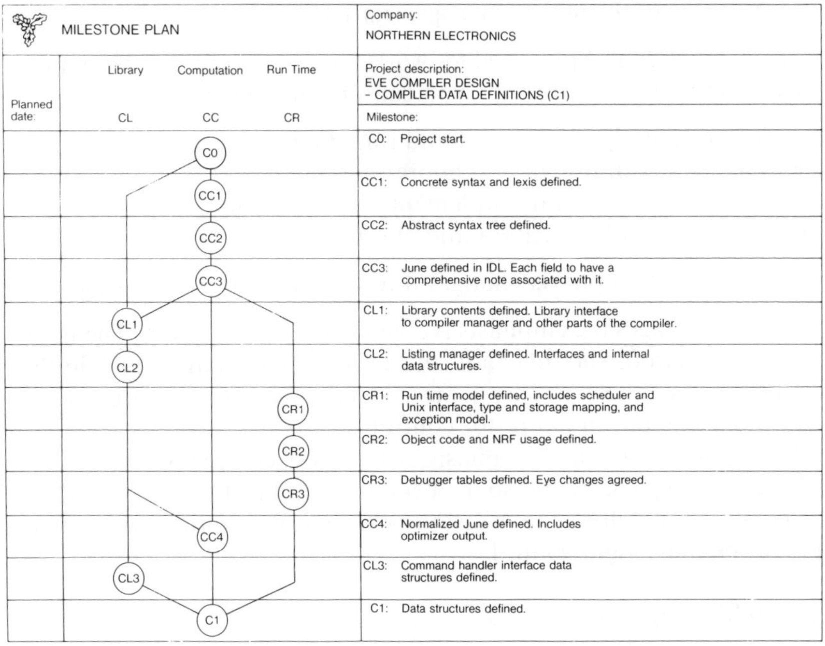

Figure 6.9   Subsidiary milestone plan for milestone C1

no natural milestone to use on the level of the milestone plan. It is not sufficient to define milestones such as:

SM1: when the work is 25 per cent complete

because that will not be measurable. In these curcumstances it may be worth while to derive a subsidiary milestone plan for that package of work. In effect the work package is treated as a mini-project. Figure 6.8 is the milestone plan for developing a compiler for a computer language. Milestone C1 is of the type described, requiring five months of work to achieve it. However, there are no natural milestones on the level of this plan to define control points through the work. The team therefore derived a subsidiary plan, Figure 6.9, for that milestone alone.

6.7 Applications

I close this chapter by describing two applications of milestone planning:

- milestone planning at different stages of the life cycle;
- milestone planning of subprojects on large, multi-disciplinary projects.

Different stages of the project management life cycle

Milestone plans can be prepared for work at all stages of the project management life cycle. For instance, you can prepare plans for:

- the feasibility study in proposal and initiation
- the design study in design and appraisal
- project implementation in implementation and control
- commissioning in finalization and closure.

The management emphasis changes throughout each of these stages:

1. At the early stages the emphasis is on encouraging creativity. The milestone descriptions should enable this by allowing maximum flexibility in the way the milestones are achieved, and the results delivered, while still providing a framework for control.
2. At the later stages the emphasis will be on completing the work. Money is being spent, and so the benefits must be obtained as quickly as possible. Therefore, the milestone names will be more prescriptive, providing more rigid control.

Large, multi-disciplinary projects

I have worked on several large multi-disciplinary projects which, for management purposes, were divided into a number of subprojects almost independent of each other, with each being the responsibility of a separate discipline. The project team derived a milestone plan for each subproject, and each discipline was then able to work virtually independently of the other, corresponding only at key milestones. I have applied this approach to construction projects, development projects and IT projects.

NORTH SEA OIL FIELD DEVELOPMENT

This development consisted of two phases each of £3.0 billion. In the first phase, the project used ARTEMIS and planned at a fairly low level of detail. Management reports were 150 pages of computer output, and the management team had no visible control. In the second phase it was recommended that they adopt a work breakdown structure. The development was divided into several contracts, and each contract into several stages, such as:

- feasibility
- design
- procurement
- construction
- link-up
- commissioning.

Figure 6.10 illustrates this work breakdown. A milestone plan was prepared for each contract stage. Figure 6.11 is an example of a typical plan. The management team monitored progress against each aspect of

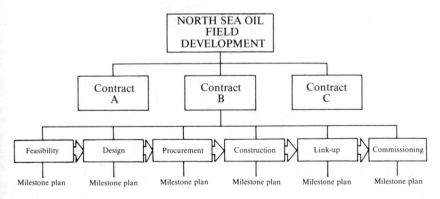

Figure 6.10   Work breakdown structure for the development of a North Sea oil field

MILESTONE PLAN

Company: NORTHERN ENERGY AND CHEMICAL INDUSTRIES PLC

Project description: NORTH SEA OIL FIELD DEVELOPMENT – STANDARD PROCUREMENT CHAIN

Project manager:	Contractor:	Contract no:
Plan issue:	Approved by:	Date:
Project procedures:		Contractor's procedure:

Planned date:

Engineering (E)	Vendor selection (V)	Procurement (P)	Lead text	Definition	Project procedures
E1		P1	Preliminary requirement raised	Transmittal of short package description with ref. to req. no. and pck. no. from engineering discipline to procurement.	
	V1		Preliminary enquiry issued	Preliminary enquiry comprising short package description issued to approved vendors (by telex).	
E2			Bidders list approved	List of all approved bidders for package.	PS-CB30 PS-CA13
		P2	Requirements for enquiry approved	Transmittal of provisional package with all necessary documentation attached.	PS-CA13
			Enquiry issued	A complete invitation to tender issued to approved bidders.	PS-CB31
	V2		Bid closure date	Deadline for bidders to submit tenders as stated in the ITT covering letter.	PS-CB32
E3		P3	Preliminary bid evaluation	Preliminary evaluation of bids by Engineering and Procurement. Joint recommendation compiled by Procurement.	PS-CB32
	V3		Bidders' short-list approved	Bidders short-listed from evaluation.	PS-CB32 PS-CA13
E4		P4	Bid evaluation	Evaluation of bids by Engineering and Procurement. More information may be obtained from vendors. Joint recommendations compiled by Procurement.	PS-CB32
	V4		Recommended vendor approved	Vendor selected and approved.	PS-CB32 PS-CA13
E5			Purchase order requirements approved	Issue of revised requisition for purchase.	PS-CA13
		P5	Purchase order issued to vendor	Issue of signed purchase order to selected vendor.	PS-CB33 PS-CA13
		P6	Purchase order acknowledgement approved	Acknowledgement of purchase order received from selected vendor and approved.	PS-CB33
		P7	'Dear John' letters issued	Unsuccessful bidders informed of decision.	

Figure 6.11 Sample milestone plan for the development of a North Sea oil field

the milestone plan. The project teams supported these with lower level plans.

The Health Authority was changing from distributing supplies through each of the 15 districts to regionally coordinated distribution. The project was divided into 22 subprojects, each with its own milestone plan, and each the responsibility of a separate discipline. There were a few, easily monitored links between each plan. The projects were:

- construction of the regional warehouse
- creation of the warehouse establishment
- implementation of computer systems
- recruitment, redeployment and training
- switching from district buying to regional buying
- switching from district revenue to regional revenue
- district implementation (15 districts)
- commissioning the warehouse.

Each discipline met once a fortnight to monitor progress against its plan. The team leaders then met every six weeks to monitor progress of the project overall, by comparing progress on each plan.

COMPUTERIZATION OF THE NORWEGIAN SECURITIES SERVICE

This project consisted of four subprojects:

- design and implementation of the computer system
- creation of a company to operate it
- registration of dealers and holders of stock
- legal basis.

An overall milestone plan was developed for the entire project. Subsidiary milestone plans were also prepared for the first two subprojects. This project involved one million people, and yet was managed to a successful conclusion using manual planning methods only by taking this structured approach. At one point the Norwegian government tried to delay passing the enabling legislation by twelve months. Using the top level plan, the project team was able to demonstrate to the Minister that that would delay the project by twelve months, and effectively kill it. The argument won the day and the bill was passed.

CUSTOMER SERVICE SYSTEM IN A REGIONAL SUPPLY COMPANY OF A LARGE PUBLIC
UTILITY

Implementation of the customer service system required several projects:

- implementation of hardware and software
- transfer of data
- networking of buildings
- estates refurbishment
- writing operating procedures
- training
- commissioning.

Again, an overall milestone plan was developed, supported by milestone
plans for each subproject.

You may notice that the last three of these projects involve a mixture
of:

- construction or building work
- information technology
- organizational change
- recruitment, redevelopment and training.

They each also had a duration of about 15 to 24 months, and each was
finished on time and to cost.

6.8 Summary

1. The purpose of scope management is to ensure that:
   - adequate work is done
   - unnecessary work is not done
   - the project's purpose is achieved.
2. There are four steps of scope management:
   - develop the concept through the project's objectives
   - define the scope through the work breakdown structure
   - authorize and execute the work, and monitor and control progress
   - commission the facility to produce the product, and obtain benefit.
3. Work breakdown is a process by which the work of the project is subdivided for management and control purposes.
4. The project is defined at the strategic level, through:
   - the *purpose*: the problem to be solved, or the opportunity to be
     exploited, or the benefit to be obtained
   - the *scope*: the solutions to the problem, and covering the inclusions
     (work within the remit of the project) and the exclusions (work out-

side the remit, because it is deemed unnecessary, or because it is shared with other projects)
- the *objectives*: the facility to be delivered, quantitative and qualitative measures of when the project is complete.

5. At the strategic level, the milestone plan:
    - shows how the intermediate products, or deliverables, build towards the final objectives of the project
    - sets a stable framework, fixed goal-posts, for the project team, and thereby provides a common vision
    - controls devolution of the management of the scope.

6. A good milestone plan:
    - is understandable to everyone
    - is controllable
    - focuses on necessary decisions
    - is logical
    - gives an overview of the project to build cooperation and commitment of all the parties involved.

7. There are seven steps in milestone planning:
    - agree the final milestone
    - brainstorm milestones
    - review the list
    - experiment with result paths (areas of work)
    - draw the logical dependencies
    - make the final plan.

8. Plans at lower levels of work breakdown include:
    - subsidiary milestone plans
    - work-package scope statements
    - activity plans developed on a rolling-wave basis.

References

1. George, D. J. (ed.), *A Guide to Capital Cost Estimating*, Institution of Chemical Engineers, 1988.
2. Anderson, E. S., Grude, K. V., Haug, T. and Turner, J. R., *Goal Directed Project Management*, Kogan Page, 1987.
3. LBMS, *PROMPT*, Learmonth and Burchett Management Systems.
4. CCTA, *PRINCE*, NCC Blackwell, 1991.

7
Managing project organization

7.1 Introduction

I now turn to the second mandatory project objective, managing organization; without an organization there are no resources to undertake the project. Through the organization the manager defines the type and level of resource input, and how they are to be managed to achieve the project's purpose. Once the organization has been defined, the project team can determine how much the project will cost and how long it will take, thus providing a baseline for managing quality, cost and time. The definition of scope and organization together make a contract between the project and the parent organization; that is, between the contractor and owner in Figure 4.1. It is through the contract that project managers negotiate their authority.

In the next section, I shall recall the purpose and principles of managing the project organization, and then identify the processes of negotiating a contract between project and business. I shall describe types of project organization available, including a range of line and matrix structures. I shall introduce the *responsibility chart* as the primary tool for defining the project organization and negotiating the contract, and show that this satisfies the principle of single-page reporting. In order to agree the contract, the responsibility chart requires the manager to identify both the type of resource input and the level of effort, the *work content*. I shall describe how to incorporate estimates of work content, and close the chapter by explaining the use of equipment and drawing registers to manage non-human resources.

7.2 Purpose, principles and processes of project organization

The purpose of project organization can be defined as follows: *to marshal adequate resources (human, material and financial) of an appropriate type to undertake the work of the project, so as to deliver its objectives successfully.* The use of the word 'adequate' implies that the resources should be of sufficient number, but only just sufficient: too few and the organization will be ineffective and the project will flounder; too many and the organization will be inefficient. This chapter focuses primarily on human resources, although material resources are considered at the end. Negotiating financial resources is beyond the scope of this book.

Three of the five principles of good project management, introduced in Section 5.5, relate to managing the project organization:

- negotiate a contract between parties involved
- assign roles and responsibilities at all levels of work breakdown
- adopt a clear and simple reporting structure.

Organizing a contract

The organization breakdown structure (OBS) runs in parallel to the WBS. Table 7.1 shows the parties involved at the three fundamental levels. The project manager must organize a contract between the parties involved at all levels (Figures 2.6 and 4.1), that is:

- between the owner and contractor at the project level: the contract
- between the parties making up the contractor at the strategic level
- between the members of the project team at the tactical level.

It is also in the project manager's interest to ensure there is cooperation between the parties which make up the owner. This is usually beyond the responsibility, but not the influence, of the project manager.

Table 7.1 Three fundamental levels of organization breakdown

No.	Level	Resource type
1	Integrative	Company, department or group
2	Strategic	Function, discipline or section
3	Tactical	Named person, group of people or skill type

I described in Chapters 4 and 5 how the project manager negotiates the contract by building a clear mission or vision for the project, and cascading that mission down to objectives at each level of the OBS.

Cooperation can then be gained by building a commitment to the objectives. The negotiation should take the following form:

- Do you believe that the purpose of the project is worth while?
- Do you believe that to achieve that purpose we need to achieve the identified end and intermediate objectives?
- Do you believe that it is the responsibility of your group to deliver some or all of those objectives?

If the answer to the first question is 'no', then you, as project manager, need to find some way of making the project of value to the people concerned. If the answer to the second question is 'no', then you can involve the group of people in the planning process to gain their views. If the answer to the third question is 'no', then you can gain their opinion on whose responsibility it might be. If you cannot gain agreement on the second and third question, then you must doubt the group's answer to the first, and work further on finding ways of making the project beneficial to them.

Defining roles and responsibilities

The contract is defined by defining roles and responsibilities of the parties involved for the work elements at each level of breakdown. Many project management systems focus on just one role: Who is to do the work? The various roles and responsibilities on a project are listed in Table 7.2.

Table 7.2 Roles and responsibilities

Responsibility	Role
For work	Who is to undertake the project's task?
For management	Who is to take decisions? Who is to manage progress? Who is to guide and coach new resources?
For communication	Who must provide information and opinions? Who may provide information and knowledge? Who must be informed of outcomes?

Keep it simple

Below, I introduce a responsibility chart as a single-page document to define resources and their input. It defines the contract at all levels of breakdown (Figure 2.6) and is the document against which the contract is negotiated and agreed. The responsibility chart can be used to build cooperation and to ensure that the novel organization of a project is brought into operation quickly and effectively. However, before describing the responsibility chart more fully, I shall describe the types of organization that can be used for managing a project.

7.3 Types of project organization

Selecting the type of project organization is the first step in its management, and is the step by which we develop the concept (Section 6.2). There are two key issues when selecting a project organization:

- line vs matrix structure
- isolated vs integrated resources.

Line vs matrix structure

There are two extremes for creating an OBS. At one extreme an existing functional hierarchy within the parent organization is used, and the WBS is massaged so that work elements fall wholly within the realm of resource units in the line management structure. This gives a project organization in which the OBS and WBS are aligned with the functional hierarchy (Figure 7.1(a)). At the other extreme, a natural WBS is developed, independent of the organization, with dedicated resources being assigned to work elements in the WBS. This gives a project organization in which the OBS and WBS are aligned with a project hierarchy (Figure 7.1(b)). Both of these structures are inflexible.

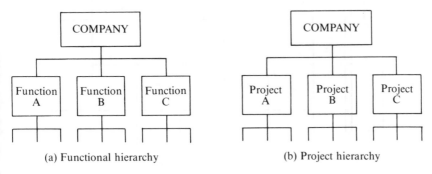

(a) Functional hierarchy   (b) Project hierarchy

Figure 7.1   Line organizations

Overlapping the two structures gives a matrix in which people have both project and functional responsibility (Figure 7.2). It is now common to consider five types of project organization,[1] with three types of matrix structure between the two extremes (Figure 7.3):

- functional hierarchy
- coordinated matrix
- balanced matrix
- secondment matrix
- project hierarchy.

Functional hierarchy: Project tasks are assigned to relevant operational areas, whose managers take responsibility for achieving tasks in their area. Unfortunately, different managers may have different views on the priority of the project, and so one area may be delayed by lack of support from another.

Coordinated matrix: A project controller is appointed with responsibility for coordinating tasks, but with limited authority for ensuring priority is

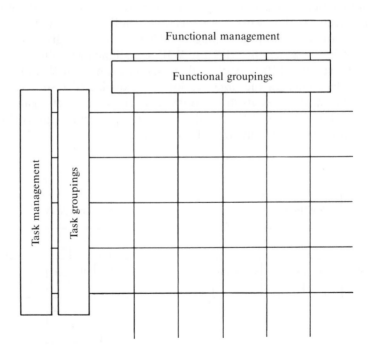

Figure 7.2   Matrix structures

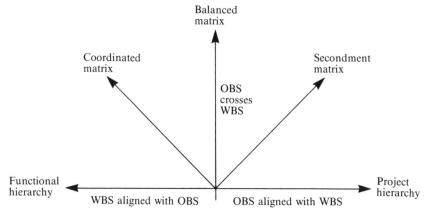

Figure 7.3   Range of matrix structures

given for resources. Having responsibility but no authority is an impossible position.

Balanced matrix: A project manager is appointed to oversee the project and responsibility is shared with the operational managers. The project manager is responsible for time and cost, the operational managers for scope and quality. The balanced matrix is probably difficult to maintain, depending on the relative strengths of the project and operational managers. By default it may become either coordinated or a secondment matrix.

Secondment matrix: The project manager has primary responsibility for tasks and the operational managers assign (second) personnel, full or part time as required. The project manager now has more effective control but the users begin to lose influence over the project's outcome.

Project hierarchy: The project manager manages a dedicated project team, and the operational managers have no involvement. The project manager now has total control, but the users have lost all influence, and this structure is inflexible.

You may have an idea about which of these five structures gives the most successful outcome of projects in your industry. The balanced matrix is probably the ideal, giving the project manager control, while maintaining user involvement. However, it depends on the relative strengths of the project and operational managers. Gobeli and Larson[1] surveyed a large number of projects, and, subject to the discussion of Chapter 5, judged whether or not they were successful. Their results are illustrated

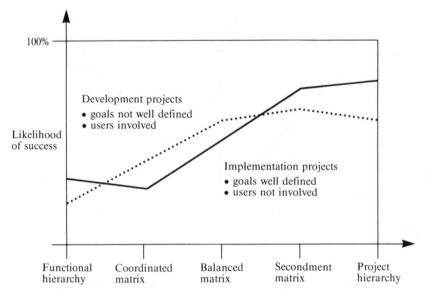

Figure 7.4   Project success rates

diagrammatically in Figure 7.4. They split projects into two types: development projects and implementation projects.

DEVELOPMENT PROJECTS

The three project structures are almost equally successful, with secondment matrix slightly ahead. The purpose of development projects is to define the products of future projects and of the organization as a whole. Therefore, user involvement is also important to gain their acceptance of the end product. It is also difficult to predict the resource requirements and so flexibility is important. The secondment matrix allows greater user involvement than the project team, and provides some flexibility while still maintaining control.

IMPLEMENTATION PROJECTS

The project hierarchy is very successful, with the secondment matrix close behind. On implementation projects the size of the team can be accurately forecast, so inflexibility does not matter, and the product is defined so user involvement is reduced. Furthermore, the project team can build a commitment to a common goal. This commitment may also explain the rise in effectiveness of the functional hierarchy. I also think that the straight line from the coordinated matrix to the secondment matrix shows that the balanced matrix will become one or other, depending on the relative strengths of the project and operational managers.

Isolated vs integrated resources

A related issue[2] arises with two of the project organizations, the secondment matrix or the project hierarchy. The issue is where to locate resources. There are two extremes (Figure 7.5), each of which has advantages and disadvantages. Resources can be:

- isolated from operations by being placed in a task force
- integrated with operations by working on the project from their normal place of work.

ISOLATED

The advantages are that the project team can work without distraction and on secret work. The disadvantages are that users seconded to the team lose contact with normal operations, users not seconded mistrust the project, operational managers are reluctant to release their best people, and it is inflexible (Example 7.1).

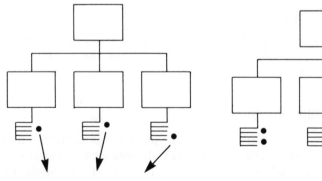

- Project members released full time to a separate project room

(a) Isolated

- Project members work in their normal environment

(b) Integrated

Figure 7.5   Locating resources

INTEGRATED

The advantages and disadvantages above are reversed. To be successful this requires the manager's subordinate to be given space to work on project tasks, to be allowed to focus on the task at hand without distraction, with no environmental problems imposed on that individual while working on project tasks.

Intermediate positions are possible, giving advantages of both models. Individuals seconded part time to a project can be given a quiet room, close to their normal place of work, to use while working on the project.

A public utility adopted the integrated approach for the design and development of their customer database system. People were seconded from the districts into a central design team. The development process took two years, at the end of which time the design was two years out of date. Furthermore, many users seconded to the development team were given temporary promotions. When they returned to operations they expected their promotions to be made substantive, but were often of less use to their districts than they were before they left as their experience was now also two years out of date. However, the alternative, the integrated team, is extremely unlikely to have delivered the design in anything like two years, so the isolated approach was the only option.

When I described this story to a group of Russian managers on a course at Henley Management College, they said the people should have taken greater responsibility for managing their own careers!!!

Example 7.1 Isolated project teams

Project Definition Report

The Project Definition Report (Chapter 13) is used to define the type of project organization to be adopted, and to detail the organization breakdown structure.

7.4 Responsibility charts

The use of responsibility charts to define the project organization is now widespread.[2,3] Typically, a chart is a matrix with work elements shown as rows and organizational units as columns (Figure 7.6). Symbols are placed in the body of the matrix to represent the involvement of each resource type in each work element. The matrix can be used at any level of work breakdown. This provides a one-to-one correspondence between the levels in the WBS and the OBS (as one might expect). Even though the responsibility chart is a matrix, it can be used to describe any one of

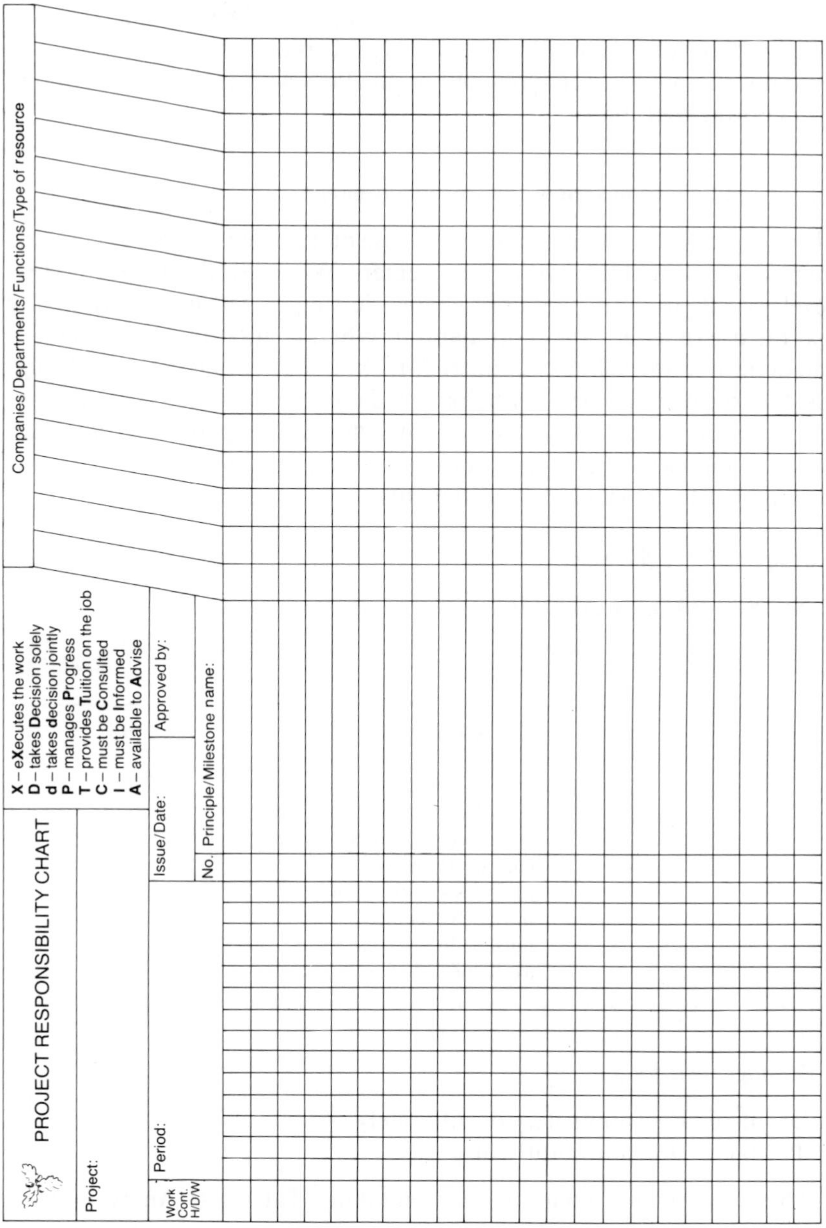

PROJECT RESPONSIBILITY CHART

Companies/Departments/Functions/Type of resource

Project:

X – eXecutes the work
D – takes Decision solely
d – takes decision jointly
P – manages Progress
T – provides Tuition on the job
C – must be Consulted
I – must be Informed
A – available to Advise

Issue/Date: Approved by:

Period:

Work
Cont.
H/D/W

No.   Principle/Milestone name:

Figure 7.6   Blank responsibility chart

the five organization types, or any mixture of them. The use of a responsibility matrix does not imply a matrix organization. I have often encountered mixed organization types, but particularly a project line surrounded by a coordinated matrix.

Use of symbols to describe types of involvement

Cleland and King[3] give examples of the use of numbers, letters or geometric shapes to represent the type of involvement. When Grude and Haug[2] first developed their chart they used geometric shapes, but found eventually that the use of letters was more natural. When facilitating project launch and definition workshops (Chapter 13), I find the use of letters which suggest the role or responsibility helps to aid communication. I would therefore recommend the use of the eight letters developed by Grude and Haug[2] to represent eight types of roles and responsibilities (Table 7.3), as they appear to cover most requirements.

1. *Responsibility for work*

   X: eXecutes the work: this is self-explanatory.

Table 7.3 Types of role and responsibility

Letter	Role or responsibility
X	eXecutes the work
D	takes Decision solely or ultimately
d	takes Decision jointly or partly
P	controls Progress
T	provides Tuition on the job
C	must be Consulted
I	must be Informed
A	available to Advise

2. *Management roles*

   D: takes Decision solely or ultimately
   d: takes Decision jointly or partly

   There are various modes of decision taking (Table 7.4). An example of D2 might be the selection of a financial management system. The financial manager agrees it meets the company's financial requirements. The IT manager agrees it meets the company's systems strategy. If they fail to agree the decision is referred to the financial director,

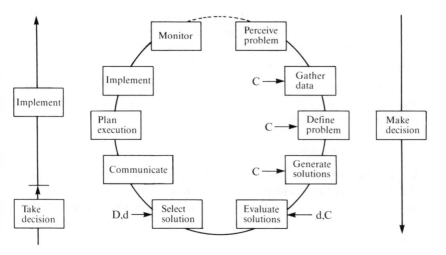

Figure 7.7 Consultation vs closing options

their joint boss. In decision D3, there can be a fine line between being consulted, 'C' (as shown in decision D4), and truly closing options, 'd'. This may be the case with the trade union representatives with no authority but significant disruptive power. If you return to the ten-step problem-solving cycle, reproduced at Figure 7.7, this distinction only occurs at step 5, 'evaluate solutions'. At previous steps, people are consulted. At step 6, decisions are taken. The symbol used will represent what you, the manager, want.

Table 7.4 Four modes of decision taking

Decision mode	Person			Description
	A	*B*	*C*	
D1	D	–	–	*A* takes the decison alone.
D2	–	d	d	*B* and *C* share the decision. If they agree the decision stands. If not it is referred up the usual management channels.
D3	D	d	d	*B* and *C* close options and recommend. *A* has the ultimate authority.
D4	D	d	C	*C*'s opinion must be sought (but can be ignored). *B* closes options and *A* has the ultimate authority.

P: controls **Progress**. This is the person responsible for ensuring that the work is planned, organized, implemented and controlled. The project manager is ultimately responsible, but uses the symbol to delegate responsibility at lower levels of the WBS.

T: provides **Tuition** on the job. This assumes that the people doing the work do not have sufficient skill, so they are coached on the job. As their skill grows, 'T' may change to 'P'.

3. *Communication channels*

C: must be **Consulted**. These people must be consulted in the course of the work. They have information or opinions that the project must take into account when doing the work or taking decisions. However, they do not have decision-taking responsibility: their opinions can be ignored.

I: must be **Informed**. These people must be provided with information about the outcome on one part of the project to enable them to do work or take a decision on another part.

A: available to **Advise**. These people may have information or opinions which the project team may want to use, but cannot know until they reach that part of the project. In effect the symbol represents 'may be consulted'.

'C', 'I' and 'A' control the flow of information. If people feel they should be consulted or informed, that is negotiable as part of the contract.

The symbols must be used flexibly and imaginatively. Nothing is served by being pedantic. The project team paint the picture they want, and use the chart as a communication tool. For instance, in a training course is the trainer 'T' and the tutee 'X', or is the trainer 'X' and the tutee 'I'? It makes no difference as long as everyone understands.

Use of the responsibility chart

The responsibility chart can be used at all levels of the WBS. In particular it can be used at the three fundamental levels, as follows:

PROJECT LEVEL: PROCEDURAL RESPONSIBILITY CHART

At this level the chart is used to define procedures, principles or policies for managing the project. For example, that may be:

- procedures for monitoring and control
- change control procedures
- quality control procedures
- configuration management procedures.

Figure 7.8 is a procedure for monitoring and control. You will see that a time chart is used to define a regular cycle throughout the project. The resources at this level are companies, organizational units (departments, groups, sections), or management functions (finance director, IT manager, project manager). It is important that someone is described by their role on the project. If the R&D manager is also project manager, and has responsibilities as both, that person should appear as both. If that individual leaves part way through the project, he or she may be replaced by one person as R&D manager, and another as project manager. Procedural responsibility charts may be included in the Project Definition Report and Manual (Chapter 13).

STRATEGIC LEVEL: MILESTONE RESPONSIBILITY CHART

At this level the chart is used to define roles and responsibilities for achieving milestones. Figure 7.9 is a chart for the CRMO Rationalization Project. The resources at this level are the same as above. This leads us to using the same version of the form for both, and calling it a *project responsibility chart*. Sometimes both milestones and procedures are included on the same page, which is why these two levels were merged into a single management level in Figure 2.6. Figure 7.9 also includes a time schedule. (We shall discuss scheduling in Chapter 10.)

TACTICAL LEVEL: ACTIVITY SCHEDULE

At this level the chart defines the roles and responsibilities of named people to do work to achieve a milestone. Because activity schedules are prepared on a rolling-wave basis during implementation planning, the people involved can now be named. They are unlikely to change on the time scale of a work package, and if they do, the work should be replanned. Furthermore, because the activities are now more certain, more effort can be put into ensuring that the chart is correct. Figure 7.10 is an activity schedule for milestone P1 in the CRMO Rationalization Project.

Developing the responsibility chart

I described in Section 6.6 how the milestone plan is best developed in a group working session, specifically at a project launch or definition work-

Figure 7.8 Procedural responsibility chart for monitoring and control

PROJECT RESPONSIBILITY CHART

Project: CRMO RATIONALIZATION

Issue/Date: Approved by:

Period: 199X — 199Y

Legend:
- X – eXecutes the work
- D – takes Decision solely
- d – takes decision jointly
- P – manages Progress
- T – provides Tuition on the job
- C – must be Consulted
- I – must be Informed
- A – available to Advise

Companies/Departments/Functions/Type of resource

No.	Principle/Milestone name	Regional Board	Operations Director	CRMO Managers	CRMO Team Leader	CRMO Staff	Project Manager	Project Support Office	Estates Manager	Estates	Network Manager	Networks	IT	Operations	Personnel	Suppliers
P1	Project Definition	D	d	dX	dX	-	PX	X	X	-	X	-	C	C	C	
O1	Communication plan	I	D	d	PX								C	C		A
T1	Technology design					C					PX	X	C	C		
O2	Operational procedures	I	D	d	PX	X									TX	
O3	Job/Management design	I	D	d	PX	C							X			
T2	MIS Functional spec.	I	D	d	dX						PX		X		TX	
O4	Staff Allocation	I	D	d	PX	C										
A1	Estates roll-out plan	D	d	C	X		C	X	XP	X	C	-	-	-	-	C
T3	Technology roll-out plan	D	d	-		-	C	X	C	-	PX	X	X	-	-	C
P2	Financial approval	D	d	-	C		PX	X	C		C	X	C	A	A	C
O5	Management changes	I	DX	X	PX	-			PX	X	-					
A2	Sites 1 and 2 available			-	-					X	-					
O6	Redeployment/Training		D	D	PX						PX	X	X		TX	
T4	Systems in sites 1 and 2	I		-	-	X	P			X		X	X	-		X
A3	Sites 1 and 2 ready	I		-	X	X				X		X	X	-		X
T5	MIS delivered	I	D	-	X						P		X			X
O7	Procedures implemented	D	d	PX	PX			X	A		A	A	A	-	X	
P3	Intermediate review	D	d	C	C		PX	X	-		-	X	A	A	A	
A4	Roll-out implemented	I	D	dX	dX	X	PX	X		-	-	X	X	A	X	X
P4	Post completion audit (benefits)	D	d	C	C		PX	X					C	C	X	X

Figure 7.9 Project responsibility chart for the CRMO Rationalization Project

ACTIVITY SCHEDULE

Project: CRMO RATIONALIZATION
Milestone No./Name: P1: PROJECT DEFINITION
Period: 199X Week Number
Issue/Date: A/2 Jan
Approved by: JRT

Key:
- X – eXecutes the work
- D – takes Decision solely
- d – takes decision jointly
- P – manages Progress
- T – provides Tuition on the job
- C – must be Consulted
- I – must be Informed
- A – available to Advise

Companies/Departments/Functions/Type of resource

No.	Activity/Task name	Regional Board	Operations Director	CRMO Managers (2)	CRMO Team Leader	CRMO Staff	Project Manager	Project Support Office	Estates Manager	Estates	Network Manager	Networks	IT	Operations	Personnel
1	Produce project proposal	C	D	d	dX		PX	A	A		A		A	A	A
2	Hold project definition workshop		DX	d	X		PX	X							
3	Define required benefits	C	D	d	dX		PX		I		I		I	I	I
4	Draft project definition report	C	D	d	dX		PX	X	X						
5	Hold project launch workshop		D	X	X		PX	X	X		X		X	A	C
6	Finalize milestone plan	D	D	d	d		PX	X	C		C		C	A	A
7	Finalize responsibility chart	D	D	d	d		P	X	C		C		C	A	A
8	Prepare estimates – time				A		P		A		A		A	A	A
9	Prepare estimates – cost			A	A		P		A		A		A	A	A
10	Prepare estimates – revenue		A	A	A		P								
11	Assess project viability		D	d	d		PX	X							
12	Assess risks	D	D	d	dX		PX	X	C		C		C	C	C
13	Finalize project definition report	D	d	d	d		PX	X	C		C		C	C	C
14	Mobilize team	D	D	d	dX	I	PX	X	I		X		IX		I

Work Cont. H/D/W — Week Number: 4, 5, 6, 7, 8, 9, 10

Figure 7.10   Activity schedule for milestone P1

shop (Chapter 13). The same applies to the responsibility chart. It is very effective to copy the blank form on to an acetate, project it on to a white board, and then complete it with the team participating. Entering the symbols directly on to a paper form can isolate members of the group, with the result that they may not accept the end product. However, I find that if everyone is involved, then when they allow symbols to remain under their names, they internalize the result, and accept that as their responsibility. Estimates and schedules can be entered on the projected form in the same way.

7.5 Incorporating work content

In negotiating the contract between project and business it is necessary to include estimates of the resource requirements. Functional managers cannot commit themselves to release resources without knowing the level of requirement. I shall explain here what consumes resources, describe how to communicate the estimates as part of the contract, and end with a cautionary remark about accounting for lost time. Estimating work content, and using that to calculate duration, is covered in Chapters 9 and 10.

Consumption of resources

Two of the eight roles and responsibilities primarily consume resources:

X: eXecutes the work
C: must be Consulted.

Many project management methodologies only include estimates of the former. However, the latter can consume as much if not more resources and must therefore be included in the estimate. The four management responsibilities are overhead resources and are considered to be part of the holders' day-to-day duties. Therefore, estimates of those items will not usually be included. The main exceptions to this will be where 'T' refers to the involvement of a trainer, or an external consultant whose bill will be charged to the project. 'D' and 'd' should consume little time if they are limited to decision taking as opposed to decision making. Unfortunately, I often come across decision takers who want to repeat the decision-making process. With the other two communication roles, 'I' should consume little time until the person starts work, especially if the reports are well constructed, and 'A' is not certain to consume resources. An allowance may be made.

Communicating the estimate

There are several ways of communicating a resource estimate, using:

- the responsibility chart
- estimating sheets
- resource histograms.

THE RESPONSIBILITY CHART

This can be used in one of two ways to communicate the estimates. There is a column at the extreme left-hand end of the chart. This will refer to the 'X' and 'C' resources. Alternatively, the estimates can be written in the body of the matrix, as in Figure 7.11.[4]

ESTIMATING SHEETS

These are commonly used for preparing the resource estimates. Figure 7.12 is an estimating sheet for the work package *P1: Project Definition* from the CRMO Rationalization Project, prepared on a PC using a spreadsheet. They can also be used to communicate the estimates. The use of estimating sheets is described further in Chapter 9.

RESOURCE HISTOGRAMS

These provide a visual picture of the estimates (Figure 7.13). However, they require a schedule for the work elements, and so are discussed further in Chapter 10. (For simplicity, the figure shows only part of the associated bar chart.)

Accounting for lost time

When agreeing resource availability, the project managers and resource providers must have the same understanding of how much time is actually required. It is quite clear that one man-day means a day's work by one person. But how much work is a man-year: 260 days or something less? Figures quoted in man-weeks, man-months and man-years are usually interpreted as a statement of both resource requirement and duration; that is how many people are needed for how long. They therefore should include an allowance for the fact that personnel working full time on a project are not available 5 days each week for 52 weeks of the year. They lose time through sickness, holidays, training, group meetings, etc. This lost time is said, on average, to be 30 per cent of the working year. When

PROJECT RESPONSIBILITY CHART

Legend:
- X – eXecutes the work
- D – takes Decision solely
- d – takes decision jointly
- P – manages Progress
- T – provides Tuition on the job
- C – must be Consulted
- I – must be Informed
- A – available to Advise

Project: HARPENDEN FACTORY - CENTRE DEVELOPMENT

Issue/Date: A 14 Dec 87 **Approved by:**

Companies/Departments/Functions/Type of resource — Resources in Man Days

No.	Principle/Milestone name	H'den - Quality	H'den - Accounts	H'den - CIB	H'den - Personnel	H'den - Engineering	H'den - Production	H'den - Factory Manager	H'den - Centre Mgt.	Engineering	Finance	Quality	MIS	Contractors	Consultants	R & D
ST1	Define structure	1	1	1	1	1	1	1								
PE1	Determine message	1	1	1	1	1	1	1								
PE2	Change attitudes	5	3	4	12	25	26	1	1							
PE3	Select managers	1	1	1	1	1	1	1								
SY1	Write job outlines	3	2	2	6	13	13	1								
SY2	Determine crewing	5	5	5	1	5	5	2	20							
PE4	Determine redeployment/recruitment	1	1	1	1	1	1	1	15							
ST2	Define factory facilities	5	5	5	5	5	5	5	15		2			25		
PE5	Define training programme	2	2	4	20	4	2		10				3	25		
SY3	Decide cost control information	2	20	20	1	2	1	20	6		10	2	10		2	
SY4	Specify computer systems	4	2	10	2	5	1	5	20		10		40	5	2	
ST3	Build facilities					20		15	15	1113				large		
SY5	Implement revised cont sys.	20	10	10	15	20	2	25	25				15			
ST4	Share rev. cost cont. resp.	1	1	1	1	1	1	2	15							
PE6	Recruitment	2	2	2	50	2	2	2	60			3		25		
PE7	Training	25	15	20	60	50	10	5	200					25		
PE8	Achieve minimum staffing	15	15	15	15	15	2	5	45							
ST5	Transfer personnel resp.	1	1	1	1	1	1	1	3							
ST6	Transfer engineering resp.	1	1	1	1	1	1	1	3							
ST7	Transfer quality resp.	1	1	1	1	1	1	1	3							
ST8	Achieve centre management							1								3

Period: FY 9X (1 2 3 4) | FY 9Y (1 2 3 4) | FY 9Z (1 2 3 4) — Work Cont. H/D/W

Figure 7.11 Responsibility chart showing resource usage

ESTIMATING SHEET		TRIMAGI COMMUNICATIONS BV			02-Jan-9X

PROJECT:	CRMO Rationalization	CODE:	C1	ISSUE:	A
WORK AREA:	Project	CODE:	C1P	AUTHOR:	LJN
WORK PACKAGE:	Project Definition	CODE:	C1P1	APPRVD:	JRT
ACTIVITY:	....	CODE:	....	DATE:	02-Jan-9X

ACTIVITY/TASK		WORK CONTENT			RESOURCES					9 People
		No of steps	Effort/ step	Total effort	Prjct Mgr	Prjct Offc	CRMO TL	CRMO Mgrs	Ops Direct	Other Mgrs
Number	Description		(days)	(days)	1	1	1	2	1	3
1	Produce project proposal	1	4	4	1	2	1			
2	Hold project definition workshop	1	4	4	1	1	1		1	
3	Define required benefits	1	2	2	1		1			
4	Draft Project Definition Report	1	8	8	2	6				
5	Hold project launch workshop, 1.5 day duration	1	12	12	1.5	1.5	1.5	3		4.5
6	Finalize milestone plan	1	2	2	1	1				
7	Finalize project responsibility chart	1	2	2	1	1				
8	Prepare estimates – time	20	0.1	2		2				
9	Prepare estimates – cost	20	0.1	2		2				
10	Prepare estimates – revenue	1	1	1		1				
11	Assess project viability	1	1	1	1					
12	Assess risks	1	3	3	1	1	1			
13	Finalize Project Definition Report	1	5	5	2	3				
14	Mobilize team	1	3	3	0.5	0.5	0.5			1.5

		SUB-TOTAL:		51	13	22	6	3	1	6
TOTAL EFFORT:	56 DAYS									
TOTAL COST: £K 22.22		ALLOWANCE %		10	10	10	10	10	10	10
DURATION: DAYS										
TARGET START:		TOTAL EFFORT:		56	14	24	7	3	1	7
TARGET FINISH:										
		UNIT RATE:	£K/day	0.5	0.3	0.3	0.5	0.8	0.5	
		COST:	£K	7.15	7.26	1.98	1.65	0.88	3.30	

Figure 7.12 Estimating sheet for milestone *P1: Project Definition* from the CRMO Rationalization Project

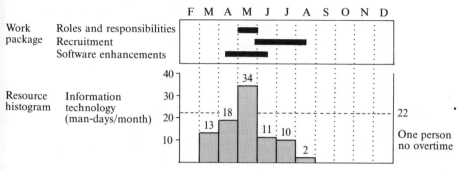

Figure 7.13 Resource histogram

converting from man-days to man-weeks, man-months or man-years I would suggest you use the following ratios:

- 5 × 0.7 = 3.5 man-days/man-week
- 22 × 0.7 = 15.5 man-days/man-month
- 52 × 3.5 = 180 man-days/man-year

If you are employing a labourer from a contractor, then you can clearly expect a person on every day you want one. If the person you had one day is not available the next, then a replacement can be sent. The contractor accounts for lost time in the rates charged. The same is not true for professional people. It is very inefficient for an engineer or software programmer or training professional to hand over part way through the design of a programme.

You must also not double account. Having used these ratios, an individual is available 260 days per year. For instance, if you have a resource calendar which allows you to account for individual holidays, then you should use a ratio of 0.8, which gives 4.0 man-days/man-week, 16.5 man-days/man-month, and 210 man-days/man-year. (A resource calendar is a calendar which identifies working days and rest days during the life of a project. It can also identify the number of hours worked per day. There can be resource calendars for the project as a whole, for individual resources within it, and for different geographical locations).

7.6 Equipment and drawing registers

Up to this point I have focused on human resources in the project organization. Other types of resources include:

- drawings representing the designs of material, plant and equipment
- materials to be consumed in the delivery of the facility
- plant and equipment to be used, but not consumed, during the work on the project
- finance to pay for the project.

Finance is beyond the scope of this book.

Drawings, materials, plant and equipment are often managed using lists or registers. These are lists of the resources against each activity in the project. Maintaining these in an electronic database enables the project manager to monitor the delivery of the resources against the start date of the activity. Often, the resources go through several stages of development before final delivery. For instance, drawings go through:

- functional, systems and detail design
- various iterations and stages of sign-off of the drawings;

and materials go through

- production of drawings
- procurement
- manufacture
- assembly
- delivery
- kit marshalling.

On a small project, these steps may be included as activities in the project plan. However, on larger projects this can become too cumbersome. The stages of development are then monitored in the registers, effectively as separate packages of work. Standard or known lead times are used to work out the due date for completion of each step, from the start date of the activity in which the resource is used.

Shortly before the start of an activity, the material register becomes a *kit-marshalling list*. This is used to check that all the materials required for the activity have been delivered, and to collect them together to ensure that they are ready for use when the activity starts.

7.7 Summary

1. The purpose of project organization is:
    - to marshal adequate and appropriate resources
    - to undertake the work of the project
    - to ensure successful delivery of its objectives.

2. The principle tools and techniques of organization management are:
   - the contract between the parties involved
   - organization breakdown structure, matching work breakdown
   - responsibility charts.
3. There are two issues in choosing a project organization:
   - type of organization structure
   - location of resources.
4. There are five types of organization structure:
   - functional hierarchy
   - coordinated matrix
   - balanced matrix
   - secondment matrix
   - project hierarchy.
5. Eight types of role or responsibility are suggested for use in the responsibility chart:

   X   eXecutes the work
   D   takes Decision solely or ultimately
   d   takes decision jointly or partly
   P   controls Progress
   T   provides Tuition on the job
   C   must be Consulted
   I   must be Informed
   A   available to Advise.

6. The contract requires recording of estimates of work content, so that resource providers can commit themselves to the release of their people.
7. Drawings, materials, plant and equipment are managed using registers and lists against the activities in which they are required.

References

1. Gobeli, D. H. and Larson, E. W., 'Project structures versus project performance', in *Proceedings of the 11th INTERNET International Expert Seminar* (ed. H. Schelle), INTERNET, 1987.
2. Andersen, E. S., Grude, K. V., Haug, T. and Turner, J. R., *Goal Directed Project Management*, Kogan Page, 1987.
3. Cleland, D. I. and King, W. I., 'Linear responsibility charts in project management', *The Project Management Handbook* (eds D. I. Cleland and W. I. King), Van Nostrand Reinhold, 1988.

4. Turner, J. R., 'Company resource planning in the food canning industry', in *Proceedings of the 12th INTERNET International Expert Seminar* (ed. S. Dworatschek), INTERNET, 1988.

8
Managing quality

8.1 Introduction

The last two chapters described methods, tools and techniques for managing the two mandatory system objectives: scope and organization. Let us now turn to the three secondary objectives or constraints: quality, cost and time. Contrary to common practice, they will be addressed in that order, which I believe is the order they should be first addressed during project definition (Figure 2.5).

This chapter addresses the first constraint: quality. Section 8.2 considers quality in the context of projects, followed by a description of the methods for assuring and controlling the quality of the project's products, the facility and the product produced by the facility. Equally important, and considered next, are methods for managing the quality of the management process. If the project is not managed properly, it is almost impossible to achieve a quality product. The chapter then describes some of the concepts, tools and techniques of total quality management (TQM) applied in a production environment and considers how they might be applied in a project environment. The chapter closes with an explanation of how quality is free, but not on individual projects.

8.2 Quality in the context of projects[1]

A project is said to be successful if the work is finished to time, to cost and to quality. We understand quite clearly how we measure time and cost – hours or days and pounds or dollars, respectively – but very few people have a clear idea of what they mean by quality in the context of projects. Indeed, in spite of it being stated as one of the major criteria for judging the success of a project, very little is written about managing quality on projects. In order to use quality as a measure of the success, we need to understand what we mean by it. This section defines quality in the context of projects, and introduces processes for its achievement.

What is quality?

The word quality is often used to mean expensive, luxurious, sophisticated, or conforming to an extremely high specification. For example, a quality car is a Mercedes or Rolls-Royce, a quality watch is a Rolex or Cartier, a quality suit is tailor made in Bond Street or Savile Row. However, by adopting this view of quality you can end up pursuing an impossibly expensive standard which is neither what the customer wants, nor what is necessary in the circumstances. Good quality does not have to mean high quality or high prices; it means supplying the customers with what they want, to the standard and specification they want, with a predictable degree of reliability and uniformity, and at a price that suits their needs.[2] There are three essential elements to this concept of quality:

- good quality vs high quality
- fitness for purpose
- conforming to customer's requirement.

GOOD QUALITY VS HIGH QUALITY

Good quality does not imply high quality. Steam raising in an electricity generating station requires high-quality water, with impurities reduced to a few parts per million, whereas for cooking in the home good-quality tap water is perfectly adequate. Indeed, for drinking purposes the high-quality water used in the power plant may not be suitable as it will be flavourless, and will not contain essential minerals. It is therefore not fit for drinking purposes, and so is poor quality in those circumstances.

FITNESS FOR PURPOSE

This concept of fitness for purpose is now often adopted as a measure of good quality,[3,4] and can be applied equally well whether the facility produced is an organizational change, an information system, or an engineering product. In the simple example of selecting a motor car above, the Ford Fiesta can be a good-quality car if its purpose is to act as an economical, reliable, family runabout. Within its own market niche, it may have a higher quality rating than the Jaguar, the *high*-quality car. Indeed in the early 1980s Jaguar had a poor reputation for reliability compared to Ford. The same can apply when comparing a Marks and Spencer suit to a Savile Row suit.

However, saying something is fit for purpose begs the question of who makes the judgement. The answer must be the customer, and this implies that quality means meeting the customer's requirement or specification.[3,5] This is the definition of quality that is now widely adopted. In order to set a measure of quality it is therefore necessary to set out the customer's requirement *in advance* in a formal document or specification. In a project, of course, the customer's requirement is for the product produced by the facility which the project delivers. The quality of the facility is only important in the efficacy with which it produces the product, and its availability to do so. (The latter in defence procurement is called *availability, reliability and maintainability*, ARM.) Therefore the specification of the customer's requirement is once removed from the work being done.

Traditionally on projects the owner has specified the facility in detail, and sometimes even the work to be done. This has had two effects: it has required the owner to be able to design the facility required to produce the product, and this has meant that operating companies have needed to maintain a large engineering design function at significant overhead; and it has absolved the contractor of any responsibility of ensuring that the facility is capable of producing the product. All the contractor has to do is deliver the facility to the owner's specification, and the owner must accept responsibility for whether or not it works.

Many owners, including the UK's Ministry of Defence, are now adopting *Cardinal Points Procurement*,[6] in which they specify the reliability of the product, and leave it to the contractor to design a facility that will produce a product of that reliability. This is good for the owner, but means that the contractor is exposed to claims for the lifetime of the facility, not just its guarantee period.

Giving customers what they want

So quality is defined as conformance to customers' requirements, and this requires the customers to state their requirements in a formal, specification document. This document may be a *Statement of User Requirements* (for organizational development projects), part of the *Project Definition Report* (for information systems projects), or a *Customer Requirements Document* (for engineering projects). However, there are two difficulties with this approach:

1. Projects are unique, and therefore carry risk and uncertainty. Customers may not be able to state their needs in full at the start of projects.

Should contractors hold them to the original specification or allow them to change?
2. Who is the customer: the owner or the user?

ALLOWING CUSTOMERS TO CHANGE THEIR MINDS

If quality is meeting the customers' requirements then they must be allowed to change their minds as new information becomes available during the project. It is no good delivering what they wanted when the specification was first drawn up; you must deliver what they want now. However, if they continually change their minds, then the project will surely fail. The need for quality must be balanced against the other four system objectives. In some circumstances, such as R&D, high technology, or management development programmes, the customers cannot know the exact form of the product at the start; what they often request is a solution stated in terms of familiar technology. The project team may also not know how the solution will be delivered as they too are treading new ground. It is only as the project progresses that the new technology becomes understood by customers and project team alike. This may cause both parties to a contract to change course. If this creates difficulty, the fault lies with the way the project was structured and in the basis of the contract, rather than with the customers' desire for change.

A strict change control procedure is important, but if this is too rigidly applied the output may be of no value to the customer. Delivering quality is a delicate balance between frozen specifications which produce still-born products, and totally fluid situations which produce at best an uneconomic product and at worst no product at all. The correct balance lies somewhere between, and this must be set before the specification is agreed. Where the methods and outputs are clearly known, a more rigid form of specification is required. This will be the case during the execution stage of most projects. Where the process and outcomes are unclear, a more flexible specification is required, calling for a strong client/contractor interaction, in which they work together towards a mutually acceptable solution. This is the approach required during the development stage of many projects. (Chapter 11 describes how the risk associated with the uncertainty of the specification can be shared between owner and contractor. The important principle is to assign risk to those best able to control it. Chapter 16 describes the use of configuration management to manage the refinement of the specification.)

SATISFYING THE OWNER OR THE USER

There is a simple answer to this dilemma; it is the owner who puts up the money to buy the facility, and so has the right to know what he or she is committing to in advance. This means that the owner must agree the specification at the end of proposal and initiation, at the end of design and appraisal, and as any changes are made. It is the champion's role to convince the owner that the specification will deliver the most cost-effective product, and that any changes are necessary to the effective operation of the product. This is not inconsistent with what was said above. It just means that the negotiations on a flexible specification involve three parties: the owner; the champion; and the contractor (Example 8.1). The ultimate arbiter, of course, is the consumer of the product produced by the facility.

On the extension to the National Gallery on Trafalgar Square, the Sainsbury family were able to donate only a fixed amount of money; the museum curators had to match their requirements to that available budget. The project manager managed the negotiation process.

Example 8.1 Tripartite negotiations

Quality and the project management life cycle

The life cycle is the vehicle by which quality is delivered to the customer. Throughout a project, the team can do it right first time, or get it wrong. Common sense says that the earlier in the life cycle errors are detected the cheaper they are to correct. Experience in shipbuilding, motor car and software industries supports this. In the first they talk about a ratio of 1:3:8 – that is, for every pound it costs to correct a mistake in design, it costs three to correct it during construction and eight during commissioning and sea trials. Again, Hitachi claim that 75 per cent of the production costs are determined by design, and Mazda find that more than 50 per cent of a product's quality is determined during design. In the software industry it has been found that the cost of correcting an error when the software is in use is at least 250 times greater than finding and correcting it at design stage. It is estimated that over 40 per cent of software errors occur during the requirement specification and design stages.

Although the initial definition of the customer's requirements are crucial to achieving quality on a project, there is opportunity throughout the life cycle for losing sight of those requirements. In Section 2.3 it was stated that there are typically four major stages to a project:

- initiation, in which the requirements are converted into a proposal
- design, in which that proposal is turned into a working design
- execution, during which the facility is developed
- finalization, during which it is commissioned and tested.

Not only can the customer's requirements become denigrated in each stage, but the stages are often performed by different groups and so attenuation can occur between stages. The design team may produce a design that meets the objectives as stated in the proposal, but does not truly address the customer's purpose. The execution team may then not implement the design correctly. Furthermore, they are primarily concerned with doing the work, and even less concerned with the customer's purpose. The people conducting commissioning trials check to ensure that the facility achieves the customer's purpose, but they usually work from a test specification produced by the design team, not by the customer, and so work to the former's interpretation of the prupose or, worse, the way they, the testers, read that interpretation. Is there any chance of achieving a quality product?

8.3 Achieving quality on projects

The process for achieving quality being adopted by an increasing number of companies in the manufacturing and service industries is called total quality management (TQM). Total quality management means[4,7] *harnessing everyone's effort to achieve zero defects at lowest cost*, and zero defects means *continually satisfying customer requirements*.

On a project, this process contains five elements (Figure 8.1):

- two of the elements concern quality: the product and the management processes
- there are two approaches to achieving this: quality assurance and quality control
- there is the attitude of mind of everyone in the organization – from senior management down – towards achieving zero defects.

Quality of the product is the ultimate goal. On a project this means meeting the customer's purpose, but achieving the quality of the facility that will produce the product is an essential stage towards that.

Quality of the management processes is another necessary condition for achieving a quality product. We saw above the impact that the life cycle can have on the interpretation of the customer's requirements. It is essen-

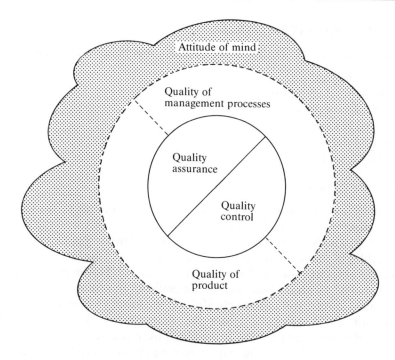

Figure 8.1   Total quality management of projects

tial that the management processes are such as to ensure the quality of the product throughout each stage and between each stage.

Quality assurance is preventative medicine. These are steps taken in advance to increase the likelihood of obtaining a quality product. Ideally this likelihood should be 100 per cent. Prevention aims to stop defects happening.

Quality control is curative medicine. These are steps taken to measure the quality of both the product and the management processes, and to eliminate any variances from the desired standard.

The attitude of mind is the commitment of everyone in the organization to achieve quality. This commitment must start at the top of the organization; it cannot be delegated.

Methods for assuring and controlling the quality of the product and the management processes are described below.

Assuring the quality of the product

In order to assure the quality of the product, it is beneficial to have:

- a clear specification
- use of defined standards
- historical experience
- qualified resources
- impartial design reviews
- change control.

CLEAR SPECIFICATION

Without a clear idea of what is to be achieved, the team has no direction. It is possible to specify both the end product of the project, and the intermediate products: milestones resulting from work packages; and deliverables of the activities at lower levels. The lower the level at which the deliverables are specified the tighter the control. However, there are risks associated with a highly detailed specification: it may be inconsistent; it may confuse rather than clarify; and the lower level products may become an end in their own right, rather than a means of achieving the facility. I described above how, if the client overspecifies, the contractor can meet the specification, but not satisfy the client's purpose. Cardinal points procurement attempts to overcome this.

USE OF DEFINED STANDARDS

These are standard designs and packages of work which, from previous experience, are known to be able to deliver results of the required specification. One of the great differences between the project environment and a routine manufacturing facility is that, in the latter, each day's production becomes a standard against which to improve the next day's production. In a project environment it may be some years before you repeat a process, and then the environmental conditions may be different. However, the use of standards will be beneficial in the long run.

HISTORICAL EXPERIENCE

Hence, the greater the historical experience, the better will be the standards and specification. For this reason, it is not always possible to create a clear specification of R&D, high technology and organizational development projects. However, the more historical data that are used the better. In the next chapter it will be shown that there is a clear learning curve in industries with time, with it taking perhaps 50 years to build up a credible body of data.

QUALIFIED RESOURCES

If the people used on the project have access to that body of data, either through their own experience or training, then that makes them better able to apply standards and achieve the specification. This applies equally to professional staff (engineers, IT staff, researchers, trainers, managers) and artisans (electricians, mechanics, programmers). It is common in the engineering industry to put artisans through strict testing procedures before allowing them to do critical work. The use of qualified resources also applies to material and financial resources, but these can be tested against the standards.

IMPARTIAL DESIGN REVIEWS

The use of auditors to check the design can ensure that the customer's requirements are properly met by the design produced. However, this can have an adverse effect (Example 8.2).

In a recent privatization, several interested parties could appoint an auditor to check the writing of the corporate software of the company being floated. This almost resulted in there being more auditors than programmers. Because auditors are there to find fault, they can tend to find it where none exists: the design is adequate, though not perfect. The programmers then spend more effort proving their design than doing new work.

Example 8.2 A possible adverse effect of auditors on a project

CHANGE CONTROLS

This is vital to achieve the specification where change is necessary. It does not mean that changes are eliminated, because that can result in a product that does not meet customer requirements, but the purpose of each change must be carefully defined, the impact on the design assessed, and the cost compared to the benefit, so that only those changes that are absolutely necessary and cost-effective are adopted.

Controlling the quality of the product

Quality control is a process of diagnosis and cure. As the facility is erected and commissioned it is checked against the specification to ensure that it is of the required standard, and any variances are eliminated. The activities by which this is done must be planned, tested, recorded and analysed.

Planned: quality control consumes resources, and so the activities must be planned so that those resources are allowed for in the project's estimates and are available to conduct the tests at the right time.

Tested: it must be known that the method of checking the specification will highlight variances.

Recorded: the results must be recorded to provide a historical record for planning future projects, and to be able to analyse trends.

Analysed: the results must be analysed to determine the cause of any variance so it can be eleminated, and the analysis of trends can indicate potential problems before they occur.

Assuring the quality of the management processes

To assure the quality of the management processes, a similar list as that for the product applies, which means having a set of defined procedures for managing projects. Procedures clearly specify how projects are to be managed by qualified resources, and are derived from standards based on historical experience. That may be the company's own experience, or standard good practice.[8] The British Standards Institute has produced standards on the management of projects, as well as standards on quality approaches to management. The most common is BS 5750, but there are several industry-specific ones. Many client organizations, such as the Ministry of Defence and British Rail, have their own, and regularly audit contractors against them. An organization is required to document and examine its policy and methods through regular, formal, detailed reviews, conducted by in-house teams. Policy, methods and procedures are scrutinized by independent assessors, initially to ensure that the organization merits registration under BS 5750, and thereafter to ensure that the required standards are maintained. The important requirement for the procedures is: they must be used. There are two reasons why they are not used, even where they exist. First, they are bureaucratic and, secondly, there is lack of management commitment. Once, when conducting a project audit, I was assured that a set of procedures existed, but when I asked to see them the interviewee took a heavy tome from a top shelf and blew the dust off before opening it.

Having good effective procedures requires the right attitude of mind; a commitment to quality management which must start at the top. Procedures usually require the production of periodic reports for senior management, who must be seen to use the reports to take decisions that affect the course of the project and the business, or the processes will fall into disrepute. (Procedures manuals are described in Chapter 16.)

Controlling the quality of the management processes

The method of monitoring the management processes is through project audits. An audit is a detailed check of the operation of the management processes against standards of good practice, such as the organization's procedures manual or that of an external agency. (Audits are described further in Chapter 16.)

The quality plan

At the start of the project, the manager should draw up a quality plan to define how quality will be achieved, how the company's procedures will work on this project, and how the manager intends to assure and control quality. In qualifying the procedures, it may contain new ones where items are either not covered or inadequately covered for this project in the overall procedures, and may include such things as: disputes, documentation, reporting mechanisms, customer liaison, etc. For the quality control process, it may contain a detailed activity and resource plan. The quality plan may form a section of the Project Definition Report (Chapter 13).

8.4 Implementing total quality[9]

Several techniques have been developed to complement the introduction of total quality management (TQM), which may be adapted to the project environment. Quality control has been an integral part of manufacturing since before the Second World War. However, quality approaches which encompass all of an organization's operations have only recently been developed. TQM is essentially *good management practice*. It is about ensuring that every task completed by every employee, from managing director downwards, is *done right first time* – an attractive concept for the manager of a complex interrelated task such as the management of a project. This section reviews the main doctrines of TQM as practised in the manufacturing industry, describes some of the techniques derived from them, and suggests how they might be used to manage quality on projects.

The philosophies of total quality

There are several fundamental doctrines on how to implement and improve quality. The main American and Japanese advocates of total quality are:

– Dr Edwards Deming
– Joseph M. Juran

- A. V. Feigenbaum
- Philip Crosby
- Kaori Ishikawa.

Deming's doctrine is based on an organization having a constant purpose to:

- improve its products or service
- develop reliable statistical methods for measuring improvements.

The whole approach is led by top management, and requires the institution of a rigorous programme of education and training. Deming's 14 points of quality management formed the basis of the Japanese quality programme following the Second World War. However, it is not a simple approach, and other less statistical methods have been developed.

JURAN'S MANAGEMENT OF THE VITAL FEW

Juran's ideas are based on a project approach to quality improvement. He suggested that errors should be identified and targeted for solution in priority order. The technique which Juran recommends is *Pareto analysis*, which focuses on the 20 per cent of the causes of problems which account for 80 per cent of failures. These *vital few* are continually improved until the process is fault free and efficient.

FEIGENBAUM'S HANDS ON

Feigenbaum's approach to quality improvement suggests that it has to be organization wide. He proposes *total quality control*, which aims to bring all the functions of the organization together to create systematic quality processes. Feigenbaum conceived the term *cost of quality* to encompass:

- product and process failures
- quality control, inspection and appraisal
- prevention programmes.

He estimated that these can account for 10 to 40 per cent of a company's annual turnover. The focus on cost of quality is believed to motivate managers to improve quality, and it allows them to gauge success by the measurement of improvement in these costs.

CROSBY'S ZERO DEFECTS

Crosby advocates a prescriptive approach, consisting of 14 steps for management to review. The basis of quality can be summarized as:

- management has the responsibility to set performance standards, and the standard should be *zero defects*
- the definition of quality is conformance to the standard
- there is no such thing as the economics of quality; it is always cheaper to do the job right first time
- the only performance measure is the cost of quality.

KAORI ISHIKAWA'S SEVEN TOOLS

The focus of Kaori Ishikawa's teaching is that all employees are responsible for their own quality output. He has developed the *7 tools* method, which uses techniques simple enough for all employees to understand and adopt. The seven tools are:

- Pareto chart
- cause and effect diagram
- check sheet
- histogram
- scatter diagram
- Schewart cycle
- Deming cycle.

Kaori Ishikawa estimates that 95 per cent of problems in an organization can be solved by the use of these simple tools. Other techniques associated with TQM are:

- statistical process chart
- quality loss function/Taguchi method.

SUMMARY

Although some of this writing is contradictory, there are a number of conclusions that can be drawn, some of which we have already met:

- Organizations need to be committed to quality from the top down: Table 8.1 shows Crosby's continuum of commitment to quality.
- Companies need to identify their most critical quality problems, and management must provide the lead in resolving them.
- In every known process, organizations need to identify the factors that indicate good quality, so that the process becomes measurable.

– Quality should be achieved through understanding and improving processes, and by prevention, not by inspection and correction.
– Organizations must develop a statistical understanding of processes, and use statistics to solve problems.

The proponents of TQM argue that the benefits of the approach are massive, and can lead to the reduction and elimination of work in progress, defects and waste. It can also aid the planning process, thus making more effective use of human and other organizational resources.

Table 8.1 Continuum of quality awareness (after Crosby[10])

Stage	Description
1. Uncertainty	No comprehension of quality as a management tool
2. Awakening	Recognize that quality may be of value, but unwilling to provide resources to make it happen
3. Enlightenment	Management becoming supportive and helpful
4. Wisdom	Participative understanding of the absolutes of quality management
5. Certainty	Quality management is an essential part of the organization's system

Techniques of total quality

Some of the techniques associated with TQM can be used by project managers to control and coordinate complex interrelated tasks. I consider the application of three of the techniques mentioned above to project-based management:

CAUSE AND EFFECT DIAGRAM

This is a technique used by quality circles throughout the world.[11] It is also known as the Ishikawa diagram or fishbone diagram. The technique consists of defining an occurrence, the effect, and then reducing it down to contributing factors, the causes. The factors are then critically analysed in the light of their probable contribution to the effect (Figure 8.2). There are essentially four steps to the construction of the diagram:

1. *Identify*: the problem area needs to be identified and specified. Techniques such as Pareto analysis can assist in this initial stage of constructing a cause and effect diagram.

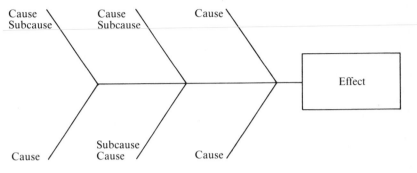

Figure 8.2 Cause and effect diagram

2. *Target*: specific targets and objectives need to be set at this stage. Every-one involved in the construction of the cause and effect diagram needs to be clear about what is to be achieved, e.g.: *The second phase of the project must be reduced by four weeks.*
3. *Construct*: the construction of the diagram is a good opportunity to involve the project team and encourage them to participate in problem-solving exercises. Individual members can contribute suggestions as to the causes of the problem, thus forming the branch lines. Subcauses can also be identified and are shown as branch lines shooting horizon-tally from the main branch lines.
4. *Contemplate*: contemplation of the ideas that emerge is necessary. This is a kind of incubation period so that individuals are able to assess the repercussions of the situation and design and develop appropriate action.

Figure 8.3 demonstrates how a cause and effect diagram can be used as part of the problem-solving process in project management. By producing a cause and effect diagram, you are able to put project problems into per-spective, and re-establish your priorities.

PARETO ANALYSIS

This is a problem-solving technique developed by an Italian economist. It is a means of isolating the *vital few* from the *trivial many*. For example, in a company store, it can usually be found that 20 per cent of the differ-

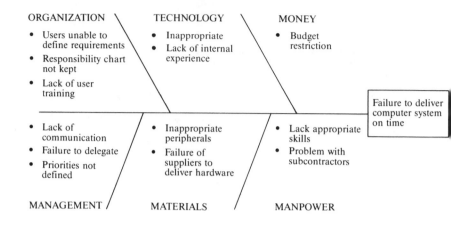

Figure 8.3 Diagram used for problem solving in project management

ent stock items account for 80 per cent of the total store value. This 80/20 relationship holds good in many situations:

- 80 per cent of the turnover from 20 per cent of the customers
- 80 per cent of the scrap from 20 per cent of the causes
- 80 per cent of the delays come from 20 per cent of the subcontractors.

Recognizing the Pareto relationships can help to rank priorities and focus resources where they have the greatest impact. This can be demonstrated by plotting the available data on a histogram (Figure 8.4).

TAGUCHI METHODS

These are based on the philosophy that you should always aim to produce a result to the highest quality, independent of the *acceptable* limits, as the value to the society as a whole will always be enhanced. Taguchi found that better results are obtained by making small variations to the input factors, often at low cost, but this requires an understanding of the effects of various inputs and their interdependence. Manufacturing operations have a wide variety of inputs, not only raw materials, but also process conditions. To vary each input, while systematically holding all the other inputs at set levels and to gauge the effect of the single input on the end product, would take a large number of experiments, except in the simplest of systems. Even taking a Pareto style selection of inputs – the 20 per cent of inputs giving 80 per cent of the impact – the amount of experimentation would probably be beyond the resources of most organizations.

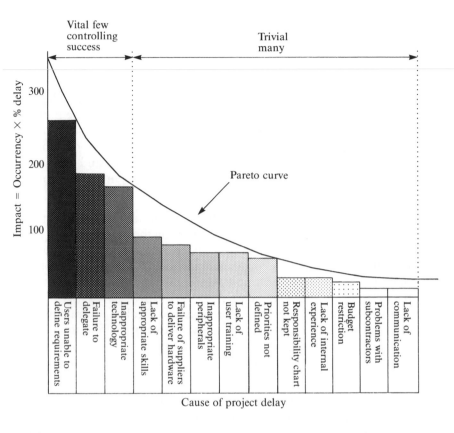

Figure 8.4 Pareto analysis of failures of computer system implementation

The Taguchi method allows simultaneous variation of a number of inputs, while allowing analysis to be performed on each individual input. The method employs several inputs varied from their normal value in a balanced matrix known as an *orthogonal array*. The essence of the method is that each experiment is designed to look at the effect of one particular input, and although the other inputs vary, they vary in such a way that they are present in equal numbers at higher and lower numbers about their norm, so that their effects cancel and leave only the input being analysed. The array of experiments can be analysed for each input in turn. The results show the strength of the effects of each input, and can also be used to show the strengths of any interactions between inputs. When used correctly, the Taguchi method can give some startling improvements, but relies on some basic requirements:

- there is a measurable quality
- there is a basic understanding of which inputs are important, and their relative effects.

Now, a project is a unique piece of work, undertaken using a novel organization (Chapter 1). I also show in the next chapter on managing costs that it is necessary to plan for the adequate outcome, because planning for the perfect outcome can cost more than doing the work itself. Furthermore, because they are novel and unique, there is no *norm* about which to vary the inputs. Does this mean that Taguchi philosophy and methods do not apply to the management of projects? The argument is fallacious for two reasons:

1. Use of the Taguchi method permits you to reduce the amount of work required to assess the impact of the inputs on the outcomes, and hence the cost of planning to achieve a better output. Effectively, you can raise the level of what is considered adequate for the same amount of planning effort. However, you must still take care that you do not seek the perfect solution at any cost.
2. The whole point of planning in projects is to break the work down into elements (inputs) that are familiar, and to use norms for estimating the time and cost of those elements. All cost estimating is based on historical data. The Taguchi method can be used to improve the efficacy of those historical data.

However, you are still faced with a dilemma in the project environment. The Taguchi analysis takes upfront investment in effort, to give greater, long-term return. That is acceptable in a manufacturing facility, because, being *eternal*, it will reap the benefit of the investment. However, projects are *transient*, so it is only later projects that reap the benefit of the analysis performed on the current project. The manager of the current project may not want to perform the analysis, because the cost cannot be recovered within the project. The optimum for the project conflicts with the optimum for the organization. For this reason, the drive for quality must come from senior levels of the organization, and quality initiatives must be funded centrally, not charged to individual projects.

8.5 The cost of quality

Applying the above techniques costs money, and so you may wonder whether the cost justifies the benefit. What is the cost of achieving quality? You will often hear people say that the cost of quality is free.[10] This is based on measured results of implementing total quality management in manufacturing companies, producing savings something like those shown in Figure 8.5. This views the cost of quality as being made up of three elements, as proposed by Feigenbaum:

- the cost of failure
- the cost of appraisal and control
- the cost of prevention.

Applying the above techniques certainly increases the cost of prevention, but it reduces the number of failures. That has an effect on the cost of failures, and as the number of failures falls the need for appraisal and control falls, reducing that cost as well. Eventually, the total cost of quality is less than it was at the start, even though the cost of prevention has risen. That, too, may begin to fall as the attitudes to quality become ingrained.

However, we now meet the first great rub of project management. In a manufacturing company, the time to show any improvement is typically about 18 months (the duration of many projects), and the time to the point where prevention costs begin to fall is typically four years. This means that if the technique is applied to a project, no return will be seen within that project's lifetime. The solution is for the prevention costs to be borne by the parent organization as an overhead, with the whole organization benefiting as savings feed back into more effective projects. That will be effective where the project team is drawn wholly from within the organization, which is the case on organizational development projects and in project-based organizations such as an engineering design consultancy, construction contractor, or software house. However, it may still be difficult to get contractors to adopt the prevention techniques if

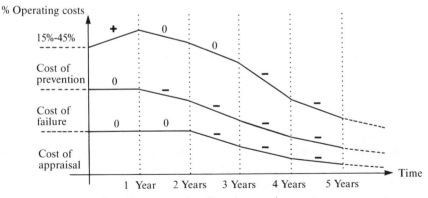

Figure 8.5   Cost of quality as a ratio of total operating costs

they have no long-term commitment to the client and the client's future projects. The solution is to develop integrated supply chains and to adopt partnering arrangements whereby the contractor has the necessary commitment. This is the approach adopted by Marks and Spencer for the supply of their clothes and food, and it is being adopted by the oil majors in the United States. However, further description of these arrangements is beyond the scope of this book.

8.6 Summary

1. Quality means giving customers what they want. On a project this may mean allowing the customer to have a change of mind as new information comes available, but this should be managed through effective change control. The owner is the ultimate arbiter of what is necessary, as it is the owner who pays for the project's output. However, the user is the owner's representative.
2. The customer's requirements can become denigrated during the project life cycle, and this must be avoided.
3. There are five elements to total quality management on projects:
   - quality of the product
   - quality of the management processes
   - quality assurance
   - quality control
   - the right attitude of mind from top to bottom.
4. Assuring the quality of the product requires:
   - a clear specification
   - use of defined standards
   - historical experience
   - qualified resources
   - impartial design reviews
   - change control.
5. Controlling the quality of the product must be:
   - planned
   - tested
   - recorded
   - analysed
   - independent.
6. Assuring the quality of the management processes requires defined procedures for managing projects, which are used. These procedures can be used to conduct audits to control the quality of the management processes.

7. Techniques of quality management that can be used by project managers include:
   - cause and effect diagrams
   - Pareto analysis
   - Taguchi methods.
8. Quality is free, but not within the lifetime of a project.

Notes and references

1. Section 8.2 incorporates material written by Mahen Tampoe. Mr. Tampoe is a research associate of the College, and his interests are in the management of knowledge workers. Previously he worked for ICL, his last job with them being managing director of a research subsidiary.
2. Deming, W. E., 'Quality, productivity and competitive position', in *MIT Charter for Advanced Engineering Study*, Massachusetts Institute of Technology, 1982.
3. Juran, J. M. (ed.), *Quality Control Handbook*, McGraw-Hill, 1974.
4. Cullen, J. and Hollingum, J., *Implementing Total Quality*, IFS/Springer Verlag, 1989.
5. Crosby, P. B., *Quality Without Tears*, McGraw-Hill, 1979.
6. Kiely, D. G., *Defence Procurement: The equipment buying process*, Tri-Service Press, 1990.
7. Anon., *How to Take Part in the Quality Revolution: A management guide*, PA Consulting Group.
8. Crosby, P. B., *Quality is Free*, McGraw-Hill, 1979.
9. Section 8.4 incorporates material written by Julie Hartley. Ms Hartley works for University of Central England, where she lectures in Quality Management.
10. PMI, *The Project Management Body of Knowledge*, Project Management Institute, 1987.
11. Sasaki, N. and Hutchins, D., *The Japanese Approach to Product Quality*, Pergamon, 1984.

9
Managing cost

9.1 Introduction

Let us now consider the fourth project objective, managing cost, by which the project manager ensures that the product of the project is financially viable and worth while. The next section will consider the purposes of estimating costs, and show how this leads to several types of estimates, of different accuracy prepared at different stages of the project management life cycle. Later sections explain how the estimate is structured through the cost control cube, and describe several methods of preparing the estimate. Finally, we shall discuss how costs are controlled by comparing actual expenditure against the value of work done, not against planned expenditure, and show how S-curves can provide a pictorial representation of this.

9.2 Estimating costs

There are several reasons why we estimate costs. The most obvious is to provide a measure against which to control costs. A list of the reasons is given below.

Basis for control

The estimate is prepared as a measure against which to control expenditure on the project. This measure is known as the *benchmark* or *baseline*. The classic control process has four steps:

- estimate future performance
- record actual performance
- calculate the difference, called the variance
- take action according to the size of the variance.

There are three basic actions:

- if the variance is zero or negligible: continue without change
- if the variance is significant but recoverable: plan recovery
- if the variance is large: revise the estimates.

As a basis for control the estimate may need to be quite detailed, prepared at a low level of the WBS.

Assess project viability

Before getting to a position where you need to prepare a control estimate, you need to determine whether the project is worth undertaking. You therefore prepare an estimate of the costs to compare with the estimates of returns. (Methods of assessing project viability are beyond the scope of this book, except where covered in Chapter 3). Furthermore, the appraisal estimate goes through various stages of increasing accuracy, at the start of proposal and initiation, at the transition from that stage to design and appraisal, and at the transition from that stage to execution and control.

Obtain funding

After approval has been obtained, the project must be financed. Again, funding will be awarded on the basis of a comparison between an estimate of costs and an estimate of returns. The accuracy will usually be similar to that required for project approval. (Obtaining finance is also beyond the scope of this book.)

Allocate resources

Work content is one element of the total cost. The need to estimate work content as part of the negotiation of the contract between project and business was introduced in Chapter 7. In a way, human resources are a special form of project funding. The business plans their allocation in advance against an estimate of the accuracy of the project approval estimate. They will be assigned to the project week by week against the control estimate.

Estimate durations

The duration of a work element is calculated by comparing the estimate of work content to resource availability, and so the cost estimates form an input to time estimating. Time estimating is performed for similar reasons to cost estimating, and so similar types of estimate are required.

Prepare tenders

Contracting firms tendering for bespoke contracts need to prepare estimates for the tender. They may use the cost estimate in several ways, including:

- to forecast the profit by subtracting the estimated cost from the market price
- to calculate the price by adding a fixed percentage to the cost
- for passing on to the client. Clients in the public sector often demand a cost breakdown.

9.3 Types of estimate

The same estimate cannot satisfy all six purposes mentioned above. Five types of estimate, of varying accuracy, are required (Table 9.1). There is another purpose against each type: to prepare the equivalent estimate of duration. The levels of accuracy in Table 9.1 are those obtainable on engineering projects: those for information technology (IT) projects are said to be half this level (double the figure). Table 9.2 summarizes an idea first introduced in Section 6.3: you obtain increasing accuracy of estimate by estimating at lower and lower levels of WBS. If the estimates are truly mean values, errors cancel out. Table 9.2 implies that to obtain an estimate to the correct accuracy at the project level, you need only estimate to the order of magnitude at the currently lowest level of the WBS. There are two provisos to this:

1. A consistent error will reinforce: if all activities are underestimated by 20 per cent, the project will be underestimated by 20 per cent.
2. The absolute error, in ±£, at the project level is probably worse than at the lower levels.

Table 9.1 Types of estimate: purpose and accuracy

Type of estimate	Range of accuracy (%)	Purpose
Proposal	±50	Appraise viability to start feasibility study
Budget	±20	Appraise viability to start systems design
Sanction	±10	Appraise viability to approve project, obtain funding, allocate resources
Control	±5	Measure progress, assign resources
Tender	±2	Prepare tender

Table 9.2 Types of estimate: level in work breakdown structure

Type of estimate	Lowest level of estimating in WBS	Accuracy of estimate (%)			
		Project	Work area	Work package	Activity
Proposal	Areas of work	±50	±100	–	–
Budget	Work packages	±20	±40	±100	–
Sanction	Work-package scope statements	±10	±20	±50	(±150)
Control	Activities	±5	±10	±25	±75
Tender	Tasks	±2	±4	±10	±30
Assumed number per project		1	4	25	200

Table 9.2 can be taken to lower levels of WBS for larger projects. On one large engineering project worth several hundred million pounds, I prepared a WBS that had approximately 100 areas of work and a ratio of 1:10 for each subsequent level of work breakdown, down to the task level. On the same project, estimators were estimating costs accurate to the nearest pound at all levels of WBS, and yet including contingencies of several hundreds of thousands of pounds at the work-package level. This is clearly absurd. It is the right level of contingency, but the wrong level of accuracy. Table 9.3 shows appropriate levels of accuracy and contingency at different levels of the WBS for a project worth £100 million. The table is based on three simple ratios: (a) the average cost of an element of work is inversely proportional to the number in the project; (b) the accuracy as a percentage is proportional to the square-root of the number in the project, or inversely proportional to the square-root of the size (the binomial theorem introduced in Section 6.3); and (c) the accuracy as an absolute value is the accuracy as a percentage multiplied by the average cost:

(a) $$\frac{C\,(\text{element})}{C\,(\text{project})} = \frac{1}{N\,(\text{element})}$$

(b) $$\frac{\pm e\%\,(\text{element})}{\pm e\%\,(\text{project})} = \sqrt{\frac{N\,(\text{element})}{1}} \quad \text{(binomial theorem)}$$

(c) $$\pm e£\,(\text{element}) = C\,(\text{element}) \times \pm e\%\,(\text{element})$$

At any level of the WBS, there is no point calculating and quoting the estimates to a greater degree of accuracy than the figure in the right-hand column, and any contingency added at that level of the WBS must be at least of this amount as a level of contingency is already included through the accuracy to which the figures are calculated.

Table 9.3 Levels of estimating in a large engineering project

Level of WBS	Number in project (N)	Average cost (C)	Accuracy	
			Ratio ($\pm e\%$)	Value ($\pm e\pounds$)
Project	1	£100 000 000	± 1	±1 000 000
Area of work	100	£1 000 000	± 10	± 100 000
Work package	1000	£100 000	± 30	± 30 000
Activity	10 000	£10 000	±100	± 10 000
Task	100 000	£1 000	±300	± 3 000

9.4 When to estimate costs

It follows from Table 9.2 that to prepare estimates of increasing accuracy requires increasing effort as you estimate at lower levels of breakdown. The binomial theorem implies that to double the accuracy at the project level requires you to estimate at a level of breakdown with four times as many work elements, requiring four times the effort. This has been measured in the engineering industry,[1] Table 9.4. When plotted (Figure 9.1) this is a learning curve, with greater effort giving greater accuracy, but with diminishing returns. This is similar to the Pareto curve (Section 8.4), but unlike the Pareto curve you can never obtain all the information: there is no 20 per cent of effort. In addition, there is a point, at 5 per cent accuracy with effort 5 per cent of project cost, where the effort does not justify the return. This has three consequences:

1. On projects internal to an organization, it is not worth while producing an estimate more accurate than the control estimate, because it costs more to produce than the value of the data. This is a consequence of the uniqueness of projects (Chapter 1). On a production line, costs may be estimated to a low level of detail, because the saving is made many times over. On projects, the saving is made once only. This is the second great rub of project-based management: it is not worth while producing plans in great detail, because the effort is not rewarded. It is better to put management effort into eliminating risk, not quantifying it. The

Table 9.4 Level of effort and stage of production of project estimates

Type of estimate	Accuracy (%)	Level of effort as % of project cost	Stage of production
Proposal	±30 to ±50	0.02–0.1	Pre-proposal and initiation
Budget	±20 to ±35	0.1–0.3	Proposal and initiation
Sanction	±10 to ±25	0.3–1.0	Design and appraisal
Control	± 5 to ±15	1–3	Implementation planning
Tender	± 2 to ±5	5–10	Tender preparation

    problem arises for contracting companies who, when tendering, must prepare estimates that will allow them to make a profit (Example 9.1).
2. The way to improve accuracy of estimates is not to put more effort into estimating, but to improve the estimating data – effectively to move the curve in Figure 9.1 to the left using historical data. However, this too suffers from the law of diminishing returns. On engineering projects, 80 years of effort has gone into preparing data.[1] The IT industry has only 20 years of experience, which is why the accuracy of estimates for

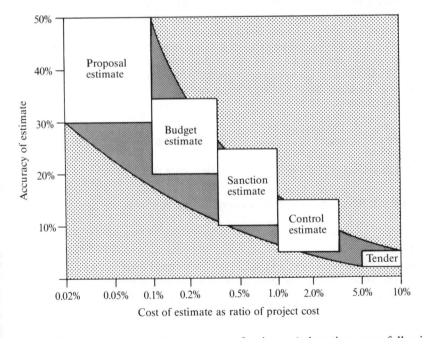

Figure 9.1 Accuracy of estimate vs cost of estimate (a learning curve following an inverse square law)

each type is only half as great (double the figure) – four times the effort doubles the accuracy.
3. The estimate at one level should not be prepared before the estimate at the previous level. Each estimate is therefore prepared at a given stage of the life cycle (Table 9.4), and these stages should be followed rigorously. Effectively, the comparison of costs and returns at the end of one stage of the life cycle justifies the commitment of resources to planning, design and estimating at the next stage. If the project is not viable at these high levels of estimate, work should not proceed to the next stage (Example 9.2).

I facilitated a bid management workshop run by one of the major IT vendors at Henley Management College. They spend 3 per cent of contract value preparing estimates, are successful at winning one contract in five, and have traditionally made profit margins in excess of 50 per cent. The contract they win pays the estimating costs of the four they do not, but the net margin is still in excess of 35 per cent. However, margins are being squeezed, and they are now lucky if they make a gross margin of 15 per cent. That means they must increase the number of contracts won, reduce the estimating costs, or make a loss. A bid manager from one of the major engineering contracting firms in the petrochemical industry spoke at the workshop. He said they had reduced the bidding costs to 0.75 per cent of contract cost. They also win one contract in five, but need to make a margin of only 4 per cent on that contract to cover the bidding costs on the five. The way they reduced bidding costs is to have a department of bid managers, who are the centre of expertise for tendering. That department can make maximum use of historical data. Effectively:

– they accelerate the learning curve
– they reduce the unique elements of projects, and therefore turn the bidding process into a repetitive operation
– they achieve quality through using historical data (Chapter 8).

Example 9.1 Recovering the cost of estimating on contracts

I worked in one company where the IT Department prepared control estimates at project initiation, only to find projects were not viable. If you expect an internal rate of return of 20 per cent on projects (at interest rates at the time of writing), you can only make that mistake three times per year until you cannot afford projects at all.

Example 9.2 Tailoring the estimate to the current stage of the project

9.5 Structuring the estimate

Cost components

The cost of a project may consist of several components, some of which are detailed below.

LABOUR

This includes the cost of people employed by the parent company involved in executing project tasks, as well as people designing and delivering the facility. I have worked with some manufacturing companies that do not attribute design labour to contracts. It is absorbed into company overheads and shared between all contracts. The result is that the company only wins contracts with a high design element, and they have no control over design costs. Some other labour costs are included under other headings.

The labour cost may be measured in monetary terms, or in man-hours. The latter is also called the work-content (Section 7.5) and is a measure of the total effort required, independent of the duration and number of people performing the task. Clearly, effort can be converted into monetary terms by applying known costs per man-hour for each resource.

MATERIALS

This should include the cost of all materials bought via the parent company and consumed in delivering the facility. They may be materials contained in the final product or consumables used on project tasks. On engineering projects materials include machinery, vessels, piping, structures, instrumentation and machinery, but also include things like welding rods and coffer dams. On information systems projects, materials include main and peripheral hardware, proprietary software and coding sheets. On organizational development projects, materials may be more peripheral to the project, but include materials used on training programmes, furniture for new offices, and stationery for new management procedures.

PLANT AND EQUIPMENT

These are materials used in delivering the facility, but as they are not consumed, they are available for re-use on subsequent projects. They may be bought or hired, but either way each project only pays a part of their price new. This cost component should only include the cost of plant and equipment borne by the parent company. On engineering projects, plant and equipment includes welding machines and earth-moving machinery. On information systems projects it includes hardware used by programmers. On organizational development projects it may include equipment used in the preparation and delivery of training programmes, temporary accommodation used during office moves, and printing equipment if hired especially for the project.

SUBCONTRACT

This includes the cost of labour and materials as above provided by outside contractors. Costs will be included in this heading where their control is not within the scope of the parent organization.

MANAGEMENT

This should include the cost of people and materials involved in managing the project. These costs are directly attributable to the project, but not to specific tasks, and include: the project manager and team leaders (integrators); the project support office; the cost of a project management information system if required; and temporary site services. The cost of the management of a project gets smaller as a proportion of the total cost as the size grows. Typically it is about 5 per cent on a project of £10 million, and 1 per cent on a project of £1 billion.[1] For projects of less than £10 million, many of the routine project management tasks must be undertaken by the manager if this is not to become a burdensome overhead, and on very small projects it may not be treated as a direct cost at all, but borne by the parent organization as an overhead. (The risk of this, of course, is the same as treating design as an overhead.)

OVERHEADS AND ADMINISTRATION

This should include the cost of administering items included in labour, materials and subcontract. These will include: costs directly attributable to some items such as transport, but included under this heading for convenience; costs shared between items such as procurement and storage; absorption of some parent company overheads.

FEES AND TAXATION

Fees may include insurance, finance or licence agreements, and taxation may be regarded as a special type of fee.

INFLATION

This may or may not be ignored in the estimates.

1. Two cases when it is ignored are on publicly funded infrastructure projects, and projects where project costs, raw material costs and revenues are expected to inflate at the same rate. In the former case it is assumed that tax revenues will rise as fast as costs, and so the project will not become a larger burden on the public purse. For projects such as roads or the Thames Barrier there are no direct revenues; the benefit is to the economy and that is expected to grow in real terms. The Thames Barrier, for instance, was 400 per cent overspent on the original budget, but it is claimed that 80 per cent of that was due to inflation.[2] Only 20 per cent of the overspend was due to unforeseen costs. In the latter case, accounting for inflation will make the returns from the project appear better than they actually are, and so it is often ignored. In fact its main impact will be to decrease financing costs as a percentage of the total cost, but to increase taxation as the project will appear to be more profitable than it actually is.

2. Two cases where it is not ignored is where there is expected to be differential inflation between project costs, raw material costs and revenues and by contractors preparing fixed price tenders. In the former case it is necessary to account for it to calculate the true return of the project (Example 9.3). In the latter case the contractor must either include inflation in the price, or agree with the client to increase the price against an agreed index, called escalation.

When preparing the case for the construction of a chemical plant in the mid-1980s, I had to account for inflation. The price of the plant was expected to rise with the construction index (CI), which was running ahead of the retail price index (RPI); the price of the gas feedstock was expected to rise faster than the CI, the price of electricity with the RPI, while it was expected that the price of the product would remain static.

Example 9.3 Allowing for inflation in the estimates

CONTINGENCY

Contingency may be added as blanket figures or calculated according to risk. In the copy of the estimate shown to the owner, contingency is usually distributed among the other headings. In the copy shown to the team, the manager should hold contingency in a project manager's reserve, and show the team just the raw estimates. Given 'Work done expands to fill the time available', if contingency is included in the sub-budgets given to work-package managers and subcontractors, then they will spend up to that amount. In fact it is common for project managers to maintain three estimates:

1. The *baseline* or *estimated prime cost* is the raw estimate, without contingency, given to the project team to spend. There is typically no chance of achieving an out-turn less than this, but it is given to the project team to provide them with a tight target. The project manager only adds contingency when there is significant variation, so the baseline is impossible to achieve, and to hold the team to it would be demotivating. Contingency is consumed to update the baseline, but this must be done through a process of strict change control. If the baseline is updated lightly, then the project is always on budget and control is lost. On the National Gallery Extension the project manager would allow no contingency to be apportioned to any of the work packages as he wanted to maintain strict control of costs.
2. The *most likely out-turn* is the estimate the project manager thinks is most likely, with contigency apportioned appropriately. There is typically a 55 per cent chance of achieving an out-turn less than this.
3. The *budget* is the amount the owner is willing to spend. This is what the project manager is measured against by the owner, and is justified by the expected returns from the project. There is typically an 80 per cent chance of achieving an out-turn less than this.

On a typical engineering project the budget will be 10 to 20 per cent higher than the baseline, with the most likely out-turn half way between. On information systems and R&D projects the contingency may be much higher.

Structuring the estimate

These seven or eight components constitute a third breakdown structure, the *cost breakdown structure* (CBS). The CBS is usually much simpler than the other two, although at least one more level of breakdown can be derived under most headings.

The three structures, WBS, OBS and CBS, combine to form the *cost control cube* (Figure 9.2). This concept was developed by the United States Department of Defense (DOD), in the 1950s, as the basis of their C/SPEC methodology for controlling project costs (sometimes called C/SCSC). All costs can be assigned to a cell of the cube, and through the cube all costs have a position in each of the three breakdown structures. A project

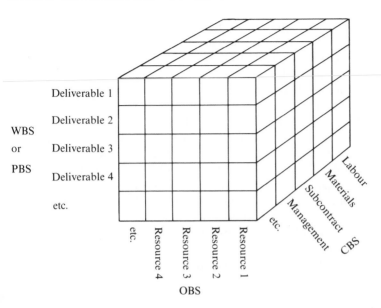

Figure 9.2   Cost control cube

aggregate can then be prepared by summing along any of the three directions. Of course a large number, often the majority, of cells in the cube will contain no costs. For instance:

– A work element may be assigned to one subcontractor, a single entity in both the OBS and CBS.
– A work element may consume labour only and of one type only.
– A work element may be created to assign management costs.

Any two of the breakdown structures taken together form a matrix:

– The matrix formed by the WBS and OBS forms the responsibility chart (Chapter 7).
– The matrix formed by the OBS and CBS is called a 'code of accounts'. It is used to apportion the costs in the parent company's accounts.
– The OBS is usually used to link the WBS and CBS (via the code of accounts), so the third matrix is seldom encountered.

The cost control cube provides a structure for the estimate, used to create it, and in the subsequent control of costs. The WBS and OBS are evolved to the current lowest level according to the stage of production (Table 9.4) and costs assigned to each element in the WBS/OBS matrix against each costs element. The estimate is then aggregated to the project level. In this way the cost control cube is amalgamated through a series of pages (Figure 9.3). Figure 9.4 shows a typical OBS for a chemical plant. A page like this would be prepared for the facility as a whole; that is, aggregated from similar pages for each part (intermediate product) of the facility and those in turn for each subassembly of the part. Figure 9.5 is the plant in Figure 9.4 at a lower level of work breakdown.

Estimates can be structured for IT projects, organizational development projects, training projects and others in a similar way. Figure 7.12 contains a simpler estimating sheet for a smaller project, in that case the CRMO Rationalization Project. This sheet has only two dimensions of the cost control cube: work and organization. It relates to only one component of the CBS: labour. If estimates were required for other components, such as materials or plant and equipment, then similar sheets could be developed, or more columns added to this sheet, especially if it is held in a spreadsheet package on a personal computer.

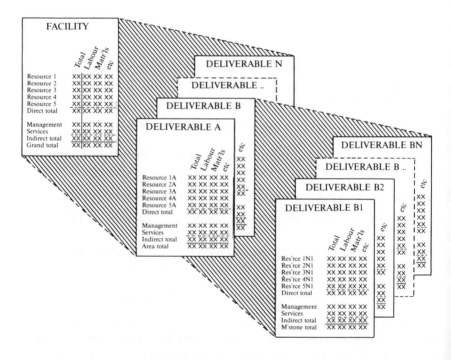

Figure 9.3 Cascade of estimates through the WBS, OBS and CBS

PROJECT ESTIMATE   NORTHERN ENERGY AND CHEMICAL INDUSTRIES PLC   02-Jan-9X

PROJECT:	Petrochemical Plant	CODE:	THNS	ISSUE:	A		
WORK AREA:	....	CODE:	....	AUTHOR:	JRT		
WORK PACKAGE:	....	CODE:	....	APPRVD:	CME		
ACTIVITY:	....	CODE:	....	DATE:	02-Jan-9X		

| | 1000 tonne per day plant | | | | SCALE EXPONENT | COST FACTOR | 1500 tonne per day plant | | | |
	Material £,000	Erection £,000	Function £,000	Plant £,000	n	$1.5^{\wedge}n$	Material £,000	Erection £,000	Function £,000	Plant £,000
Main plant items										
– Vessels	13.33	0.63	13.96		0.65	1.30	17.35	0.82	18.17	
– Furnace and boiler	2.89	0.14	3.03		0.70	1.33	3.84	0.18	4.02	
– Machines and drives	9.73	0.46	10.19		0.75	1.36	13.19	0.62	13.81	
– Vendor packages	6.77	0.32	7.09		0.75	1.36	9.18	0.43	9.61	
– Other	0.00	0.13	0.13		0.70	1.33	0.00	0.17	0.17	
MPI total: Materials	32.72	—	32.72				43.55	—	43.55	
MPI total: Erection	—	1.67	1.67				—	2.22	2.22	
Bulk Items										
– Piping	1.22	1.88	3.10		0.70	1.33	1.62	2.50	4.12	
– Instruments	0.64	1.10	0.74		0.60	1.28	0.82	0.13	0.94	
– Computer control system	1.56	0.88	2.44		0.70	1.33	2.07	1.17	3.24	
– Electrical	1.82	0.53	2.35		0.70	1.33	2.42	0.70	3.12	
– Structural		0.26	0.26		0.65	1.30	0.00	0.34	0.34	
– Civil		2.11	2.11		0.65	1.30	0.00	2.75	2.75	
– Painting		0.10	0.10		0.65	1.30	0.00	0.13	0.13	
– Insulation		1.50	1.50		0.65	1.30	0.00	1.95	1.95	
– Buildings		0.12	0.12		0.65	1.30	0.00	0.16	0.16	
– Plant modification		0.70	0.70		0.70	1.33	0.00	0.93	0.93	
Bulk items total	5.24	8.18	13.42				6.93	10.75	17.68	
TOTAL DIRECT COSTS				47.81						63.45
Engineering – Design			8.40		0.50	1.22			10.29	
– Software			0.53		1.20	1.63			0.86	
Construction – Management			3.22		0.65	1.30			4.19	
– Services			1.50		0.65	1.30			1.95	
Works – Start-up			6.70		0.65	1.30			8.72	
– Working capital			9.56		1.00	1.50			12.69	
Contingency			4.78						6.34	
TOTAL INDIRECT COSTS				34.69						45.05
CAPITAL COST OF ERECTED PLANT				82.50						108.50
Inflation				4.13						5.42
Licence fees and royalties				0.41						0.54
Insurance				0.83						1.08
TOTAL OVERHEADS				5.36						7.05
TOTAL CAPITAL COST				87.86						115.55

Figure 9.4 Sample OBS for a chemical plant (plant level)

PROJECT ESTIMATE		NORTHERN ENERGY AND CHEMICAL INDUSTRIES PLC					02-Jan-9X
PROJECT	Petrochemical Plant		CODE:	THNS	ISSUE:	A	
WORK AREA:	Synthesis		CODE:	THNS5	AUTHOR:	JRT	
WORK PACKAGE:	....		CODE:	....	APPRVD:	CME	
ACTIVITY:	....		CODE:	....	DATE:	02-Jan-9X	

	Material £,000	Erection £,000	Function £,000	Plant £,000	Parametric ratio Function %MPI	Plant %MPI
Main plant items						
- Vessels	4.85	0.23	5.08			
- Furnace and boiler	0.00	0.00	0.00			
- Machines and drives	3.67	0.17	3.84			
- Vendor packages	1.55	0.07	1.62			
- Other	0.00	0.00	0.00			
MPI Total: Materials	10.07	—	10.07		100.0%	
MPI Total: Erection	—	0.47	0.47		4.7%	
Bulk items						
- Piping			1.21		12.0%	
- Instruments			0.23		2.3%	
- Computer control system			0.82		8.1%	
- Electrical			0.81		8.0%	
- Structural			0.09		0.9%	
- Civil			0.76		7.5%	
- Painting			0.03		0.3%	
- Insulation			0.50		5.0%	
- Buildings			0.06		0.6%	
- Plant modification			0.24		2.4%	
Bulk items total			4.74		0.47	
TOTAL DIRECT COSTS				15.29		1.52
Engineering - Design			1.72		17.1%	
- Software			0.09		0.9%	
Construction - Management			0.80		7.9%	
- Services			0.33		3.3%	
Works - Start-up			1.43		14.2%	
- Working capital			3.06		30.4%	
Contingency			1.53		15.2%	
TOTAL INDIRECT COSTS				8.96		0.89
CAPITAL COST OF ERECTED PLANT				24.24		2.41
Inflation						
Licence fees and royalties						
Insurance						
TOTAL OVERHEADS				0.00		
TOTAL CAPITAL COST				24.24		

Figure 9.5 Sample OBS for a chemical plant (plant area level)

9.6 Estimating techniques[3]

There are several ways of preparing estimates for the various cost components. The most direct is to break the work down to a lower level of detail, estimate the cost at that level and sum back up. However, the arguments of Section 9.4 imply that that level of detail cannot always be justified, especially at earlier stages of the project life cycle. It is therefore necessary to use other methods which enable estimates to be produced at higher levels of work breakdown.

Methods of estimating

The engineering and civil construction industries have well-advanced methods of estimating at all levels of work breakdown.[1] These rely heavily on historical data and include step-counting, exponential, parametric, and detailed and computerized methods. The IT industry is now developing similar techniques, and it is possible to postulate similar approaches for organizational development projects.

STEP COUNTING METHODS

These methods assume that cost is a function of the number of functions and plant throughput. In the engineering construction industry standard formulae and tables have been derived from empirical data. Some of these formulae are still valid after 20 years. The formulae exist at several levels of the WBS, the plant level, plant area level or main plant item, (MPI) level. Similar methods can be used for software projects based on the number of data elements and processes, or management development projects based on the number of managers or training requirements.

EXPONENTIAL METHODS

These methods assume that cost is proportional to the size of the facility, to some power. In the chemical industry, this is called the *two-thirds power law* because the exponent is usually between 0.6 and 0.75. If you know the cost of a plant of standard size, the cost of a larger or smaller one can be derived. The law can be applied at several levels of WBS or OBS; the lower the level, the more accurate the estimate at the plant level. Figure 9.4 contains exponents from George[1] for chemical plant, applied at the first level of OBS, showing how they can be used to convert from a 1000 tonne/day plant to a 1500 tonne/day plant. In software projects, the method should be called the *six-fifths power law*: according to the widely used COCOMO cost model (the COnstructive COst MOdel),[4, 5] the cost is proportional to the number of data items to the 1.2 power; that is, the unit cost actually increases with the increasing amount of data!!!

PARAMETRIC METHODS

Parametric methods assume that all costs are proportional to some core cost. On chemical plants this is the MPI. Tables of ratio exist giving the cost of other items as ratios of the MPI, dependent on the value of the MPI, its type and the severity of duty. These tables exist at several levels of WBS. Figure 9.5 contains data at the plant area level, from George.[1] With parametric methods, the estimates are based on:

- estimates of MPI costs
- vendors quotes
- prices of placed orders.

The techniques are so advanced in the engineering construction industry that estimates based on prices of placed orders and derived at the equipment levels are sufficiently accurate for the control estimate. It is in this way that the cost of estimating is being reduced. Parametric data are now being derived in the electronic and IT industries.[5]

DETAILED ESTIMATES

These are prepared by contracting companies tendering for work, where the level of accuracy is of the same order of magnitude as the expected profit margin. At the lowest levels the costs are derived from standard cost books or from parametric data.

COMPUTER AIDED ESTIMATES

These estimates have been derived to support parametric estimating and detailed estimating. These are often based on a bill of materials (BOM) or a bill of quanitities (BOQ) for standard components.

Table 9.5 shows which estimating methods are used to prepare the different types of estimate.

Sources of Data

Possible sources of data for preparing estimates are:

- suppliers' quotations (typical, budget, detailed)
- trade literature, technical literature, textbooks

Table 9.5 Estimating methods used to prepare types of estimate

Type of estimate	Accuracy (%)	Estimating methods
Proposal estimate	±50	Step counting; exponential (plant level)
Budget estimate	±20	Exponential (MPI level); parametric (plant level)
Sanction estimate	±10	Parametric (MPI level, vendor quotes)
Control estimate	± 5	Parametric (MPI level, firm prices)
Tender estimate	± 2	Detailed estimating; computer-based methods

- company historical data, standard costs
- computer systems
- black books
- government figures.

Updating estimates

Estimating data is only valid at a certain time, in a certain place and in a given currency. It will almost certainly be necessary to allow for inflation. It may also be necessary to convert from one country to another and from one currency to another. Tables of ratios exist for these conversions.[1] For example, to calculate the cost in one year given the cost in the second, you merely need to multiply by the ratio of the price index in the two years (usually calculated with respect to a base year):

$$\frac{\text{Cost in year 1}}{\text{Cost in year 2}} = \frac{\text{Price index in year 1}}{\text{Price index in year 2}}$$

Without any other guidance you can use the retail price index, RPI. However, tables exist for many industries giving inflation rates different to RPI. Tables are published for most countries of the world. They also exist for ratios of exchange rates for years past, and for differences in labour and material costs between different countries. Therefore, given the price of a project in one country in its local currency in a year past, you can calculate the cost of the same project in another country in its local currency in another year past. The tables also predict future rates.

9.7 Controlling costs: obtaining value for money

Up to this point of the chapter we have discussed estimating costs. Let us now discuss the control of costs. This was stated as the first purpose of preparing the estimate, and so the structure has been derived to facilitate this process. In Section 9.2, it was stated that the estimate is prepared as a measure against which to compare actual performance. In this section let us consider:

- the appropriate measure for cost control
- when to make the comparisons
- using the comparison to forecast cost to completion
- the use of S-curves to provide a visual representation.

We shall not discuss how to overcome variances (differences) identified for now, but leave that to Chapter 14 where we shall discuss execution and control.

The measure for cost control

The commonest mistake of cost control is to use as the measure or base-line for control the predicted rate of expenditure with time, and to compare the actual rate of expenditure with this. A cost estimate is prepared against the work breakdown structure. This is then scheduled in time by scheduling the work elements to produce an expenditure profile. (How to schedule the work will be discussed in Chapter 10.) This predicted rate of expenditure is variously called:

- scheduled cost
- predicted cash flow
- baseline cost of work scheduled (BCWS)
- planned cost of work scheduled (PCWS).

The last two are the most descriptive. As work is done, actual expenditure is recorded. This actual rate of expenditure is variously called:

- the accrual
- the actual cash flow
- the actual cost of work complete (ACWC).

To determine whether the project is over- or underspent, actual expenditure is compared to the scheduled cost, and, if less, all is assumed to be well. However, this assumption may be false because no measure is made of what work has been done for the expenditure. In the most extreme case no work may have been done, and yet expenditure accrued. I conducted a post-completion audit on a project where the company's finance director realized something was wrong when all the project's budget had been spent and yet only 40 per cent of the work was done. To control costs you must compare the actual expenditure not to the schedule of expenditure, but to some measure of the value of work done. The WBS provides the means to do this. As an element of work is complete, you can compare how much it actually cost against what it was estimated to cost. This estimated cost of the actual work done is variously called:

- earned value
- baseline cost of work complete (BCWC)
- planned cost of work complete (PCWC).

The *earned value* for a work package or the whole project is the sum of the estimate of the completed activities which constitute it. Cost is controlled by comparing the earned value to the actual expenditure, and calculating a *cost variance*:

> Cost variance = Accrual − Earned value
> % Variance   = Variance/Earned value

If this variance is positive, the project is overspent, and if it is negative it is underspent. Action is taken if this variance is non-zero (positive) – Section 9.2.

If we used the strict definition of earned value given above, based only on work complete, a bias would be introduced, because no allowance is made for work in progress. At the work package or project level some allowance must be made for activities started but not finished. A subjective estimate of percentage completion of activities can be made, but this is usually an overestimate (always 99%!) It is more accurate to assume that, on average, activities in progress are half finished. We therefore have:

- for activities:
> % Completion = 0%, 50% or 100%

- for the project and work packages:
> % Completion = Earned value/Original estimate
> where
> Earned value = Sum of (% Completion × Original estimate)
> with the sum taken over the constituent activities.

It was implied above that the comparison between the scheduled cost and actual cost is meaningless. If the actual cost is less than scheduled cost it does not tell us whether the project is underspent or late. It was shown that the comparison between earned value and actual cost indicates whether the project is over- or underspent. The comparison between the earned value and the scheduled cost tells us whether the project is early or late; if the earned value is greater than the scheduled cost, the project is on average early, and if it is less, it is on average late. I say on average, because it gives us no information about progress on the critical path. Critical work can have been delayed, but a larger, non-critical job brought forward, and the project appear to be early. We can calculate a second variance, the *volume variance*, as:

Volume variance = Earned value − Scheduled cost
% Variance = Variance/Scheduled cost

Consider a very simple example of a 'project' to make 100 pairs of shoes at £10 per pair. At the end of the period, only 80 pairs have been made at £12 per pair. In this simple case we have:

Scheduled cost = 100 pairs @ £10 per pair = £1000
Actual cost = 80 pairs @ £12 per pair = £960
Earned value = 80 pairs @ £10 per pair = £800

Cost variance = £960 − £800 = £160 unfavourable;
= 20% unfavourable;

Volume variance= £800 − £1000 = £200 unfavourable;
= 20% unfavourable

Example 9.4 Earned value calculation

Example 9.4 presents a simple earned value calculation for a project to make 100 pairs of shoes. Accountants talk about variances being favourable or unfavourable, rather than positive or negative, since the latter can be misleading. In this simple production model, it would be more common to talk about the cost variance as being £2 per pair (or 20% on the *standard cost* of £10 per pair; and the volume variance as being 20 pairs (or 20%) on a production target of 100 pairs. Because projects are unique, it is not possible to talk of 'standard costs', and because they are usually made up of quite a variety of work, the only standard for comparison is in expenditure, either of money or man-hours, and so everything must be translated to this standard for control purposes.

When to make the comparisons

A second mistake in cost control is to record accrual and earned value only as invoices are paid. Although this provides a valid comparison, it is too late to overcome problems. You must therefore record accrual and earned value at an earlier time. This is usually as the cost is committed, when effective action can be taken. The cost may be committed when the order is placed or when the work is done.

1. The cost is committed when the order is placed for:
   - large material items
   - fixed price contracts.
2. The cost is committed when the work is done for:
   - labour
   - cost plus contracts
   - bulk materials.

For cost control purposes it does not matter what is assumed for individual cost elements, as long as the same assumption is made throughout for each element; that is, the cost is accrued and the value is earned together, and at the same time as the expenditure was planned. However, the above gives the most effective means of control.

Forecasting completion

The variance calculation can be used to forecast the likely cost to complete the project. There are two simplifying assumptions:

1. The absolute variance at completion equals the variance to date:

   Cost at completion = Original estimate + Variance to date

2. The percentage variance at completion equals the percentage variance to date:

   Cost at completion = Original estimate $\times$ (1+% Variance to date)

The latter is more realistic, but it is common to use the former because:

- some cost overspends are unlikely to be repeated
- those likely to be repeated may be reduced using experience to date
- some cost savings will be made to balance further overspend.

In fact the most accurate forecasts are obtained by applying the second formula above at lower levels of the WBS, using as the '% variance to date' that on similar work elements modified in the light of experience.

Figure 9.6 is a cost report at a point during the CRMO Rationalization Project, showing estimates of percentage completion and expenditure to date against both labour and materials, and comparing these to the scheduled percentage completion, planned cost of work scheduled (SCHEDULED COST) and planned cost of work complete (EARNED VALUE). Table 9.6 contains an explanation of abbreviations used. At the time of the report, the project was behind schedule, marginally underspent on labour and overspent on materials.

PROJECT COST REPORT

TRIMAGI COMMUNICATIONS BV

31-Aug-9X

PROJECT: CRMO RATIONALIZATION
WORK AREA: —
WORK PACKAGE: —

WORK PACKAGE NO	PACKAGE DESCRIPTION	ORG DUR (D)	REM DUR (D)	BASE COMPL (%)	PERCT COMPL (%)	BASELINE			CURRENT ESTIMATE			SCHEDULED COST			EARNED VALUE			ACTUAL COMMITMENT		
						LABOUR (£,000)	MATL (£,000)	TOTAL (£,000)	LABOUR (£,000)	MATL (£,000)	TOTAL (£,000)	LABOUR (£,000)	MATL (£,000)	TOTAL (£,000)	LABOUR (£,000)	MATL (£,000)	TOTAL (£,000)	LABOUR (£,000)	MATL (£,000)	TOTAL (£,000)
P1	Project definition	30.0		100.0%	100.0%	11.2	6.4	17.6	11.2	6.4	17.6	11.2	6.4	17.6	11.2	6.4	17.6	11.0	6.3	17.3
T1	Technology design	40.0		100.0%	100.0%	12.8		12.8	12.8	0.0	12.8	12.8	0.0	12.8	12.8	0.0	12.8	12.1	0.0	12.1
O1	Communication plan	5.0		100.0%	100.0%	1.2	2.5	3.7	1.2	2.5	3.7	1.2	2.5	3.7	1.2	2.5	3.7	1.2	2.4	3.6
02	Operational proc.	15.0		100.0%	100.0%	9.6		9.6	9.6	0.0	9.6	9.6	0.0	9.6	9.6	0.0	9.6	9.8	0.0	9.8
03	Job/Management desc.	20.0		100.0%	100.0%	12.8		12.8	12.8	0.0	12.8	12.8	0.0	12.8	12.8	0.0	12.8	12.5	0.0	12.5
T2	MIS function spec.	15.0		100.0%	100.0%	4.8		4.8	4.8	0.0	4.8	4.8	0.0	4.8	4.8	0.0	4.8	4.5	0.0	4.5
04	Staff allocation	15.0		100.0%	100.0%	3.6		3.6	3.6	0.0	3.6	3.6	0.0	3.6	3.6	0.0	3.6	3.7	0.0	3.7
A1	Estates plan	10.0		100.0%	100.0%	1.6		1.6	1.6	0.0	1.6	1.6	0.0	1.6	1.6	0.0	1.6	1.6	0.0	1.6
T3	Technical plan	10.0		100.0%	100.0%	0.8		0.8	0.8	0.0	0.8	0.8	0.0	0.8	0.8	0.0	0.8	0.8	0.0	0.8
P2	Financial approval	15.0		100.0%	100.0%	3.6	1.5	5.1	3.6	1.5	5.1	3.6	1.5	5.1	3.6	1.5	5.1	3.6	1.5	5.1
A2	Sites 1&2 available	15.0		100.0%	100.0%	8.4	6.6	15.0	8.4	6.6	15.0	8.4	6.6	15.0	8.4	6.6	15.0	7.5	6.9	14.4
05	Management changes	10.0		100.0%	100.0%	2.4		2.4	2.4	0.0	2.4	2.4	0.0	2.4	2.4	0.0	2.4	2.4	0.0	2.4
06	Redeployment/train	40.0	10.0	100.0%	75.0%	25.6	55.2	80.8	24.4	52.6	77.0	24.4	52.6	77.0	18.3	52.6	70.9	17.9	52.2	70.1
T4	System in sites 1&2	30.0	20.0	100.0%	33.3%	19.2	44.0	63.2	19.2	44.0	63.2	19.2	44.0	63.2	6.4	44.0	50.4	4.5	42.4	46.9
A3	Sites 1&2 ready	15.0	15.0	50.0%	0.0%	8.4	60.0	68.4	9.2	66.0	75.2	4.6	66.0	70.6	0.0	0.0	0.0	0.0	0.0	0.0
T5	MIS delivered	15.0	9.0	50.0%	40.0%	4.8	38.0	42.8	4.8	38.0	42.8	2.4	38.0	40.4	1.9	38.0	39.9	1.6	40.2	41.8
07	Procedures implem.	10.0	10.0	0.0%	0.0%	4.0		4.0	4.0	0.0	4.0	0.0	0.0	0.0	0.0	0.0	0.0	0.0	0.0	0.0
P3	Intermediate rev.	40.0	40.0	0.0%	0.0%	1.6	10.8	14.8	1.6	10.8	14.8	0.0	0.0	0.0	0.0	0.0	0.0	0.0	0.0	0.0
A4	Roll-out implem.	80.0	80.0	0.0%	0.0%	64.0	240.0	304.0	70.4	264.0	334.4	0.0	0.0	0.0	0.0	0.0	0.0	0.0	0.0	0.0
P4	Benefits obtained	60.0	60.0	0.0%	0.0%	2.4		2.4	2.4	0.0	2.4	0.0	0.0	0.0	0.0	0.0	0.0	0.0	0.0	0.0
						202.8	465.0	667.8	208.8	492.4	701.2	123.4	217.6	341.0	99.4	151.6	251.0	94.7	151.9	246.6

Table 9.6 Explanation of abbreviations in Figure 9.6

Abbreviation	Meaning
ORG DUR	is the originally planned duration of each work package
REM DUR	is the remaining duration with some work done
BASE COMPL	is the expected (baseline) percentage completion of each work package at the time of reporting
PERCT COMPL	is the actual percentage completion, calculated as:

$$(ORG\ DUR - REM\ DUR)/ORG\ DUR$$

BASELINE LABOUR MAT'L TOTAL	are the original estimates of labour and material costs, and the sum of the two
CURRENT ESTIMATE LABOUR MAT'L TOTAL	are updated estimates: the project manager has consumed some contingency through a process of change control
SCHEDULED COST LABOUR MAT'L TOTAL	is the scheduled completion calculated as: = BASE COMPL * CURRENT ESTIMATE LABOUR; = CURRENT ESTIMATE MAT'L if the work is planned to have started, otherwise zero
EARNED VALUE LABOUR MAT'L TOTAL	is the actual completion (earned value) calculated as: = PERCT COMPL * CURRENT ESTIMATE LABOUR. = CURRENT ESTIMATE MAT'L if the work is started, otherwise zero
ACTUAL COMMITMENT LABOUR MAT'L TOTAL	is the exenditure to date against each cost item

S-curves

It is common to plot earned value and accrual on a time chart at each reporting period. As the project progresses they form the customarily shaped curve, called an S-curve. The shape is caused by the work of the project taking some time to accelerate at the start, and slowing down towards the end. It provides a visual representation of whether the project is under- or overspent as it progresses. If the originally planned expenditure profile also happens to be plotted on the curve, then the comparison of earned value to planned expenditure tells you whether the project is ahead or behind schedule (on average) and so provides an element of

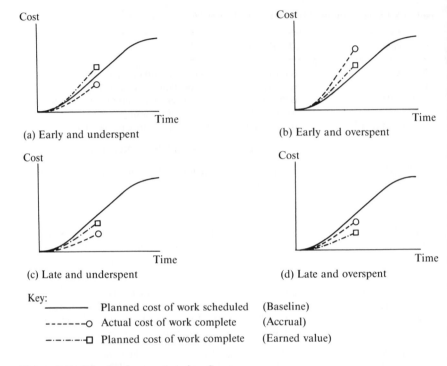

Key:

——————— Planned cost of work scheduled (Baseline)

------o Actual cost of work complete (Accrual)

—·—·—·—□ Planned cost of work complete (Earned value)

Figure 9.7 Monitoring costs using S-curves

time control. Figure 9.7 shows S-Curves for the four cases of projects over- and underspent and ahead and behind schedule.

9.8 Summary

1. A cost estimate is prepared:
   - as a basis for control
   - to assess the project's viability
   - to obtain funding
   - to allocate resources
   - to estimate durations
   - to prepare tenders for bespoke contracts.
2. There are five types of estimate of increasing accuracy requiring pro-portionately more work to prepare:
   - proposal estimate
   - budget estimate

- sanction estimate
- control estimate
- tender estimate.

3. The proposal estimate is prepared before proposal and initiation to commit resources to the first stage of the project.
4. The budget estimate is prepared during proposal and initiation to initiate the project, and commit resources to design and appraisal.
5. The sanction estimate is prepared during design and appraisal to gain funding for the project, or approval from the project sponsor.
6. The control estimate is prepared during implementation planning.
7. A tender estimate is prepared as part of the process of bidding for a contract.
8. There are over ten types of cost to be estimated, including:
   - labour
   - materials, plant and equipment
   - subcontract
   - management, overhead and administration
   - fees and taxation, inflation, and other contingencies.
9. The cost control cube, a three-dimensional matrix of the WBS × OBS × CBS, provides a structure for estimating and controlling costs.
10. The estimate is prepared by breaking the work down to an appropriate level of WBS, and then estimating the cost of each element in the cost control cube. Methods of estimating include:
    - step-counting methods
    - exponential methods
    - parametric methods
    - detailed and computerized methods.
11. Cost is controlled by comparing the earned value, a measure of the amount of work performed to date, to the actual expenditure to date. A comparison of earned value to the originally planned spend helps to control elapsed time. S-Curves provide a visual representation.

Notes and references

1. George, D. J. (ed.), *A Guide to Capital Cost Estimating*, Institution of Chemical Engineering, 1988.
2. Morris, P. W. G. and Hough, G. H., *The Anatomy of Major Projects: A study of the reality of project management*, Wiley, 1987.
3. Section 9.6 contains ideas contributed by Dr Alan Oliver. Dr Oliver is a project manager with SD-Scicon.
4. DeMarco, T., *Controlling Software Projects: Management, measurement and estimation*, Yourdon Monograph, Prentice-Hall, 1982.
5. Garvey, P. R. and Powell, F. D., 'Three methods of quantifying software development effort uncertainty', *Journal of Parametrics*, 1988.

10
Managing time

10.1 Introduction

Let us now discuss the last of the five system objectives, managing time, by which the project manager coordinates the efforts of those involved, delivers the facility to meet market opportunities, and so ensures revenues are derived at a time which gives a satisfactory return on investment. All three of these purposes for managing time imply it is a soft constraint on most projects. Being late reduces the benefit; it does not cause the project to fail absolutely. There are only a few projects for which there is an absolute deadline. Project Giotto, the spacecraft to Halley's comet, was one: there was a very small time window in which to make the *rendezvous*, and if missed it would not recur for 75 years. Another is the reconstruction of the Glyndebourne Opera House; the opening night has been booked. However, on most projects, timely completion is a benefit that must be balanced against the cost of achieving it. Unfortunately many project managers treat time management as being synonymous with project management, and much of the project management software is written on this assumption.

In the next section we shall consider the purpose of managing time, define the concepts and terminology of the time schedule, and introduce tools for communicating the schedule, including activity listings and bar charts. We shall discuss how to calculate the duration of work elements, and how to use networks to calculate the overall project duration, and show how to adjust the schedule by balancing resource requirements and resource availability. We shall conclude the chapter by describing the use of the schedule in controlling the duration of a project.

10.2 The time schedule

The time schedule is a series of dates against the work elements in the work breakdown structure, which will record our forecast of when the work will occur and when the work actually does occur.

Purpose of the schedule

The purpose of recording these dates and times is

- to ensure that the benefits are obtained on a time scale that justifies the expenditure
- to coordinate the effort of resources
- to enable the resources to be made available when required
- to predict the levels of money and resources required at different times so that priorities can be assigned between projects
- to meet a rigid end date.

The first of these is the most important. It addresses the *raison d'être* of project management, achieving the overall purpose and mission. The second is the next most important as it enables the project to happen, and the third and fourth are variations of this. It is the fifth item that gets most attention from project managers: they set themselves a rigid end date, sometimes unnecessarily, and focus on this at the detriment of cost and quality. Chapter 12 will describe techniques for achieving an appropriate balance between time, cost and quality.

The schedule

On a simple level, the schedule records the planned and actual start date, finish date and duration of each work element. We may also record whether there is any flexibility in the start of each element without delaying the completion of the project. This is called the *float*. In most sophisticated schedules we record up to five versions of each of the start date, finish date, duration and float. These are the early, late, baseline, scheduled and actual dates.

THE DURATION

This is the time to do the work. It is common to treat a work element's duration as an immutable figure. For some it is dependent on external factors beyond the control of the project team. For others it is a variable that can be changed by varying the number of people working on the activity. Methods of estimating durations are described in the next section and of balancing durations and resource levels in Section 10.5. For now we shall assume that they are fixed. Therefore, before work starts we have for each activity an *estimated* duration. Once work starts, but before it finishes, we can estimate a *remaining* duration. This may be equal to the planned duration less the time since the activity started, or we may re-estimate the remaining duration based on the knowledge gained from doing the work so far. Once work is complete we can record an *actual* duration. It is useful to record actuals because a comparison of planned and actual figures may indicate trends that may be useful in the control process.

EARLY AND LATE DATES

These can be forecast from an estimated duration of all activites. In Chapter 6 it was stated that the start or finish of an activity may be dependent on finishing other work. Therefore there is an earliest date by which a work element may start, known as the *early start date*. The early start date plus the estimated duration is the *early finish date*, the earliest date by which the work can finish. Similarly, other work may be dependent on the element's being finished, so there is a latest date by which it can finish and not delay completion of the project. This is known as the *late finish date*, and correspondingly the *late start date* is this less the estimated duration. If the late start date is different to the early start date, there is flexibility about when the element can start, the *float*:

Float = Late start date − Early start date

If the duration is immutable, then the difference between the early and late start and the early and late finish is the same (and indeed this is the assumption made in most scheduling systems). However, it is not too difficult to imagine situations in which the duration is dependent on the time of year the work is done.

A work element with zero float is said to be critical; its duration determines the project's duration. If a project is tightly scheduled with minimum duration, then running through it will be a series of work elements with zero float. This series is known as the *critical path*. Work elements with large float are known as *bulk work*. They are used to smooth forecast resource usage, by filling gaps in the demands made by the critical path. There are also work elements with very small float. These are *near critical*, and should receive as much attention as the critical path. In Section 10.4, CPM (critical path method) networks are described, which are mathematical tools for calculating early and late start and finish and float.

PLANNED, BASELINED AND SCHEDULE DATES

These are dates between the early and late dates when we choose to do the work. These are *planned dates*. However, the date we planned to do a work element at the start of the project may be different to our current plan. It is important to record the original plan, because that is the measure against which we control time. This original measure is commonly known as the *baseline date*, and the current plan as the *scheduled date*. (Baselining will be described in Chapter 12.) If the baseline start is later than the early start, then the planned or baseline float will be less than the available float. Likewise, as a project progresses, if the start or finish of a work element is further delayed, then the remaining float will be less than the original float.

THE TOTAL SCHEDULE

Hence, in a full scheduling system, there are up to 15 dates and times associated with a work element (Example 10.1). The process of scheduling the project is the assignment of values to these dates and times. The first step is to estimate the duration and the second is to assign start and finish dates. This is usually done by calculating the early start and late finish dates and then assigning baseline dates somewhere between these two, after taking account of other factors such as resource smoothing. It is sometimes necessary to assign a finish date after the late finish and thereby delay the project. If the logic is correct, it will be impossible to schedule the start before the early start.

Early start	Duration	Early finish
Late start	Float	Late finish
Baseline start	Baseline float	Baseline finish
Schedule start	Remaining float	Schedule finish
Actual start	Remaining duration	Actual finish

where

Planned duration = Planned finish − Planned start;

Planned float   = Late finish − Planned finish.

Example 10.1 Scheduled dates associated with a work element

For some projects with a well-constructed WBS, it is possible to schedule the project manually, by nesting the schedule at lower levels within that at higher levels. To be able to do this it must be possible to break the project into discrete work areas and work packages, with few logical links between them and little sharing of resources. The large multi-disciplinary projects described in Section 6.7 were four such projects. In the Regional Health Authority warehouse and the Norwegian Security Centre projects, the project managers positively resisted computer systems because they felt they retained greater visibility without them. Where there are complex interdependencies and multiple shared resources, it may be necessary to use computer-aided support tools.

The processes of estimating durations and calculating and assigning dates, including the use of computer-aided network planning systems will be described in the following sections. However, first it is appropriate to describe tools by which the schedule is communicated.

Communicating the schedule

There are two accepted ways of communicating a project's schedule:

- activity listings with dates
- bar charts (or Gantt charts).

ACTIVITY LISTING WITH DATES

This is a list of some of the work elements at a given level of the WBS, with some or all of the dates and times above listed beside them. This method of communicating the schedule can give a comprehensive checklist, but is not very visible. Figure 10.1 is an activity listing for a simple project to erect a statue by early start/early finish. Although this list shows the float, I believe it should not be shown as it tends to be consumed.

LANDSCAPE LTD
ACTIVITY LISTING

PROJECT NAME: ERECT STATUE

Activity No Name	Duration (days)	Early start (day)	Early finish (day)	Float (days)
A Grade site	3	0	3	0
B Cast plinth	2	3	5	0
C Plant grass	3	3	6	1
D Set concrete	2	5	7	0
E Place statue	1	7	8	0

Figure 10.1   Activity listing

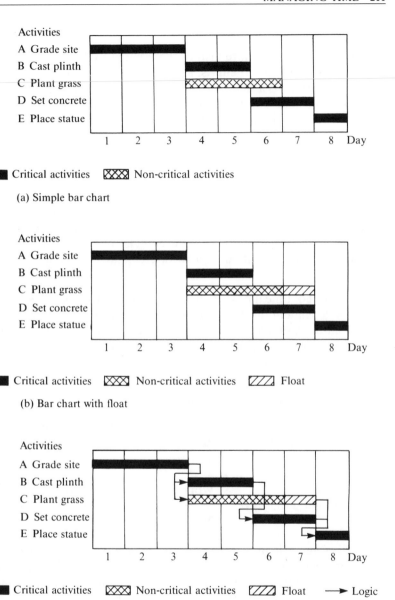

Figure 10.2 Bar charts for the activity listing in Figure 10.1

BAR CHARTS

The schedule can be more visibly represented by the use of bar charts (sometimes called Gantt charts, after Henry Gantt who pioneered their use). Figure 10.2(a) is a simple bar chart for the project in Figure 10.1. Figure 10.2(b) is the same bar chart with the float shown. It is also possible to show the logic in a bar chart (Figure 10.2(c)).

10.3 Estimating durations

The duration of work elements is central to the scheduling process, not only in relating the start and finish of a given work element, but in calculating its earliest start from the cumulative duration of the preceding activities, and the latest finish from the cumulative duration of the succeeding activities. The duration of a work element is dependent on one of three things:

- the amount of time it physically takes to do the work involved, which in turn is dependent on the number of people available to do it
- the lead-time, or waiting time, for the delivery of some item, which is independent of the number of people doing the work
- some mixture of the two.

Duration dependent on work content

It is normally assumed that the duration of work element depends on the amount of work to do and the number of people available to do it. Nominally:

$$\text{Duration (days)} = \frac{\text{Work content (man-days)}}{\text{Number of people available}}$$

I described the role of work content in negotiating the contract between project manager and resource providers in Chapter 7, and how to estimate it as a labour cost in Chapter 9. It is always necessary to add allowances to this raw estimate of duration, to calculate the actual duration. These allowances are to account for various factors, which include:

- time lost through non-project activities
- part-time working
- interference between people doing the work
- communication between people doing the work.

LOST TIME

Someone nominally working full time on a project is not available 5 days per week, 52 weeks per year. They lose time through holidays, bank holidays, sickness, training, group meetings, etc. It was shown in Section 7.5, that for the average project worker these consume 80 days per year; someone assigned full time to a project does, on average, 180 days of project work a year, equivalent to 70 per cent availability. To allow for this, 40 per cent is added to the nominal duration (1.4 = 1.0/0.7). A smaller ratio will be added if the project's resource calendar allows for some lost time.

PART-TIME WORKING

Individuals may be assigned to a project part time. Therefore, the number of people should be based on the number of full-time equivalents (FTE). However, you must be careful not to double account. If someone is assigned two days per week to a project (40 per cent), you must be clear whether those two days include or exclude a proportion of the lost time above before adding the 40 per cent allowance.

INTERFERENCE

Doubling the number of workers does not always halve the duration, because people doing work can restrict each other's access to the workface, and so reduce their effectiveness. For instance, if the task requires access to a limited space with room for just one person, adding a second person will not double the rate of working. Two will work faster than one, because they can step each other off, but only one can work at a time. Adding a third person will not increase the rate of working, and may even reduce it by distracting the other two. A third person would be most effectively used to extend the working day through a shift system.

COMMUNICATION

Where more than one person works on a job, they need to communicate details of the work to each other to make progress. This is especially true of engineering design and writing software. With two people there is just one communication channel, so they may work almost twice as fast as one. With three people there are three channels, with four people six, and as the number of people grow, the channles grow exponentially. Hence, you reach a point where adding another person in fact reduces the amount of effective work (Example 10.2). The way to overcome this is to find ways of reducing the channels of communication, by using a central administrator or Project Support Office (Chapter 16). In the office in Example 10.2, the pool was split into four pools of three secretaries.

In an office in which I worked, there were three managers each with a secretary. As the office grew, and new managers joined, the number of secretaries grew, until there were about twelve working in the same pool. We reached a point where adding a new secretary seemed to make no difference to the amount of work done in the pool. If we assume that a new secretary spends a quarter of an hour each day talking to each of the others (not an unreasonable amount of time for social interaction), then each conversation consumes half an hour's work, and since she has twelve conversations, six hours is lost, equal to the effective working day.

Example 10.2 Communication consumes time

Hence, for work-dependent work elements:

$$\text{Duration (days)} = 1.4 \times \frac{\text{Work content (man-days)}}{\text{Full-time equivalents}} \times \text{Interference}$$

where the interference allows for both the physical interaction and the communication.

Duration dependent on lead time

For some work elements the duration depends on the lead time or waiting time to obtain some item of material or information or to wait for some change to take place. This may include:

- delivery time for materials in procurement activities
- preparation of reports
- setting of concrete
- negotiations with clients or contractors
- obtaining planning permission or financial approval.

In these cases the likely duration will be known from historical data or the known cycle of events.

Duration dependent on work content and lead time

In some instances a work element contains lower level activities, some of which are work-content dependent and some lead-time dependent (Example 10.3). The duration of the work package must be calculated from the duration of each of the activities and their logical dependence, perhaps using the networking techniques described in the next section in more complex cases. (Note, if you are adopting a rolling-wave approach to planning, at the start of the project you will estimate the duration of the work package as a whole, working from a work-package scope statement and making use of previous experience, and only do the more detailed analysis when you are about to start the work.)

The work package, *O5: Redeployment and Training*, from the CRMO Rationalization Project, may consist of the following activities:

- identify training needs of staff
- develop training material
- conduct courses
- transfer staff to new posts.

The first two of these are work-content dependent. The number of trainers assigned will depend on the number of people requiring training and the amount of material to be developed. However, two people will not work twice as fast as one since they will need to keep each other informed of progress. The duration of the third activity depends on the availability of the training facilities, and the fourth on how quickly people can be assimilated into new work environments.

Example 10.3 A work package from the CRMO Rationalization Project containing activities of mixed type

Estimating sheets

The estimating sheet (Figure 7.12) was introduced in Section 7.5 as a tool for estimating work content. The same sheet can be used for estimating durations (Figure 10.3). Example 10.4 provides a rationale.

---

1. The person with the most work to do is the project control officer, with 24 man-days.
2. Therefore the duration of the work package will be determined by his or her availability.
3. It is assumed that during Project Definition the officer will not take a holiday. Therefore, his or her availability will be greater than the average 70 per cent. A figure of 80 per cent is assumed.
4. The duration is, therefore, 30 days (24/0.8).

Example 10.4 Rationale for the duration of the work package *P1: Project Definition*

ESTIMATING SHEET			TRIMAGI COMMUNICATIONS BV					02-Jan-9X
PROJECT:	CRMO Rationalization		CODE:	C1		ISSUE:	A	
WORK AREA:	Project		CODE:	C1P		AUTHOR:	LJN	
WORK PACKAGE:	Project Definition		CODE:	C1P1		APPRVD:	JRT	
ACTIVITY:	....		CODE:	....		DATE:	02-Jan-9X	

ACTIVITY/TASK		WORK CONTENT			RESOURCES					9 People
		No of steps	Effort/ step (days)	Total effort (days)	Prjct Mgr	Prjct Offc	CRMO TL	CRMO Mgrs	Ops Direct	Other Mgrs
Number	Description				1	1	1	2	1	3
1	Produce project proposal	1	4	4	1	2	1			
2	Hold project definition workshop	1	4	4	1	1	1		1	
3	Define required benefits	1	2	2	1		1			
4	Draft Project Definition Report	1	8	8	2	6				
5	Hold project launch workshop, 1.5 day duration	1	12	12	1.5	1.5	1.5	3		4.5
6	Finalize milestone plan	1	2	2	1	1				
7	Finalize project responsibility chart	1	2	2	1	1				
8	Prepare estimates – time	20	0.1	2		2				
9	Prepare estimates – cost	20	0.1	2		2				
10	Prepare estimates – revenue	1	1	1		1				
11	Assess project viability	1	1	1	1					
12	Assess risks	1	3	3	1	1	1			
13	Finalize Project Definition Report	1	5	5	2	3				
14	Mobilize team	1	3	3	0.5	0.5	0.5			1.5
	SUB-TOTAL:			51	13	22	6	3	1	6
	ALLOWANCE % 10				10	10	10	10	10	10
	TOTAL EFFORT: 56				14	24	7	3	1	7
	UNIT RATE: £K/day				0.5	0.3	0.3	0.5	0.8	0.5
	COST: £K				7.15	7.26	1.98	1.65	0.88	3.30

TOTAL EFFORT: 56 DAYS
TOTAL COST: £K 22.22
DURATION: 30 DAYS
TARGET START: 01-Feb-9X
TARGET FINISH: 15-Mar-9X

Figure 10.3 Estimating sheet with durations entered for the milestone *P1: Project Definition* from the CRMO Rationalization Project

10.4 Calculating the schedule with networks[1]

Having estimated duration, we assign dates to work elements. Until 1950, that was done manually using bar charts (Section 10.2). With the increasing size and complexity of projects this became more difficult, until computer-aided tools were introduced in the 1950s. Since then, these have grown in power. The mathematical technique on which they are based is the critical path method (CPM), sometimes called critical path analysis (CPA) or the programme evaluation and review technique (PERT). The initials CPM, CPA and PERT are used interchangeably. Networks are a mathematical technique used to calculate the schedule. They are seldom useful for communicating the schedule. Bar charts or activity listings (Section 10.2) are best used for that. Networks will only be used where the project is too complex to be scheduled manually through the WBS and so will only be used in conjunction with computer-aided systems. This section describes the mathematical technique of networking. Computer-aided project management information systems (PMIS) are described in Chapter 17. Networks and the terminology used are described in two British Standards.[2, 3]

Types of network

There are three types of network:

- precedence networks
- activity-on-arrow networks
- hybrid networks.

PRECEDENCE NETWORKS

In precedence networks, work elements are represented by boxes, linked by logical dependencies, which show that one element follows another. Figure 10.4 is a simple precedence network with four activities A, B, C and D. B and C follows A and D follows B and C. Four types of logical dependency are allowed (Figure 10.5):

- *End-to-start:*   B cannot start until A is finished.
- *End-to-end:*   D cannot finish until C is finished.
- *Start-to-start:*   D cannot start until C has started.
- *Start-to-end:*   F cannot end until E has started.

End-to-start dependency is the most common (a hangover from IJ networks). End-to-end and start-to-start dependencies are the most natural and allow overlap of succeeding work elements in time. It is not uncom-

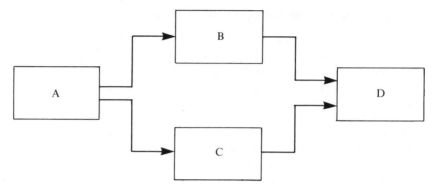

Figure 10.4   A simple precedence network

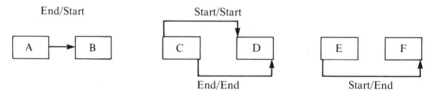

Figure 10.5   Four types of logical dependency

mon to build ladders of activities like C and D. It is the use of end-to-end and start-to-start dependencies that allows fast track or fast build construction (Section 5.4). Start-to-end are only defined for mathematical completeness. I have only encountered one case in which it might have been used.

The milestone plan (Section 6.5) is a precedence network. The circles (nodes) represent the work elements. The lines are dependencies, but only end-to-end dependencies, linking the milestones, are used.

ACTIVITY-ON-ARROW NETWORKS

These are often called IJ networks, because each activity is defined by an IJ (start/finish) number. In this type of network a work element is represented by an arrow between two nodes. The activity is known by the number of the two nodes it links. Figure 10.6 is Figure 10.4 drawn as an IJ network. Activity A becomes 1–2 etc. Because activities must be uniquely defined two cannot link the same two nodes. Therefore B and C finish in

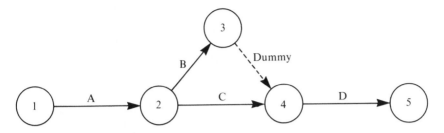

Figure 10.6   Activity-on-arrow network

nodes 3 and 4 respectively and these nodes are linked by a dummy activity. Because activities are linked through nodes, end-to-start logic is imposed. However, it is possible to introduce dummy activities to represent the other three logical links.

HYBRID NETWORKS

These mix the two previous types. Work is represented by either a box (node) or a line (arrow). Furthermore there may be boxes and lines that do not represent work, just events in time and logical dependency. A line need not join a box at its start or finish, but at any time before, during or after its duration. In advanced hybrid networks, even the distinction between nodes and lines disappears. The mathematics of hybrid networks is fairly new so they will not be discussed further.

PRECEDENCE VS ACTIVITY-ON-ARROW NETWORKS

You will find some people fervently committed to one or the other. The early work in the 1950s was done with arrow networks, whereas precedence networks were not introduced until the 1960s. Therefore arrow networks tend to be the more widely used. However, precendence networks are gaining wider preference with practising project managers for several reasons:

1. It is more natural to associate work with a box.
2. It is more flexible for drawing networks. All the boxes can be drawn on a page and the logical dependencies inserted later. In Section 6.5, I described how to develop a precedence network (milestone plan) by moving Post-It slips around a flip chart or white board. The same is not possible with an arrow network since the activities are only defined by two nodes, and that imposes logic.

3. It is easier to write network software for precedence networks. Most modern software is precedence only, or both. Software written for both has an algorithm to convert from precedence to IJ.
4. It is easier to draw a bar chart showing precedence logic with the bars representing the activity boxes and vertical lines showing the logical dependencies (Figure 10.2(c)). With an arrow network either more than one activity must be drawn on a line or dummies must be used to show logic, which virtually gives a precedence network. (This last statement reintroduces hybrid networks, and shows that the distinction between precedence and IJ networks really is slight.)
5. The work exists independently of the logic, and so you can draw a work breakdown structure and overlay the logic later. If you use the C/ SPEC methodology and the approach described in this book – i.e. you define the work of the project first – then you are almost forced to use precedence networks. (People who use IJ networks have to draw the network before developing the work breakdown structure.[4]) For this reason precedence networks have been adopted as standard at Henley Management College, and so are treated more fully here.

Networking technique

All that networks do is to calculate the early start and finish, the late start and finish and the float of work elements in a project given their duration and logical dependency. The reason this is so powerful is it allows you to explore many different options, called conducting a *what-if* analysis, assuming different durations and logical dependencies of the work elements. As the networking technique is introduced, I will illustrate it by scheduling a simple project, represented by the network in Figure 10.4. An activity listing for the network is given in Figure 10.7. This is a modified Figure 10.1, and you will see shortly that the activity 'set concrete' has been replaced by a lag on the logical dependency from B to D.

NOTATION

In a precedence network, each work element is represented by a box with seven internal boxes (Figure 10.8). The top three segments contain the early start, duration and early finish respectively. The bottom three contain the late start, float and late finish. The central one contains a description of the activity. Figure 10.9 is Figure 10.4 with durations entered. In an arrow network the node has four segments: the identifier, the early and late times and the float. The time is the start of the succeeding activity and

LANDSCAPE LTD
ACTIVITY LISTING

PROJECT NAME: ERECT STATUE

Activity		Duration	Preceding	Lead/Lag
No	Description	(days)	activities	(days)
A	Grade site	3	—	0
B	Cast plinth	2	A	−2
C	Plant grass	3	A	0
D	Place statue on plinth	1	B, C	+2,0

Figure 10.7   Activity listing for a project to erect a statue

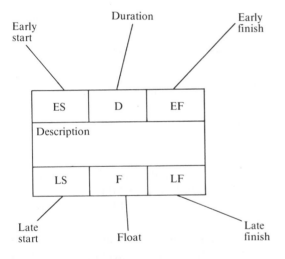

Figure 10.8   Activity in a precedence network

the finish of the preceding activity. The duration is still associated with the activity (Figure 10.10).

LEADS AND LAGS

The dependencies connecting the activities in a precedence network usually have zero duration. However, they can be given positive or negative duration, and this is called *lag* or *lead* respectively. In Figure 10.7 the concrete

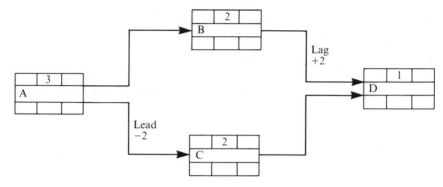

Figure 10.9   Precedence network: durations entered

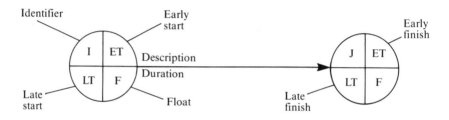

Figure 10.10   Activity in an IJ network

must be left for two days to dry before erecting the statue. These two days can either be added to the duration of B (taking it to 4 days), or shown as a lag on the dependency. Similarly, it might be possible to start planting grass on the second day after the first third of the site has been graded. This can be shown as a start-to-start dependency with a lag of 1 or a finish-to-start with a lead of −2. The latter is chosen. The leads and lags are also shown in Figure 10.9.

FORWARD PASS

Early start and finish are calculated by conducting a *forward pass* through the network. The early start of the first activity is zero and the early finish is calculated by adding the duration. The early finish is transferred to subsequent activities as the early start, adding or subtracting any lead or lag, assuming a finish-to-start dependency. For a start-to-start dependency it is the start time that is transferred to the start, for a finish-to-finish

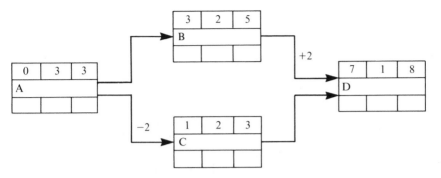

Figure 10.11 Network after forward pass

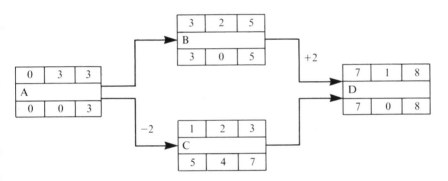

Figure 10.12 Network after back pass

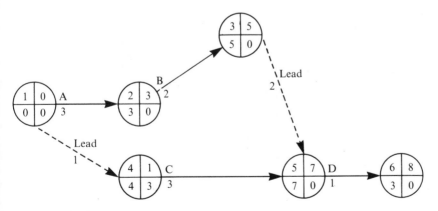

Figure 10.13 Arrow network after forward and back pass

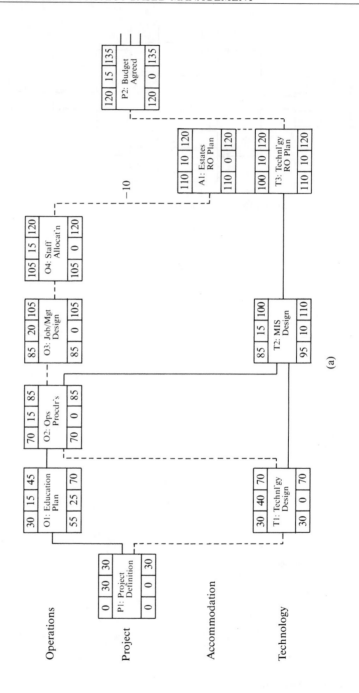

(a)

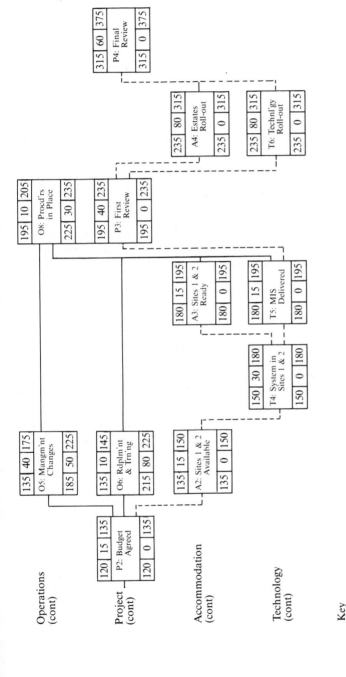

Key

------ Critical Path

Figure 10.14 Precedence network at work-package level for CRMO Rationalization Project

(b)

dependency the finish time is transferred to the finish, and for a start-to-finish the start time is transferred to the finish. Where an activity has two or more preceding activities the largest number is transferred. The process is repeated throughout the network. Figure 10.11 on page 223 shows the example network after a forward pass.

Figure 10.11 on page 223

BACK PASS

The late start and finish and float are calculated by conducting a *back pass*. The early finish of the last activity becomes its late finish. The duration is subtracted to calculate the late start. The late start is transferred back to the late finish of preceding activites. Again it is the start or finish time that is transferred to become the start or finish time depending on the type of dependency. Where an activity has two or more succeeding activities it is the smallest number that is transferred (after adding lags or subtracting leads). The process is repeated throughout the network. The float of each activity is calculated as in Section 10.2. (This should be the same for both start and finish.) The float of the first and last activities should be zero. Figure 10.12 shows the network after the back pass.

IDENTIFYING THE CRITICAL PATH

This is the series of activities with zero float, here A–B–D. Some textbooks suggest you find the critical path not by conducting a forward and back pass, but by identifying every possible path and finding that with the longest duration. This works with small networks, but it does not take many activities before this becomes an impossible task. The methods of forward and back pass are designed to cope with networks of limitless size. Since you only need to use networking on large projects, this is the approach recommended.

ARROW NETWORKS

Figure 10.13 shows the arrow network after a forward and back pass.

CASE STUDY PROJECT

Figure 10.14 is the precedence network (at work-package level) for the CRMO Rationalization Project.

SOFTWARE PACKAGES

Some software packages assume that if an activity has a start date of day 6 (Monday, say) and duration 3, then it will finish on Wednesday evening, day 8. Therefore the finish is:

Finish date = Start date + Duration −1

However, if there is no delay to the start of the next activity, it starts on Thursday morning, day 9. Therefore, a day is added as the finish date is transferred to the start of the next activity. The start date of the first activity is taken as day 1, Monday morning, rather than zero, as used above. The overall effect is just to add one to all the start dates you would obtain using the method proposed above.

Scheduling the project

The network only calculates early and late dates. The baseline or scheduled dates must be chosen taking account of other factors. Hopefully they will be between the early and late dates. There are three options:

- *schedule by early start (hard-left):* used to motivate the workforce
- *schedule by late finish (hard-right):* used to present progress in the best light to the customer
- *schedule in between:* done either to smooth resource usage (Section 10.5) or to show management the most likely outcome.

Using networks

Networks are a mathematical tool to be used as appropriate. This does not depend on the size of the project. Section 6.7 gave examples of multi-million pound projects where they were not used. Their use depends on the complexity of the interdependencies and resource sharing and the manager's ability to analyse these without computer support. As a mathematical tool, they help the manager to calculate the schedule and analyse the impact of changes (*what-if* analysis). However, except as a milestone plan, networks should not be used to communicate the plan or schedule. Bar charts should be used in that instance.

10.5 Resource histograms and resource smoothing

Using a network, you can calculate the early and late start and finish for work elements. However, in order to set the baseline or scheduled dates, it is necessary to take account of other constraints. Resource constraints are the most common. If the resource requirements for all activities of a projects are known then, once the project has been scheduled, you can calculate a resource profile for the project as a whole. This is known as the *resource schedule* and is either listed as a table of resource levels with time or is drawn as a resource histogram. This resource schedule can be compared to the known availability of each type of resource, and if the requirement exceeds availability it may be necessary to adjust the time schedule to reduce the requirement. It may be possible to do this by consuming some of the float on non-critical activites. Alternatively, it may be necessary to extend the duration of the project.

The method of calculating the duration of the activity was shown in Section 10.3. Although no mention was made at the time, this calculation of the duration assumed either a constant or stepped resource usage during the activity. Figure 10.15 illustrates four possible resource profiles for an activity: constant, stepped, triangular and normal. Constant or stepped profiles are almost always used at the activity level, and indeed the errors introduced by these simplifying assumptions cancel out at the work package or project level. Using triangular or normal profiles is something that is quite easy with modern computer systems but adds little extra information, and indeed tends to confuse rather than clarify.

Figure 10.16 is an activity listing for a small project that will be used to illustrate the concept of resource scheduling. There are two resource types: analysts and programmers. Figure 10.17(a) shows the bar chart and resource histogram for both resource types with the project scheduled by early start. This produces quite wildly varying resource levels. If only one analyst was available, he or she would be overloaded during the first two months of the project. One person can work up to 22 days in a month without overtime. To overcome this problem we can try to use the float associated with some of the work elements to smooth the resource profiles. Figure 10.17(b) shows the bar chart and resource profiles for the project scheduled by late start. This is no better as the analyst is still overloaded, but now in months 3 and 4.

Concentrating on the analyst, Figure 10.17(c) shows a schedule which gives the least variability of the analyst's utilization, giving a maximum level of 24 days in month 3. This can be easily met by overtime. It also illustrates two further points:

- the danger of imposing a rigid resource constraint of 22 days which would delay the project
- the need to encourage the analyst to take his or her annual holiday in months 5 and 6 rather than months 1 to 3.

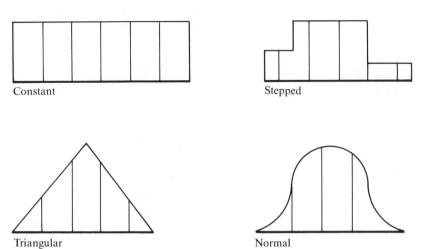

Figure 10.15   Resource profile for an activity

TRIMAGI COMMUNICATIONS BV
ACTIVITY LISTING

PROJECT NAME: CRMO RATIONALIZATION
WORK AREA: MIS DESIGN AND DELIVERY

Acty	Durn	Early	Late	Early	Late	Resource requirement	
		start	start	finish	finish	Analyst	Programmer
	(mths)	(mth)	(mth)	(mth)	(mth)	(days)	(days)
A	3	0	1	3	4	24	—
B	2	0	2	2	4	24	—
C	2	0	2	2	4	16	16
D	1	3	4	4	5	—	12
E	1	0	3	1	4	—	4
F	4	0	0	4	4	16	—
G	1	4	4	5	5	12	8
H	1	5	5	6	6	4	8

Figure 10.16   Activity listing for an IT project

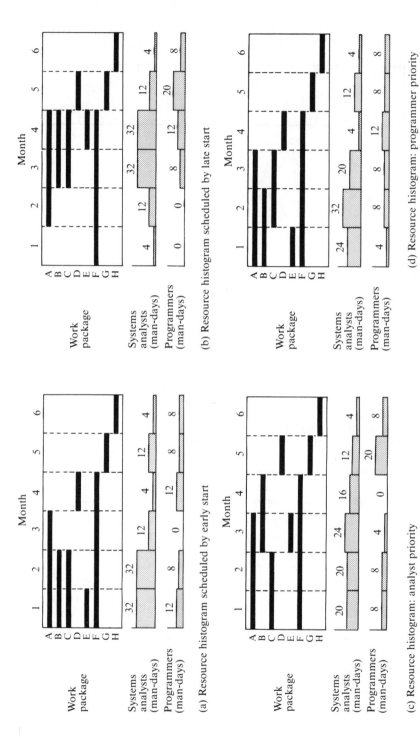

(a) Resource histogram scheduled by early start

(b) Resource histogram scheduled by late start

(c) Resource histogram: analyst priority

(d) Resource histogram: programmer priority

Figure 10.17 Resource smoothing

Alternatively, you can take the programmer as priority. Figure 10.17(d) shows the schedule and resource profiles in that case. However, this overloads the analyst again.

10.6 Controlling time

Up to this point, I have explained how to calculate and communicate the schedule. Let us conclude by discussing how to use the schedule to control the project's duration, which is the primary purpose of setting the schedule. There are four steps in the control process (Section 9.2).

- set a measure
- record progress
- calculate the variance
- take remedial action.

Only the first three of these, together with the use of S-curves to produce a visual representation of progress, will be discussed here. The subject of remedial action will be dealt with in Chapter 14.

Set the measure

The planned, or baselined, dates set the measures for control of time. I shall discuss baselining further in Chapter 12. It is vital to measure progress against a fixed baseline. If you measure progress against the most recent update of the plan you lose control. It is not uncommon to come across projects that are always on time, because the schedule is updated at every review meeting, and people very quickly forget what the original schedule was; they can remember that the schedule has been updated, but not by how much.

Record progress

Progress is recorded by reporting actual start and finish dates. It is common to measure progress against start and finish dates only (as opposed to trying to assess percentage completion part way through a work element) at a level of the WBS and on a frequency to provide adequate control. Typically, on a project of a year's duration, progress is measured fortnightly against activities of two weeks' duration (Section 6.3). Progress is fed up to higher levels of the WBS on a longer frequency.

Calculate the variance

The variance is calculated either in the form of delays to completion of critical, or near critical, work, or as the remaining float of subsequent activities. There is a tenet of project management that you cannot do anything about the past; you can only affect the future. Therefore, it is better to focus on the remaining float of subsequent work, or on future delays to the start of critical or near critical work. Delays to critical or near critical work have an impact on the remaining float of subsequent work, and when the remaining float of a subsequent work element becomes negative, that extends the *forecast completion date* of the project. It is important to monitor near critical work, and not focus solely on *the* critical path. The mathematical exactitude of the network can produce an undue focus on *one* area of the project, whereas it may be one of several other near critical paths which determines the duration of the project, and it was only estimating error that caused one of these to be identified as *the* critical path. Indeed, if you focus all your management attention on one path, you can guarantee another will determine the duration.

Where delays occur to bulk work, it will have little effect on the remaining float of future activities, until it has been delayed so much that it is itself critical. Indeed, resources may be switched from bulk work to critical work to maintain progress on the latter.

In order to determine the impact of any delays on the project, and any proposals for eliminating them, it is necessary to analyse the effect of each on the overall project. This is a repeat of the *what-if* analysis described above. If the WBS has been well constructed this analysis can often be conducted manually, by analysing the effect of the delay on the work package within which it occurs and then the effect of the work package on the overall project. The milestone plan is a powerful tool for determining whether a work package is critical and its effect on the project. This approach gives greater management control. Alternatively, where there are complex interdependencies and multiply shared resources, the analysis can be performed using the network. This provides a more accurate picture of the effect of changes, but it is difficult to determine the appropriate changes in the first place. The network does provide a valuable support to the manual approach, avoiding oversights.

S-Curves

S-Curves (Section 9.8) provide a pictorial representation of whether the project's progress is on schedule, ahead of schedule or behind schedule. The volume variance introduced in that section is another time variance, in addition to the remaining float on critical activities.

10.7 Summary

1. The purpose of scheduling time on a project is:
   - to obtain timely benefits which justify the expenditure
   - to coordinate resource inputs
   - to schedule resource availability
   - to assign priority for resources between projects
   - to meet a specified end date.
2. The schedule specifies the duration, start and finish date, and float of the activities in the project. Several dates are recorded against each activity:
   - early date
   - late date and float
   - baseline date and baseline float
   - most likely date and remaining float
   - actual date and remaining duration.
3. The schedule can be communicated as:
   - an activity listing
   - a bar chart
4. The duration is calculated by comparing the work content to the number of people available and allowing for:
   - lost time
   - part-time working
   - interference
   - communication
   - lead times
   - sequencing of tasks within activities.
5. The early and late dates can be calculated from the durations and logical sequence of the activities using a critical path network. There are two types of network:
   - precedence network
   - activity-on-arrow network.
6. Given the initial schedule and resource requirements for each activity, a resource schedule can be calculated showing the requirements for each type of resource with time. This can be smoothed by delaying bulk work to fill peaks and troughs, or by extending the duration of the project. The resulting schedule is frozen as the baseline.
7. Progress against the schedule can be monitored by:
   - recording progress on the critical or near critical paths
   - recording progress on S-curves.

Notes and references

1. Section 10.4 contains ideas contributed by Simon Bissel. Mr Bissel is a project manager with British Aerospace Dynamics.
2. BSI, *Use of Network Techniques in Project Management*, BS 6064, British Standards Institute, 1984.
3. BSI, *Glossary of Terms used in Project Management*, BS 4335, British Standards Institute, 1987.
4. Kerzner, H., 'Pricing out the work', in *The Project Management Handbook* (eds D.I. Cleland and W. R. King), Van Nostrand Reinhold, 1988.

11
Managing risk

11.1 Introduction[1]

The last five chapters have described methods, tools and techniques for managing the five system objectives: scope, organization, quality, cost, and time. We shall now consider the management of the risk inherent in each of these. Developing the project model requires us to make assumptions about future performance, and this introduces an element of uncertainty. There is a risk that the project will not turn out as expected, arising directly from the uniqueness of projects. Successful completion requires this risk to be managed. Effective project management aims to reduce the risk in two ways, either by developing a project model which, by thorough design and planning, minimizes the inherent uncertainty, or by implementing a project strategy which makes the team better able to respond to deviations as they occur. The first of these is only of limited efficacy, as it is not possible to eliminate risk entirely from a project. In Section 9.3 it was shown that to do so can be more expensive than the possible impact of the risk itself. It is therefore necessary to implement management approaches that address the risk directly.

I shall start by defining risk and risk management, explain the difference between business and insurable risk, and introduce five steps of risk management. I shall then identify the types of risk, and show how to determine their impact on the project. Finally, I shall describe how to assess the overall effect of the significant risks, explain methods of reducing risks, and introduce techniques for risk management.

11.2 Risk and risk management

Risk can be defined as: *hazard, chance of bad consequence or loss, exposure to mischance.*[2] This definition captures the essence of project risk, except that it implies that things are only expected to go wrong. On projects, some risks carry an inherent chance of profit or loss, and some carry a chance of loss only. The former are called *business risks* and the latter *insurable risks*.[3]

Business risks

The majority of risks are business risks. That is true for any part of the operation, but especially for projects. On a project, business risk may include: response of the market to a product; inflation; weather; or the performance of technology and resources. The manager's role is to increase the chance of profit and reduce the chance of loss. However, the expectation is that on average the risks will turn out worse than better, because, although the likelihood of profit and loss may be the same, the maximum possible loss is very much greater than the maximum profit. The weather may be kind as often as it is unkind. However, bad weather can stop work completely or even destroy previous work, but good weather seldom allows work to proceed at double the normal pace.

Insurable risks

Insurable risks lead to loss only, and are usually caused by external, unpredictable factors. These are called insurable, but it is not always possible to find a company to provide cover. For example, war and civil disturbance are insurable risks, but are excluded from most policies. Insurable risks fall within four areas:

– direct property damage
– consequential loss
– legal liability
– personal loss.

Direct damage can be to the facility, or to plant and equipment being used in its delivery, and may be caused by fire, flood, bad weather, or damage during transportation. Consequential loss is lost production arising from the facility's being unavailable due to direct property damage. It may be lost revenue, or the cost of providing temporary cover. Legal liability may arise for damage to property, or injury to a third party, or may be due to the negligence of others. It will also cover liability under a contract for the failure of the facility to perform, either because it is late or because it fails to meet its specification. Finally, there is the risk that members of the team may suffer injury arising directly from their work on the project.

Risk management

Risk management is the process by which the likelihood of risk occurring or its impact on the project is reduced. It has five steps:

1. Identify the potential sources of risk on the project.
2. Determine their individual impact, and select those with a significant impact for further analysis.
3. Assess the overall impact of the significant risks.
4. Determine how the likelihood or impact of the risk can be reduced.
5. Develop and implement a plan for controlling the risks and achieving the reductions.

11.3 Identifying risk

One way of classifying risk is by where control of the risk lies. However, project managers must have the right mental attitude to risk, and expect risks where they are least expected. In that way they will be better able to respond to risks as they occur. They must also be aware that exposure to risks can vary throughout the project management life cycle.

Classifying risks

There are five classifications of risk according to where control lies:

EXTERNAL: UNPREDICTABLE

These are risks beyond the control of managers or their organizations; and are totally unpredictable. They can be listed, but we cannot say which will be encountered on a given project. They arise from the action of government, third parties, or acts of God, or from failure to complete the project due to external influences. Government or regulatory intervention can relate to supply of raw materials or finished goods, environmental requirements, design or production standards, or pricing. Many projects have been killed by the unexpected requirement to hold a public enquiry into environmental impact. Whether a change of government at an election falls in this or the following category is a moot point. Actions of third parties can include sabotage or war, and acts of God are natural hazards such as an earthquake, flood, or the sinking of a ship. Failure to complete can arise from the failure of third parties to deliver supporting infrastructure or finance, or their failure through bankruptcy, or a totally inappropriate project design. By their nature, these risks are almost all 'insurable' risks.

EXTERNAL: PREDICTABLE BUT UNCERTAIN

These are risks beyond the control of managers or their organizations. We expect to encounter them, but we do not know to what extent. There is usually data that allow us to determine a norm or average, but the actual impact can be above or below this norm. There are two major types of risk in this category: the first is the activity of markets for raw materials or finished goods, which determines prices, availability and demand; the second is fiscal policies affecting currency, inflation and taxation. However, they also include operational requirements such as maintenance, environmental factors such as the weather, and social impacts – which are all 'business' risks.

INTERNAL: TECHNICAL

These are risks arising directly from the technology of the project work, of the design, construction or operation of the facility, or the design of the ultimate product. They can arise from changes or from a failure to achieve desired levels of performance. They can be 'business' or 'insurable' risks, although in the latter case the risk is borne by the parent organization, not by an outside insurance company. (The premium paid is the investment in other products which far exceed expectations.)

INTERNAL: NON-TECHNICAL

These are risks within the control of project managers, or their organizations, and are non-technical in nature. They usually arise from a failure of the project organization or resources (human, material or financial) to achieve their expected performance. They may result in schedule delays, cost over-runs or interruption to cash flow. These are usually 'business' risks.

LEGAL

Legal risks fall under civil and criminal law. Risks under civil law arise from contractual arrangements with clients, contractors or third parties, from licences, patent rights, contractual failure or *force majeure* (a unilateral claim by one party to a contract that its requirements cannot be met through an act of God). Risks under the criminal law are duties imposed on both the owner and contractor. Under the Health and Safety at Work Act (1974), all employers, not just in the engineering industry, have a duty of care for their employees and for the public. Therefore, project managers, their employers (the contractors) and design teams can be held responsible if their negligence causes injury to any of the parties involved with the project, including: the project team while working on the project; users while operating the facility; and consumers using the product produced by the facility. There have been successful prosecutions in the engineering industry. I am unaware of a software error leading to injury of a user or consumer, but with some of the modern uses of computer systems, programmers must be aware of this risk. I worked with programmers on an air traffic control system who were concerned about their liability.

Table 20.5 on page 479 contains ten sources of risk for software projects. Many also apply to engineering and organizational development projects.

Techniques for identifying risk

There are five techniques for identifying risk. They are listed separately, but are in practice used interactively:

1. *Expert judgement* uses personal intuition and awareness. This is the simplest technique, but is sufficient only on the simplest projects. The use of checklists against the categories identified above can help.[3]
2. *Plan decomposition* shows risks inherent in the interdependency of work. Any event that lies at the start or completion of many activities is a potential risk. These occur at bottlenecks in the network. When analysing the plan, you should also look at all external interfaces, such as external supply, for potential failure of third parties.
3. *Assumption analysis* is win/lose analysis, and focuses on events that might be detrimental, considering both events we want to occur but may not, and events we do not want to occur but may. Expert judgement is needed to foresee these events and check for completeness. Table 11.1 contains an assumption analysis on the purchase of a computer system.
4. *Decision drivers* are influences that might determine whether or not certain events may occur (inside and outside the project). Win/lose analysis can be used to derive the list of decision drivers. It can be particularly damaging if decisions are made for the wrong reason: political versus technical; marketing versus technical; solution versus problem; short term versus long term; new technology versus experience.
5. *Brainstorming* uses social interaction to enhance the above techniques.

Expecting the unexpected

The secret of clear risk identification is to be able to predict possible causes of divergence from plan. It is the experience of many people that failure occurs on a project where they least expect it. This is known as *Sod's law*, or *Murphy's law*. It is sometimes stated as: *if something can go wrong, it will; if something can't go wrong, it will*!

Table 11.1 Win/lose analysis for the purchase of a computer system

System offered vs system specified	Winners	Losers
Quick, cheap product	Developer Sponsor	User
Lots of 'nice to haves'	Developer User	Sponsor
Driving too hard a bargain	Sponsor User	Developer

The value of this attitude is that if you expect things to go wrong, you will be on your guard for problems, and will be able to respond quickly to them. The failures may be ones you had predicted, or ones you least expect. If you anticipate problems, and plan appropriate contingency, you will not be disrupted when those problems occur. If the unexpected then also occurs, you will be able to focus your management effort into the areas that might now cause greatest disruption (Example 11.1). This attitude of expecting risks and being ready to respond is sometimes known as *risk thinking*. To some people it comes naturally; others require structured, logical processes of risk identification and analysis to support their response.

Variation of risk with the project management life cycle

Like quality, the impact of risk varies throughout the project management life cycle. The later in the cycle risks occur, the more expensive are their consequences, but to counteract that, the less likely they are to occur. Section 8.2 gave figures for the variation of the cost of correcting quality problems through the life cycle. Similar figures apply to risk. After all, quality problems are one type of risk. If the design stage is managed well, any *show-stoppers* (technical problems that will cause the project to fail) should be found then, before real money is spent. Risk can be reduced at the design stage by choosing a proven design rather than an untested one, or during the implementation stage by choosing proved methodologies. Whenever novelty is introduced, the risk of failure grows throughout the life of the project.

Isolating risk in the work breakdown structure

Similarly, it is usually possible to isolate risk in the work breakdown structure, by identifying it as being associated with a certain part of the project (Figure 6.1).

In 1983, I managed an area of work on the overhaul of an ammonia plant. We were uprating the steam system, and this required us to run a line between the 50 bar and 30 bar steam mains shown in Figure 11.1. On the overhaul, we just had to make break-ins into the two mains at each end of the line. These consisted of T-sections, together with an isolation valve. The new line would be run between the two valves once the plant was back on line. The break-in to the 30 bar main was simple. We made an 8 in. by 6 in. T-section in advance of the overhaul. In the overhaul we just had to cut the line, weld in the T-section, and install the isolation valve. The other break-in, however, carried greater risk. It was to be made in a 12 in. line just downstream from the main isolation valve, separating the plant main from the factory main. This valve had not been closed in 12 years, and so we did not know if it would shut tight. If it did not, the job would be more difficult, or even impossible. We put considerable effort into drawing up contingency plans in the event of a partial or full leak of the valve. In the event it shut like a dream. However, when we offered up the T-section at the other end, we found it had been made 6 in. by 6 in. instead of 8 in. by 6 in. We therefore had to make a new T-section in a hurry, and 8 in. pipe of the right pressure rating was not immediately available. That particular job almost extended the duration of the overhaul. However, the time spent planning the other job was not wasted. I knew that so well, I could leave it to run itself and focus my attention on procuring 8 in. pipe.

Example 11.1 Expecting the unexpected

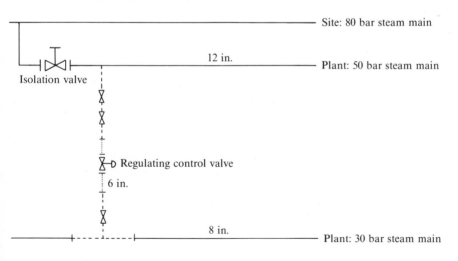

— Existing line

---- Line added or replaced during the shutdown

.... Line added post shutdown

Figure 11.1   Break-ins to the steam mains of an ammonia plant

11.4 Assessing risk

Having identified possible sources of risk to the project, we need to calculate their impact on the project. First we calculate the impact of individual risks, and then determine their combined impact.

The impact of risk

The impact of a risk factor depends on its likelihood of occurring and the consequence if it does occur:

Impact of risk = (Likelihood of risk) * (Consequence of risk)

To illustrate this concept, consider the question of whether buildings in the British Isles have earthquake protection. The answer is: very few do. Multi-storey office blocks in London do not. The consequence of an earthquake in London of Force 7 on the Richter Scale would be severe loss of life. However, the probability of such an earthquake is so small, virtually zero, that it is considered unnecessary to take any precautions. However, one type of building that does have earthquake protection is a nuclear power station. The likelihood of an earthquake has not changed, but the consequences of that occurrence are now unacceptably high. The consequence of an earthquake of Force 7 in the Heysham area would

---

Perhaps the consequence of an earthquake under a nuclear power station would not be as severe as suggested, but the public perception is that it would. Several years ago, the civil design consultants, Ove Arup and Partners, put considerable effort into designing and testing railway wagons for transporting low-level nuclear waste around the country. There were some highly publicized experiments in which a locomotive was slammed into a wagon at 100 miles per hour. In this case, the likelihood that an accident would cause a release of radiation was small, and the consequence was also small – no immediate deaths but, perhaps, one or two additional cancer cases resulting in early death several years later. However, this is a highly emotive public issue, and hence the need for indestructible wagons. On the other hand, quite lethal chemicals are transported around in relatively flimsy wagons. In the early 1980s I worked close to a railway line along which, twice each day, passed a train towing two wagons filled with cyanide gas. The consequence of a crash involving a leak in the centre of a city could be instant death to thousands of people, but this is not a public issue. A thousand instant deaths from cyanide gas seems to be more acceptable than two lingering deaths from radiation-induced cancer.

Example 11.2 Public perception of risk

make Liverpool uninhabitable for 10 000 years (or that at least is the public perception). Perhaps you should include the public perception of the consequence of the risk in the equation as well (Example 11.2):

$$\text{Impact of risk} = (\text{Likelihood of risk}) * (\text{Consequence of risk})$$
$$* (\text{Public perception})$$

Combining the impact of several risks

It is a rare project that has only a single source of risk, so to determine the total impact of risk on a project, the elements must be combined. If we include all possible sources of risk into the model, it will become impossibly complicated, and so we limit our attention to the significant few, the 20 per cent that have 80 per cent of the impact. As I suggested earlier, the work breakdown structure is a key tool in this integration of the risk. In practice there are two approaches:

- a top-down approach, in which key risk factors are identified and assessed at a high level of work breakdown, and managed out of the project
- a bottom-up approach, in which risks are identified at a low level of work breakdown, and an appropriate contingency made to allow for the risk.

The top-down approach

The top-down approach can provide managers with checklists of potential risk factors based on previous experience,[4] and can help them to determine each risk's relative importance. Furthermore, by identifying the controlling relationships at a high level, it enables project managers to find ways of eliminating the most severe risks from their projects.[5]

Table 11.2 Project to erect a warehouse

No.	Name of work package	Preceding package	Duration (months)
A	Design building and foundations	–	3
B	Prepare site and foundations	A	2
C	Procure steelwork	A	2
D	Erect steelwork	B, C	2

Figure 11.2 is the top-level network for a simple project to build a warehouse. There are four packages of work (Table 11.2). Assuming end-to-start dependencies only, the duration of the project is seven months. It

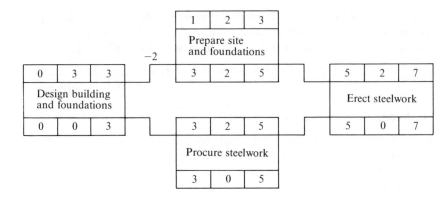

Figure 11.2 Simple precedence network for constructing a warehouse

might be possible to fast track the project by overlapping work packages. However, let us assume that that is impossible on the path A–C–D: it is not possible to buy the steel until the design is finished, and because all the steel will arrive at once, erection cannot begin until the steel has arrived. It might be possible to start work on the site before the design is finished, but there is no need, because the duration will be determined by the delivery of the steel.

Now let us consider the risks. Let us assume that the project will start at the beginning of September, after the summer vacation. The risks are as follows:

1. The design of the building may take more or less than three months. From previous experience we may be able to say it will take two, three or four months with the following probabilities:

   – 2 months: 25 per cent
   – 3 months: 50 per cent
   – 4 months: 25 per cent

   Hence it may be finished as early as the end of October, or may stretch to the end of December.

2. The site cannot be prepared if there is snow on the ground. Snow occurs in four months of the year with the following probabilities:

   – December: 25 per cent
   – January: 25 per cent
   – February: 50 per cent
   – March: 25 per cent

   The duration of this work package is dependent on when it starts. If it starts in October, it will take only two months; if it starts in November, it will have the following range of durations (see Figure 11.3):

- 2 months: 75 per cent
- 3 months: 19 per cent
- 4 months: 3 per cent
- 5 months: 2 per cent
- 6 months: 1 per cent

There will be similar tables if the work were to start in December or January, but with the probabilities weighted towards the longer durations. In some circumstances the preparation of the site will become critical. Now it may be worth while trying to fast track the design of the foundations. If the design could be completed by the end of September, we could eliminate this risk entirely. If it is finished by the end of October, there is a 75 per cent chance of the work being finished on time. If the start of this work is delayed to December, there is only a 50 per cent chance. The choice will depend on the cost of fast tracking the design of the foundations. There will be additional financial charges if this work is completed early, it is unlikely that the cost of the design will be greater *per se*, but there is a risk of re-work, as described in Section 11.3 above. In the event, you may actually make the decision on the day, depending on how the design of the steelwork is progressing, and other factors below.

Nov	Dec	Jan	Feb	Mar	Apr	Total
1.0	0.75					75%
	0.25	0.25 * 0.75				19%
		0.25 * 0.25	0.06 * 0.50			3%
			0.06 * 0.50	0.03 * 0.75		2%
				0.03 * 0.35	1.0	1%

Key

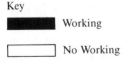

Working

No Working

Figure 11.3 Calculating the duration of work package B with November start

3. There may be two possible suppliers of steelwork: the more expensive one can deliver in one month or two months with equal probability; and the cheaper in two months or three months also with equal probability. The delivery time therefore has the following distribution:

- 1 month: 25 per cent
- 2 months: 50 per cent
- 3 months: 25 per cent

On the face of it this appears the same as the design. However, the power of this top-down approach is you can decide what to do on the day, when you know how long the design has taken, and how you are progressing with the foundations. To understand this we need to address the fourth risk.

4. This is that the steelwork cannot be erected if there are strong winds, and these occur with the following probability:

- February: 25 per cent
- March: 50 per cent

The duration of this work will also depend on when it starts, as with preparing the site. However, what we can see is that if the design work finishes at the end of October, then it will be better to use the more expensive supplier. There will then be a 50 per cent chance that erection can begin in December and finish in January without any delay, or a 50 per cent chance that it will begin in January, in which case it will finish in February with a 75 per cent chance. This is, of course, dependent on the foundations being ready, and so if it looks as though the steelwork design will be completed early, then it will be worth while fast tracking the foundations. On the other hand, if the design takes four months, it would be better to use the cheaper supplier, and just plan to start erecting the steelwork in April, saving on extra cost of the foundations and on having erection fitters standing idle.

This simple case shows that the top-down approach allows you to analyse the interrelationships between elements of risk, and management decisions based on that analysis and the actual out-turn. Following a top-down approach, you are able to develop additional detail in some areas. In the case above, for instance, you could introduce a lower level of work breakdown to find out how to fast track the design of the foundations. The concept of fast track was mentioned in Section 5.4 and 10.4. Indeed, Section 5.4 differentiated between fast track and fast build, and it is in fact fast build we should use here to reduce the risk. That requires the design to be broken into smaller packages of work, subject to strict design parameters at the top level.

Influence diagrams

Influence diagrams are tools – derived from a systems dynamics approach – that can assist a top-down analysis. They show how risks influence one another: some risks reinforce others (+), and some reduce others (−). Figure 11.4 is an example of an influence diagram. The power of the technique is to identify loops of influence. 'Vicious cycles' have an even (or zero) number of negative influences, and 'stable cycles' an odd number. In Figure 11.4, loop ADEKLIBA is vicious, and loop ADEGHJIBA is stable. In a 'vicious cycle' an externally imposed influence can be amplified indefinitely.

The bottom-up approach

The bottom-up approach analyses risk at a low level.[6] It can identify several critical paths, and calculate a range of outcomes for cost and duration to enable the project manager to allow appropriate contingency. However, it is essentially a negative approach to risk, as it assumes that risk elements are beyond the control of managers. It does nothing to help the manager to quantify or convey information for developing an appropriate management response to reducing or eliminating risk.

The approach develops a detailed project model, at a low level of breakdown. Variable durations and/or costs are assigned to work elements, as in the above example. However, at a low level it is not possible to calculate the various outcomes manually, as they were above. Instead, we perform a *Monte Carlo* analysis. The project model is analysed many times; 100 to 10 000 is typical, depending on the size of the model. Each time, a random number is drawn for each parameter for which there is a range of values, and a value selected accordingly. (This makes the simplifying assumption that the risk elements are unrelated, which may not be the case – see Figure 11.4.) The cost and duration are then calculated using those values, and a range of possible outcomes calculated for the project. Effectively, the project is sampled however many times the analysis is performed. The results of the Monte Carlo analysis are presented as a probability distribution for time, cost, or both. This may be a simple or cumulative distribution. Figure 11.5 shows both distributions for the duration of the warehouse project, assuming the logic given in Table 11.2. For this simple case, the critical path may go through either A–B–D or A–C–D, and the duration can be anything from 6 to 11 months. The likelihood that either or both of the routes will be the critical path is:

Critical path:	A–B–D	Both	A–C–D
Likelihood:	52%	24%	24%

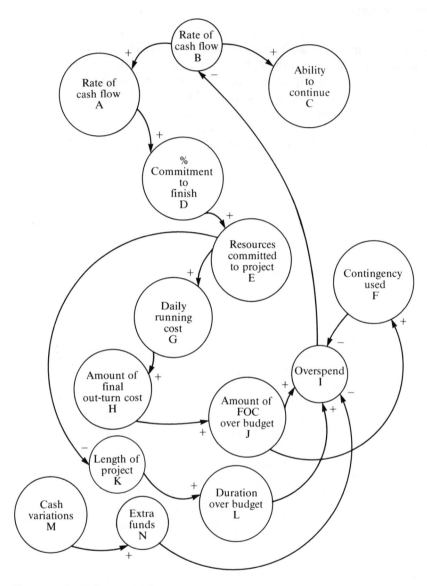

Figure 11.4   Influence diagram

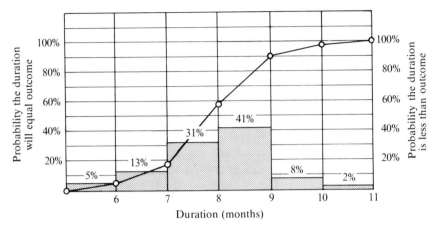

Figure 11.5 Simple and cumulative probability distributions for the duration of the project to build a warehouse

and the range of all possible outcomes is:

Duration (months):	6	7	8	9	10	11
Probability:	5%	13%	31%	41%	8%	2%
Cumulative:	5%	18%	49%	90%	98%	100%

With a project this small, it is just possible to calculate these numbers by hand: it took me an hour. With anything larger, the figures have to be determined using a Monte Carlo analysis. From this we see that the median outcome is eight months (half the time the duration will be this or less), and that 90 per cent of the time the duration will be less than nine months. The most likely duration (the mode) is nine months. If a nine-month duration is acceptable, we may accept these figures. If not, we would need to shorten the project. The critical path figures show that the most useful effort may be put into shortening A–B–D, and that may suggest fast tracking the design of the foundations. However, from this we do not see the effect of the two suppliers. That can only be analysed by the top-down approach.

Accounting for increased costs or reduced revenues

Monte Carlo analysis can also be applied to the costs and revenues of a project, to produce a range of likely returns. However, with the costs and revenues, the risk can be accounted for directly by allowing a contingency, as suggested in Section 3.4.

The owner's view of the risk

I should like to reinforce a point made in Section 3.4. The quantitative methods described above produce a value for the project. However, in the final analysis, the true value of the project is not the figure calculated by the project team, using these methods. It is the value the owner puts on the project, and that reflects his or her perception of the risk, and to a certain extent the public's perception as well (if the owner is concerned about public opinion – Example 11.3).

In the early 1980s, NIREX proposed storing medium level nuclear waste in a redundant mine under ICI's factory at Billingham. It may have been one of the safest proposals for storing medium level waste. The project would cost ICI nothing (but see Example 11.4), but earn them an income; an attractive project with *no* risk attached. However, ICI would not allow the project to proceed because that was not the way the local community viewed it, and ICI was concerned about local opinion. The ironic thing was ICI used to operate one of the country's largest private nuclear sources on the Billingham site.

Example 11.3 The owner's perception of risk

It is almost certainly incorrect to say that the project described in Example 11.3 would have 'cost ICI nothing'. It was causing a loss of goodwill in the local community, and so the 'cost' was whatever value the company put on that goodwill. Clearly they did not think that 'cost' was worth the returns.

This is part of a wider viewpoint that is gaining credence. The environment itself has a value, and if a project we undertake reduces that value, we should take that into account when assessing the value of a project. In the case described in Example 11.3, that loss of value had a monetary impact in that house prices were falling in Billingham. The cost of the project would therefore not have been borne by ICI, but by the local community.

In this case the loss in value was caused by a fear of anything nuclear. A case in which the environment has suffered a real loss in value is the Adriatic coast of Italy. Algae blooms have reduced its ability to earn tourist revenues. Economic activity up the Po valley for the last 20 to 30 years have caused the blooms. However, the people who have received the benefit of that activity have not paid the price. The solution is an environment tax. That can be levied in Italy in the latter case, but should Switzerland pay a tax to Germany for the water flowing down the Rhine? The answer to that question is beyond the scope of this book.

Example 11.4 Putting a cost on the loss of value of the environment

Communicating the risk analysis

The ultimate purpose of the risk model is to communicate the analysis to all the parties involved with the project:

- to the owners for them to assess its value
- to the champions, so they can give their support and commitment to the project
- to the project managers so that they can develop their project strategies and perform *what-if* analyses
- to the integrators, to enable them to manage the risks during implementation
- to people joining the project at a later time, so they know what assumptions have been made
- to the users, so that they know the commitments they are making.

To be an effective communication tool, the model must be simple, robust, adaptable and complete. Achieving this requires considerable effort. Structuring the model in order to achieve these requirements can take 60 per cent of the total effort of risk analysis.

11.5 Reducing risk

Having identified and assessed the risk, you are in a position to consider ways of reducing it. There are three basic approaches[3]:

- *avoidance*: having identified the risk, you replan to eliminate it
- *deflection*: you try to pass the risk on to someone else
- *contingency*: you take no action in advance of the deviations occurring, other than to draw up contingency plans should they occur.

Pym and Wideman[3] use an analogy of a man being shot at. He can take cover to avoid the bullets; he can deflect them using a shield or divert the bullets by placing someone else in the firing line; or he can allow them to hit him, and plan to repair the damage.

Avoidance

The warehouse project above showed how to avoid the risk of snow holding up the preparation of the foundations by starting the work early enough, so that it is finished before the snow comes. Under avoidance, you change the plan for any one of the five system objectives, or any combination of them, to reduce the risk or eliminate it entirely.

Deflection

There are three ways of deflecting risk:

- *through insurance*: by which it is passed on to a third party
- *through bonding*: by which a security is held against the risk
- *through the contract*: by which it is passed between owner, contractor and subcontractors.

1. *Insurance* A third party accepts an insurable risk (Section 11.2) for the payment of a premium, which reflects the impact of the risk, the likelihood combined with the consequence.
2. *Bonding* One or both parties to a contract deposit money into a secure account so that if they or either party defaults the aggrieved party can take the bond in compensation. This is a way of transferring the risk of one party defaulting to that organization.
3. *Contract* Through contracts, the risk is shared between owner, contractor and subcontractors. There are two common principles of contracts:
   (a) *Risk is assigned to that party most able and best motivated to control it* There is no point passing risk onto a contractor or subcontractor if neither has the power or the motivation to control it. The Institution of Civil Engineers is currently revising its standard forms of contract around this principle.[7] There are four styles of contract for different approaches to sharing risk:
      - fixed price
      - cost-plus
      - cost reimbursable
      - target cost.

   Under *fixed price contracts*, Figure 11.6(a), the contractor accepts all the risk by taking a fixed fee for the work, regardless of how much it costs. It is assumed that the owner has completely specified the requirements, and as long as they do not change, the contractor can meet a given price. This approach is adopted for *turnkey contracts*, where the contractor takes full responsibility, and delivers to the owner an operating facility. The owner has no role in its construction. Often in fixed price contracts the owner and contractor haggle over every change, arguing over which one of them caused it, and whether it is within the original specification.

   When the owner cannot specify the requirements, the contractor should not accept the risk, but it should be borne by the owner. The simplest way is through *cost-plus contracts*, Figure 11.6(b). The owner refunds all the contractor's costs, and pays a percentage as profit. The disadvantage is that the contractor is still responsible

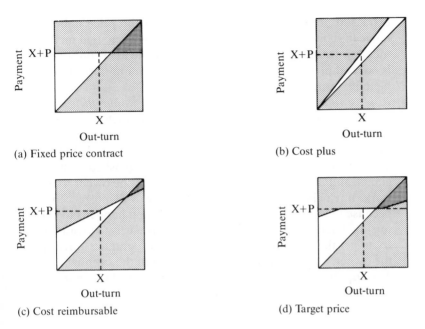

Figure 11.6   Four types of contract

for controlling costs, and yet the higher the costs the higher the profit. This is a recipe for disaster, as the party responsible for control is not motivated to do it; in fact the exact opposite. It is possible to adopt strict change control, and that passes responsibility for controlling costs back to the owner, but can lead to strife. Typically, cost-plus contracts are used on research contracts.

Another way of overcoming the problem is to pay the contractor a fixed fee, as a percentage of the estimate, instead of a percentage of the out-turn. This is a *cost reimbursable contract*, Figure 11.6(c). The contractor can be motivated to control costs if paid a bonus for finishing under budget, or charged a penalty if over budget. However, the parameters for the bonus or penalty must be carefully set to ensure that the accepted risk is not beyond the contractor's control. Even without a bonus the contractor may be motivated to control costs, as that increases the percentage return.

A related approach is target cost, Figure 11.6(d). The contractor is paid a fixed price if the out-turn is within a certain range, typically ±10 per cent of the budget. If the cost goes outside this range, then the owner and contractor share the risk, at say 50p in the pound. If the costs exceed the upper limit, the owner pays the contractor an extra 50p per pound of overspend, and if the price is below the range the contractor reduces the price. This is often used on development projects, where there is some idea of the likely out-turn, but it is not completely determined. The contractor may also share in the benefits from the product produced.

(b) *Risk is shared with subcontractors if it is within their sphere of control* To achieve this, back-to-back contracts are used: the clauses in the contract between owner and contractor are included in that between contractor and subcontractors. I have come across instances where the contractor feels squashed between two giants, and accepts quite severe clauses from the owner to win the work, but believes that the subcontractors will not accept them because they do not need the work. This often happens to contractors on defence or public sector projects. The way to avoid this is to try to get the subcontractors to make their contracts directly with the owner, and use the owner's power to pull the supplier into line. The supplier may not need the business from the contractor, but may have a better respect for the owner.

Contingency

The third response to risk is to make an allowance for it by adding a contingency. You can add an allowance to any one of the five system objectives, but typically there are two main approaches:

– make an allowance by increasing the time and/or cost budgets
– plan to change the scope, by drawing up contingency plans should the identified risks occur.

TIME AND/OR COST

You can either add the allowance as a blanket figure, calculated through a bottom-up approach as above, or you can add it work element by work element. Either way, the project manager should maintain at least two estimates, as described in Sections 9.5 and 10.2: a raw estimate without contingency, and an estimate with contingency. The former, called the baseline, is communicated to the project team as their working 'budget', and the latter to the owner for the provision of money and resources. The project manager may also maintain two further estimates, the most likely out-turn, the figure to which they are working, and the current estimate, which is the baseline with some contingency already consumed. The reason for giving the project team the baseline or current estimate as their working figure is that their costs will seldom be less than the estimate, and will consume contingency if it is given to them. The reason for communicating the estimate with contingency to the owner is they want to budget for the maximum likely time and cost.

CONTINGENCY PLANS

These are alternative methods of achieving the milestones, to be used in different circumstances. The alternative plans may or may not cost more money to implement, though presumably if they cost less it would be better to follow them in the first place. On the extension to the steam system on the ammonia plant above, it was shown how alternative plans were available should the valve shut tight, shut partially, and not shut at all. The latter plans each would have cost more than the first, which is the one we followed, although the second would have only been marginally more expensive.

However, it is better to plan to eliminate the risk than to plan how to overcome it, and it is better to plan how to overcome it than to increase the cost and extend the duration to pay for it.

11.6 Controlling risk

Having identified ways of reducing risk, you can implement a plan to control the reduction. Section 9.2 listed four basic steps in control:

- draw up a plan
- monitor progress against the plan
- calculate variances
- take action to overcome variances.

The risk management plan

The risk management plan identifies the risks associated with a project, the means by which they have been assessed, and the strategy for their reduction. A risk item tracking form (Figure 11.7) provides a framework for recording the relevant information for each risk. The form, which may be held in a spreadsheet or computer database, describes:

- *why* the risk is significant
- *what* is to be done to reduce it
- *when* the risk will have its impact on the project
- *who* is responsible for resolving the risk
- *how* the reduction will be achieved
- *how much* it will cost to resolve the risk.

TRIMAGI COMMUNICATIONS BV

RISK ITEM TRACKING FORM   PAGE 1 OF 2

PROJECT: CODE

WORK PACKAGE   CODE

ACTIVITY   CODE

RISK NUMBER: RISK IDENTIFIER

NATURE OF RISK

SOURCE: EU/EP/IT/IN/L   TYPE: BUSINESS/INSURABLE

CATEGORY   CONTRACTUAL/MANAGEMENT/TECHNICAL/PERSONNEL

DESCRIPTION:

IMPACT DATE: LIKELIHOOD   LOW/MEDIUM/HIGH

SUBSIDIARY RISKS

ACTIVITY   RISK IDENTIFIER

ACTIVITY   RISK IDENTIFIER

RISK IMPACT

SEVERITY: VL/L/M/H/VH   SEVERITY SCORE   ....../5

LIKELIHOOD SCORE   ...../3   RISK SCORE   SS * LS = .../15

IMPACT AREA

SCHEDULE:

COST:

PERFORMANCE:

RISK MONITORING

MONTH										
RANK										

Figure 11.7 Risk item tracking form

TRIMAGI COMMUNICATIONS BV

RISK ITEM TRACKING FORM   PAGE 2 OF 2

CORRECTIVE ACTION   PROPOSED/APPROVED

DESCRIPTION:

RISK REDUCTION COST

RESPONSIBLE MANAGER

REVISED DATE   LIKELIHOOD   LOW/MEDIUM/HIGH

START DATE: CLOSURE DATE:

REVISED IMPACT

SEVERITY: VL/L/M/H/VH   SEVERITY SCORE   ....../5

LIKELIHOOD SCORE   ...../3   RISK SCORE   SS * LS = .../15

IMPACT AREA

SCHEDULE:

COST:

PERFORMANCE:

MONTH	ACTION TAKEN	NEXT ACTION	BY WHOM

ISSUE: DATE: AUTHOR   APPROVED

Figure 11.7   (continued)

TRIMAGI COMMUNICATIONS BV
MONTHLY TOP RISK ITEM REPORT

PROJECT: CRMO RATIONALIZATION PROJECT   MANAGER: RODNEY TURNER
WORK AREA: TECHNOLOGY   DATE: 26 FEBRUARY 199X

RANK THIS MONTH	RANK LAST MONTH	MONTHS ON LIST	RISK ITEM	POTENTIAL CONSEQUENCE	RISK RESOLUTION PROGRESS
1	4	2	Replacement for team leader for MIS software development team	Lack of expertise in team. Delay in code production, with likelihood of lower quality – less reliable operation even after testing	Chosen replacement unavailable
2	6	2	Requested changes to user-interface	Now realized may impact h/w–s/w interface definition. If not cleared up at next week's user evaluation of prototype, will delay delivery date	User evaluation of latest prototype set for next week – attendance of some key users still to be confirmed
3	2	5	Resolution of network diagnostic software problems	Delay in completion of software detailed design and coding	New version of diagnostics appears to clear most problems but still to be fully checked
4	3	6	Availability of workstations for main test phase	Lack of sufficient workstations will restrict progress on testing	Delay in deliveries being discussed with supplier
5	5	3	Testbed interface definitions	If not finalized by end of next month, will delay availability of testbed	Delayed items now being worked on. Review meeting scheduled
6	1	3	Tighter fault tolerance requirements impact on performance	Performance problems could require change to h/w–s/w architecture with major impact on cost and schedule	Latest prototype demonstrates performance within specification
7	—	1	Delay in specification of network data transmission	Could delay availability of hardware subsystems for integration	Meeting scheduled to consider alternatives
8	8	4	Tech author required	Insufficient time for programming staff to produce quality manuals	Requirement with agency
—	7	4	CM assistant required	Inadequate effort for rising CM workload with resulting costly errors	CM assistant joined team full-time
—	9	4	Re-usable database software uncertainties	Potential increase in estimates of coding effort	Uncertainties resolved in latest prototype

Figure 11.8 Monthly top ten risk items report

As previously stated, the risk varies throughout the life cycle of the project, and hence the priorities for risk reduction will change. Having each risk recorded on a separate sheet of paper or in a computer database allows them to be sorted into appropriate order each month.

Monitoring risk

The risks are then monitored on a regular basis (weekly, fortnightly, monthly, or at other predetermined intervals) to determine how far each risk has actually been reduced. At each review, the risk tracking forms are sorted into their order of current importance. A list of the most significant risks, usually the 'top-ten', is produced, giving rank this period, rank last period, and periods on the list. Figure 11.8 shows a completed report.

Risk reassessment

Reassessment should be carried out whenever new risks are identified in the course of risk monitoring. In addition, there should be explicit reassessment at key milestones in the project, and at transition between stages. The launch meetings for subsequent stages (Chapter 13) are ideal media for this reassessment. All the above techniques are used for reassessment. It is always easier to improve on an existing plan, but there is the disadvantage that new risks may be ignored.

11.7 Summary

1. There are two types of risk:
   - *business* risk
   - *insurable* risk.
2. There are five steps in risk management:
   - identify sources of risk
   - determine impact of individual risks
   - assess overall impact of risks
   - determine how the risk can be reduced
   - control the identified risks.
3. There are five sources of risk:
   - external: unpredictable
   - external: predictable but uncertain
   - internal: technical
   - internal: non-technical
   - legal.
4. Techniques for identifying risks include:
   - expert judgement
   - plan decomposition
   - assumption analysis
   - decision drivers analysis
   - group brainstorming.
5. The impact of individual risks is a product of the likelihood they will

occur, the consequence if they do occur, and the public perception of that consequence.

6. In assessing the combined effect of several risks, you can use:
   - a top-down approach, a management decision-making tool
   - a bottom-up approach, and Monte Carlo analysis
   - influence diagrams.
7. There are three ways of reducing risk:
   - avoidance
   - deflection
   - contingency.
8. Contracts should be drawn up with the policy that risk should be assigned to the party best able and best motivated to control it, and to this end there are four types of contract:
   - fixed price
   - cost-plus
   - cost reimbursable, with or without bonus
   - target cost.
9. There are four steps in controlling risk:
   - draw up a risk management plan consisting of risk item tracking forms
   - monitor progress against the top ten risks
   - reassess risks at regular intervals, and at key milestones or stage transition
   - take action to overcome any divergence from plan.

Notes and references

1. This chapter includes material written by Dr Alan Oliver. It also uses ideas contributed by Mahen Tampoe and Bob Thomas. Mr Thomas is a consultant with WS Atkins Project Management.
2. Fowler, H. W. and Fowler, F. G. (eds), *The Concise Oxford Dictionary of Current English*, Oxford University Press, 1964.
3. Pym, D. V. and Wideman, R. M., 'Risk management', in *The Revised Project Management Body of Knowledge*, Project Management Institute, 1987.
4. Ashley, D. B., 'Project risk identification using inference, subjective expert assessment and historical data', in *Proceedings of the INTERNET International Expert Seminar on Project Risk Management* (eds D. B. Ashley and S. Dworatschek), INTERNET, 1989.
5. Cooper, D. F. and Chapman, C. B., *Risk Analysis for Large Projects*, Wiley, 1987.
6. Hertz, D. B. and Thomas, H., *Risk Analysis and its Applications*, Wiley, 1983.
7. The Institution of Civil Engineers, *The New Engineering Contract: The need for and features of the NEC*, A Consultative Document, Thomas Telford, 1991.

12
Structuring the plans

12.1 Introduction

I have now completed the review of the management of the five system objectives and the risks inherent in all of them. In Part Four of this book our attention will switch to the management processes through which the manager integrates the five objectives to undertake the work of the project. However, I wish to close this part by reinforcing three concepts associated with the management of all five system objectives. Section 12.2 will describe the value of defining the relative importance of scope, quality, cost and time at the start of a project as a basis for all decision making throughout the project, and show how this is done pictorially. Section 12.3 will then describe how the technique of nesting the plans in the work breakdown structure provides a basis for single-page reporting at all levels, and limits the impact of risk and changes during the planning and control process. Section 12.4 then describes how and why we freeze the plan as the measure, or baseline, against which progress is monitored and controlled throughout the project.

12.2 Balancing the system objectives

In most projects, the five system objectives are in conflict. Priority cannot be given to one without compromising one or more of the others. For instance, shortening the duration may cost more money, will usually threaten the scope or quality of the work, and may have an impact on the organization. Hence, when making decisions during the planning, risk analysis or control process of the project, it is important to know which objectives have priority so that appropriate emphasis can be given to different actions. Priority must be set during project definition, otherwise priority will usually be given to time by default.

Time/cost/quality

Traditionally, priority has been traded between time, cost and quality, shown pictorially by placing a mark in the time/cost/quality triangle

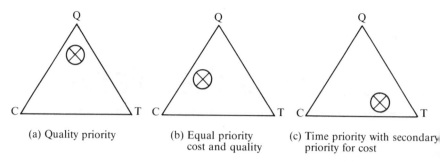

(a) Quality priority   (b) Equal priority   (c) Time priority with secondary
                            cost and quality   priority for cost

Figure 12.1 Placing a marker in the quality/cost/time triangle

shown in Figure 12.1. Priority can be given to (a) one objective alone; (b) equally to two; or (c) primarily to one but with secondary emphasis to another. All subsequent decision making, during project definition, risk analysis or control, must take this into account.

Time/cost/performance

In Chapter 8 it was stated that satisfying the customer means not compromising quality below the adequate specification set during project definition. This may appear to say that the mark should always be placed in the quality corner of the triangle. I once gave a seminar to people from a company committed to total quality management. When I described the project control process, I said that if it was not possible to keep to the original plans then you sacrifice one of time, cost or quality. One of the audience challenged me, saying that under the TQM philosophy you cannot sacrifice quality. When I looked closely at my slide, it did not in fact say that it was quality you sacrifice; it said 'reduce the level of ambition', that is scope. The priority is not set in the time/cost/quality triangle, but in another face of the pyramid of project objectives (Figure 1.1), the time/cost/scope face. We may indeed set the priorities in any one of the four faces of the pyramid, or any plane through it. Sometimes you will hear people talking of the time/cost/performance triangle. In the diamond model introduced by the Project Management Institute of North America[1] (Figure 1.4), scope/cost/time/quality appear as the four corners of a diamond. Performance appears in this as the balance between scope and quality. The time/cost/performance triangle therefore implies that the balance has already been made between scope and quality in setting the adequate specification. The setting of priority is then between time, cost and performance. If subsequently it is necessary to compromise the performance, this is achieved by compromising scope, not quality.

Time/cost

It was stated above that you may spend more money to reduce the duration of the project. This in fact goes against many people's experience of projects, for two reasons:

1. It takes a certain amount of effort to complete some work. It does not matter whether 5 people take 2 days or 2 people take 5 days, the level of effort is 10 man-days.
2. Projects that are late are usually overspent; those that are on time are on budget. Therefore it costs more to delay a project, not to shorten it.

The first statement is not necessarily correct. Section 10.3 showed that an increase in the number of people may reduce their efficiency. Therefore, 5 people may take 3 days, or 15 man-days. However, the second is correct for two reasons. Projects are usually delayed by changes or poor quality, both of which require additional work at greater cost. Associated with a project there will be an overhead required to run the project, arising from project management costs and temporary services, which are usually constant with time. Therefore the longer the project takes, the more it costs. There are two cost elements associated with a project. There is the direct element required to complete the scope of work. Given sufficient time this will cost some fundamental amount. However, as you shorten the duration, the efficiency will fall and the project will cost more. Then there is the overhead element, being the cost of additional work and project management. This rises uniformly with time (at least initially before accelerating). When these two costs are added together, they give some minimum cost of doing the project (see Figure 12.2), achieved during an optimum time window. Hopefully, the original project duration will have been set in this time window. Shortening the project's duration will then incur additional cost, but lengthening it will also incur cost.

12.3 Nesting the plans

It was stated in Chapter 6 that the work breakdown structure (WBS) is the back-bone of project management. Throughout this part we have seen its role in:

- defining the scope of work
- defining the project organization
- setting the quality and specification of the project's product
- estimating and controlling costs
- estimating durations and scheduling times.

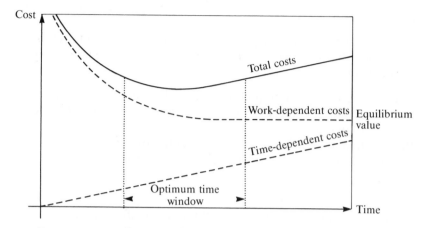

It costs money to shorten the duration
It costs money to extend the duration

Figure 12.2   The optimum time window for a project from the balance of cost and time

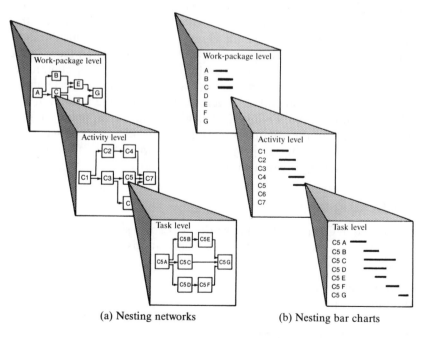

(a) Nesting networks   (b) Nesting bar charts

Figure 12.3   Nesting networks and bar charts

The project manager is able to obtain greater management control over the project if, through the WBS, the project can be broken into discrete elements with little interdependency or sharing of resources. This is especially true when managing cost and time. The impact of any changes can be minimized by carefully nesting plans at each level of the WBS, within the plans at the higher level. Figure 12.3 illustrates the nesting of networks (a) and the corresponding bar charts (b) at several levels of the WBS. If changes do occur at one level of the WBS, the project manager can try to limit the impact within the element of work at the level the change occurred. If this is impossible then the impact may be limited within the element at the level above.

This can be difficult if there are complex interdependencies between activities in several work packages. However, given the management advantage, it may be better to draw idealized logic than to draw pedantically correct logic. For example, in Figure 12.3 it may be that the start of C7 is actually dependent on the completion of C5E, and the end of C7 is dependent on C5G. It is better to draw on finish-to-start dependency from C5 to C7, with a lead equal to the duration of C5G, than to complicate the network with a dependency from C5E to the first task in C7, and another from C5G to the last task in C7.

12.4 Baselining

Chapters 9 and 10 introduced the control process, the first step of which is to set a measure against which to judge progress. For effective control this measure must be frozen at some point before the end of project definition and held constant for the duration of the project. If the measure is updated to reflect current progress, then it will be impossible to calculate variances, and control will be lost. I have often seen projects that are always on time and within budget because the plan has just been updated at the latest meeting, and no one can remember what the original targets were.

The frozen measure is called the *baseline* (a term that is now widely accepted). There will be a baseline for each of the five project objectives, scope, organization, quality and specification, cost and time. The first three must be baselined before the fourth and fifth.

For both cost and time it is common to maintain two measures, the baseline and the current estimate. The former is used for control, the latter to predict out-turn, manage cash flow and schedule work. The baselined cost is often known as the *estimated prime cost*, or *planned cost of work scheduled*, and the current estimate as that. The baselined dates are sometimes known as the *planned* dates, and the current estimate as the *scheduled* dates.

Although the baseline should be frozen and maintained constant as far as possible, there are occasions when it may need to be changed, and some when it must be changed. When it is changed this must be subject to a strict change control procedure. Reasons for changing the baseline include:

1. When work is switched between one work package and another then the baselined cost of that work must be switched (Example 12.1).
2. When new work is added to the project, the estimated cost of that work may be added to the baseline, but without changing the baseline for the existing work. Changing the baselined dates is more difficult, because it may be impossible to isloate the impact of the new work from previous delays.
3. If the project becomes significantly overspent or delayed, then the baseline may no longer represent a sensible measure for control. Using it for control can then actually be demotivating. It may then be necessary to update the baseline. This should be treated as a serious exercise not to be undertaken lightly (Example 12.2).

I audited one project, where an activity within a work package had been switched from in-house supply to subcontract. However, the baselined cost was not switched, and the in-house resources spent up to the original estimate on the remaining work.

Example 12.1 Packet switching

I worked in one company where it was assumed that all projects would 'go to the right'. This became a self-fulfilling prophecy, with people working to rumoured new time scales, even while the project manager was still trying to maintain the original schedule. On one occasion a major payment milestone was missed because people has assumed that the project was late.

Example 12.2 Updating the baseline through change control

12.5 Summary

1. The priority between the five system objectives – scope, organization, quality, cost and time – must be set at the start of the project, and become the basis for all decision making. If priority is not set at the start, decisions will be influenced by the situation.

2. Single-page reporting is obtained by nesting the plans in the work breakdown structure.
3. There are up to four plans:
   - the baseline, the fixed measure for control
   - the current estimate, including some contingency
   - the most likely out-turn
   - the budget, the most that can be consumed (in time and money).

Reference

1. Wideman, R. M., 'The framework', in *The Revised Project Management Body of Knowledge*, Project Management Institute, 1987.

PART FOUR
UNDERTAKING
PROJECTS

13
Project definition

13.1 Introduction

Part Three described methods, tools and techniques for managing the first dimension of project management, the five objectives – scope, organization, quality, cost, time – and the inherent risk. We shall now turn to the second dimension, the management processes, and describe how the methods, tools and techniques are applied to undertake projects. In Chapter 2 I explained that because projects are of finite duration, project management is said to have a *life cycle*, going through several stages of development from germination of the idea to commissioning of the facility. During the life cycle, management emphasis changes. The definition of the project evolves in a controlled way, so that the best solution to the owner's requirements is achieved, and money and resources are committed only as uncertainty is reduced. This part will describe how the methods, tools and techniques are applied at different stages of the life cycle, following the four-stage life cycle introduced in Chapter 2 (see Figure 13.1 and Table 13.1).[1] (Later chapters will consider other variants of the life cycle.)

This chapter will describe the first two stages, 'proposal and initiation' and 'design and appraisal', commonly merged as the project definition. I

Table 13.1 The four-stage life cycle

Stage	Name	Chapter	Topic
Germination	Proposal and initiation	13	Project definition; feasibility
Growth	Design and appraisal	13	Planning and design; appraisal
Maturity	Execution and control	14	Implementing measuring progress; forecasting completion; taking action
Death	Finalization and close-out	15	Project close-out

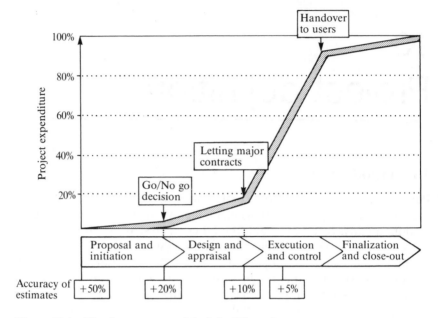

Figure 13.1 The four-stage model of the life cycle

shall start by explaining the process of *project start-up*, which may be used to initiate any stage of the project, even close-out. I shall describe proposal and initiation, and explain how to conduct a feasibility study to achieve the objectives of the stage. I shall then describe design and appraisal, and explain the use of initiation meetings and the Project Definition Report and Manual as tools to start project definition and record decisions made.

13.2 Project start-up[2]

A project requires the undertaking of a unique task using a novel organization, which must be created from scratch at the start of the project. When new teams are formed, the members take some time to learn how to work together before becoming truly effective. Typically, a team goes through four stages of formation in which its effectiveness first falls and then rises[3] (Figure 13.2):

– *forming*: the team members come together;
– *storming*: they find areas of disagreement;
– *norming*: they agree principles of cooperation;
– *performing*: they achieve the task effectively.

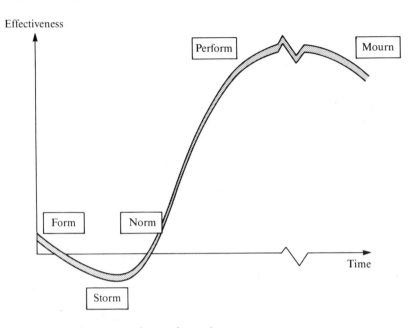

Figure 13.2   The stages of team formation

(A fifth stage, *mourning*, when the team is disbanded at the end of the task, is introduced in Chapter 18.) A project is subject to time constraints, and so this process of team formation must be undertaken in a structured way to ensure that it happens quickly. Furthermore, it may be done at several stages throughout the project management life cycle, since the team may change from one stage to the next.

The structured approach to creating the project organization is called *project start-up*.[4,5] The term 'project start-up' is used to differentiate from 'project start'; the former is a structured process for team formation, the latter is an action at an instant in time. Fangel[6] draws the analogy of starting the engine of a car and starting-up the diesel engine in a ship. The former is achieved by flicking the ignition switch, the latter by a structured series of activities, a start-up process, which gives the most efficient and economical operation. The same applies to projects.

This section will clarify the concept of project start-up, and discuss its timing in the project management life cycle. It will describe the objectives of the process, show how these change throughout the life cycle, and review methods of start-up and their effectiveness for achieving the various objectives. Finally, it will describe how to schedule the start-up process.

Initiating projects

The approach used for initiating a project and its activities depends on the nature of the project and on the current position in the life cycle. There are three typical procedures (Figure 13.3):

- smooth transition from a previous stage
- crystallization of the project over a period of time
- project start-up for rapid launch.

Smooth transition or crystallization were the approaches traditionally used, but the trend in recent years has been to project start-up. The reason may be the promotion of the start-up concept, but is more probably attributable to:

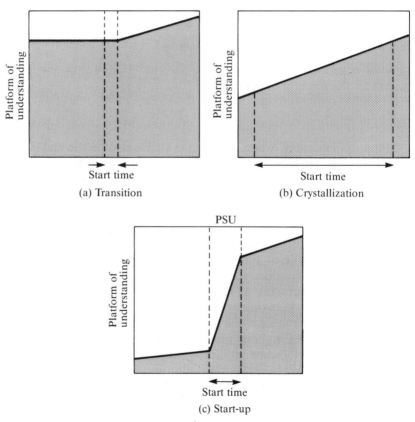

Figure 13.3 Procedures for project initiation

- the increasing complexity of technologies used
- the use of qualified project management earlier in the life cycle
- new patterns of cooperation in projects, including the need for team building and cross cultural cooperation (Chapter 4)
- a need for increased effectiveness caused by shorter product life cycles
- changes in the way projects are managed, including the use of goal-directed approaches,[7] which reinforce the setting of objectives and scope, the use of group methods for building cooperation, and the management of the team through the use of a clear and common mission.

To achieve start-up, it is necessary to create a shared perception of the project and its context, to gain acceptance of the plans, and to get the team functioning. These objectives are achieved by an intensive process over a short period of time, unifying the parties involved, their efforts, and the decision-making processes, and thereby creates a common basis for planning, organizing, implementing and controlling the project or stage.

Start-up and the management life cycle

Depending on the character of the project, the start-up process may be undertaken once only or repeated several times throughout the life cycle:

1. One start-up (Figure 13.4(a)) is typical of system development projects (see Section 20.4). Subsequent stages are initiated by planning the work at the end of the previous stage.
2. Multiple start-up (Figure 13.4(b) is typical of major engineering construction projects (see Section 20.3), where a different team of people works on each stage.

The figures illustrate levels of cooperation and understanding throughout the project, which increases at the start of and during each stage. They also indicate a close-out process (Chapter 15). For some project personnel close-out occurs at the end of earlier stages, and this is illustrated by the dipping in understanding at the end of each stage, caused by a (partial) change in the project organization. It is when a significant portion of the organization changes that project start-up is required. Perhaps unsurprisingly, this can be important at the start of the close-out stage, when the team members may have lost sight of the purpose, and when their motivation can start to wain as the work of the project begins to run down. The start-up process will be timed to achieve maximum benefit from reducing the level of uncertainty and increasing the level of energy of the team (Figure 13.5). The uncertainty is reduced either by taking key decisions, or by clarifying the consequences of those decisions. The start-

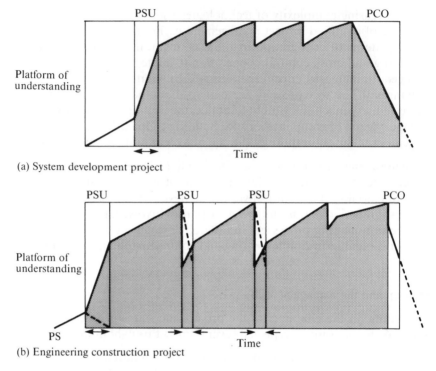

Figure 13.4   Project start-up in the life cycle

up process should therefore be held when the project team have matured enough to understand the basis of the decisions. This should also correspond to the time when the increased energy can be usefully harnessed. This means that project start-up can be done too early, but it is almost never too late.

Objectives of start-up

For a systematic approach to start-up to be successful, the participants must understand the objectives of the process at any stage, and must be aware of the specific outputs needed to achieve the necessary level of understanding. These objectives might be:

- to create a shared vision or mission for the project, by identifying the project's context, its purpose and objectives
- to gain acceptance of the plans, by defining the scope of work, project organization, and constraints of quality cost and time

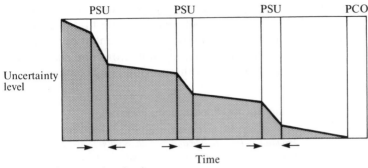

(a) Trends in uncertainty level

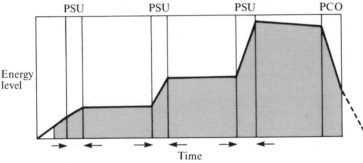

(b) Trends in energy level

Figure 13.5 Timing project start-up

- to get the project team functioning, by agreeing its mode of operation and the channels of communication
- to refocus the project team onto the purpose of the project, and the method of achieving it.

The first three objectives correspond to Parts Two, Three and Four, respectively; the fourth runs throughout. As they move through the stages of a project, the team's understanding of these develops in turn (Figure 2.5). At the start, the emphasis is at the top level, identifying the project's context, developing the shared vision and project strategy. As that is achieved, the emphasis shifts to the second level, developing the project model for the five system objectives, the first dimension of project management. In the third stage, the emphasis changes again into pulling the strands of the project model together, to undertake the work. This is done through the project management life cycle, the second dimension. Finally, as the facility is commissioned, and handed over to the client, the emphasis changes back to the purpose of the project, the benefit expected from the facility and the product it produces, to ensure that is achieved. Hence, the objectives of project start-up will be different at each stage of the life cycle (Table 13.2), although as you move from one stage to the next, you may review the objectives of the previous stage, and look forward to those of the next.

Table 13.2 Shift of the start-up objectives throughout the life cycle

Objective	Proposal and initiation	Design and appraisal	Execution and control	Finalization and close-out
Context and objectives	Main	Review		Monitor
The project model	Draft	Main	Review	
The management approach		Draft	Main	Review
Commission and handover	Prepare		Draft	Main

Table 13.3 Fifteen subsidiary management objectives and their effect on the working of the team

Subsidiary objectives	Analyse	Plan	Communicate	Motivate
Context and objectives				
Impact of context	A		C	M
Business purpose	A	P		
Objectives of project		P	C	M
The project model				
Milestone plan	A	P		
Responsibility chart		P	C	M
Detailed work plans		P	C	M
Resource allocation		P	C	M
The management system				
Management system		P		
Principles of cooperation			C	M
Control processes		P	C	
Commission and handover				
Timely, efficient end		P	C	M
Disband team		P	C	M
Handover to client		P	C	
Obtain benefits		P	C	
Record data	A		C	

Below the four main objectives in Table 13.3 are fifteen subsidiary objectives. These in turn may influence the emphasis of the work of the project team depending on the type of activity and decisions undertaken. The emphasis of the team's work may be:

- *analysis* of the project's context, previous plans, future tasks, and management routines;
- *planning* of objectives, scope of work, organization and routines;
- *communication* between participants of the results of the analysis and plans;
- *motivation* of participants to carry out work or make decisions.

Table 13.3 relates the emphasis of the team's work to the fifteen subsidiary objectives. When linked to Table 13.2, this shows that during the life cycle the emphasis shifts from analysis and planning to communication and motivation until the end when it switches back to analysis, which will probably match the experience of most people.

Methods of start-up

Another requirement of a systematic approach to project start-up is the use of appropriate methods. There are three standard techniques:

- *holding project or stage launch workshops* where key people develop project plans in a joint team building process
- *developing a start-up or stage review report* which collates the results of the analysis undertaken during start-up or from a previous stage in accessible form for use during the subsequent stage
- *using ad-hoc assistance* from project management professionals.

These three techniques may be used individually or in combination. The choice depends on several factors. First, the different methods require varying amounts of time, so you must ensure that key team members are willing to devote that time; without it most methods will fail. Secondly, the methods have different efficacy in achieving the objectives in Tables 13.2 and 13.3. Table 13.4 shows the different impact of each method. Thirdly, through project start-up, you should try to build as much historical experience into the project definition as possible, to minimize the uncertainty. You should choose a method that does that for the case in hand.

A *launch workshop* held at the start of proposal and initiation is often called a *Project Definition Workshop*, and at the start of design or execution an *Initiation* or *Kick-off meeting*. The objectives of the workshop, the

Table 13.4 Effectiveness of the techniques for project start-up

Start-up technique	Analyse	Plan	Communicate	Motivate
Launch workshop	High	Medium	High	High
Review report	Low	High	High	Medium
Ad-hoc assistance	Medium	High	Low	Medium

agenda and the people invited depend on the stage being launched, and are discussed more fully in Section 13.6.

The *Start-up* or *Stage Review Report* is prepared at the end of one stage to launch the next. A report for launching proposal and initiation may be a one- or two-page *Project Scope Statement* (see Section 6.4 and Example 6.1). During the feasibility study, this is expanded into a Project Definition Report or Client Requirements Definition, used to launch design and appraisal. At the end of that stage, a full Project Manual or Project Requirements Definition may be produced in support of the design package, and that used to launch project execution. The contents of each of these reports depend on the stage being reviewed, and are described in Section 13.7.

Ad-hoc assistance may be from:

- internal professionals, such as the Project Support Office
- external consultants
- team members from similar (earlier) projects.

The advantage of this method is it provides additional resources with special skills, who may motivate key people. Having someone to share ideas with can be stimulating. A disadvantage is that there can be some confusion over responsibilities, which can lead to wasted effort.

Other methods of start-up include case studies, study tours, social events, education programme, and other media such as videos.

Scheduling start-up

A schedule of the start-up activities helps to focus attention on the process, and acts as a means of implementing the chosen techniques. The schedule may take the form of a responsibility chart (Figure 13.6) with both a definition of roles and responsibilities, and a time scale. The schedule for starting-up design and appraisal may be included in the Project Definition Report. A comprehensive checklist of items that may be included in the project start-up schedule is suggested by Archibald.[8]

PROJECT RESPONSIBILITY CHART

X – eXecutes the work
D – takes Decision solely
d – takes decision jointly
P – manages Progress
T – provides Tuition on the job
C – must be Consulted
I – must be Informed
A – available to Advise

Project:

Period: WEEK   Issue/Date: Approved by:

Work Cont H/D/W   1 2 3 4 5 6 7 8 9 10 11 12 13 14   No. Principle/Milestone name:

Companies/Departments/Functions/Type of resource

Principle/Milestone name	Environment	Purpose	Objectives	Work breakdown	Responsibilities	Detailed plans	Resource allocn	Pm system	Co-operation	Information	Steering cttee	Project manager	Project office	Participants	Consultants
Project description	O	●	●	●	●	●						DX	C	C	I
Definition workshop	O	O	O	O	O	O	O	O	O	O			PX	X	X	T
Draft issue of plan	●	O	O	O	O	O	●	●	●	●	●	I	PX	X	I
Meeting with consultants			O		O					O			PX	X	X	A
First issue of plan	●	●	●	●	●	●	O	O	O	O	O	I	PX	X	I
Invitations to start-up W/S														X
Start-up workshop														
· Part 1	●	●	●	●	●	●	O	O				DX	PX	X	X	T
· Part 2	O	O	O	O	O	O	●	●	●	●	●	DX	PX	X	X	T
Final editing of plan	●	●	●	●	●	●	●	●	●	●		I	PX	X	I
Approval of plan	●	●	●	●	●	●	O	O	O	O	O	D	P	I	I
Issue of definition report	●	●	●	●	●	●	●	●	●	●		D	PX	X	C

● Main issue
O Subsidiary issue

Figure 13.6 Responsibility chart used as a start-up schedule

13.3 Proposal and initiation[9]

The first stage of the life cycle is proposal and initiation, which deals with the definition of the project and its context (Table 13.2). Although the majority of a project's expenditure occurs in execution and control, the greatest influence over cost is during proposal and initiation. Decisions made here have a lasting impact on later expenditure (Figure 13.7). Hence, although only 0.1 per cent of costs may be incurred during proposal and initiation (Table 9.4), perhaps 90 per cent of the expenditure has actually been determined by the end of this stage. The ability to influence cost falls off rapidly during the design stage, so changes made later are impossible to implement without incurring considerable additional cost. This is the relationship between the life cycle and the risk and quality described in Chapters 8 and 11. Proposal and initiation form the key to the later success of the project. We secure the foundation of this success by:

- setting project objectives and scope
- developing the project model at the integrative level
- defining the project organization.

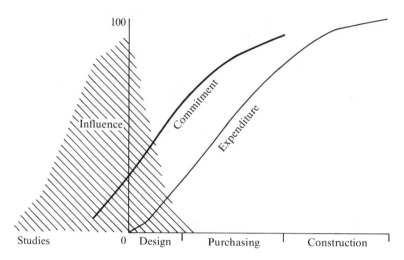

Figure 13.7 The time at which the out-turn cost of a project is set, and the ability to influence it

Setting project objectives and scope

The setting of clear, unambiguous objectives is the key to success; little progress can be made until this is done. The objectives and initial definition of the scope can be developed through the process described in Section 6.4. Section 4.2 described how people have covert objectives that differ from the stated purpose. Even the sponsor may have a hidden agenda. Hence the interpretation of the sponsor's ambitions is unlikely to be the subject of unanimous or even objective judgement. This makes this first step particularly difficult, and means it must be done in a way that leaves little margin for misunderstanding. The Project Definition Workshop (Section 13.6) is a powerful medium for flushing out covert objectives (see Example 4.1).

Developing the project model at the integrative level

Having defined the project's objectives, we can set constraints for its cost and duration, and the performance of the facility. The purpose indicates parameters for the facility's value and the time window in which it has that value, and from these we determine the maximum cost and latest completion date of the project. The value of the facility depends on the completion date: the later the completion, the lower the value (as calculated at the start of the project), as shown in Figure 13.8. The decrease in

Value

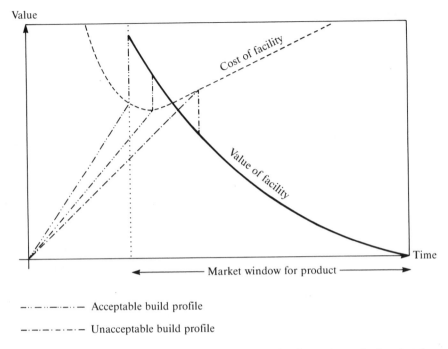

—··—··—··—··— Acceptable build profile

—·—·—·—·—·— Unacceptable build profile

Figure 13.8   Present value of the facility produced by the project calculated at the start of the project as a function of completion date

value represents two things: revenues from the facility having lower present value; and lost revenue if the product has only a limited life. This decrease may allow several build programmes, with a minimum achieved in some optimum time window (Figure 12.2). Three build programmes are illustrated in Figure 13.8. There may be some indication at this stage whether these times and costs are realistic for achieving the objectives set, but it is not until the feasibility study is completed that you can begin to match the costs to the definition of the work to be done.

Defining the project organization

The owner will also begin to consider the source of the resources for the project: whether internal or external contractors, the type of project organization to be adopted (Section 7.3) and a possible project manager. It is better to appoint the project manager early in this process, because that person will be more committed to the project strategy if he or she is involved in determining it. This is a very extensive area, and is best achieved using responsibility charts (Section 7.4). Remember that the process of project organization is one of negotiation, winning people's commitment to the project by demonstrating that it can be of benefit to them.

13.4 Conducting a feasibility study[10]

Much of the above work takes place at the start of proposal and initiation, and leads to an initial proposal, corresponding to the first line in Table 9.4 (p. 185). To develop a full proposal, to initiate the project and so commit resources to systems design, it is necessary to develop the definition further, and refine estimates to the level implied by the second line in Table 9.4. This is done through a feasibility study, which occupies the remainder of the stage. It is during the feasibility study that the range of possible options is examined, and potential issues identified. The aim is to narrow the range of options, provide an assessment of each one remaining, and propose solutions to issues confronting the project. This section will describe the objectives of the feasibility study and the factors that should be addressed. It will also describe how to set up the study, manage it and bring it to a successful conclusion.

Aims of the feasibility study

Feasibility studies involve time and money, and so it is essential that they are well managed. By understanding the aims of the study and the criteria for its success we can focus effort on its key aspects. The objectives of the study will be specific to the project, but should be based broadly on the following considerations:

- exploring all possible options for implementing the project
- achieving a clear understanding of the issues involved
- producing enough information to be able to rank the options
- obtaining a clear picture of the way forward.

THE OPTIONS

As many ideas as possible should be explored to render the best solution. Each option should be thoroughly reviewed to determine whether it can be improved, within the limitations of market and technical conditions. The original specification should act as a guide to the extent of the study, but it should not stifle imagination and creativity.

THE ISSUES

The feasibility study must give a clear understanding of the issues involved. In particular, associated with each option still being considered should be: estimates of costs and revenues; an understanding of the views and objectives of the various sponsors and institutions involved; confirmation of both technical and financial viability; and estimates of the likely economic and financial returns, as described above.

RANKING THE OPTIONS

The study should produce enough information to rank options. The criteria used are based on the strategic factors, described above. Their weighting in the overall ranking of options depends on the sponsor's goals; the public sector will usually give more weight to social and environmental factors than the private sector (Section 3.4).

THE WAY FORWARD

The study should result in a clear idea of future stages. It helps to think of the feasibility study as a funnelling and filtering exercise, directing a wide range of possible ideas into a much narrower range of options, with those which clearly fail to meet objectives sifted out. The study should aim to provide for the next stage – design and appraisal – both a new, refined specification and a work plan. It may also result in a draft plan for the design or execution stages (Example 13.1).

I worked on a three-month feasibility study to assess the efficacy of a new process in the petrochemical industry. We launched the feasibility study with a two-week workshop. At the end of that workshop we had a clear objective for the feasibility study, but we had produced no plan, not even at the strategic level, for the feasibility study or the year-long systems design stage that followed. The first plan produced was at the end of that year, for the detailed design and construction of the plant.

Example 13.1 Produce a clear definition of the way forward

The factors addressed

The study must provide an understanding of factors influencing success, and assess the advantages and disadvantages of each option to enable them to be ranked. The following factors influence the feasibility of the project.

MARKET CONDITIONS

Expectation of returns depends on satisfying demand for the project's product at a certain price level. Usually neither future demand nor future prices can be predicted very accurately. If there is a limited portfolio of potential buyers, or the market is volatile, or demand is price-sensitive (as with commodity products), the project is vulnerable to many adverse circumstances over which the project manager has little influence. However, the existing market environment provides a wealth of information on which to base sales forecasts, establish price structures, understand potential purchasers and consumers, evaluate expected trends in demand and the actions of potential competitors, learn about the expected quality of the product or service, and assess a range of other information.

SUPPLY CONSIDERATIONS

Existing supply conditions are also important sources of information. The feasibility study should assess the cost, quality and availability of capital equipment, raw materials and labour of the required skill levels. Different technical options should also be explored, and specialist technical advice obtained on their feasibility.

FINANCIAL PROSPECTS

The profitability of the project can be analysed by applying economic evaluation techniques (Section 3.4). The financial feasibility also depends on whether the expected return from a project is sufficient to finance debt and provide shareholders with an adequate return to compensate them for their risk. Financial feasibility is influenced by economic conditions such as interest and exchange rates prevailing when costs are incurred and income received. The approach differs for projects in the private or public sector. The latter often take account of non-monetary benefits and costs, as well as factors such as environmental impact. Shadow prices are used where the market price is considered not to reflect the economic cost or benefit of an input or output of the project. The private sector usually places more weight on purely monetary return, although legislation, tax benefits or subsidy, and public relations considerations may encourage it to place value on non-monetary factors.

Adequate consideration must be given to risk and uncertainty (Chapter 11). Risk and uncertainty cannot be eliminated, but they can be managed and reduced by prudent project design and management, and taken into account in comparison of project options. You should also remember that the shareholders' evaluation of the project, and hence the share price of the company, depends on their assessment of the risk.

Initiating the study

There are five steps to setting up a feasibility study:

1. Appoint an experienced manager and management team. The make-up of the team depends on the nature of the project. For the feasibility study, the team should include technical, financial and marketing expertise, and for larger projects may also have economists, legal and environmental experts, human resources experts, etc. It is essential that a good balance is struck between specialists, as assessment of the options may be biased if one specialism dominates. For example, if technical experts dominate, they may emphasize technically exciting options that may not provide the required financial return. It is often helpful to limit the size of the core management team, as far as the size of the project allows. Compact teams are usually easier to organize and coordinate than larger groups. The manager of the study will usually not be the project manager for subsequent stages. However, it is usually a good idea for the latter to be a member of the management team for the study, and thus have greater ownership and commitment to the results of the study, the decisions made and the strategy set.
2. Examine the scope of the study to assess the work involved and any constraints imposed (quality, cost, time, etc). The manager must determine exactly what the decision makers require to guide them in their choice of the project options, and in what form the information is needed. A work plan with the delivery time and content of interim and final reports should as far as possible be agreed in advance with decision makers.
3. Appoint external advisers, if required, to supplement the expertise of the core team in specific areas. It might also be necessary to obtain certain permission and consents, if only on a provisional basis. It would be prudent, for example, to obtain outline planning permission for any construction work envisaged in the project.
4. Draw up a plan for the study, including a milestone plan and responsibility chart. The milestone plan should pin-point steps through which the study must pass (interim and final reports, meetings, data collection, etc.), and on what dates. The plan can highlight different lines of enquiry involved and their interdependence, enabling the different aspects of the study to be coordinated. It should be robust, but sufficiently flexible to cope with any unexpected changes. Adequate allowance

should be made for the time required to request and collect data as well as processing and interpreting results.
5. Set the timetable and budget for the study. These must be sufficient to enable options to be properly explored and refined, without endangering the feasibility of the whole project. It is important to budget for an adequate exploration of the options without going to the depth of investigation required for the design and appraisal stage.

The Project Definition Workshop (Section 13.6) can be used to undertake steps 4 and 5 in particular, as well as developing the initial project definition and strategy.

Managing the study

Once it has been adequately planned, there are three main elements to managing the feasibility study:

1. *Organization* This involves the adoption of a clearly focused but flexible structure based around the milestone plan. The team should be aware of what is expected, and by when. They should understand how they fit into the study framework and to whom they need to report results and problems. Hence, roles and responsibilities must be clearly defined. The responsibility chart is the tool that effectively achieves this.
2. *Implementation* This requires efficient communications within the study team. The manager should maintain frequent contact with sponsors to ensure that the study remains on target and that any change in decision-makers' goals is identified. The team should maintain good internal communications to ensure that delays are reported to minimize any knock-on effect, to avoid duplication, and to confirm that all information received has been made available to all members of the team. It is particularly important that good communication is maintained between team members in different fields of expertise to ensure that any interdependencies are taken into account.
3. *Control* This is the responsibility of the manager who must ensure that milestones are being reached on time, and that the milestones adopted lead to punctual report delivery. Likewise, costs should be monitored to ensure that the study remains within budget. Control involves both monitoring of timing and budgets, and rapid and effective corrective action when targets are not met, either by revising targets or by restructuring present plans within the existing targets.

The detail of how work is assigned to people and their progress monitored and controlled, during the feasibility study or any other stage, will be postponed until the discussion on execution and control in later chapters.

Completing the study and transition to the next stage

The feasibility study should act as a spring-board for design and appraisal, ensuring that it is able to commence in a focused way. The end product should therefore comprise a clear, concise report, the Project Definition Report (Section 13.7), which presents the original specification and objectives, with the conclusions and recommendations for use in the next stage. The report should highlight advantages and disadvantages – cost, revenue, strategic considerations, economic benefits, etc. – for each of the options that deserve further consideration and the proposed solutions to issues confronting the project. Furthermore, the report should indicate sensitivities to variations from the assumed base case.

13.5 Design and appraisal[11]

The second stage of the life cycle is 'design and appraisal'. The primary emphasis in this stage is the development of the project model shown in Table 13.3. The original outline requirements, as expressed by the client in the Project Definition Report, are subjected to more rigorous examination to define exactly what is to be done to achieve the project's objectives. A systems design is developed for the facility, the product it will produce, and the method of building it. This last defines the scope of work for the project at the strategic level (Chapter 6). The project organization is developed at that level, and roles and responsibilities of departments, functions, disciplines, or their managers, are described (see Chapter 7). The quality specification, the cost of the project, the time scale and the risk are all planned and estimated at the corresponding level of detail, as in Chapters 8, 9, 10 and 11. From this information we determine whether or not the project is viable and represents a good investment at the level of refinement implied by the third line in Table 9.4 (p. 185). This appraisal process is vital, as it is the last chance the sponsor has to decide whether to proceed with the project before committing scarce resources to execution (cf. Figures 13.1 and 13.7). Many of the issues investigated in design are the same as in the feasibility study, but at a lower level of detail. We shall not repeat the discussion of what is investigated, but focus on the special management problems arising in the design and appraisal process.

The design is developed at several levels of the project and stages of the life cycle. It is common to show the life cycle as a serial process, beginning with feasibility and continuing through design and construction, until the facility is commissioned and producing the desired output. Most of the life cycles described in Chapter 2 and in Part 6 follow this model.

However, the reality of most projects is different. Design in particular is an iterative process, proceeding through several levels, as our understanding is refined. It has already been shown that there are at least four levels, corresponding to the first four lines of Table 9.4:

- outline requirements
- functional design
- systems design
- detail design.

At each level, the designs must be checked back to the assumptions set in the project's strategy. Even at one level, there may be several iterations, as the design proceeds through several formats. In ship-building, the paper design is converted into a plastic model, then into a wooden model from which fabrication jigs are made, before the first vessel of the class is made. The ship is thus made four times before it is completed: once in paper (design), plastic (scale model) and in wood (full scale model); and then the first time in metal. The design process is therefore not a single activity, but a set of activities ranging from the outline requirements to the detail design, and these cover all the stages of the life cycle. The computer industry has developed a spiral model of the life cycle (see Section 20.4) which reflects the reality of the design process, and perhaps has applications elsewhere.

The concerns of the project manager during the design process include:

- managing the urgency
- managing the designers
- managing the user
- design, estimation and risk
- managing the appraisal process.

Managing the urgency

There is often a tendency to try to shorten the design process to begin work on a project. In Chapter 2 it was stated that people may tend to jump from perceiving a problem to selecting a solution, or worse to implementing one. They then never truly determine the cause of the problem or the best method of solving it; they do little more than paper over cracks. It is always important to put adequate time and effort into the design process, and the way to ensure this is to have a proper project plan for the design stage, which measures the progress of the design towards completion against a series of milestones. Those people who are keen to begin execution can then follow this plan and progress their work accordingly.

There can also be a tendency to overlap implementation and design to make better use of available skilled resources. This is what was described in Section 5.4 as *fast build, fast track* or *concurrency*, which are associated with increasing risk. The importance of allowing the design stage to take its course cannot be overemphasized. However, we shall now see that the project manager must guard against the opposing risk, namely the desire of the designers to develop the ideal solution or prolong the design period because of the inherent job interest it offers.

Managing the designers

Design is a creative skill, and designers may argue that creativity cannot be rushed. Whether this is true or not for a given project needs to be judged by the manager. To a certain extent, design depends as much on inspiration as on effort. However, to be of value, the facility must be obtained by a certain time (Figure 13.7) and so the creative process must be managed. There is a continual balance between doing the job well, and doing it within a time that is worth while. Again a thorough plan for the design process, with measurable milestones, provides a framework for monitoring achievement of the design. However, it is better to spend a little longer in design to get an optimum solution, than to spend money correcting mistakes during execution.

Designers are also in a better position than anyone to incorporate their covert objectives into the project definition. This highlights the need for thorough quality control of the design process, with clear specifications and thorough design reviews (refer to Chapter 8 on quality and Chapter 16 on configuration management).

Highly complex projects may need teams of designers. The increased number of interfaces increases the complexity of the design process and can weaken the manager's ability to control quality, cost and time. Where a multi-disciplinary team operates there is the potential for a difference of opinion between team members, creating the need for arbitration which is fair, but does not demoralize or demotivate the team.

It may be necessary to allow the project team access to designers during execution, so they can question the assumptions. However, this must be balanced against the cost of keeping designers on the project beyond the completion of their work. It is common for designers to remain throughout the execution process, to deal with technical problems and design changes as they arise. This is the case on fast track or concurrent build, where changes during construction are expected. However, the devil makes work for idle hands, and designers often tinker with their designs, making small 'improvements'. Although these changes may be technically correct, they can cause the costs to escalate. It is actually better to transfer the designers to a new project, and create a system that allows them to be returned quickly, if necessary, to the project in construction.

Managing the user

Throughout design, designer, client and end user must remain in close dialogue to ensure that the design meets the user's needs. This has been stated (Chapter 8) to be the ultimate measure of quality. However, it is important that the designer and user are not allowed to change the requirements so frequently that no progress is made. Managing the user is vital. The challenge is to ensure that essential changes are incorporated, but that 'nice to haves' are avoided. Many people suggest freezing user requirements at an early stage. However, that can lead to ineffective solutions, as the process of designing the facility and its product can help to clarify user requirements (see Section 20.4). What is actually needed is the application of effective change control to enable the design to move steadily forward until a viable design is produced that also meets the user's needs.

Design, estimation and risk

As the design develops, it is possible to refine estimates of cost and time. This is because they can be gauged with greater certainty once the detail is confirmed. When the cost of delivering the facility as designed is estimated, reference should be made to the risks set out in the Project Definition Report, to ensure that adequate emphasis is given to them. As risks are avoided, then contingency can be released, either to be removed from the estimate, or to allow for problems elsewhere. Referring to records of similar projects is a good way of checking the estimates. Similarly, seeking a second opinion or comparing estimates with those from other suppliers (if the project is subject to tender procedure) may be beneficial.

Managing the appraisal process

Appraisal is the process by which the viability of the project is finally checked before money is committed to its implementation. If the appraisal process results in approval for the project, the sponsor gives authority for the project to proceed and raises finance for it. The appraisal of the project is based on many of the issues identified in the feasibility study, and the methods of analysis outlined in Section 3.4. The project may be compared against quantitative criteria: first, that it meets certain minimum investment criteria; and, secondly, that it compares favourably with other projects competing for the same scarce finance. However, it may also be compared against qualitative criteria, such as its impact on the business, its impact on the environment, and its popularity with the stakeholders.

At this stage, it is important to perform a thorough analysis of the risk so that appropriate risk reduction measures can be implemented (Chapter 11). It can also be useful to appoint an independent team to audit the risk, as the people who have performed the design and undertaken the initial appraisal may be too close to the project to take a dispassionate view. They may be just unable to see the obvious risks. The team of auditors may be external consultants, or a separate team of internal designers who have not been involved with the project to date. The latter may be preferable – see Example 8.2.

13.6 Initiation, launch and kick-off meetings

Launch workshops were introduced in Section 13.2 as a way of initiating the current stage. Indeed, mini workshops may be held at the start of work packages, in accordance with the rolling-wave principle. A workshop held at the start of proposal and initiation is called a *Project Definition Workshop*, and at the start of design and appraisal a *design initiation* or *kick-off meeting*. (A similar meeting, a project initiation meeting, may be held at the start of execution and control.) In this section, the objectives, attendees, agenda and timetable of these workshops will be described.

Workshop objectives

The main objectives of the workshop are given below.

1. *Gain commitment and build team spirit*   This is the primary objective of a workshop. Many of the others can be achieved by people working alone or meeting in smaller groups. By coming together, they may develop a common understanding, and resolve items of confusion, disagreement, or conflict through discussion. If people are briefed after a meeting (presented with a *fait accompli*), they may nod their heads in agreement, but you often find they do not truly accept what they are told. If people agree to a course of action in a meeting, you usually find they have internalized that agreement, but if they have not, it is difficult for them to avoid their commitments later because several people have witnessed them.

2. *Ratify earlier project definition*   Whatever stage is being launched, it is vital for the team to agree on what the current level of definition entails, and that it represents a true interpretation of the user's requirements.
3. *Plan the current stage*   The workshop is used to launch the current stage, and so producing a plan for the stage is a key objective. This should consist of a milestone plan and responsibility chart at a minimum.
4. *Prepare preliminary plans for execution*   It is usually worth while to prepare a draft milestone plan for execution, as this can be a useful basis for the feasibility study or design, even if the subsequent project follows a slightly different course.
5. *Prepare preliminary estimates*   These give the project team some idea of the expectation of the cost and benefit of the project. Although their subsequent work should not be constrained by the estimates, they can help to set the basic parameters.
6. *Start work promptly*   The workshop should be used to plan the initial work of the current stage, so that the team members can made a prompt start.
7. *Agree a date for reviewing the stage deliverables*   Ideally the plan should contain a time scale and budget for the stage. An end date, at least, should be set for completion of the stage, to ensure that it does not remain open ended.

Workshop attendees

The workshops should be attended by key managers, including:

- the project sponsor and champion
- the manager of the current stage
- the manager designate of future stages, especially execution
- key functional managers whose groups are impacted by the project, including technical managers, user managers, and resource providers
- a Project Support Office manager
- a facilitator.

The sponsor may attend the Project Definition Workshop, but is unlikely to attend later ones. Possible attendees for a Project Definition Workshop on the CRMO Rationalization Project are given in Example 13.2.

The *sponsor* may be a main board director or regional managing director.
The *champion* may be the regional managing director, the operations director, the financial director or the technical director.
The *manager of the feasibility study* may be the champion.
The *project manager designate* may be the customer services manager, the network manager or the IT manager.
Key *functional managers* will include these three: the estates manager, the finance manager, and the sales and marketing manager.
There may already be a *Project Support Office* in the IT or Networks Department, otherwise a field Planning Office could fulfil the role.

Example 13.2   Project Definiton Workshop attendees for the CRMO Rationalization Project

Workshop agenda

A typical agenda for a workshop is:

1. Review the current project definition.
2. Define the objectives of the current stage.
3. Develop solutions and criteria for evaluation.
4. Assess risks and assumptions.
5. Prepare a milestone plan for the current stage.
6. Prepare a responsibility chart against the plan.
7. Estimate work content and durations for the work packages.
8. Schedule the work packages.
9. Prepare initial activity schedules.
10. Prepare a management and control plan.

Most effort usually goes into the milestone plan and responsibility chart, as they provide the most effective use of group working. Sections 6.5 and 7.4 described how to develop these systems using whiteboards, flip charts, Post-Its, and an overhead projector. Involving everyone present around a whiteboard, gains their commitment to the plans produced. Working around a table with pen and paper can isolate members of the team from the working process. Estimates and schedules are best agreed through a process of negotiation immediately after the workshop. The initial activity schedules are prepared so that the team members know what to do immediately following the meeting; it is an initiation meeting (Example 13.1). The management and control plan agrees the approach to be used in managing the project and the mechanisms, priorities and frequency of the control process. It may be the basis of the management approach outlined in the Project Manual.

Workshop timetable

A workshop typically lasts one to four days. I usually allow two hours per item, except items 5 and 6 above for which I allow four hours. However, it is important not to stick rigidly to a timetable, but to allow discussion to come to a natural conclusion, as people reach agreement and a common understanding. I sometimes include project management training as part of the timetable, which extends the duration by about a day. It is useful to schedule a break in the middle of agenda item 5. When developing a milestone plan, people often reach a blank; the plan will just not make sense. However, when left for a while, it just seems to fall into place.

13.7 Project Definition Report and Manual[12]

Section 13.2 introduced the Start-up or Stage Review Report, which gathers the results from the work of one stage, and is used to launch the next stage. The report produced at the end of proposal and initiation is called the Project Definition Report, and that at the end of design and appraisal the Project Manual. In this section I shall describe the objectives and content of these two reports.

Objectives of the Project Definition Report

The Project Definition Report, sometimes called the Client's Requirements Definition or Statement of User Requirements, gathers the results of the feasibility study into a readily accessible document. It is a handbook for the management, design and execution teams, which defines what the owner expects from the project, and the reasoning behind the chosen options and strategies. This reasoning can always be open to question. It is healthy that the teams involved in later stages question earlier decisions. However, by having earlier reasoning recorded, the project teams can avoid repeating work and, more importantly, avoid following previous blind alleys. The Project Definition Report will also be used to launch design and appraisal, and may be the input to a kick-off meeting at the start of that stage. Hence, the objectives of the Project Definition Report are:

– to provide sufficient definition, including costs and benefits, to allow the business to commit resources to design and appraisal
– to provide a basis for design and appraisal
– to provide senior management with an overview of the project's priority alongside day-to-day operations and other projects (both proposed and on-going)

- to communicate the project's requirements throughout the business
- to define the commitment of the business to the project.

Most of these objectives look forward; the report is not produced as a bureaucratic exercise to record the feasibility study, but as a basis for the future stages.

Contents of the Project Definition Report

The suggested contents of the report are:

1. *Preface*: outlines the objectives of the document, as described above.
2. *Management summary*: a one-page summary for senior managers.
3. *Background*: sets the context of the project as it exists, and may describe the purpose of the higher level programme of which the project is a part.
4. *Purpose, scope and objectives*: the reason for undertaking the project, with expected returns, the sort of work needed to achieve that, and the product to be produced by the project in order to achieve the returns.
5. *Work breakdown structure*: initiates work breakdown, stating the areas of work and including a milestone plan. A target schedule may also be included.
6. *Project organization*: defines the type of project organization, including:

   - organizational units within the business involved in the project
   - their involvement in different areas of work
   - managerial responsibility for different areas of work
   - the type of project organization to be used
   - the location of project resources
   - the source of the project manager
   - the source and limits of authority of the project manager

   and describes the responsibilities of key managers and groups in the business, including:

   - project sponsor, champion and manager
   - work area and work-package managers
   - project steering board
   - quality assurance board and Project Support Office manager.

It may be necessary to include a tentative resource schedule, so the project can be assigned priority. This schedule is derived from high level assumptions, applied to areas of work or work packages. It should not be based on a detailed definition of work, except in areas of high risk, because that requires an investment in planning resource before the business has agreed to commit it.

7. *Project management system*: defines the tools and techniques for planning and controlling the project, and supporting computer systems. This may include preliminary quality plans and control procedures.
8. *Risks and assumptions*: stated for future reference, and to allow adequate account to be taken in the investment appraisal.
9. *Project budgets*: the initial estimates for the project, and a statement of the maximum amount that can be spent to justify the expected benefits.
10. *Project justification*: an investment appraisal performed using the estimates as they exist, against defined investment criteria. This will justify the commitment of resources to the design and appraisal stage.
11. *Appendices*: contain many of the preliminary plans.

Example 6.1 contains items 3, 4 and part of 5 for the CRMO Rationalization Project. Item 5 may include a milestone plan for later stages, and work-package scope statements (Example 6.3). Item 6 will be partly descriptive, but may include a responsibility chart. Item 7 may also include responsibility charts, such as that in Figure 7.9, and a recommendation of how to use a computer-based project management information system. Part Five of this book covers the contents of item 7.

The report is typically 10 to 40 pages long, depending on the size and complexity of the project, and its impact on the organization. It is developed throughout proposal and initiation. However, once ratified by senior management at the end of that stage, it should be sacrosanct, and only modified by formal change control.

Objectives of the Project Manual

The results of design and appraisal are recorded in a Project Manual. This is a definitive document which explains how the owner's requirements set out in the Project Definition Report are to be delivered by describing the objectives, scope and management strategy for the project as they are defined at the end of the stage. It is used as the briefing document for all people joining the project team in execution and control.

The manual is developed progressively by the project manager from the Project Definition Report throughout design and appraisal. The draft manual is reviewed by the owner and project manager together, until it is signed off at the end of the stage as reflecting their mutual understanding of how the owner's requirements are to be delivered. When the manual is signed off, the project manager must accept responsibility for delivering the project as defined in the manual, and from that point on changes to the manual can only be made through strict change control. The development of the Project Manual, and the master plan it includes, often represents the largest proportion of the project manager's efforts during design after the management of the actual design process itself.

Throughout execution and control, the manual is extended down to the work-package level, as part of the start-up of individual work packages. The manuals at the work package level must be derived from the Project Manual, but they may highlight the need for modifying the Project Manual.

Contents of the Project Manual

The contents of the manual may include the following items:

1. *Project description and objectives*: summarizes the Project Definition Report, as modified by the design and appraisal process (Example 13.3).

I had a discussion with managers attending a course at Henley Management College about whether the manual would contain the Definition Report in its entirety, or whether it would be summarized into a single section as a background. We decided on the latter for two reasons. First, it is the job of management to summarize the instructions from the level above when passing them on to the level below, so the next level down can focus on those things that enable them to do their jobs effectively. You inform people on the next level on a 'need to know' basis. This does not mean you need to be excessively secretive. You tell the next level enough to motivate them, and make them feel part of the overall management team, without overburdening them with unnecessary information. Secondly, taken to the extreme, you would include the entire corporate plans in the briefing documents to every project.

Example 13.3   Summarizing the Project Definition Report in the Project Manual

2. *Master project plan*: forms the major part of the manual. The design and appraisal process will result in this master plan for the project at the strategic level. The contents of this plan, which cover the definition of scope, organization, quality, cost and time in the project model, are summarized in Table 2.4 (p. 28).
3. *Management plan*: describes how the project is to be planned, organized, implemented and controlled, although the first two of these will now only need to be done at lower levels of work breakdown.
4. *Performance specification*: defines the required levels of performance of the facility and its product. This is one of the major elements of the

quality specification of the project, and will have been developed and refined during the design process.

5. *Technical specification*: explains the technology to be used in the development of the facility, and how that will function to deliver the required output.

6. *Acceptance tests and acceptance criteria*: are derived from the previous two, and form an important part of the manual. They must be defined before work starts for two reasons: (a) they must be independent – that is, the project team members must not be allowed to develop testing procedures which match the facility built; (b) the project team must know how they are to be judged if they are to deliver a quality product. In Chapter 8, quality was defined as meeting customer's requirements. These must be defined in advance so that the team members know what their objective is, and they do not produce a product that is either *over*- or *under*-specified.

7. *Project constraints*: are derived throughout the first two stages, and so must be recorded for all people joining the project at a later date.

8. *Risks and assumptions*: must also be recorded for two reasons. So people joining the project later know what has been addressed, and so others, especially owners, sponsors, financiers and auditors, can see they have been properly addressed and that adequate weight has been given to them.

Many cover or result from topics discussed at the design initiation meeting. It is to be expected that the meeting initiates the preparation of the manual, and will lay the foundation for it. Fangel[4] gives the contents of a manual for a project to electrify the Danish railways. The manual is the document that initiates execution and control.

13.8 Summary

1. Part Four follows a four-stage cycle:
   - proposal and initiation
   - design and appraisal
   - execution and control
   - finalization and closure.
2. There are four stages of team formation:
   - forming
   - storming
   - norming
   - performing

3. Project start-up is a structured way to moving the project team quickly and effectively through these four stages, so as to:
   - define the project's context and objectives
   - develop the project model
   - define the management approach
   - commission the facility and hand it over.
4. The methods of project start-up include:
   - stage launch workshops
   - start-up reports
   - ad-hoc assistance.
5. The foundation of the success of the project is secured during the proposal and initiation stage by:
   - setting project objectives and scope
   - developing the project model at the integrative level
   - defining the project organization.
6. A feasibility study is an initial study into the solutions for achieving the project and has four objectives:
   - to explore all options
   - to understand all the issues
   - to rank the options
   - to plan the way forward.
7. The feasibility study will address the following issues:
   - market conditions
   - supply considerations
   - financial prospects.
8. The concerns of the manager during the design process include:
   - managing the urgency
   - managing the designers
   - managing the user
   - design, estimation and risk
   - managing the appraisal process.
9. Appraisal is the process by which the viability of the project is finally checked, and is the last chance to stop the project before significant amounts of money are spent on its delivery.
10. A stage launch workshop may be held with the objectives:
    - to gain commitment and build the team spirit
    - to ratify the project definition as produced in the previous stage
    - to plan the current stage of the project
    - to prepare preliminary plans for the execution stage
    - to prepare preliminary estimates for the project
    - to ensure that work starts promptly
    - to agree a date for review of the stage deliverables.

11. A Project Definition Report may be prepared with the objectives:
    - to commit resources to design
    - to provide a basis for design
    - to set the project's priority
    - to inform all those effected by the project
    - to gain commitment.
12. The contents of the report may include:
    - backgound
    - purpose, scope and objectives
    - work breakdown structure
    - project organization
    - project management system
    - risks and assumptions
    - project budgets
    - project justification.
13. The systems design produced during the design and appraisal stage may be summarized in a Project Manual, which may have as its contents:
    - project description and objectives
    - master project plan
    - management plan
    - performance specification
    - technical specification
    - acceptance tests and criteria for acceptance
    - project constraints
    - risks and assumptions.

Notes and references

1. Morris, P. W. G., 'Interface management: an organisational theory approach to project management', *Project Management Quarterly*, **10** (2), June 1979.
2. The material of Section 13.2 is derived from the work of the INTERNET Committee for Project Start-up, and especially Morten Fangel, its chairman (Fangel, 1987). Mr Fangel is a consultant in project management based in Copenhagen, and is currently President of INTERNET, the International Association of Project Managers.
3. Handy, C., *Understanding Organisations*, Penguin, 1986.
4. Fangel, M. (ed.), *Handbook of Project Start-up: How to launch projects effectively*, INTERNET, 1987.
5. Fangel, M., 'The essence of project start-up: the concept, timing, results, methods, schedule and application', in *Handbook of Project Start-up: How to launch projects effectively* (ed. M. Fangel), INTERNET, 1987.
6. Fangel, M., 'To start or to start-up?' That is the key question of project initiation', *International Journal of Project Management*, **9** (1), 1991.

7. Andersen, E. S., Grude, K. V., Haug, T. and Turner, J. R., *Goal Directed Project Management*, Kogan Page, 1987.
8. Archibald, R. D., *Managing High-Technology Programs and Projects*, Wiley, 1976.
9. Section 13.3 incorporates material written by John Dingle.
10. Section 13.4 incorporates material written by Nick Aked and Roger Sharp. Messrs Aked and Sharp are consultants with Coopers & Lybrand, and work in the area of economic assessment of infrastructure projects.
11. Section 13.5 incorporates material written by Mahen Tampoe.
12. Section 13.7 incorporates material written by Paddy Lewis and Martin Samphire. Messrs Lewis and Samphire work for Nichols Associates, Project Management Consultants.

14
Execution and control

14.1 Introduction

The third stage of the life cycle is execution and control. During this stage, the majority of the work to deliver the objectives (build the facility) is undertaken, and thus the majority of the expenditure committed. The stage is started by the completion of the detail design. At the previous stage, sufficient design (a systems design) has been done to prove the concept, and obtain financing for the project. The detail design shows how the work of the project will be implemented, and from this a cost estimate corresponding to the fourth line of Table 9.4 (p. 185) is developed. A corresponding project plan is also produced. This plan and design may require three or four times as much effort as the systems design developed at the previous stage, but it is only done after the project has been proved and the finance raised. Once sufficient design has been done, work can begin. If fast build or fast track is possible, this may be before the detail design is complete. Resources are selected, and they plan the detail work on a rolling-wave basis. Work is authorized by the project manager, and allocated to teams or individuals. As work is done, progress is measured to ensure that the desired results are achieved; that is, the required facility is delivered within the constraints of quality, cost and time, and that this will achieve the required benefit. If there is a shortfall, appropriate recovery action is taken. This may mean doing nothing because the variances are small, replanning the work to recover the original plan, or revising the plan to accept the current situation. *In extremis*, it may mean terminating the project, if the original objectives are unobtainable.

In this chapter, I shall describe the management of execution and control and explain the selection of resources, implementation planning, and the allocation of work. I shall then describe the requirements for effective control, how to monitor progress and analyse variances to forecast completion of all five project objectives, and how to take action to respond to deviations from plan. The chapter ends with a description of an integrated control cycle. I said in the last chapter that this control cycle applies to the management of feasibility, and design and appraisal. It is described here because it is the major emphasis of this stage. I shall not describe the detail design process, as it is merely a refinement of what was covered in Chapter 13.

14.2 Resourcing a project

One of the recurrent questions of project management is: 'Do you assign work to people or people to work?' In one approach – assigning work to people – you form a project team, decide what work needs to be done and assign it to the people in the team. There is a risk that you may find the skills of the people in the team to be inappropriate for the task. In the other approach – assigning people to work – you define the scope of work and then form a project team of appropriate skills. In this case there is a risk that the project manager will not be a technical expert, and so will be dictating to experts how they should undertake the task.

To overcome this dilemma, you develop the definition of scope and organization in parallel down the project hierarchy (Figure 2.5). During proposal and initiation, you define the areas of work and the functional areas of the organization involved in the project (Sections 13.3, 6.4 and 7.3). During design and appraisal, you work with functional managers to develop the milestone plan and responsibility chart at the strategic level (Sections 13.5, 6.5 and 7.4). From the responsibility chart you determine the skill types required and form a project team. The team determine how they think the work should be done, and so define the scope at the tactical level. The project manager and work-package manager agree and authorize the work and assign it to the team. Hence, the people to do the work are selected from a resource pool, which is identified by planning the work at the strategic level in the project hierarchy.

The process of resourcing a project includes the following steps:

1. *Identify what is to be achieved*   That is done through the milestone plan and project responsibility chart.
2. *Identify the skills and skill types required*   From the milestone plan and project responsibility chart you can identify the skills and skill types required to do the work. They include technical skills, craft skills, professional skills, functional skills and managerial knowledge.
3. *Identify the people available*   The manager identifies the people available with the resource providers. It is important to obtain people with the correct skills. There is a danger, especially with a fixed project team, of selecting people to do work because they are available, not because they have the right skills. There is also a danger that the resource pro-

viders may try to provide their least competent people to the project team, and retain their best individuals within their own sphere. You should take account of people's true availability. A person may only be available to a project part time, and be retained for the remainder of the time on normal duties. In Section 10.3 it was stated that someone working nominally full time on a project will do on average only three and a half days work per week throughout a year.

4. *Assess the competence of the people available*   Even after selecting people with the correct skills, it is unlikely that there will be a complete match to requirements. The manager, therefore, needs to identify any short-fall in skills of the people available.

5. *Identify any training required*   If there is a shortfall, training may be required to overcome the deficiency. Training may be in the form of open or bespoke courses, or on-the-job coaching.

6. *Negotiate with the resource providers*   Throughout this process you must negotiate with the resource providers – i.e. the line managers of the people who will do the work – so that they willingly release their people to the project. If the resource providers will not freely release people, the manager can bring pressure to bear via the project's sponsor. However, even then they may not cooperate, and block their people working on the project, so it is best to win the resource providers' support. This can be done by gaining their commitment to the project's goals, and helping them to understand how the project is of benefit to them.

7. *Ensure that appropriate facilities and equipment are available*   At the start of execution and control, the facilities and equipment required by the project team should be made available. Facilities may include office space, meeting rooms, security arrangements and transport. Equipment may include computers and other office equipment, computer software (including word processing, spreadsheets, and project management information systems), telephone, modems and facsimile.

14.3 Implementation planning[1]

Having identified the people to do the work, the team can then define the details of the work to be done, and to assign work to people for execution. The detail work should be planned on a rolling-wave basis, as it is only when you are about to start the work that you have all the information required to plan activities in detail. In this way you can also allow people to plan their own work. However, I suggested in Section 6.6 that you can create a preliminary activity definition through work-package scope statements for early estimating. In this section, I shall consider the process of implementation planning, including:

- planning and scheduling the activities to be done
- authorizing the work
- representing the activity schedule
- representing the programme.

Planning and scheduling activities

There are five steps in planning and scheduling activities:

1. *Define activities to reach a milestone* The team start by listing the activities required to deliver a milestone. When selecting activities, you must chose those that are controllable. This means they should:

    (a) *Produce a measurable result* It must be possible to determine when an activity is finished. It is no good dividing a work package into five activities each equal to 20 per cent of the work. In those circumstances the last activity often takes 80 per cent of the effort.

    (b) *Have average duration roughly equal to the frequency of review* See Section 6.3.

2. *Ratify the people involved* The people to do the work have been chosen as described above. However, once the activities have been defined it may be necessary to review the team to ensure that it contains all the necessary skills, and no redundant skills.

3. *Define roles and responsibilities* The involvement of each of the team members in the activities is then identified. A responsibility chart can be a useful tool for this exercise.

4. *Estimate work content and durations* The work content and durations are estimated applying the processes used at the work-package level.

5. *Schedule the activities within the work package* Finally the activities are scheduled within the work package to deliver the milestone on time. This can be done manually, or by building the activities into a nested network, as illustrated in Figure 12.3.

If you adopt rolling-wave planning, estimates of work content and duration at the activity level will be made at a later stage of the project than those at the work-package level, after sanction has been obtained. Some people are uncomfortable with this, fearing that the activity estimates will turn out to be different from, and higher than, the work-package estimates. What should happen, of course, is that the range of possible out-turns for the total project after activity estimating, should fall within the range after work-package estimating. Table 9.4 shows that the range of accuracy for the project after estimating at the work-package level may be of the order of ±10 per cent, and after estimating at the activity level may be ±5 per cent. Figures 14.1(a) and (b) show acceptable activity estimates, and Figures

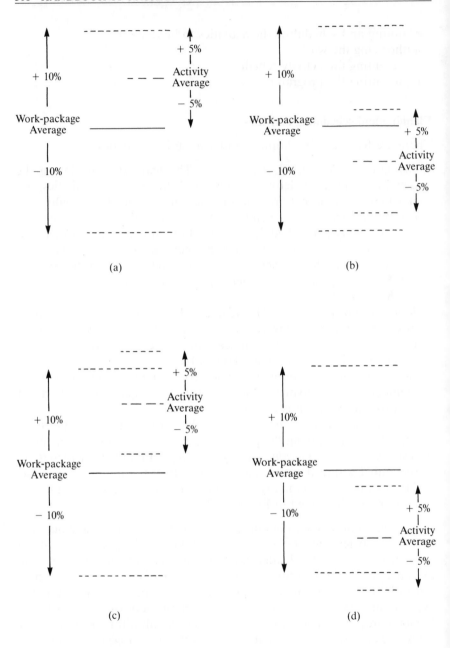

Figure 14.1 Comparison of total project estimates following estimating at the work-package level and activity level

14.1(c) and (d) unacceptable activity estimates. Figure 14.1(d) is unacceptable because overestimating can lead to viable projects being cancelled, or capital being tied up and unavailable to fund other worthwhile projects. If the estimates consistently fall outside the allowable range of those prepared at the work-package level, then the estimating data used for the latter need to be improved. It is therefore important to feed the results back to the estimators so that they can improve their data.

If it is not possible to schedule the activities to deliver the milestone on time (subject to Figure 14.1) then the delay to the plan must be subjected to change control. The change can be to declare a variance between the current schedule and the baseline, or, if the delay is severe, to update the baseline.

Authorizing the work

The newly created activity schedule is entered into the master plan and then, at appropriate intervals, current work is allocated to individuals. Both of these steps must be authorized.

AUTHORIZING INCLUSION IN THE MASTER PLAN

Although the project manager may delegate the creation of the activity schedule to the project team, or experts, its inclusion in the master plan must be authorized because:

- the team, or experts, must agree to any variances of the estimates at the work-package level as a result of the lower level planning
- experts will sometimes plan for a Rolls-Royce solution rather than an adequate solution within the quality constraints, and so the project manager must have an opportunity to ratify the plan
- the experts may sometimes allow themselves excessive contingency.

In all of these circumstances the project manager must negotiate an agreed estimate with the project team.

AUTHORIZING ALLOCATION OF WORK

Including the activity schedule in the master plan does not automatically give the project team the authority to do the work at the planned time. The project manager may need to reschedule the work for a variety of reasons:

- it may be dependent on other delayed work
- other resources may need to work in the same space at the same time

- the work may be rearranged as part of a larger recovery plan
- there may be financial or resource constraints.

The project manager must therefore authorize all work before it commences. Often the issuing of 'work-to lists' as part of the allocation of work will give this authority. Work-to lists are discussed further below.

Representing the activity schedule

There are several ways of representing the activity schedule:

RESPONSIBILITY CHARTS

The responsibility chart provides a complete picture of the schedule of activities that make up a work package. Figure 14.2 shows the activity schedule for milestone P1 in the CRMO Rationalization Project.

ESTIMATING SHEETS

The responsibility chart is an effective tool for representing the people involved, but is weak for estimating work content. An estimating sheet (Figure 14.3) can be used for the latter. This is often usefully developed in a spreadsheet, and it:

- lists the activities
- lists the people involved
- breaks the activities into repeated events
- sums the work content of the events to the activities
- spreads the work content between resources
- sums for the work package as a whole
- calculates the duration and cost of the work package.

An estimating sheet only shows the resources represented by an X or C on the responsibility chart. It can be augmented to show start and finish dates for activities. However, it is a tool for calculating the work content and schedule, not for communicating them. A responsibility chart or bar chart is better for that purpose.

NESTED NETWORKS

You can draw a network of the activities that make up a work package. Figure 12.3(a) illustrates nested networks. If you are using computer-supported tools, the nested network can either be included as a ham-

ACTIVITY SCHEDULE

Project: CRMO RATIONALIZATION	Milestone No./Name: P1: PROJECT DEFINITION
Issue/Date: A/2 Jan	Approved by: JRT

Legend

- X – eXecutes the work
- D – takes **D**ecision solely
- d – takes decision jointly
- P – manages **P**rogress
- T – provides **T**uition on the job
- C – must be **C**onsulted
- I – must be **I**nformed
- A – available to **A**dvise

Companies/Departments/Functions/Type of resource

No.	Activity/Task name	Regional Board	Operations Director	CRMO Managers (2)	CRMO Team Leader	CRMO Staff	Project Manager	Project Support Office	Estates Manager	Estates	Network Manager	Networks	IT	Operations	Personnel
	Produce project proposal	C	D	d	dX		PX	A	A		A		A	A	A
	Hold project definition workshop		DX		X		PX	X							
	Define required benefits	C	D	d	dX		PX								
	Draft project definition report	C	D	d	dX		PX	X							
	Hold project launch workshop			X	X		PX	X	X		X		X		
	Finalize milestone plan		D	d	d		PX	X	C		C		C	A	C
	Finalize responsibility chart		D	d	d		PX	X	C		C		C	A	A
	Prepare estimates – time				A		P	X	A		A		A	A	A
	Prepare estimates – cost		A	A	A		P	X	A		A		A	A	A
	Prepare estimates – revenue		A	A	A		P								
	Assess project viability		D	d	d		PX	X	C		C		C	C	C
	Assess risks		D	d	dX		PX	X	C		C		C	C	C
	Finalize project definition report	D	d	d	d	I	PX	X	X	I	X	I	IX	C	C
	Mobilize team		D	d	dX		PX	X			-			-	-

Period: 199X — Week Number: 4, 5, 6, 7, 8, 9, 10

Work Cont. H/D/W

Figure 14.2 Activity schedule for milestone P1 in the CRMO Rationalization Project

ESTIMATING SHEET		TRIMAGI COMMUNICATIONS BV			02-Jan-9X

PROJECT:	CRMO Rationalization	CODE:	C1	ISSUE:	A
WORK AREA:	Project	CODE:	C1P	AUTHOR:	LJN
WORK PACKAGE:	Project Definition	CODE:	C1P1	APPRVD:	JRT
ACTIVITY:	....	CODE:	....	DATE:	02-Jan-9X

ACTIVITY/TASK		WORK CONTENT			RESOURCES					9 People
		No of steps	Effort/ step	Total effort	Prjct Mgr	Prjct Offc	CRMO TL	CRMO Mgrs	Ops Direct	Other Mgrs
Number Description			(days)	(days)	1	1	1	2	1	3
1	Produce project proposal	1	4	4	1	2	1			
2	Hold Project Definition Workshop	1	4	4	1	1	1		1	
3	Define required benefits	1	2	2	1		1			
4	Draft Project Definition Report	1	8	8	2	6				
5	Hold project launch workshop, 1.5 day duration	1	12	12	1.5	1.5	1.5	3		4.5
6	Finalize milestone plan	1	2	2	1	1				
7	Finalize project responsibility chart	1	2	2	1	1				
8	Prepare estimates – time	20	0.1	2		2				
9	Prepare estimates – cost	20	0.1	2		2				
10	Prepare estimates – revenue	1	1	1		1				
11	Assess project viability	1	1	1	1					
12	Assess risks	1	3	3	1	1	1			
13	Finalize Project Definition Report	1	5	5	2	3				
14	Mobilize team	1	3	3	0.5	0.5	0.5			1.5
	SUB-TOTAL:			51	13	22	6	3	1	6
	ALLOWANCE %			10	10	10	10	10	10	10
	TOTAL EFFORT:			56	14	24	7	3	1	7
	UNIT RATE: £K/day				0.5	0.3	0.3	0.5	0.8	0.5
	COST: £K				7.15	7.26	1.98	1.65	0.88	3.30

TOTAL EFFORT: 56 DAYS
TOTAL COST: £K   22.22
DURATION: 30 DAYS
TARGET START: 01-Feb-9X
TARGET FINISH: 15-Mar-9X

Figure 14.3   Estimating sheet representing the activity schedule for milestone P1: *Project Definition* of the CRMO Rationalization Project

mocked network in the master network, or kept as a separate subnetwork linked to the master network.

NESTED BAR CHARTS

Similarly, you can draw a bar chart of the activities that make up a work package. Figure 12.3(b) illustrates nested bar charts, and responsibility charts at several levels contain nested bar charts. As discussed in Chapter 10, the bar chart is the best communication tool. As a communication tool it may be augmented by:

- baseline start and finish
- current planned actual start and finish
- estimated work content
- work done to date.

All the above tools conform to the principle of single-page reporting. All the activities that make up a work package are shown together, *and alone*, on a single page. This can be repeated at lower levels of work breakdown if required.

Table 14.1   Different representations of the programme

Representation	Owner	Use/format/source
Summary master programme	Client	Typically in bar-chart format; Project Definition Report
Master programme	Project manager	Detailed version for overall control; usually network and bar-chart format; Project Manual
Stage programme	Project/resource managers	Detailed development of one-stage; usually network format
Supporter's programmes	Internal/external contractors/suppliers	Detailed control of contractors; usually network or bar-chart format
Work-package programmes	Work-package managers	Detailed programmes; usually in bar-chart or list format; Project Manual, work-package level
Activity schedules	Individuals	Daily scheduling; bar charts or work-to lists
Other specific programmes	Individuals/contractors	For example, contractors own programme; bar charts or work-to lists

Representing the programme

The activity schedules represent the programme at the lowest level of work breakdown. In fact, the programme will be represented in many different ways depending on the level of planning and for whom it is being prepared. It is worth while at this point to summarize the different representations shown in Table 14.1.

14.4 Allocating work

After authorization of the work, it is allocated to the project team. It is often allocated via *work-to lists*. A work-to list is a list of activities to which a person or resource is assigned. The activities may be listed by:

1. *Work package*   The people or resources are given all the activity schedules for work packages on which they are working;
2. *Time period*   They are given a listing of the activities to which they are assigned for a given period of time from across all work packages on which they are working. The period is typically the current control period and one or two control periods into the future. That will be six weeks if reviews are held fortnightly. The work-to list contains:
   – all activities started but not finished
   – all activities due to start in the period.

The work-to list may be in the form of a responsibility chart (Figure 14.2) or output from a computer system (Figure 14.4). The latter may contain some or all of the following information:

– activity number and name
– baselined dates and duration
– current estimate/actual dates and duration
– estimated work content
– work to date
– bar chart of baselined dates
– bar chart of current estimate/actual dates.

Some people also include float, but I do not agree with this. The team do not need to know the float, and they will invariably consume it. At the end of the control period the work-to list will become a *turn-around document* (Section 14.6) through which the project team report progress. The processes of drawing up the activity schedules, including them in the master plan, and issuing work-to lists are shown in the procedure for monitoring and control (Figure 7.8).

   The equivalent list for gathering materials on a project is called a *kit-*

WORK-TO LIST AND TURN-AROUND DOCUMENT TRIMAGI COMMUNICATIONS BV   15-Feb-9X

PROJECT: CRMO RATIONALIZATION   REPORT AUTHOR: PAGE: 1
WORK PACKAGE: PROJECT DEFINITION   APPROVED: PRINT DATE: 15-Feb-9X
                                                                  REPORT DATE:

ACTIVITY NUMBER	DESCRIPTION	ORG DUR (D)	REM DUR (D)	BASE START	BASE FINISH	SCHED START	SCHED FINISH	ACTUAL START	ACTUAL FINISH	WRK EST (D)	WRK DNE (D)	WRK REM (D)	COMMENTS
P1A	Project Proposal	5.0		01Feb9X	05Feb9X			01Feb9X	05Feb9X	4.0	5.0		
P1B	Definition WShop	1.0		10Feb9X	11Feb9X			11Feb9X	11Feb9X	4.0	4.0		
P1C	Define Benefits	5.0		08Feb9X	12Feb9X			08Feb9X	12Feb9X	2.0	2.0		
P1D	Draft Defn Report	10.0	5.0	08Feb9X	19Feb9X		19Feb9X	08Feb9X		8.0	3.0		
P1E	Launch WShop	1.5	1.5	23Feb9X	24Feb9X	25Feb9X	26Feb9X			12.0			Workshop Delayed
P1F	Milestone Plan	2.5	2.5	24Feb9X	26Feb9X	01Mar9X	02Mar9X			2.0			
P1G	Respbl'ty Chart	2.5	2.5	24Feb9X	26Feb9X	01Mar9X	02Mar9X			2.0			
P1H	Estimate Time	5.0	5.0	24Feb9X	02Mar9X	01Mar9X	05Mar9X			2.0			
P1I	Estimate Costs	5.0	5.0	24Feb9X	02Mar9X	01Mar9X	05Mar9X			2.0			
P1J	Estimate Revenue	5.0	5.0	24Feb9X	02Mar9X	01Mar9X	05Mar9X			1.0			
P1K	Assess Viability	2.5	2.5	03Mar9X	05Mar9X	03Mar9X	05Mar9X			1.0			
P1L	Assess Risks	2.5	2.5	08Mar9X	10Mar9X	08Mar9X	10Mar9X			3.0			
P1M	Final Defn Report	15.0	15.0	22Feb9X	12Mar9X	22Feb9X	12Mar9X			5.0			
P1N	Mobilize Team	2.5	2.5	10Mar9X	12Mar9X	10Mar9X	12Mar9X			3.0			

Figure 14.4 Computer-generated work-to list

marshalling list. This lists all the materials required for an activity, and the date they are required by. If the materials are held in a store, then the list may be issued in the reporting period before that activity, so that the materials can be collected together (marshalled) at a central point, ready for use. If they need to be procured, then clearly the list must be issued earlier still. The planning system needs to record the lead time. A computer system can be very useful for this.

14.5 Requirements for effective control

Everything covered until now has brought us to the point where we are doing work. However, as the work is done we must ensure that we achieve the planned results and that we deliver the facility to the specification we designed, within the cost and time at which it was thought to be worth while. Furthermore, as the facility is commissioned, we must ensure that it delivers the expected benefits that were used to justify the money spent. We can be sure that this will not occur in a haphazard fashion. The structured process by which we check progress and take action to overcome any deviations from plan is *control*. There are four essential steps to the control process:

1. Plan future work and estimate performance.
2. Monitor and report results.
3. Compare results to the plan and forecast future results.
4. Plan and take effective action to recover the original plan, or to minimize the variance.

The book so far has dealt with the first step. In the remainder of this chapter, we shall deal with the other three steps in turn. Let us start with an explanation of the requirements for effective control. For control to be effective, each step in this four-step process must be effective.

Effective plans

I have discussed the requirements of effective planning throughout the book. Five principles of good project management, all of which relate, at least in part, to the development of the plans, were listed in Section 5.5. In particular, the plans must be comprehensive, and frozen into a baseline to provide a fixed measure for control. If the plans are updated frequently, without the application of strict change control, then there will be no measure for control. The project will always be on time, because the plans have just been updated. Team members may develop new activity schedules, but the project manager must authorize them before they are included in the master plan. Work is done against current work-to lists, issued regularly.

Effective reporting

If reporting mechanisms (discussed in Section 14.6) are to be effective, they should satisfy the following requirements:

REPORTS SHOULD BE MADE AGAINST THE PLAN

To ensure that people are interpreting the reports in the same way, they should be made against the plan. Example 5.3 described a case in which the project manager and team members were working to different plans. The team members were making verbal reports and reporting satisfactory progress. The project manager could not understand why they were not achieving his milestones. Turn-around documents are mentioned below as a tool for reporting against the plan.

THERE SHOULD BE DEFINED CRITERIA FOR CONTROL

Likewise it is important to have defined criteria for control. If people are asked to make ad-hoc reports, they usually tend to report the good news and hide the bad news. If asked to report against set questions, they will usually answer honestly. If they report dishonestly, it will become obvious at the second or third reporting period. Defined criteria are given in the next section.

THE CONTROL TOOLS SHOULD BE SIMPLE AND FRIENDLY

Project members should spend as little time as possible filling in reports. Typically an hour each reporting period would be a reasonable amount of time. If submitting reports takes an excessive amount of time, people rightly complain that they are being distracted from productive work (Example 14.1). Simple friendly tools means two things:

– single-page reporting nested in the WBS
– reports against the plan, against defined criteria for control, requiring simple numeric or yes/no answers.

Reports are often filed against work-to lists. These are the *turn-around documents* mentioned above. The work-to list contains space for the report, and is returned at the end of the reporting period. The turn-around document may even have expected answers entered.

REPORTS SHOULD BE MADE AT DEFINED INTERVALS

Just as it is necessary to report against defined criteria, it is also necessary to report at defined intervals. You should not ask people to report only when there is something to discuss. People hate to volunteer failure, so they will not ask for help until it is too late to recover. If people know that they must report both good news and bad at defined intervals, then they will report more freely. The frequency of the reporting period depends on:

- the length of the project
- the stage in the project
- the risk and consequence of failure
- the level of reporting.

At the start of a year-long project, you may report fortnightly at the activity level and six weekly at the milestone level. In areas of high risk you may report more often. Towards the end of the project you may report weekly, or even daily.

I used to work on ammonia plant overhauls, each a four-week project. Every day, supervisors came to a one-hour control meeting in the morning, a two-hour meeting in the afternoon, and spent one hour after work completing daily returns. They complained, with justification, that they should spend more time on the patch motivating their men.

Example 14.1 Simple friendly tools

REPORTS SHOULD BE DISCUSSED AT FORMAL MEETINGS

To be effective the reports must be made and discussed at formal meetings. Passing the time of day at the coffee machine is part of effective team building, but not of effective control. Formal meetings have an agenda, and a chairperson to maintain control. To keep the meetings short and effective, the discussion should also focus on identifying problems, and responsibility for solving them, but you should not attempt to solve the problem at meetings.

THE REPORTS SHOULD STIMULATE CREATIVE DISCUSSIONS

To link into the next steps of control the reports must generate creative discussion, so the team can identify where variances are occurring, and possible ways of taking effective and timely action.

Effective reviews

Having gathered the data, the team must determine whether the project is behaving as predicted, and if not to calculate the size and impact of the variances. The two quantitative measures of progress are cost and time, and so receive significant attention. The team uses the reports to forecast time and cost at completion, and calculates any differences (variances) between these figures and the baseline. It may simply be that work is taking longer and costing more than predicted. Or delays or additional effort may be caused by variances in quality, people failing to fulfil their responsibility, externally imposed delays, or changes in scope. Therefore the variances in time and cost can point to a need to control one or more of the five system objectives. The defined criteria, formal meetings and creative discussions are the key elements in this process.

Effective action

To close the control loop, the team must take effective action to overcome the variances. This may mean revising the plan to reflect the variances, but hopefully it means at least taking timely and effective action to stop them getting worse, and preferably reducing or eliminating them. Effective action requires two things:

- being able to calculate the impact of any changes in the plan on the project's outcome
- having the resolve to take action.

REPLANNING

This is often called *what-if* analysis. The team calculates the impact of action it may take. The most effective management information is obtained by doing this through plans nested in the WBS (single-page reporting). The impact of a change in one activity on related activities can be analysed at the activity level, and on other work packages at the milestone level. However, in complex situations the what-if analysis may be done with computer systems. To be able to perform this what-if analysis it is vital that the project's plans have been kept up to date.

THE RESOLVE TO TAKE ACTION

This is dependent on managers using their sources of authority, and being able to motivate and persuade their teams. To motivate and persuade the teams the manager must build their commitment to the common mission, and help them to understand how the project will be of benefit to them. Teams are discussed further in Chapter 18. Recovery planning and taking action are discussed further in Section 14.7.

14.6 Gathering data and calculating progress

The first step in the control process after doing work is to gather data on progress. Data, as stated above, are most effectively gathered against defined criteria using turn-around documents.

Table 14.2 Criteria for control, and required data

Criteria for control	Quantitative data	Qualitative data
Time and cost	Revised start/finish Actual start/finish Effort to date Effort remaining Other costs to date Other costs remaining	
Quality		Quality problems
Organization		Externally imposed delays Responsibility chart kept?
Scope		Changes to scope Special problems

Defined criteria

Satisfactory progress on the five system objectives are the suggested defined criteria for control. The data required to control them are given in Table 14.2. These are usually collected at the activity level but may be collected at the work-package or task levels. When collected at a lower level they can be summarized to report at a higher level. The use of these data in the control process is described below.

Turn-around documents

These are work-to lists issued at the start of the reporting period and then used at the end of the period to gather data. They provide:

- reports against the plan
- defined criteria
- simple friendly tools.

They can also be used as the focus for formal meetings as described above. I find it very effective to photocopy the turn-around document onto a transparency, and project that on to a white board. The team can then fill in the document on the board in a group meeting. This process encourages the creative discussions to identify any problems, but also enables the meeting to be kept short. Figure 14.5 is a manual turn-around document encompassing the activity schedule from Figure 14.2. Figure 14.6 contains a computer-generated turn-around document.

Calculating progress

The data gathered are used to calculate progress on all of the five system objectives: time; cost; quality; project organization; scope. In particular, with the first two we try to forecast the final out-turn, the time and cost to completion, as this gives better control than reporting the actual time and cost to date. This concept is part of the forward looking control of which project managers speak.

Forecasting time to completion

This is the simplest system objective to monitor and that is perhaps why it receives the greatest attention. If critical milestones have been delayed, or if the critical path has been delayed (and no other path has become 'more critical'), then it is likely that the project has been delayed by that amount. If the team has maintained an up-to-date network for the project, that can be used to forecast the completion date for the project in exactly the same way it was used to predict the end date initially.

The record of effort to date versus effort remaining can also be used to control time, in one of three ways:

- by revising estimates of duration
- by indicating the cause of delays
- through an earned value calculation.

REVISING ESTIMATES OF DURATION

If there is a consistent estimating error, this will be indicated by a trend. The estimates of duration can be revised accordingly.

INDICATING THE CAUSE OF DELAYS

Table 14.3 shows four possible outcomes of duration and effort. (1) Both may be on (or under) budget. In this case all is well. (2) The project may

PROGRESS REPORT

Consequence for Milestone Plan:

Suggested text on Milestone Report: WORK ON TARGET FOR PLANNED COMPLETION FOR 12TH MAR

ACTIVITY SCHEDULE

Project: CRMO RATIONALIZATION

Milestone No./Name: P1: PROJECT DEFINITION

X – eXecutes the work
D – takes Decision solely
d – takes decision jointly
P – manages Progress
T – provides Tuition on the job
C – must be Consulted
I – must be Informed
A – available to Advise

Period: 199X Week Number 4 5 6 7 8 9 10

Issue/Date: A/2 JAN

Approved by: JRT

Named Functions/Named Persons/Named Resources

Work done	Work to do	Est'd compl'n	Quality accept	Resp'y chart kept	Change req'd	Waiting time	Special problem	Work Cont H D W	No.	Activity/Task Name	Regional Board	Operations Director	CRMO Managers (2)	CRMO Team Leader	CRMO Staff	Project Manager	Project Support Office	Estates Manager	Estates	Network Manager	Networks	IT	Operations	Personnel
5	0							4		PRODUCE PROJECT PROPOSAL	C	D	d	dX		PX	A	A		A		A	A	A
4	0							4		HOLD PROJECT DEFINITION W'SHOP		DX		X		PX	X							
2	0							2		DEFINE REQUIRED BENEFITS	C	D	d	dX		PX								
7	0							8		DRAFT PROJECT DEFINITION REPORT	C	D	d	dX		PX	X	I		I		I	I	I
13	0							12		HOLD PROJECT LAUNCH W'SHOP			X	X		PX	X	X		X		X		
2	1	3/3						2		FINALIZE MILESTONE PLAN		D	d	d		PX	X	C		C		C	A	C
1	1	3/5						2		FINALIZE RESPONSIBILITY CHART		D	d	d		PX	X	C		C		C	A	A
1	1	5/3						2		PREPARE ESTIMATES-TIME				A		P	X	A		A		A		A
1	1	5/3						2		PREPARE ESTIMATES-COST				A		P	X	A		A		A		A
0	1	5/3						1		PREPARE ESTIMATES-REVENUE		A	A	A		P	X							
0	1	✓						1		ASSESS PROJECT VIABILITY		D	d	d		PX								
0	3	✓						3		ASSESS RISKS		D	d	dX		PX	X	C		C		C	C	C
0	5	✓						5		FINALIZE PROJECT DEFINITION REPORT	D	d	d	d		PX	X	C		C		C		C
0	3	✓						3		MOBILIZE TEAM		D	d	dX	I	PX	X	X	I	X	I	IX		I

Additional comments

– problem description: LAUNCH WORKSHOP DELAYED 3 DAYS
MILESTONE PLAN REQUIRED ADDITIONAL MODS

– likely cause: OPERATIONS DIRECTOR UNAVAILABLE
CRMO I HAD ADDITIONAL COMMENTS

– possible consequence: COMPLETION DELAYED 3 DAYS

– suggested action: NONE-TIME CAN BE RECOVERED

– supporting information

Signed: LJN Date: 26/2/9X

Manager's comments:

MONITOR

Signed: [signature] Date: 1 MAR 9X

Figure 14.5 Manual turn-around document encompassing the activity schedule

WORK-TO LIST AND TURN-AROUND DOCUMENT						TRIMAGI COMMUNICATIONS BV							15-Feb-9X
PROJECT: CRMO RATIONALIZATION													
WORK PACKAGE: PROJECT DEFINITION													
						REPORT AUTHOR: _WJ_ APPROVED: _JRT_				PAGE: 1 PRINT DATE: _26/2/9X_ REPORT DATE: 15-Feb-9X			

ACTIVITY NUMBER	DESCRIPTION	ORG DUR (D)	REM DUR (D)	BASE START	BASE FINISH	SCHED START	SCHED FINISH	ACTUAL START	ACTUAL FINISH	WRK EST (D)	WRK DNE (D)	WRK REM (D)	COMMENTS
P1A	Project Proposal	5.0		01Feb9X	05Feb9X			01Feb9X	05Feb9X	4.0	5.0		
P1B	Definition W'Shop	1.0		10Feb9X	11Feb9X			11Feb9X	11Feb9X	4.0	4.0		
P1C	Define Benefits	5.0		08Feb9X	12Feb9X			08Feb9X	12Feb9X	2.0	2.0		
P1D	Draft Defn Report	10.0	5.0	08Feb9X	19Feb9X		19Feb9X	08Feb9X	_24/2/9X_	8.0	_7.30_		
P1E	Launch W'Shop	1.5	1.5	23Feb9X	24Feb9X	_25Feb9X_	26Feb9X	_25/2/9X_	_26/2/9X_	12.0	_3_		_Workshop Delayed_
P1F	Milestone Plan	2.5	2.5	24Feb9X	26Feb9X	01Mar9X	02Mar9X		_3/3/9X@_	2.0	_2_		_Extra Person_
P1G	Respb'ty Chart	2.5	2.5	24Feb9X	26Feb9X	01Mar9X	02Mar9X		_3/3/9X@_	2.0			
P1H	Estimate Time	5.0	5.0	24Feb9X	02Mar9X	01Mar9X	05Mar9X		_5/3/9X@_	2.0			
P1I	Estimate Costs	5.0	5.0	24Feb9X	02Mar9X	01Mar9X	05Mar9X		_5/3/9X@_	2.0			
P1J	Estimate Revenue	5.0	5.0	24Feb9X	02Mar9X	01Mar9X	05Mar9X		_5/3/9X@_	1.0			
P1K	Assess Viability	2.5	2.5	03Mar9X	05Mar9X	03Mar9X	05Mar9X			1.0			
P1K	Assess Risks	2.5	2.5	08Mar9X	10Mar9X	08Mar9X	10Mar9X			3.0			
P1M	Final Defn Report	15.0	15.0	22Feb9X	12Mar9X	22Feb9X	12Mar9X			5.0			
P1N	Mobilize Team	2.5	2.5	10Mar9X	12Mar9X	10Mar9X	12Mar9X			3.0			

Completion Expected on time

Figure 14.6 Computer-generated turn-around document

be on time, but effort over budget. In this case there may be some minor estimating errors, but the project team is managing to cope, perhaps by working some unplanned overtime. Estimating errors will be indicated as above. (3) The project may be late, but no additional effort has been expended. In this case the cause of the delay must have been due to external factors, perhaps other people failing to fulfil their responsibilities, or late delivery of some materials, or perhaps the project team have been occupied on work of higher priority (to them). The qualitative control data, Table 14.2, may help to indicate the cause. (4) If both time and effort are over budget then the cause may be:

- serious estimating errors
- rework due to poor quality
- rework due to change.

A trend will indicate the first as described above, and so you will need to monitor effort and duration over several reports. The qualitative control data, Table 14.2, will indicate the second or third cause. You can see from Table 14.3 how the complete set of control data can help initiate discussion over the likely causes of delays, and help in their elimination.

Table 14.3 Determining the cause of delays by comparing effort and completion dates

	Duration	
Effort	*On time*	*Late*
As predicted	No problem	External delays Responsibility chart not kept
Over budget	Minor estimating errors	Estimating errors Quality problems Changed scope

EARNED VALUE CALCULATION

The volume variance, calculated as part of the cost control process, will indicate whether the project is, on average, ahead of or behind schedule.

Forecasting cost to completion

The simplistic approach to controlling costs is to compare costs to date to the baseline cost to date. However, it was shown in Section 9.8 that this comparison is of little value. If actual cost is less than baseline cost we do not know if the work is underspent, late or even late and overspent. I therefore introduced the concept of *earned value*, or *baseline cost of work complete* (BCWC). This is what was planned to have been spent on the work complete, and so is a measure of the amount of work done for the money spent. With the earned value we can calculate two variances:

Cost variance   =   Actual cost – Earned value
Volume variance =   Earned value – Baselined cost.

These figures can be calculated for the reporting period, or as cumulative figures over all reporting periods to date. The cost variance indicates whether the project is over- or underspent. The volume variance indicates whether it is (on average) early or late. With the variances calculated as shown, a positive cost variance will be unfavourable; the project is overspent, and is therefore likely to turn out over budget. However, a positive volume variance is favourable, the project is (on average) ahead of schedule, and is likely to be completed early. (I say 'on average', because it is possible for a large non-critical item to be early, and a small critical item late, and the project will appear to be ahead of schedule according to the volume variance, but behind according to the network.) The actual cost, earned value and forecast of cost to completion can be calculated from the data gathered as follows:

ACTUAL COST

The actual cost in the period is the sum of the man-hour costs and other costs in that period:

Actual cost   =   Effort × (Man-hour rate) + Other costs

Obviously if there is more than one resource then the sum over all resources must be used.

An additional complication arises when the costs are assumed to be incurred (Section 9.8). It is too late for control purposes when the invoices are paid. In Chapter 9 I described typical assumptions, and I would only reinforce here that the important items for control purposes are actual cost, baselined cost and earned value, all of which incorporate the same assumptions.

EARNED VALUE

This calculation is more complex. For work finished the earned value is clearly the baselined cost of that element of work. For work in progress, some estimate of the percentage completion must be made. This can be done in four ways:

- by summing the percentage completion of work elements at low levels of work breakdown; for instance, by adding over the activities in a work package
- by making a visual inspection
- by assuming that (at a low level of work breakdown) all work in progress is on average 50 per cent complete
- by using the effort accrued and effort remaining to calculate percentage complete.

Visual inspections are subjective. People usually overestimate percentage completion when using a visual inspection. Indeed, I was told once that in the civil construction industry it is common for a contractor's quantity surveyors to deliberately overestimate percentage completion to improve the contractor's cash flow. Most of the profit is made by investing money obtained for work that is not yet done. Effort accrued and remaining can be used to calculate the percentage complete as follows:

$$\text{Percentage complete} = \frac{\text{Effort to date}}{\text{Effort to date} + \text{Effort remaining}}$$

The sum of effort to date and remaining are used on the lower line, rather than the original estimate, because that provides a better estimate of percentage complete. The validity of this is shown if you consider the case where effort to date is already greater than the original estimate. However, the estimate of effort remaining can be subjective, and may sometimes be obtained by just subtracting effort to date from the original estimate (until such time as the former is the greater). Percentage completion can also be calculated by replacing effort by duration in the above formula. The two are the same for a single-resource activity. For an activity with internal lead times, or several resources working at different times, effort gives a more accurate answer. When calculating percentage completion at work-package or project level by summing over activities at a lower level of work breakdown, it does not matter too much what assumptions are made at a lower level, because errors cancel out as you sum at higher levels (as long as there is not a consistent error, such as from deliberate overestimating, which will reinforce at higher levels). Hence, in most cases the 50 per cent assumption for activities in progress is as accurate as you will need. Figures 14.7 and 14.8 are computer-generated cost reports for the CRMO Rationalization Project, showing the costs for each work-package and the aggregate for the project overall. Figure 14.7 shows the

PROJECT: CRMO RATIONALIZATION
WORK AREA: —
WORK PACKAGE: —

PAGE: 1
PRINT DATE: 31-Aug-9X
REPORT DATE: 31-Aug-9X

WORK PACKAGE NO	DESCRIPTION	ORG DUR (D)	REM DUR (D)	BASE COMPL (%)	PERCT COMPL (%)	BASELINE			CURRENT ESTIMATE			SCHEDULED COST			EARNED VALUE			ACTUAL COMMITMENT		
						LABOUR (£,000)	MATL (£,000)	TOTAL (£,000)	TOTAL LABOUR (£,000)	MATL (£,000)	TOTAL (£,000)	TOTAL LABOUR (£,000)	MATL (£,000)	TOTAL (£,000)	TOTAL LABOUR (£,000)	MATL (£,000)	TOTAL (£,000)	TOTAL LABOUR (£,000)	MATL (£,000)	TOTAL (£,000)
P1	Project definition	30.0			100.0%	11.2	6.4	17.6	11.2	6.4	17.6	11.2	6.4	17.6	11.2	6.4	17.6	11.0	6.3	17.3
T1	Technology design	40.0			100.0%	12.8		12.8	12.8	0.0	12.8	12.8	0.0	12.8	12.8	0.0	12.8	12.1	0.0	12.1
O1	Communication plan	5.0			100.0%	1.2	2.5	3.7	1.2	2.5	3.7	1.2	2.5	3.7	1.2	2.5	3.7	1.2	2.4	3.6
O2	Operational proc.	15.0			100.0%	9.6		9.6	9.6	0.0	9.6	9.6	0.0	9.6	9.6	0.0	9.6	9.8	0.0	9.8
O3	Job/Management desc.	20.0			100.0%	12.8		12.8	12.8	0.0	12.8	12.8	0.0	12.8	12.8	0.0	12.8	12.5	0.0	12.5
T2	MIS function spec.	15.0			100.0%	4.8		4.8	4.8	0.0	4.8	4.8	0.0	4.8	4.8	0.0	4.8	4.5	0.0	4.5
O4	Staff allocation	15.0			100.0%	3.6		3.6	3.6	0.0	3.6	3.6	0.0	3.6	3.6	0.0	3.6	3.7	0.0	3.7
A1	Estates plan	10.0			100.0%	1.6		1.6	1.6	0.0	1.6	1.6	0.0	1.6	1.6	0.0	1.6	1.6	0.0	1.6
T3	Technical plan	10.0			100.0%	0.8		0.8	0.8	0.0	0.8	0.8	0.0	0.8	0.8	0.0	0.8	0.8	0.0	0.8
P2	Financial approval	15.0			100.0%	3.6	1.5	5.1	3.6	1.5	5.1	3.6	1.5	5.1	3.6	1.5	5.1	3.6	1.5	5.1
A2	Sites 1&2 available	15.0			100.0%	8.4	6.6	15.0	8.4	6.6	15.0	8.4	6.6	15.0	8.4	6.6	15.0	7.5	6.9	14.4
05	Management changes	10.0			100.0%	2.4		2.4	2.4	0.0	2.4	2.4	0.0	2.4	2.4	0.0	2.4	2.4	0.0	2.4
06	Redeployment/train	40.0	10.0	100.0%	75.0%	25.6	55.2	80.8	24.4	52.6	77.0	24.4	52.6	77.0	18.3	52.6	70.9	17.9	52.2	70.1
T4	System in sites 1&2	30.0	20.0	100.0%	33.3%	19.2	44.0	63.2	19.2	44.0	63.2	19.2	44.0	63.2	6.4	44.0	50.4	4.5	42.4	46.9
A3	Sites 1&2 ready	15.0	15.0	50.0%	0.0%	8.4	60.0	68.4	9.2	66.0	75.2	4.6	66.0	70.6	0.0	0.0	0.0			
T5	MIS delivered	15.0	9.0	50.0%	40.0%	4.8	38.0	42.8	4.8	38.0	42.8	2.4	38.0	40.4	1.9	38.0	39.9	1.6	40.2	41.8
07	Procedures implem.	10.0	10.0	0.0%	0.0%	4.0	10.8	14.8	4.0	10.8	14.8	0.0	0.0	0.0	0.0	0.0	0.0			
P3	Intermediate rev.	40.0	40.0	0.0%	0.0%	1.6		1.6	1.6	0.0	1.6	0.0	0.0	0.0	0.0	0.0	0.0			
A4	Roll-out implem.	80.0	80.0	0.0%	0.0%	64.0	240.0	304.0	70.4	264.0	334.4	0.0	0.0	0.0	0.0	0.0	0.0			
P4	Benefits obtained	60.0	60.0	0.0%	0.0%	2.4		2.4	2.4	0.0	2.4	0.0	0.0	0.0	0.0	0.0	0.0			
						202.8	465.0	667.8	208.8	492.4	701.2	123.4	217.6	341.0	99.4	151.6	251.0	94.7	151.9	246.6

Figure 14.7 Cost report using duration to calculate percentage completion.

327

PROJECT COST REPORT

TRIMAGI COMMUNICATIONS BV

31-Aug-9X

PROJECT: CRMO RATIONALIZATION
WORK AREA: —
WORK PACKAGE: —

PAGE: 1
PRINT DATE: 31-Aug-9X
REPORT DATE: 31-Aug-9X

WP NO	DESCRIPTION	ORG DUR	REM DUR	BASE COMPL	PERCT COMPL	BASELINE			CURRENT ESTIMATE			SCHEDULED COST			EARNED VALUE			ACTUAL COMMITMENT		
		(D)	(D)	(%)	(%)	LABOUR (£000)	MATL (£000)	TOTAL (£000)	TOTAL LABOUR (£000)	MATL (£000)	TOTAL (£000)	TOTAL LABOUR (£000)	MATL (£000)	TOTAL (£000)	TOTAL LABOUR (£000)	MATL (£000)	TOTAL (£000)	TOTAL LABOUR (£000)	MATL (£000)	TOTAL (£000)
P1	Project definition	30.0		100.0%	100.0%	11.2	6.4	17.6	11.2	6.4	17.6	11.2	6.4	17.6	11.2	6.4	17.6	11.0	6.3	17.3
T1	Technology design	40.0		100.0%	100.0%	12.8		12.8	12.8	0.0	12.8	12.8	0.0	12.8	12.8	0.0	12.8	12.1	0.0	12.1
O1	Communication plan	5.0		100.0%	100.0%	1.2	2.5	3.7	1.2	2.5	3.7	1.2	2.5	3.7	1.2	2.5	3.7	1.2	2.4	3.6
O2	Operational proc.	15.0		100.0%	100.0%	9.6		9.6	9.6	0.0	9.6	9.6	0.0	9.6	9.6	0.0	9.6	9.8	0.0	9.8
O3	Job/Management desc.	20.0		100.0%	100.0%	12.8		12.8	12.8	0.0	12.8	12.8	0.0	12.8	12.8	0.0	12.8	12.5	0.0	12.5
T2	MIS function spec.	15.0		100.0%	100.0%	4.8		4.8	4.8	0.0	4.8	4.8	0.0	4.8	4.8	0.0	4.8	4.5	0.0	4.5
O4	Staff allocation	15.0		100.0%	100.0%	3.6		3.6	3.6	0.0	3.6	3.6	0.0	3.6	3.6	0.0	3.6	3.7	0.0	3.7
A1	Estates plan	10.0		100.0%	100.0%	1.6		1.6	1.6	0.0	1.6	1.6	0.0	1.6	1.6	0.0	1.6	1.6	0.0	1.6
T3	Technical plan	10.0		100.0%	100.0%	0.8		0.8	0.8	0.0	0.8	0.8	0.0	0.8	0.8	0.0	0.8	0.8	0.0	0.8
P2	Financial approval	15.0		100.0%	100.0%	3.6	1.5	5.1	3.6	1.5	5.1	3.6	1.5	5.1	3.6	1.5	5.1	3.6	1.5	5.1
A2	Sites 1&2 available	15.0		100.0%	100.0%	8.4	6.6	15.0	8.4	6.6	15.0	8.4	6.6	15.0	8.4	6.6	15.0	7.5	6.9	14.4
O5	Management changes	10.0		100.0%	100.0%	2.4		2.4	2.4	0.0	2.4	2.4	0.0	2.4	2.4	0.0	2.4	2.4	0.0	2.4
O6	Redeployment/train	40.0	10.0	100.0%	75.0%	25.6	55.2	80.8	24.4	52.6	77.0	24.4	52.6	77.0	18.3	52.6	70.9	17.9	52.2	70.1
T4	System in sites 1&2	30.0	20.0	100.0%	33.3%	19.2	44.0	63.2	19.2	44.0	63.2	19.2	44.0	63.2	6.4	44.0	50.4	4.5	42.4	46.9
A3	Sites 1&2 ready	15.0	15.0	50.0%	0.0%	8.4	60.0	68.4	9.2	66.0	75.2	4.6	66.0	70.6	0.0	0.0	0.0	0.0	0.0	0.0
T5	MIS delivered	15.0	9.0	50.0%	40.0%	4.8	38.0	42.8	4.8	38.0	42.8	2.4	38.0	40.4	2.4	38.0	40.4	1.6	40.2	41.8
O7	Procedures implem.	10.0	10.0	0.0%	0.0%	4.0		4.0	4.0	10.8	14.8	0.0	0.0	0.0	0.0	0.0	0.0	0.0	0.0	0.0
P3	Intermediate rev.	40.0	40.0	0.0%	0.0%	1.6	10.8	12.4	1.6	0.0	1.6	0.0	0.0	0.0	0.0	0.0	0.0	0.0	0.0	0.0
A4	Roll-out implem.	80.0	80.0	0.0%	0.0%	64.0	240.0	304.0	70.4	264.0	334.4	0.0	0.0	0.0	0.0	0.0	0.0	0.0	0.0	0.0
P4	Benefits obtained	60.0	60.0	0.0%	0.0%	2.4		2.4	2.4	0.0	2.4	0.0	0.0	0.0	0.0	0.0	0.0	0.0	0.0	0.0
						202.8	465.0	667.8	208.8	492.4	701.2	123.4	217.6	341.0	97.0	151.6	248.6	94.7	151.9	246.6

percentage completion of the work packages calculated on the duration, and Figure 14.8 calculated making the 50 per cent assumption.

FORECAST COST TO COMPLETION

This is calculated using the cost variance. The forecast cost to complete of activities is estimated in one of the ways just described. At the project or work-package level it is possible to make one of three simplifying assumptions:

1. All remaining activities will be done at baseline cost:

   Cost at completion = Original estimate + Cost variance to date

2. Overexpenditure will continue at the current rate:

   Cost at completion = Original estimate * (1 + % Cost variance to date)
   % Cost variance   = Cost variance/Earned value.

3. Some activities in the future will be overspent but it will be possible to make savings in other areas. Using the WBS, a second estimate can be maintained alongside the baselined cost, the current best estimate, and this can be used to forecast the cost to completion.

Figures 14.7 and 14.8 also show the forecast cost to completion. The forecasts are made using the current best estimate.

S-CURVES

Introduced in Section 9.8, S-curves can be used to represent these concepts graphically (Figure 14.9). This figure also differentiates between the budget estimate and the baseline estimate. The baseline is the measure for control, the budget is the most you expect to spend, and the difference is the contingency. You will often hear people referring to budget and baseline as the same thing.

Controlling quality

The data gathered (Table 14.2) can show where deviations have occurred from the specification. These quality variances may have been identified as part of the quality control process, or they may have been noticed by the project team members. The impact of these quality problems on time and cost is indicated by Table 14.3.

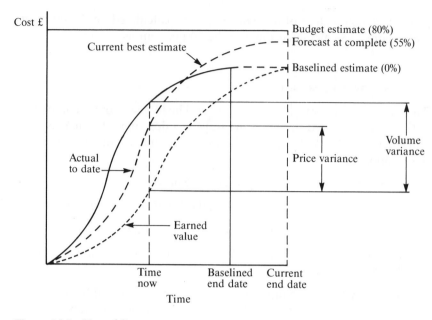

Figure 14.9   Use of S-curves

Controlling organization

Similarly, the data gathered may indicate where the project organization is not performing as planned. This may specifically be caused by people not fulfilling their roles or responsibilities as agreed in the responsibility chart. Table 14.3 also shows how the control process can indicate the impact of these organizational delays on time and cost.

Controlling scope

Finally, the data gathered (Table 14.2) can indicate that changes in scope have occurred. These especially will have an impact on the time and cost of a project (Table 14.3). Changes in scope are usually inevitable. However, they should be rigidly controlled, and this requires a change control procedure. Change control is a six-step process:

1. Log the change.
2. Define the change.
3. Assess the impact of the change. Seemingly simple changes can have far-reaching consequences.
4. Calculate the cost of the change. This is not just the direct cost, but the cost of the impact.

5. Define the benefit of the change. This may be financial or non-financial. The latter includes safety.
6. Accept or reject the change based on marginal investment criteria. A return of 40 per cent per annum is possible for marginal criteria, compared to 20 per cent for the project as a whole.

If this procedure is applied rigorously, many changes do not get past step 3. Figure 14.10 is a form to aid this process. *Configuration management*, a version of change management, is described in Section 16.3.

TRIMAGI COMMUNICATIONS CHANGE CONTROL FORM			
PROJECT: CRMO RATIONALIZATION............................ WORK PACKAGE: .... ACTIVITY: .... ORIGINATOR:			
DESCRIPTION OF CHANGE			
IMPACT OF CHANGE			
COST OF CHANGE: £ .... VALUE OF CHANGE: £			
	NAME	SIGNATURE	DATE
PROPOSED BY:	....	....	....
CHECKED BY:	....	....	....
APPROVED BY:	....	....	....

Figure 14.10   Change control form

14.7 Taking action[2]

Once we have identified that a project is deviating from plan, we must plan and take appropriate action. The earlier action is taken the better, because the cheaper it is to recover, or to abort it should it prove non-viable. This relationship between project recovery and the life cycle was described earlier in the chapters on risk and quality. In this section I shall describe how to take appropriate action to recover a project.

Recovering a project

The response to the variances can be carefully managed, or unmanaged and reactive. The most effective approach depends on the circumstances. There are cases which demand an immediate response. However, in most cases there is time to reflect and recoup. A structured approach to problem solving (Figure 2.2) is the best means of recovery. Here I shall describe a six-step version for planning recovery. Not surprisingly, this is similar to the six-step life cycle for total quality projects (Figure 2.3).

1. *Stop* Regardless of the size of the variance and its impact, everyone should pause. Unfortunately, the most common reaction is to seek an instant remedy. Some common solutions, such as adding more resources, or sacking the project manager, do more harm than good. While this reaction is understandable, it is often wrong because of the emotional state of the team. I once attended a recovery review where the chairman listened to the team, sympathized with them, made no undermining statement and gave them three days off to recover. The result was electric. The team came back remotivated to set things right. The project was back on the rails in very quick time and the product became a best seller. Keep cool, calm and collected.

2. *Look, listen and learn* It is important to undertake a thorough review in the presence of all team members and the client. Effective recovery must be based on a clear understanding of the cause of the divergence, and possible ways of overcoming it. Seeking views on what went wrong, and what action the team proposes, is important in rebuilding commitment.

3. *Develop options and select a likely course* Explore every avenue and develop a range of solutions. Establish decision criteria so that options can be evaluated against any agreed conditions. If necessary return to the original financial evaluations, re-cost and re-time each option, air them with the client and then select the one that best meets the decision criteria.

4. *Win support for the chosen option*   It is important that there is total support from all those involved. There is hard work ahead and uncommitted team members will falter at the first hurdle.
5. *Act*   Once the agreed course of action has been accepted every effort must be made to implement it. Deviations from the agreed plan will only add to the confusion and make the situation worse.
6. *Continue to monitor*   The impact of any actions should be monitored to ensure that they have the desired effect. If not, then the recovery process must be repeated.

Options for action

There are five basic options for taking action:

FIND AN ALTERNATIVE SOLUTION

This is by far the best solution. The plan is recast to recover the project's objectives in a way that has no impact on the quality, cost, time or scope. It may be that two activities were planned sequentially, because they share the same scarce resource. If the first is delayed for other reasons, it may be possible to do the second activity first, and hopefully when it is complete it will then be possible to do the other.

COMPROMISE COST

This means adding additional resource either as overtime or additional people, machines or material to recover the lost time. This is usually the instant reaction to project delays. However, recall the discussion in Section 10.3, describing how to calculate durations: doubling the number of people on a project does not usually double the rate of work. Brooks's law[3] states:

Adding resource to a late software project makes it later still!

The rationale is that the existing people must take time out to bring the new people up to speed.

COMPROMISE TIME

This means allowing the dates to slip. This may be preferable, depending on whether cost or time is the more important constraint on the project. This decision should have been made during the feasibility study, and communicated to the project team as part of the project strategy.

COMPROMISE SCOPE

This means reducing the amount of work done, which in turn means taking less on time to achieve some benefit. Notice I did not say compromise the quality. The latter is very risky once the initial specification has been set, and should therefore be discouraged.

ABORT THE PROJECT

This is a difficult decision. However, it must be taken if the future costs on the project are not justified by the expected benefits. Project teams are often puzzled that their recommendation to terminate a project is ignored; a decision which seems obvious is avoided, and good money is poured after bad, depriving other projects. It takes courage to abort a project. During their lives, projects absorb champions and supporters. Senior people may have become associated with its success and feel if the project fails it may damage their reputations. There is often a feeling that 'with a little more money and a bit of luck the project can be turned around'. The fact is that once an organization makes an emotional commitment to a project, then that project is very hard to abandon. Another argument often put forward to support a failing project is that 'as we have already spent so much on it we should finish it'. Unfortunately, this argument is fallacious: future costs must be justified by the expected benefit, no matter how much has been spent so far. If the project's outcome is still important to the organization it may be more effective to abort a project, learn from it and start afresh.

14.8 The control cycle

Building the control processes above into a cycle of monitoring and control can be complex. During a control period you must:

- issue work-to lists
- gather the turn-around documents
- analyse the data
- hold a review meeting
- update the plan

all in time for incorporation into the new work-to lists. Timing these control activities within a control period is a delicate balance between conflicting requirements. If the turn-around documents are gathered too late, then changes to the plan cannot be incorporated until the next but one control cycle. If they are gathered too early, the reports will be based on predictions

PROJECT RESPONSIBILITY CHART

Project:

PROCEDURE FOR PROJECT MONITORING & CONTROL

Legend:
- X – eXecutes the work
- D – takes Decision solely
- d – takes decision jointly
- P – manages Progress
- T – provides Tuition on the job
- C – must be Consulted
- I – must be Informed
- A – available to Advise

No.	Principle/Milestone name	Project Manager	Team Leaders	Project Members	Project Support Office	Steering Committee	Project Sponsor
	Develop milestone plan	PX	X		I	d	D
	Create high-level network	PX			X		
	Develop new activity schedules	DP	X	X	I		
	Update network	P	C	C	X		
	Issue work-to lists			I	X		
	Do work	P	PX	X			
	Return turn-around documents		P	X	I		
	Activity review meeting	I	PX	X			
	Identify variances (activities)	I	PX	X			
	Plan recovery	DP	X	X	I		
	Issue activity progress reports	PI	X		I		
	Review progress against milestones	PX		X	X	I	
	Milestone progress meeting	PX		X	X	X	
	Identify variances (milestones)	PX		X	X	DX	
	Plan recovery	PX		X	X	D	
	Issue milestone progress report	PX	X	X	X	C	I
	Approve progress						D

Period: Six Weekly Cycle (columns 1 2 3 4 5 6 1)

Work Cont. H/D/W

Companies/Departments/Functions/Type of resource

Issue/Date: Approved by:

Figure 14.11   Procedure for monitoring and control

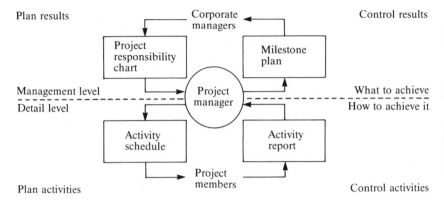

Figure 14.12   Nesting of control cycles in the work breakdown structure

to the end of the control period. Furthermore, if attendance at review meetings is to be compulsory, they should not be scheduled for a Friday or a Monday, which people may take off as a long weekend. Likewise, the meeting at the activity level should be held just before the less frequent meeting at the work-package level. Figure 14.11 shows a procedure for monitoring and control which achieves this balance, while holding reviews fortnightly at the activity level and six weekly at the work-package or milestone level. This concept of nesting the reporting cycles is further illustrated in Figure 14.12.

14.9 Summary

1. The process of resourcing a project includes the following steps:
   - identify what is to be achieved
   - identify the skills and skill types required
   - identify the people available
   - assess their competence
   - identify any training required
   - negotiate with the resource provider
   - ensure that appropriate project facilities are available.
2. The five steps of activity planning are:
   - define the activities to achieve a milestone or work package
   - ratify the people involved
   - define their roles and responsibilities
   - estimate work content and durations
   - schedule activities within a work package.

3. After creation of the activity schedule, it is entered into the master plan, and at appropriate intervals work is allocated to people. Both these steps must be authorized by the project manager.
4. Activity schedules may be represented by:
   - responsibility charts
   - estimating sheets
   - nested networks
   - nested bar charts.
5. Work is allocated to people via work-to lists, by:
   - time period
   - work package.
6. The four steps in the control cycle are:
   - plan future performance
   - monitor achievement against plan
   - calculate variances and forecast out-turn
   - take action to overcome variances.
7. For control to be effective, each step in this cycle must be effective. Requirements for effective planning have already been described, and in particular are stated in the five principles of project management at the end of Chapter 5.
8. Requirements for effective reporting include:
   - reports against the plan
   - defined criteria for control
   - simple, friendly tools
   - reporting at defined intervals
   - formal review meetings
   - creative discussions.
9. This can be achieved by gathering data using turn-around documents, which can be used to gather data to control the five objectives:
   - time
   - cost
   - quality
   - organization
   - scope.
10. Time is controlled by recording progress on the critical or near critical paths, or by comparing the cost of work actually completed to that planned to have been completed. In order to do this, the following progress data are collected:
    - revised start/finish
    - actual start/finish
    - effort to date
    - effort remaining

- costs to date
- costs remaining.

11. Cost is controlled by comparing costs incurred to the planned cost of work actually completed. In order to do this, the same data are required. Costs are said to be incurred when the expenditure is committed, not when the invoices are paid, because at that time the plan can still be recovered.

12. S-Curves provide a visual representation of progress against both cost and time.

13. When the divergence of achievement from the plan becomes too great, the project must be recovered. The ten-step problem-solving cycle can be applied to find the solution to plan recovery. Possible courses of action include:
    - rearranging the plan
    - compromising time
    - compromising cost
    - compromising scope
    - aborting the project.

Notes and references

1. Section 14.3 contains ideas contributed by Paddy Lewis and Martin Samphire.
2. Section 14.7 incorporates material written by Mahen Tampoe.
3. Brooks, F. P., *The Mythical Man-Month*, Addison-Wesley, 1974.

15
Finalization and close-out

15.1 Introduction

The last stage of the life cycle is finalization and close-out. During the closing stages of a project, the team must maintain their vigilance, to ensure that all the work is completed, and that it is completed in a timely and efficient manner. It is very easy for the good effort of execution and control to be lost, as some team members look forward to the next project, and others become 'demob happy' or 'demob unhappy'. Furthermore, during this stage, the team's focus must switch back to the purpose of the project, as implied in Table 13.3. During execution and control, the team concentrate on doing the work within time, cost and specification. Now they must remember why they are undertaking the project; they are not doing the work for its own sake, but to achieve some business benefit. It is very easy to complete the work within the constraints, and think that is a successful project, while failing to use the facility delivered to obtain the expected benefits that justified the money spent on it. There are a very small number of projects, mainly in information technology (IT), where the facility is not utilized at all, and no benefit is obtained. However, there are many where it is utilized to less than its full capacity, and the project team often do not see it as their responsibility to ensure that it is. They are more interested in their next project. At this time, the project team must also remember that it may be the closing stage of the project, but it is also the start of the operational life of the facility. Therefore, adequate mechanisms must be put in place to support the facility throughout its life.

As the project comes to an end the team disbands. If the project is to be completed efficiently, the team may be run down over some time. As this happens, it is important to ensure that it is done in a caring way. Project team members may have made significant contributions, or even sacrifices, to the success of the project. If this is not recognized, the project will at best end on an anti-climax, at worst it will leave lasting resentment that will roll over into the next project. You must ensure that project team members are given due reward for their contribution, and that the end of the project is marked appropriately.

Finally, there are items to be recorded or lessons to be learned for the operation of the facility, or for the design, planning, estimating and management of future projects. Because the team's attention may be focused on completing the task and looking forward to the next project, this often remains undone. Completing records of the last project is a distraction from the next. It also costs money; and as this money is spent after the facility has been commissioned it provides no immediate benefit, and can be easily saved, especially if the project is overspent. However, it is precisely when a project is overspent that it is important to find out why that happened, so that the information can be used for the planning and estimating of future projects.

In this chapter, I shall describe how to bring the project to a timely and efficient completion, and explain how to hand the facility over to the users, while ensuring (a) that it is fully commissioned to obtain the benefits and (b) that a proper support mechanism is put in place as it moves into its operation phase. I shall describe how to disband the project team in a caring way, and identify the key data to be recorded at the end of the project, how they are obtained and the purpose for which they are used. This is the second most critical stage of a project. No one remembers an effective start-up, but everyone remembers an ineffective close-out; the consequences are felt for a long time.

15.2 Finishing the work

As the project draws to a close, the team must ensure that all work is completed in a timely and efficient manner. The following can aid this process:

- producing checklists of outstanding work to ensure that all loose ends are tied up
- planning and controlling at lower levels of work breakdown to provide tighter control
- holding more frequent control meetings to ensure that problems are identified and solved sufficiently early
- planning the run-down of the project team as the work runs down to ensure that people are released for other work

- creating a task force with special responsibility for completing outstanding work
- closing contracts with suppliers and subcontractors to ensure that no unnecessary costs are booked
- replacing the project manager by a deputy with finishing skills.

The original plan is a checklist of outstanding work. However, as you approach the end of the project you begin to look at the tasks that need to be done to complete outstanding work. Instead of waiting for a fortnight to find out what work has been achieved, you create daily lists of work to be done to complete the facility, hand it over to the client and commission it. This leads naturally to planning at a lower level of work breakdown, and holding more frequent control meetings. At the end of a project, the risk of delay becomes greater, and so it becomes appropriate to review progress more frequently, weekly, daily, or even twice daily. It has previously been stated that whatever the frequency of control, that should be the average duration of activities, and hence you plan against shorter tasks. The checklists are just these more detailed plans.

As the project nears its end, you will require fewer resources. This is what gives the S-curve its classic shape. However, to ensure the most efficient completion, you must plan the release of resources in advance. You do not want them turning up and sitting around until you realize they are not needed, because that is inefficient for both the project and the organization as a whole. You must tell people one or two weeks in advance that they will not be required on a certain date. You must also tell the resource providers, so that they can make full use of their people when they are released.

As the teams run down, it also becomes essential to combine them into task forces, to retain natural *hunting packs*. These teams may be of about 6 to 15 people, depending on the task at hand. The reasons for this are twofold. People work best in teams of a certain size, and as the number of people reduce, the number of managers must be reduced, with teams merged. It is also natural to given these task forces the checklists to complete, rather than spread the work over disparate groups. Closing contracts with suppliers and subcontractors is another way of planning the run down of the project team.

The skills required to finish a project can be different to those required to start it up and run it. Therefore it may be appropriate to change managers in the final stage. However, if this change is to be seamless, the new manager must be a former deputy, who has been involved with the project for some time. This approach was successfully adopted on the construction of the Sainsbury Wing of the National Gallery.

15.3 Transferring the product

Key issues in transferring the facility to the users include:

- planning for the transition
- ensuring that the users accept the product
- training the users in the operation of the facility
- ensuring a definite cut-over
- recording the as-built design
- ensuring continuing service or maintenance of the facility.

PLANNING FOR THE TRANSITION

There must be a clear understanding of how responsibility for the facility is to transfer from the project manager to the operations manager. This will happen during the commissioning process, which, as we saw above, should be planned at a lower level of work breakdown than its fabrication.

ENSURING THAT THE USERS ACCEPT THE PRODUCT

I spoke earlier about involving users in the decision-taking processes. That will win their acceptance of the specification of the facility. At the end of the project the users must be given the opportunity to agree that the facility meets that specification. On a strict contractual relationship the owner should sign completion certificates to accept the product. When I worked in ICI, the operating works signed completion certificates even when the plant was built by internal resources.

TRAINING THE USERS IN THE OPERATION OF THE FACILITY

The users will usually not be experts in the operation of the facility. They will therefore require training in its use. This should be planned as part of the project. Indeed, it is probably too late if it is not addressed until close-out. However, it is in this transition stage that much of the training takes place. Training will be in the use of the facility, but may also include simple maintenance procedures. Training can be a significant proportion of the cost of a project. When converting a typewriter factory to robotic manufacture, IBM spent 25 per cent of the budget on training.

ENSURING A DEFINITE CUT-OVER

The planned transition and signed completion certificates should result in a definite cut-over, at which responsibility is transferred and final payments made (Example 15.1).

I conducted an audit in a company that had taken 18 months to complete a contract, but they had not obtained sign-off three years later. The client was always finding fault, and had effectively had three years' free maintenance. At this point, the contractor switched the equipment off, and very quickly agreed a final snagging list and obtained sign-off.

Example 15.1   Signing-off completion certificates

RECORDING THE AS-BUILT DESIGN

To ensure on-going efficient operation of the project's product, it is important that the as-built design is recorded. This requires the incorporation of all design changes into the final configuration of the product. This is part of the process of configuration management (Chapter 16).

ENSURING CONTINUING SERVICE OR MAINTENANCE OF THE FACILITY

The users may be able to undertake simple service or maintenance, and the operating manuals may help them in this. However, it is usually ineffective if not impossible for them to become experts in the 'technology' of the facility, and so it is necessary to ensure that appropriate mechanisms are in place to provide back-up service. This requires channels of communication between owner and contractor throughout the life of the facility. These channels should be defined as part of the hand-over process. In the engineering industry, many contractors make little or no profit from the construction of the facility, but large profits from its service. The construction contract is almost a loss leader to win the service contract.

15.4 Obtaining the benefits

Many project managers view their job as finishing when the facility is handed over to the users. However, obtaining the benefit from the project is the final step in the control process, undertaken at the top of the project hierarchy, the integrative level (Figure 2.5). Whether this final step is the responsibility of the project manager or project champion will depend on the circumstances, but it should be agreed as part of the project strategy at the start. It will probably be the champion who will be held accountable if the owner does not receive adequate return on the investment, and so the onus rests on the champion to ensure that it happens. There are four steps in any control process:

- create a measure
- monitor achievement of that measure
- calculate variances between the measure and achievement
- take action to remove those variances.

Create a measure

From the start there must be a clear definition of the project's purpose and the benefits expected from the operation of the facility. This is a clear statement of the criteria by which the project will be judged to be successful, stated as part of the project strategy.

Monitor achievement

Following commissioning of the facility, the expected benefits must be audited. If the facility is an IT system, you must check whether it is delivering the expected returns. For example, if it is a manufacturing planning system, you must check to see whether the inventory is falling, the work in progress is falling, and the lead times are being reduced, as predicted. Often, after the system is commissioned, no noticeable change is achieved. If the facility is a new product, you must check to see whether the predicted levels of sales are being achieved. If it is a management training programme, you must check to see if there is any noticeable improvement in management performance. (The last of these is the most difficult to check.)

Calculate variances

Determine the cause of any difference between the expected benefits and those obtained. This requires measuring the revenue stream and profitability of the project. The cause may be that the users are not using the product to its full capacity, either deliberately or inadvertently.

Take action

Hopefully a small amount of fine tuning of the design of the facility, or a small amount of additional training of users, is all that is required to achieve the actual benefit. Projects involve considerable risk, because they are novel and unique, and so it is quite likely that the design carried some small imperfections that can be very easily corrected. Sometimes, improvement will require another project. (That was why the problem-solving cycle (Figure 2.2) was drawn as a circle.)

15.5 Disbanding the team[1]

Over the last three sections, I have concentrated on the work-related and strategic issues of close-out. However, the team members may face the end of the project with mixed feelings. They may look forward to future opportunities, or they may face unemployment. This can have a debilitating effect on them and the project. It is the task of both line and project managers to manage this emotional conflict, so that staff are retained and re-introduced into the normal work environment. When considering the motivation and management of project staff, it must be remembered that they belong permanently to the organization and only temporarily to the project. This means that while the project may not need the staff once their contribution to the project has finished, the organization for which they work may value the team members even more because of new skills they learned while working on the project. Retaining project team members after the project is over is vital even if it is not so important to the specific project, and so the process of disbanding the project team must be managed in a caring way. Key elements in this process include:

- planning the run-down of resources
- returning resources promptly to their line managers
- holding an end-of-project party
- holding a debriefing meeting
- rewarding achievement
- disciplining under-achievement
- counselling staff.

Planning the run-down of resources in advance

This, as explained above, is important to achieve an efficient end to the project. It is also important for the motivation of the project team. People feel more motivated to complete their work if they know they are to be transferred immediately to new work. That is only possible if their release has been planned, so that their line managers have been able to plan their future work.

Returning resources promptly to their line managers

The organization gets the optimum use of its resources if they are returned promptly to normal duties after completion of the project. Line managers of people seconded to the project are more likely to treat future requests for resources favourably if those people are used efficiently, which means releasing them at the earliest possible opportunity.

An end-of-project party

The use of 'festivals' is an important motivator on projects. They should be used to mark important project milestones, especially the end of the project. The difficulty is chosing the timing of a party so that the maximum number of people can come before being dispersed to new jobs. Also, they should actually have something to celebrate.

A debriefing meeting

A project close-out meeting can be as important as a launch meeting, as part of the life cycle of the project team. It marks the end of the period of working together, and allows people to show their grief, or frustration, or pleasure at having been a member of the project (Example 15.2).

I worked on the overhaul of ammonia plants in the early 1980s. We held a debriefing meeting after each overhaul. They served a very useful purpose of allowing us to let off steam in advance of the next overhaul. For the four weeks of each overhaul, we used to suspend our feelings, to allow work to progress. We would talk to each other bluntly about what work we wanted done, what it would take, and how we felt about having been let down. It was necessary to make progress in the intensity of the overhaul. In the process, feathers got ruffled, but we had to bite our lips and get on with it. At the debriefing meeting, it all came out; we said all the things we had bottled up for four weeks. It was all laid bare, forgiven, and we were ready to start afresh on the next overhaul.

Example 15.2 Releasing frustration at debriefing meetings

Rewarding achievement

The team members are likely to react favourably to future requests to work for the project manager if their contribution to the project is suitably rewarded and praised. End-of-project festivals are part of that. However, it is equally important that a person's achievement is recognized by those who matter, especially the manage who is to write the individual's annual appraisal, so that the person's contribution to the business can be recognized. An important part of this process is winning the appraising manager's commitment to the project, so that that person can view a contribution to the project as an important achievement during the year.

Disciplining under-achievement

It is also important to discipline poor performance on a project so that good performers do not feel their effort was in vain and that the poor performers understand how to improve in the future. For this latter reason the disciplining process should be treated positively, guiding people on how to perform better in the future. Of course, it might be possible to take corrective action during the project, so the earlier this is done the better.

Counselling all staff

The fifth stage of team development is mourning, as the project fades into history and the team with it. This is not very good for the ego or self-esteem of the team members who find that overnight they may be reduced to 'has-beens' unless they go immediately to another project or line job. For those who are not so lucky, a counselling session can be of tremendous value. While this may incorporate some of the activities mentioned above, it often encompasses much more. For example:

- it offers a chance for the individual to review career objectives
- it offers scope for skills consolidation in the form of theoretical training to supplement the practical experience
- it shows caring by the organization, which is perhaps the key factor in the whole exercise.

Recalling the case in Example 7.1, perhaps the individuals should have been given counselling well before the end of the two-year period, into planning their re-entry into the line organization. The individuals could then have taken responsibility for their own career development, and perhaps have found opportunities for themselves within the organization where their new skills would have been of great value.

15.6 Post-completion reviews

The control process at the top level of the project hierarchy (Section 14.8) might seem to be the point at which to stop. However, there is a level above this in the corporate hierarchy (Figure 3.3). We also need to control at this level. The data gathered at this level include:

- as-built design (final configuration)
- a comparison of final costs and benefits for feeding back to the estimating process, and to the selection of future projects
- a record of the technical achievement on the project for feeding back to the design and selection of future projects

- a review of the successes and failures of the project and the lessons learned, for feeding back to the management of future projects.

There are several ways of reviewing the success and failures of projects, but two include debriefing meetings and post-completion audits.

Debriefing meetings

I have already described the role of these in disbanding the project team. It is worth while on most projects to hold a meeting of all people who attended the project launch workshop to review the assumptions made. This meeting may last from two hours to a day, depending on the size of the project. On particularly large projects they may amalgamate up from a low level, reversing the cascade of project launch workshops.

Post-completion audits

On large projects it may also be worth while to conduct a post-completion audit. This is a formal review of the project against a checklist. An audit is often conducted by external consultants. It is also common only to audit projects that have gone radically wrong. However, better lessons are often learned from successes, so it can be useful to audit projects that have gone well. (The holding of audits is described more fully in Chapter 16.)

15.7 Summary

1. The key requirements for effective project close-out are:
   - finishing the work
   - transferring the product to the users
   - obtaining the benefits
   - disbanding the team
   - reviewing progress.
2. The work must be finished in a timely and efficient manner. The following can aid this:
   - checklists of outstanding work
   - planning and controlling at lower levels of work breakdown
   - more frequent control meetings
   - planned run-down of the project team
   - use of task forces
   - changing the project manager
   - closing contracts with suppliers.

3. Effective transfer of the product to the users is facilitated by:
   - planning the transition
   - ensuring user acceptance
   - training the users
   - obtaining definite cut-over
   - recording the as-built design
   - ensuring maintenance of the facility.
4. The facility must be commissioned to obtain the required benefit, and this can be controlled by:
   - setting a measure
   - monitoring performance against the measure
   - calculating variances
   - taking action to overcome variances.
5. The project team must be disbanded in an efficient manner, and yet in a way that takes care of their motivational needs. This can be achieved by:
   - planning the run-down
   - returning resources promptly to line managers
   - holding an end-of-project party
   - holding a debriefing meeting
   - rewarding achievement
   - disciplining under-achievement
   - counselling staff.
6. Post-completion reviews must be held to:
   - record the as-built design
   - compare achievement to plan
   - record technical data
   - learn successes and failures for the future.

Note

1. Section 15.5 incorporates material written by Mahen Tampoe.

PART FIVE
MANAGEMENT
PROCEDURES AND
SYSTEMS

16
Project administration

16.1 Introduction

Parts Two to Four have described the principles and methods of managing change through projects: Part Two described the context of the project, why organizations undertake them, the relationships between the parties involved, and strategies for managing projects; Part Three explained the management of the five system objectives, scope, organization, quality, cost and time; and Part Four identified the management of the four stages of the project life cycle, proposal and initiation, design and appraisal, execution and control, and finalization and close-out. In the process, I also introduced many of the tools and techniques associated with the management of projects, and showed how they were applied to the management of the various objectives and stages. Many of the tools and techniques have become formalized into standard systems and procedures, and some of them will be described in this part. In this chapter, I shall explain some of the administrative procedures used, and Chapter 17 will identify how they have been computerized into project management information systems. We shall look at what the systems can do, the different types of system available, and how to select and implement a system. In Chapter 18 we shall discuss the role of the project manager in building and maintaining the project team.

The sections of this chapter are self-contained. I shall start by describing *programme management*, the management of the level of work breakdown above the project. Next, we shall consider *configuration management*, the procedure whereby the project's deliverables are controlled. The use of procedures manuals to record project management routines used by an organization will then be described, and the section will explain how to conduct audits into the efficacy of the procedures. I shall end this chapter by describing the Project Support Office (PSO), the central pool for administering the project management systems and procedures. In Chapter 1 projects were said to be unique, and therefore carried considerable risks. These systems can reduce this uncertainty by converting administrative procedures into a routine.

16.2 Programme management[1]

I showed in Section 3.2 how the business planning process leads to programmes of work: programmes for the continued operation of existing businesses; or programmes for the development of new businesses. These new developments, which by their nature involve the implementation of beneficial change, are managed through projects. Sometimes a programme consists of just a single project; one project delivers the required development. However, more often than not, programmes consist of several projects. Section 3.2 indicated that an organization may take several views of its programmes. They may:

- cover an annual business cycle
- deliver a development objective in the long-term (five-year) plan
- be the work undertaken by a single function, or discipline, such as marketing or R&D.

Some people also label a major project, broken down into a number of subprojects, as a programme. However, I like to maintain the distinction. A project has clearly definable (unitary) objectives: to deliver a facility, which itself will produce a product, from which benefit can be derived. The objectives of a programme are to create business development, but they are more diffuse (Example 16.1).

The objective of the Apollo Project was:

'to send a man to the moon, and bring him back safely, by the end of the 1960s'
(John F. Kennedy)

The objectives of the American Space Programme should have been wider: to develop a credible programme of activity in space that would be of benefit to the United States in particular, and mankind in general. Perhaps it was because NASA aligned the objectives of the Space *Programme* totally with those of the Apollo *Project* that the former failed after the 1960s, whereas the latter was successful.

The objective of the Channel Tunnel Project is to build a fixed link between France and Britain. The objectives of the programmes of which it is a part are to develop a portfolio of products for Eurotunnel plc, to build a pan-European high-speed rail network, and to link Britain's rail network to those on the continent. Again, perhaps it is because people have focused on the single project objective that Britain's rail network will not be fully prepared for the opening of the tunnel in 1993.

Example 16.1 Programmes versus major projects

In this section we shall consider:

- the definition of a programme and programme management
- the benefits of programme management
- selecting programmes
- coordinating interfaces
- assigning priorities for resources.

The management of multi-projects, and the role of the programme manager (or director of projects) is described in Section 21.2.

Definition of programmes and programme management

In Section 1.4 a project was defined as:

> an endeavour in which human, material and financial resources are organized in a novel way, to undertake a unique scope of work, of given specification, within constraints of cost and time, to achieve beneficial change defined by quantitative and qualitative objectives.

A programme can be defined as[2]:

> a group of projects which are managed in a coordinated way, to deliver benefits that would not be possible were the projects managed independently.

The essential feature is that the benefit of the whole is greater than the sum of the parts, although the benefit may be hard to define precisely. We can then define programme management as:

> the process of coordinating the management, support and setting of priorities across individual projects, to deliver additional benefits and to meet changing business needs.

There are three major elements of this definition:

- selecting programmes
- coordinating the projects by managing interfaces
- assigning priorities to projects.

Each of these will be described in turn. However, let us first look at the benefits, or possible benefits, of programme management.

Benefits of programme management

The benefits can come from three sources[2]:

DELIVERING CORPORATE OBJECTIVES

It is not always possible to justify projects in isolation. The benefits of an individual project may be quite small, but the project may be an essential part of a larger development. The project can only be justified as part of the programme. It is common in these circumstances to find that projects are not justified at all. There is then no control of the project selection procedure, and a lot of unnecessary projects are undertaken, or too many projects are adopted (Example 3.5). If projects are grouped into programmes, they can be adopted with due regard to the corporate strategy and priorities.

INCREASED EFFICIENCY

Efficiency savings can be of two types. I have said throughout this book that projects are unique, and so require a novel organization. By grouping projects into programmes, you reduce the novelty, and share systems, procedures and resources across projects. This reduces the time spent developing norms and procedures at the start of each project. Secondly, resources may not be fully utilized on any one project, and so they can be shared between projects to improve efficiency. However, the risk of this is that their priorities may not be clear, and they may never be able to settle properly on any one project. These problems can only be solved through multi-project management (Section 21.2).

REDUCED RISK

Specific risks associated with programmes of projects include lack of priority for any one project; inefficient use of resources; and a failure to recognize interfaces between project. These can all be reduced through the coordination provided by programme management.

Selecting programmes

If an organization follows a strict, top-down approach to its business planning (Section 3.2), its programmes should fall out of that. However, to reduce the number of interfaces between programmes, companies may group projects that share:

- objectives
- resources or skill types
- engineering or software technology
- markets or products
- contractors.

Techniques for making this selection are in an early stage of development.[2]

Coordinating interfaces

An interface can be defined as:

> a link between work elements in the work breakdown structure of two or more programmes, projects or sub-projects (adapted from BS 4335).[3]

The interface can be between one level of the WBS and the next within a single project, or between the same level of WBS in different projects. The link may be:

- a common deliverable
- shared resources (people, materials, equipment, or subcontracts)
- shared information or data, either input data or output data
- shared technology.

The definition of interfaces point the way to their management. It is a five-step process, although these steps are not necessarily sequential.

1. Identify the links that exist.
2. Group projects into programmes to minimize the links between programmes. Managing the interfaces then becomes the responsibility of the programme manager.
3. Determine the impact of the link from one project to the other. Computer-based networking techniques which allow the transfer of data between networks can aid this process (see Chapter 17).
4. Divide the links into major and minor links. Major links are those that are on or near the critical path for either project. Minor links are those that are well off the critical path. (Previously termed, 'bulk work' in Section 10.2.)
5. Develop plans for managing the major links.

Throughout the course of the programme you must repeat the steps to identify new links – and to ensure that no minor links become major.

Because programme management is a coordinating function, it will often occur at a higher level of management than project management, with several project managers working for a programme manager or director (Section 21.2). However, it can be a federal system of management, with several project managers being supported by a (subordinate) project controller or Project Support Office (Section 16.6).

Assigning priorities for resources

The primary concern when scheduling projects in a programme is the sharing of scarce resources between projects, called 'capacity planning'. Many people approach this problem by merging the networks of several projects into one giant network, and assigning priorities to projects. This does not work, because the highest priority network grabs all the resources it needs, and the other projects are left to fight for what remains. The second highest priority project grabs what it needs from what is left, and so on. The lower priority projects only get very patchy resources, and lurch along, usually starved of resources and occasionally flooded with them, but when they are flooded, the people spend most of their time trying to remember what they were doing when last on that project. Progress is inefficient and ineffective at best, and non-existent at worst (Example 3.5). The problem is exacerbated if different groups give a different priority to different projects. None of the projects then gets all the resources it needs, which means that none of them progresses, but a lot of effort is expended. The problem is solved by maintaining plans on at least two levels:

– the individual project level
– the company resource or programme level.

On individual projects, the basic unit of work is the individual activity, which has the usual characteristics of duration, start date, resource requirement, etc. At the company resource level, a multi-project programme may contain 10 or 100 projects. The basic unit of work is no longer the activity, but each self-contained project. In the company resource plan, each project is represented as a single unit of work, and assigned a resource profile (which also implies a duration). Each project must then be managed individually within its assigned resource profile. If individual managers cannot achieve their project objectives within the constraints imposed, they return to the company resource plan to negotiate additional resources. (I call this company resource plan a *rough-cut capacity plan*, or *master project schedule*, MPS, by analogy with the manufacturing industry.) Before new projects can be accepted, their impact on the rough-cut capacity plan must be analysed and agreed, and the new project assigned priority within the plan. This is particularly important in organizations undertaking projects for third parties, where a balance has to be struck by the client's time objectives and the availability of resources. The scheduling of multi-projects in a corporate programme is therefore a six-step process[4]:

1. Develop individual plans for all projects (at the strategic level). The plans can be developed according to the principles described in Part Three.
2. Determine the resource requirements of individual projects. A realistic schedule can be determined for each project, independently of all others, based purely on its own resource requirements. A responsibility chart can be used to develop the resource requirement (Figure 7.11).
3. Incorporate each individual project into the master project schedule, as a single element of work assuming the duration and resource profile determined at step 2. (Particularly small projects may be merged into the background, bulk work.)
4. Assign a priority to each project according to its resource requirements and its importance in the company's strategic development. Resource hungry projects of high strategic importance may be given priority, whereas projects of lower strategic importance requiring fewer resources may be rejected.
5. Schedule projects in the MPS according to their priority and the resource availability. Projects are assigned a time window and a resource profile in the MPS. It may be necessary to reject some projects and to curtail or delay others in order to satisfy the resource constraints. However, it is better to know that at the start, and not discover it part way through the company's development programme; and where third party projects are concerned, it is better to decline the commission than fail to achieve agreed goals.
6. Schedule the individual project plans within the time window and resource profiles assigned. Hopefully, most projects will be achievable within the assigned profiles. If not, then additional resources must be negotiated from the MPS.

The MPS can be maintained manually, or by the use of a computer system. I saw a manual system on a planning board on the wall in a ship repair yard. Computer systems may be based in proprietary database software, such as a spreadsheet, or database management system. Alternatively, you may use one of the available project management packages mentioned in Chapter 17.

When assigning projects a time window, several different selection criteria can be used to determine priorities. Typical criteria include:

1. *For time*: Minimum project slippage is often the most crucial, particularly in the construction industry, as penalty costs are involved in most projects. Slippage on one project may cause others to slip and non-completion on time may result in loss of good will or future work.
2. *For resources*: Optimum resource utilization is required in organizational

and manufacturing projects, where the efficient utilization of resources is important as peaks and troughs need to be smoothed out.
3. *For cost*: Minimum work in progress is important in the bespoke manufacturing industry where it is critical to keep the time work is kept waiting to a minimum, as work in progress creates a heavy burden in the form of working capital, which must be financed.

All three criteria will lead to different results, and so cannot be optimized at the same time.

16.3 Configuration management[5]

Configuration management was developed in the engineering industry to control changes to, and the versions of, components as they are configured in the facility. In particular, on development projects, where several prototypes are being produced, configuration management controls and keeps track of the design, or configuration, of each prototype. With rapid changes in technology and communication, identified at the start of this book, configuration management has become desirable, if not essential, to all development projects: organizational, software, technology, engineering, or a combination of the four.

So what is configuration management, and how can the control of a physical, tangible configuration be of use in a development project? Configuration management controls the specification of the product breakdown structure, it expresses the facility delivered by a project, as a configuration of component parts. The configuration can take various forms: a car, space shuttle, design, plan, software system, training programme, organizational structure. Each component may then be regarded as a configuration in its own right, made up of other components. This process, of course, develops the bill of materials, or product breakdown, of the project. Figure 16.1 illustrates the concept using a book as the configuration. The components are chapters: the subcomponents sections; etc. In this section, I explain the organization and implementation of configuration management.

Organization

Configuration management is not a radical discovery that revolutionizes the way the facility is developed and maintained. It is a set of good working practices for coping with change. Many projects use elements of configuration management, especially in the application of change control. However, to be effective, it must be a systematic, consistent approach to man-

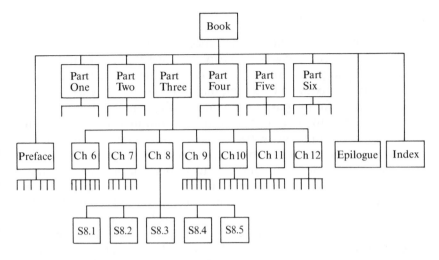

Figure 16.1 Configuration for a book

aging change on complex projects. From the outset, structures must be put in place to support it. These include specified individuals with responsibility for configuration management, and procedures supported by senior management. It also involves all project participants. There may be one or more project review boards, with responsibility for approving the specification of the facility, and to approve changes to the specification. Depending on the size and complexity of the project, there may be a group of people dedicated to the function of configuration management.

Implementation

Implementing configuration management requires the definition of tasks to be performed and procedures to be adopted. The tasks must be allocated, which requires the organization to be established, responsibilities assigned, and appropriate resources (people, money equipment, accommodation) obtained and deployed. The appropriate procedures depend on the specific project, its size and complexity, but typically configuration management comprises four functions:

- configuration identification
- configuration reviews
- configuration control
- status accounting.

CONFIGURATION IDENTIFICATION

Configuration identification is the process of breaking a system into its component parts, or *configuration items*, each of which can be individually documented and placed under change control. Ideally, each configuration item will have maximum cohesion; that is, it would not be useful to subdivide it further for the purpose of documenting it or controlling changes to it. Also, the configuration items will have minimal coupling; that is, it would not be useful to merge two or more items to form a single item for documentation and change control (Example 16.2).

In its simplest form, configuration identification involves locating all the configuration items required to deliver the facility so that nothing is overlooked, and then establishing the information to keep track of those items throughout the life of the project. Most systems can be broken down using a hierarchical product breakdown structure (PBS). When the system has been broken down to its lowest level, the resultant configuration items form the project inventory, or bill of materials. All deliveries and revisions are tracked and controlled against two forms of configuration item recording: the planned set of items; and the produced/approved set.

The identification of the sets of items for the project should cover the entire development life cycle for both the facility and the supporting documentation. The definition and recording provided will support the activities of configuration control and status accounting. A complete list of all configuration items will be derived from the design specification. The configuration is complete when all items have been delivered. If extra configuration items are delivered, or some are not delivered, then this will only be acceptable if the design specification, and therefore the list of items, has been amended accordingly.

When I was writing this book, my list of configuration items was the list of section headings, as recorded in the Table of Contents (Figure 16.1). However, I must admit that the sections did not conform precisely to the principles of cohesion and decoupling. In this chapter, the definition of the section headings was quite stable. In others, Chapter 18 for instance, the definition changed as I wrote the chapter. The chapter was perhaps therefore the configuration item. Some chapters were not configuration items on their own. Chapter 13 started life as four, which were merged because each was too small on its own. Chapter 14 was originally to be one, was split, and then remerged.

Example 16.2   Configuration identification of this book

CONFIGURATION REVIEWS

The configuration management control procedures manage the movement of configuration items from one stage of the life cycle to the next. This is done through formal review processes conducted at the end of each stage. At the end of proposal and initiation, the initial configuration review audits that the specifications are:

– *up to date*: they accurately reflect the concept of the product
– *complete*: all the configuration management documentation that should exist at this point in the life cycle actually does exist.

At the conclusion of this stage, a requirements definition is produced, as part of the Project Definition Report (Chapter 13) and reviewed, approved, baselined and handed over to configuration management before it moves on to the design and appraisal stage. Similarly, at the end of design, the design specifications are produced, as part of the Project Requirements Definition or Project Manual, which are again reviewed, approved, baselined and handed over. Once the configuration identification moves into execution, it evolves from documentation into actual deliverables, whether physical or abstract. These are again reviewed at the end of this stage, to draw up the list of outstanding items for finalization and close-out, and yet again at the end of this last stage, before the documentation is archived as the *as-built design*. Configuration management is the central distribution point for each stage of the life cycle of the project, but it becomes more critical during the last stage, finalization and close-out, as the facility is tested and commissioned.

CONFIGURATION CONTROL

Controlling the baselined configuration items through each stage of the life cycle is the basis of configuration management. The project depends on the baselined items and the record of any changes. Periodically during the life of an item, the baseline may need to be revised. It should be revised whenever it becomes difficult to work with the baseline documentation and authorized changes to it. All authorized changes to the documentation should be consolidated, as should that relating to any authorized repairs and emergency modifications. When the documentation has been completed, reviewed and approved, the baseline becomes revised. All subsequent change proposals should be made to the revised baseline.

Changes may arise internally or externally. External ones come from changes to business requirements; internal ones from forgotten requirements or problems found during the project. A procedure is required to report problems with baselined configuration items. Change control is the process of proposing, reviewing, approving and, where necessary, implementing changes to the approved and maintained items within the PBS. Through the process of change control, the impact of all changes is properly assessed, prior to deciding whether to authorize the change. Impact assessment will determine the changes in scope the change will bring about, not just in the immediate area of the change, but on the whole project. Often the change can have a far-reaching impact. The consequences for organization, quality, costs and benefit, and schedule are also assessed. It can help to have a standard form, such as that shown as Figure 14.10, to guide this assessment. It is important not to place items under change control too early, as unnecessary inflexibility and delay may occur. The steps of change control are listed in Section 14.6.

Review boards may differ for changes at different stages of the life cycle. Prior to the change review, the team determines what impact changes to configuration items has on resource requirements, and prioritize change against requirements for all projects in the organization. The impact is documented for the board. Once a change has been approved, the person responsible for the item makes the change, and passes the rebaselined documentation to configuration management. Information on revisions to the item is recorded. The revised specification for the item is passed to all interested parties, and then secured by configuration management.

For major changes, it is sometimes desirable to adopt a top-down approach in which changes to the requirements specification are agreed prior to any work being done to define consequential changes to the specification. This, in turn, is agreed prior to changes being made to the product and component specifications. Configuration management can handle this by defining the major enhancement as a separate configuration with its own baseline. When a major enhancement becomes operational, it supersedes the current system. Until then, the current operational system continues to have its own baseline changed as necessary. This can be taken one step further, where several prototypes have their separate baselined configurations operational in parallel, each subject to separate change control. When a change is made to one, it may or may not be made to some or all of the others.

STATUS ACCOUNTING

Status accounting is the fourth function of configuration management. It supplies information on request about baselines, configuration items, their versions and specification, change proposals, problem reports, repairs and modifications. For example, status accounting may identify authorized repairs and modifications awaiting the completion of amended documentation. Unless documentation is amended to be consistent with the facility, it is not accepted as being valid. Status accounting also keeps track of the complexities caused by superseding (major enhancement) configurations.

Status accounting enables people on large, volatile projects to avoid confusion by unwittingly using outdated versions of documents and components. This is important for contracting companies responsible for components that need to interface with each other. It is also important for people responsible for user acceptance tests. They need the most current version of the requirements specification, and of the agreed functional and physical characteristic of the configuration, so they can determine whether or not the specification (quality) requirements of the contract have been met; that is, that the facility functions as envisaged within its environment to produce the required product and benefit.

Summary

Configuration management is the primary tool for delivering systems that meet the specifications and are within time and budget. It manages changes to an engineering, IT or organizational facility so that:

- an up-to-date master documentation is maintained
- no change is authorized unless the impact on agreed delivery dates and costs has been assessed
- interrelated changes are synchronized
- only authorized changes are made to the facility.

16.4 Procedures manuals

I have described a range of principles, methods, tools and techniques of project management. I have also said, in Section 4.6, that to manage effectively through projects, organizations should adopt a company-wide approach. Without one, communication and cooperation can be difficult. A company-wide approach may just be a few guiding principles. However, differences of interpretation and emphasis are possible, usually just representing different people's involvement in projects (Example 16.3). In order to avoid this sort of confusion, many project-based organizations have procedures manuals for the management of projects. Organizations may develop their own procedures manuals, or use standard, documented approaches. This section will consider the purpose and structure of such manuals and describe some of the standard approaches available.

I worked in one organization where the word 'commissioning' was taken by the mechanical engineers as the period during which M&E trials (mechanical and electrical testing) are conducted, by the process engineers as the period following M&E trials during which the operation of the plant is tested, by the plant operators as the period following testing during which the plant is run up to 60 per cent name-plate capacity, and by the software engineers as the entire period during which the computer control system is tested and commissioned.

Example 16.3   The need for a company-wide approach

Purpose of procedures manuals

There are several reasons why organizations have procedures manuals, some of which are given below.

A GUIDE TO MANAGEMENT PROCESSES

Even the most experienced of managers may occasionally need to remind themselves of the procedures to be followed in certain circumstances. A procedures manual can be a useful aide-mémoire.

TRAINING NEW STAFF

Project managers often first learn their profession by 'sitting next to Nellie'. Following what they are doing in a procedures manual can help to reinforce their learning. Furthermore, if training courses are structured around the manual, it can serve to remind them of what they learned as they begin to apply it in the working environment.

DEMONSTRATE OPERATING PROCEDURES TO CLIENTS

Often, as part of their terms and conditions of contract, clients will demand to see proof of best practice in project management. This is an assurance to the client that the contractor is able to meet the agreed goals (of quality, cost and time). A procedures manual goes some way towards providing that proof.

QUALITY ACCREDITATION

Another way of demonstrating that the organization adheres to best practice is to be accredited against a defined quality standard. These standards were described in Section 8.3.

Structure of procedures manuals

The typical contents of a procedures manual may be:

PART 1: INTRODUCTION

This explains the structure and purpose of the procedures manual.

PART 2: PROJECT STRATEGY

This describes the approach to project management to be adopted by the organization, and the basic philosophy on which it is based. It will cover issues such as those described in Chapters 4 and 5. It describes the project model, introduces the stages of the life cycle to be followed (Part Four) and explains why they are adopted. It also explains the need to manage the five system objectives.

PART 3: MANAGEMENT PROCESSES

This describes the procedures to be followed at each stage of the life cycle. The inputs and outputs are listed, and the management processes required to convert the former to the latter are listed sequentially. Some processes may be broken into lower levels in a hierarchical structure. Example 16.4 presents the contents page of a manual for an information systems project, which shows that in some areas the breakdown was taken to between one and three levels below the project level. It is adapted from manuals I have prepared for clients. The inputs and outputs from each step may be:

- elements of the project plan
- data or information
- reports.

Each may have standard formats, and it may be useful to include examples of these, and the blank forms, in the appendix. Clearly, if you break the processes down to lower level, the inputs and outputs may be broken down into subcomponents.

In the procedures manuals described above, I drew pictorial representations of the processes to achieve each stage or substage in the life cycle. Figures 16.2 and 16.3 are those for successive levels of breakdown. Where there is a lower level of definition, the process is shown as a fine box. Where the process is the lowest level, it is shown as a bold box. Against each bold box were listed the inputs, outputs and steps required to achieve it.

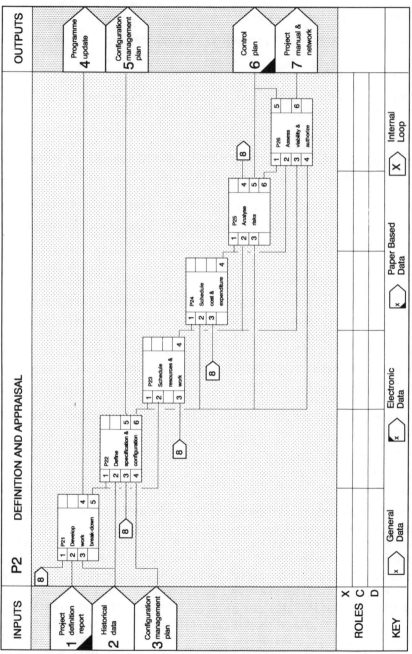

Figure 16.2 Pictorial representation of stage P2: *Definition and appraisal*

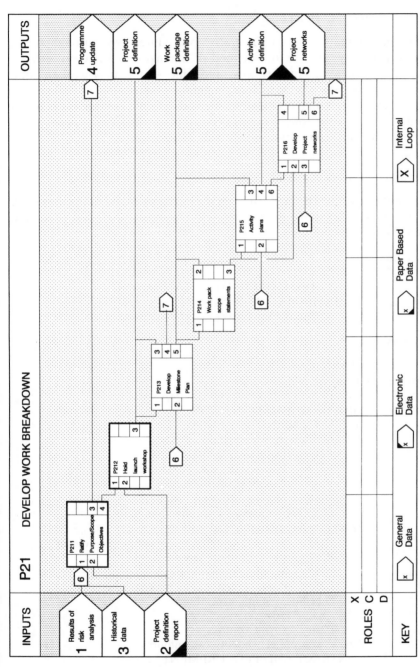

Figure 16.3 Pictorial representation of step P21: *Develop work breakdown*

PART 4: SUPPORTING PROCEDURES

This part explains the administrative procedures used throughout the project. It may describe the method of managing the five objectives – scope, organization, quality, cost and time – or it may explain some administrative procedures, such as programme management, configuration management, risk management, or methods of data collection (including time sheets), or the role of the project support office. Only those important in the particular environment will be necessary.

APPENDICES: BLANK FORMS AND SAMPLES

A blank copy of each standard form should be included in the appendix, together with an illustration of the form completed. Copies of sample reports are also useful.

TRIMAGI COMMUNICATIONS BV
INFORMATION SYSTEMS DEPARTMENT
Project Management Procedures Manual

CONTENTS

       P36   Make Payments
P4   EXECUTION AND CONTROL
       P41   Finalize project model
       P42   Execute and monitor progress
       P43   Control duration
       P44   Control resources and materials
       P45   Control changes
       P46   Update project model
P5   FINALIZATION AND CLOSE-OUT

APPENDICES

A   Project planning and control forms
B   Supporting electronic databases
C   Sample reports
D   Staff abbreviations (OBS)
E   Resource and material codes (CBS)
F   Management codes (WBS)

ADDENDA

1   Current resource and material codes
2   Current management codes

AUTHOR: JRT   ISSUE: A   DATE 30 APRIL 199X

Example 16.4 Contents page for a procedures manual for an IT project

Standard approaches

Most organizations develop their own procedures manual. However, there are some standard approaches, and most of these are industry based. The IT industry has at least three:

1. **PROMPT**   This was the standard for the management of IT projects in government and the Civil Service. It was written by consultants Learmonth and Burchett Management Systems.[6] It has the major disadvantage that it requires the project team to complete the work breakdown structure before any work is done, and so people seem to spend more time planning and replanning than they actually spend doing the work.
2. **PRINCE**   This has now replaced PROMPT, and was developed from it by the CCTA.[7] It is based on the principle of rolling-wave planning, and so overcomes the problem just described.

3. PRISM   This was developed by the firm of consultants and software engineers, Hoskyns.[8] It is used more in the private sector.

An example of a standard procedure used in another industry is the RIBA Plan of Work,[9] used in the building construction industry.

16.5 Conducting audits

Audits have been used throughout history as a way of ensuring that operations are being conducted in a correct way. There are records of audits conducted in Egypt during the time of the Pharaohs, 4000 years ago. We are most familiar with financial audits, and these are usually conducted in a policing sense, to ensure that businesses are being conducted:

– in the best interests of the shareholders (or creditors)
– in a way that will ensure achievement of the objectives
– in accordance with the law, and without fraudulent activity.

Financial audits must be conducted by independent qualified accountants. However, organizations may conduct detailed reviews of their non-financial activities, or the activities of suppliers or subcontractors, for very similar reasons. These 'audits' may be conducted by internal staff or external consultants, with the objective of ensuring that:

– activities are conducted in an efficient manner
– they will deliver the organization's objectives
– they will not lead to waste, loss or theft
– there are no mistakes in the design of the activities.

Audits are conducted on projects for all these reasons, and they may be conducted at several points throughout a project. In this section I shall explain the purpose of conducting audits on projects, identify the different types of audit conducted on projects, and when they are conducted, and describe how audits are conducted.

Purpose of audits

In order to achieve these objectives on a project, audits are conducted on projects with one of the specific aims listed below.

CHECK THAT THE DESIGN IS CORRECT

It was stated in Section 5.2 that one of the primary contributing factors to the success of a project is to ensure that it is correctly established and designed in the first place. This means that:

- the purpose of the project has been correctly identified
- the objectives set will deliver that purpose
- the facility chosen will achieve those objectives
- the facility is designed in accordance with the inherent assumptions
- the design information used, including any research data, is valid.

An audit conducted at key milestones throughout the project, especially at the end of proposal and initiation or design and appraisal, can confirm that the project, as designed so far, meets all of these requirements.

ENSURE THE QUALITY OF THE MANAGEMENT PROCESSES

A second major contributor to success is the use of qualified management processes. A project that is well designed, but badly managed, can fail on any one of the system objectives, and thereby fail to achieve its purpose. A project that is well designed and well managed is more likely to be successful. An audit can be conducted at any point throughout a project to determine whether it is being managed in accordance with best practice, and that usually means in accordance with defined procedures, perhaps as set out in a manual. Such an audit is most effective when conducted about one third of the way into a stage, as the pattern of management has been set by that time, but work is not so far advanced that mistakes cannot be recovered.

LEARN FROM PAST SUCCESS

If a project has gone particularly well, perhaps better than recent projects, then a review can help to identify what was done properly. That can be recorded as a basis for future projects. These reviews are usually best conducted at the end of a project, although it can then be difficult to gain people's commitment as they are keen to move on, as discussed in Section 15.5. However, it is usually easier to get people to review their successes than their failures.

AVOID PAST MISTAKES

Likewise, if a project has gone particularly badly, then it is usually very instructive, perhaps even mandatory, to determine what mistakes were made, so they can be avoided in the future. However, people can be very defensive in these circumstances (unsurprisingly). My own experience is that there is usually a string of excuses about why this project was unique, and the mistakes would not normally occur, even if the project is one of a series of failures.

Types of audit

These four purposes imply three types of audit:

PROJECT EVALUATION AUDIT

A project evaluation audit is an independent check of the feasibility or design studies. It is an enforced review of the investment appraisal as it currently stands, and the assumptions on which it is based. It is conducted by independent auditors to see whether they reach the same conclusion as the original design team. The audit covers similar ground as the original feasibility or design study (Chapter 13). The auditors check the validity of the data used in the original studies, and the conclusions drawn from them (Section 13.4). Often the original design team will be over-optimistic, because they have a certain subjective commitment to the project. It is important that the auditors are truly independent, and that they do not share the same commitment to the project, or they may merely repeat the mistakes.

INTERNAL AUDIT

An internal audit is a quality control check of the management processes, conducted either by independent auditors, or by the project team, to ensure that best practice is being followed, and hence that the project as defined will be delivered to quality, cost and time. (Usually only the design or execution stages will be audited.) As I said above, when conducted by external consultants, it will be conducted about one third into the stage. The project team may also make random spot checks on themselves, to ensure that they are maintaining best practice throughout the project, but especially as they near the end of execution, or the beginning of close-out. During an internal audit, the auditors will check:

- the validity of the data being gathered
- how the data are being used to generate management reports
- how those reports are being used to take timely and effective action, to ensure that the project meets its quality, cost and time targets.

This will cover everything from progress of the work itself, to the procurement and marshalling of materials and resources.

POST-COMPLETION AUDIT

The successes and failures of a project are reviewed in a post-completion audit. The scope of a post-completion audit may be very similar to an internal audit, but now the auditors are checking past practice with the knowledge, in hindsight, of how the project actually turned out. A post-completion audit may be conducted:

– as an informal review by the project manager and the project team
– at a formal debriefing meeting
– 'down the pub'
– as a detailed review by external (independent) consultants.

The first three were described in the last chapter; the fourth is discussed below.

Conducting audits

There is a seven-step process to conducting an internal or post-completion audit:

1. Conduct interviews
2. Analyse data
3. Sample management reports
4. Compare against a standard of best practice
5. Repeat steps 1 to 4 as necessary
6. Identify strengths and weaknesses of the management approach
7. Define opportunities for improvement.

CONDUCT INTERVIEWS

How you conduct interviews is a matter of style. You should always have some agenda of topics you wish to cover. Some people prefer to use a questionnaire, either a written one or a list of questions to be asked in a face-to-face interview. They work through the questions in methodical order. My own preference is for face-to-face interviews. I have a list of broad topics to cover, which I explain to interviewees at the start, but I then allow them to have free rein. Before closing the interview I ensure that all topics have been covered. I find that I learn more this way. Like Agatha Christie's detective, Hercule Poirot, I find that nobody can spin a consistent web of deceit, so if you let them talk, they must eventually tell you the truth. However, if you ask a set of closed questions, it is very easy for them to be economical with the truth. The topics covered should address the standards of good practice that you are using as your basis, as described below.

ANALYSE DATA

You should check the data being used on the project, to determine their validity. The data gathered must be relevant, give a true representation of progress, and be processed in such a way that errors are not introduced. For data which are handled manually, there can be errors of transcription. These are usually unwitting, but they can be deliberate. It is the norm to find that when data are entered manually into several computer systems they do not tally. I once spoke to a project manager in a firm of engineering contractors who said it was common for project accounts and company accounts to differ by up to 5 per cent, which he thought acceptable. To avoid errors of transcription, electronic means of data entry are now used, including bar coding. Furthermore, data may be entered into a single computer system, and distributed to all those who need them.

SAMPLE MANAGEMENT REPORTS

Reports used by managers to monitor progress are checked to ensure that they are relevant and truly representative of progress, and enable the manager to spot divergences from plan easily so that quick, effective action can be taken. The reports may be used by the project manager, work-package managers, or senior managers including the sponsor, champion or steering committee.

COMPARE AGAINST A STANDARD OF BEST PRACTICE

The information gathered about how the project is being managed is compared to a model or standard of best practice. Clearly, while you are conducting the early steps, you bear your model in mind. However, I find it is better to gather the information freely, because you then actually find out what is going on. If you merely ask whether the standard is being followed it is very easy to miss the gaps, and it is very easy for people to mislead you. The standard of best practice will be a procedures manual used by the organization, or a diagnostic procedure prepared by a firm of consultants. The standard will be hierarchical, presenting a series of important issues and questions at each stage throughout the life cycle of a project, or against each element of work in a standard work breakdown. This enables the auditor to focus on those areas that are important to the project at hand, rather than wading through a list of irrelevant questions. Figure 16.4 shows a seven-stage life cycle used for auditing contract management[10] (from the contractor's viewpoint), and gives key issues and the important parameters at each stage. Each stage of this life cycle is sup-

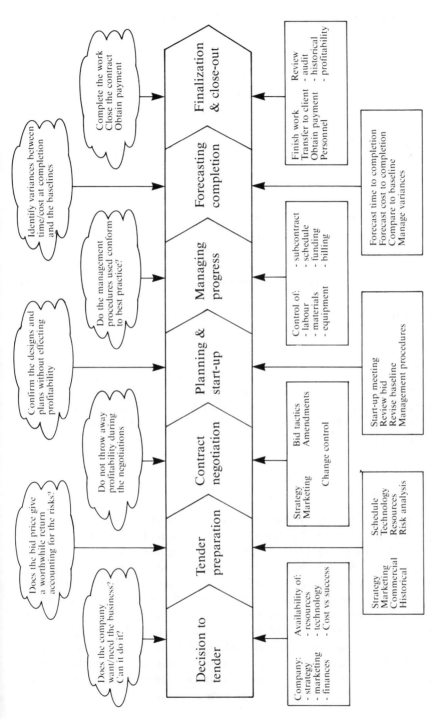

Figure 16.4 Life cycle followed in an audit procedure for contract management

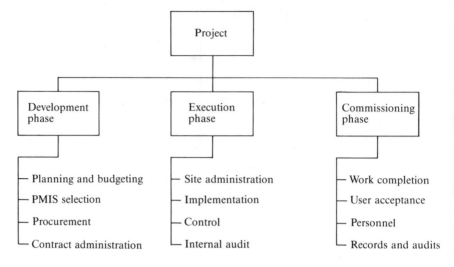

Figure 16.5   Work breakdown used in an audit procedure for project management

ported by a series of questions against each parameter. Figure 16.5 shows a work breakdown for auditing project management (from the owner's viewpoint), and Example 16.5 gives a further breakdown under *planning and budgeting*. (This follows the contents of the Project Definition Report, Chapter 13.)

REPEAT STEPS 1 TO 4 AS NECESSARY

The comparison may raise further questions about the data, or the management processes used. Alternatively, as a result of the comparison, you may realize there are things that were not adequately covered during the initial interviews. You may need to return to one or more of steps 1 to 4, until you are satisfied everything has been adequately covered. My style is to conduct a preliminary set of interviews with senior managers to try to establish their views of the problems. As a result of that initial set of interviews, and my experience of similar organizations, I draw up a more detailed audit plan covering selected topics from the audit procedure. I then work through steps 1 to 4 according to that plan. After these interviews I typically have 80 per cent of the information I require. One or two more selected interviews may then give me all the information I can reasonably expect to get.

TRIMAGI COMMUNICATIONS BV
Project Management Audit Procedure

A10 PLANNING AND BUDGETING
  A100   Introduction
  A101   Undertake feasibility study
  A102   Evaluate options
  A103   Develop statement of purpose, scope and objectives
  A104   Establish key performance criteria
       A1041   Scope
       A1042   Organization
       A1043   Quality
       A1044   Cost
       A1045   Time
  A105   Choose organizational structure
  A106   Define design/engineering tasks
  A107   Define execution management tasks
  A108   Develop milestone plan
  A109   Develop responsibility chart
  A110   Establish quality assurance procedures
  A111   Develop project schedule
  A112   Develop project budgets
  A113   Obtain project financing
  A114   Identify major risks
  A115   Select project management system
  A116   Establish project administration
  A117   Staff Project Support Office
  A118   Identify licensing/regulatory requirements

AUTHOR: JRT   ISSUE: A   DATE 30 APRIL 199X

Example 16.5 Activities under the work package: *Planning and budgeting*

IDENTIFY STRENGTHS AND WEAKNESSES OF THE MANAGEMENT APPROACH

Through comparison of the information gathered with the audit procedure, you can identify strengths and weaknesses of the management approach used on projects in the organization, either on the project being audited or in general. I always believe it is important to identify both strengths and weaknesses, for two reasons:

1. You learn as much by reinforcing strengths as you do by eliminating weaknesses.

2. People are more receptive to bad news if you start by giving them good news. Even when reviewing an utter disaster it can be a good idea to make people feel that not everything they did was wrong.

DEFINE OPPORTUNITIES FOR IMPROVEMENT

From the strengths and weaknesses you can identify areas where improvements can be made. Clearly you should aim to eliminate weaknesses. However, the application of the good points may be patchy, and so you can look to widen their scope, or you can find ways of improving their efficiency, and thereby make their application stronger still. Identified opportunities can be implemented via *improvement projects* (see Section 17.5).

16.6 The Project Support Office

Many project-based organizations use a Project Support Office (PSO) to administer project management routines. The advantage is it removes some uncertainty from projects if experienced people operate the control procedures. Large to major projects often have a dedicated office comprising people who move from project to project. Smaller projects cannot afford the overhead of a dedicated office, so they share one with projects from related programmes. Often managers of small- to medium-sized projects undertake all the administrative tasks themselves, or share them among people working on the project, with the result that they do not get done, as the technical work of the project begins to consume all the team's efforts. Hence the services of a PSO can be just as valuable to a small project as to a large one. Indeed, since it will be servicing all the projects of the organization, it can ensure that all projects receive adequate priority, that only projects for which there are adequate resources are started in the first place, and consistent approaches are used across all projects within the organization. In this section I shall describe the role of the Project Support Office, and identify the personnel it contains.

Duties of the Project Support Office

The duties of the Project Support Office include:

- maintaining the master project and programme plans
- maintaining the company-wide resource plan
- providing resource data to the project initiation process
- issuing work-to lists and kit-marshalling lists

- facilitating the control process
- issuing progress reports
- operating document control and configuration management
- producing exception lists
- purchasing and administration of subcontracts
- maintaining the client interface
- acting as a conscience.

MAINTAINING THE MASTER PROJECT AND PROGRAMME PLANS

The PSO maintains the master project and programme plans on a central (computer) system:

- for a large project, that will be a stand-alone plan
- for a major project, it may be broken down into subproject plans
- for a programme of projects, the PSO will maintain both a programme plan and individual project plans (Section 16.2).

In all cases there must be clearly defined levels of access for different managers. Almost all managers will be able to interrogate the plans at all levels. However, they will only be able to make changes at their level of responsibility: work-package managers at that level; project managers at that level; and programme directors at that level. Changes must obviously be within the constraints set at the higher level. If that is impossible, then the approval of the higher level manager must be sought. Sometimes, the ability to make changes is limited to the PSO staff. Managers can only recommend. In this way the integrity of the system is maintained.

MAINTAINING THE COMPANY-WIDE RESOURCE PLAN

The resource aggregation at the project level provides the company-wide resource plan. The PSO can take a company-wide view of the resource availability, and assign resources to individual projects (within the constraints set by the programme directors). Individual projects are not in a position to do this, unless they have a dedicated resource pool.

PROVIDING RESOURCE DATA TO THE PROJECT INITIATION PROCESS

When the organization is considering whether to initiate a new project, the PSO can compare the resource requirements to projected availability. This information can then be used as part of the feasibility study. The PSO does not have the power to veto a project; it is up to senior management to accept or reject it. However, if there are insufficient resources, senior management must decide whether to stop another project, or buy in resources from outside. That is extremely valuable information. It is better not to start a project, than to stop it half finished, especially a client contract.

ISSUING WORK-TO LISTS AND KIT-MARSHALLING LISTS

At regular intervals, as agreed with the project managers, or as set by the company's procedures, the PSO will issue work-to lists and kit-marshalling lists (Section 14.4). Giving this work to the PSO ensures that it is done regularly, and that it is done to a consistent style, in a way that people from across the organization can readily understand.

FACILITATING THE CONTROL PROCESS

The PSO can manage the control process. Indeed, it can ensure that this is done, and relieve project staff of some of the bureaucratic processes, allowing the latter to concentrate on the project work. This activity requires the project office to:

- progress, receive and process the turn-around documents
- analyse the consequences of the progress information
- perform the what-if analysis
- revise the plan with the appropriate manager
- re-issue work-to lists for the next period.

Figure 7.8 is a responsibility chart showing a procedure for this control cycle. The PSO will, of course, facilitate the control of time, cost, quality, scope, resource usage (organization), and risk.

ISSUING PROGRESS REPORTS

Following on from the control process, the PSO can issue progress reports. These may go to:

- project managers
- programme directors
- other senior managers
- the client.

The reports issued will be defined by a procedures manual. The data gathered in turn-around documents may be used for other purposes, such as:

- pay-roll
- recording of holidays and flexitime
- raising of invoices
- recording project costs for the company's accounting systems.

For the last, it is vital for control purposes that costs are recorded by the project and sent to the accounts system, and not vice versa. With the latter, information can be received several months after costs are incurred, which is far too late for control. The data can be recorded separately for each system, but then they almost never agree. The despatch of these data, which may be electronic, will be done by the PSO as part of the reporting process. It is important to review the data before despatch, rather than allowing them to go automatically, to ensure their integrity. However, this can be simplified by building in automatic checks.

OPERATING DOCUMENT CONTROL AND CONFIGURATION MANAGEMENT

Projects can involve the transmittal of a large amount of information. The PSO can coordinate that transmittal, which may include some of the items mentioned below.

1. Keep a library of progress reports for ready access by any (authorized) personnel.
2. Record all correspondence to and from clients and subcontractors. As part of this process, the PSO may include acknowledgement slips, and monitor their return to ensure receipt of the correspondence. Technical personnel can be lax in the recording of correspondence, which can cause problems later if there is a claim. To avoid this, some organizations insist that all outward correspondence goes via the PSO, and a copy of all inward correspondence is logged with that office.
3. Monitor all correspondence between project personnel. On a large project, this can drastically reduce the channels of communication. However, it is more efficient to have a central clearing point for communication on projects with as few as four people. This can be essential if the people have not worked together before, on projects involving tight time scales, and on projects involving research scientists, who do not tend to be very communicative.
4. Maintain the records for quality control and configuration management, to ensure they are properly completed, before work commences on the next stage. This can also include change control.
5. Monitor the despatch of design information to site or subcontractors, to ensure it is received and the latest information used. I have known

of cases where drawings are lost in the post, and of course the intended recipients have no way of knowing they should be using new data. Acknowledgement slips solve this problem.
6. Issue management. Issues can arise on a project, which may or may not lead to a change or a claim. The PSO can manage the decision-making process.

PRODUCING EXCEPTION LISTS

As part of the control process, the PSO may produce exception reports. Clearly they will produce variance reports at each reporting period. However, exception lists will highlight items that have become critical.

PURCHASING AND ADMINISTRATION OF SUBCONTRACTS

Where there is not already a purchasing department within the parent organization, the PSO can take over the procurement function. There is a view that in some project-based organizations a very high proportion of total expenditure on projects is through purchased materials or subcontract labour, and so this function should be within the control of project or programme management.

MAINTAINING THE CLIENT INTERFACE

The PSO may manage the relationship with the client. This includes the issuing of progress reports, the control of communications, and the despatch of invoices. It also involves producing reports against agreed project milestones, and the maintenance of links with opposite numbers in the client organization so that any threats to the contract can be worked through together. The project manager must also maintain close links with his or her opposite number and the client's sponsor, to help maintain a good working relationship. Contacts with the sponsor and the other key decision makers can help to ensure continued support for the current contract, which will ease its delivery and help to win new work.

ACTING AS A CONSCIENCE

Effective project management requires all the control procedures described above to be well maintained. Some of them can become bureaucratic, and distracting for the technical staff. While the project is running smoothly, they can seem unnecessary, and not receive adequate attention. However, if the project does go wrong, then the data and plans are required to plan recovery or defend a claim. However, it is then too late to start recording the data and maintaining the plans. This must be done from the start. The PSO can relieve project staff of the bureaucratic burden. Because they maintain the plans as one of their day-to-day duties, they become efficient at it, so the cost of the administrative overhead is less than if project personnel do it. Indeed, the service and support they give can speed up the work of the project even further. In fulfilling this role, the PSO act as a conscience, because they ensure that the regular reports are filed, and they will not let certain major milestones be met until appropriate documentation is completed.

Personnel of the Project Support Office

The number and skills of people in the PSO depends on the scope of the operation.[11] Possible personnel include:

- planners
- administrators
- cost controllers
- materials planners
- purchasing, progress and expediting
- contract administration.

Planners   At its simplest, there may be just one or more planners (called project controllers or planning engineers). They can fulfil all the planning and control functions described above, but not procurement or client liaison.

Administrators   If the document control is particularly complex, then it may be appropriate to include an administrator, clerk or secretary.

Cost controllers   For larger operations, the cost control function may be split from the remainder. The cost controller is called a cost engineer or project accountant. A cost controller should also maintain links with the estimating function. If the turn-around documents are also used to gather pay-roll data, they may also maintain links with the personnel function.

Materials planners   Again, for larger operations, or ones with a large material content, it is common to split out the materials management function. The materials planners maintain the material and design schedules, and issue the kit-marshalling lists. They also liaise with procurement and stores, and may issue work-to lists to design.

Procurement clerks   When the PSO is fulfilling the procurement function, purchasing, progress and expediting clerks may be included in the staff.

There may also be inspectors and quantity surveyors. The latter will judge performance of subcontractors.

Contract administrators When the PSO also manages the client interface, then the staff will include contract administrators or managers.

16.7 Summary

1. A programme is a portfolio of projects managed together to deliver additional benefits. Programme management is the process of coordinating the management of the projects and assigning priorities to them to achieve the benefits.
2. There are five steps to coordinating the projects:
   - identify links
   - group projects into programmes to minimize links
   - determine the impact of links
   - prioritize into major and minor links
   - manage the major links.
3. There are six steps for assigning priorities to projects for resources:
   - plan individual projects
   - calculate individual project's resource requirements
   - place each project into the master project schedule
   - assign each project priority
   - assign it a time and resource window in the MPS
   - manage each project within its window.
4. There are four steps to implementing configuration management:
   - configuration identification
   - configuration reviews
   - configuration control
   - status accounting.
5. Procedures manuals typically have four parts and an appendix:
   - introduction and purpose
   - project strategy
   - management processes at each stage of the life cycle
   - supporting procedures
   - blank forms and samples.
6. Project audits may be conducted as:
   - project evaluation audits
   - internal audits
   - post-completion audits.
7. There are seven steps to conducting an audit:
   - conduct interviews

- analyse data
- sample management reports
- compare to a standard
- repeat as necessary
- identify strengths and weaknesses
- identify opportunities for improvement.

8. The role of the Project Support Office is to:
   - maintain the master project and programme plans
   - maintain the company-wide resource plan
   - provide resource data to the project initiation process
   - issue work-to lists and kit-marshalling lists
   - facilitate the control process
   - issue progress reports
   - operate document control and configuration management
   - produce exception lists
   - purchase and administration of subcontracts
   - maintain the client interface
   - act as a conscience.

9. The personnel contained in the Project Support Office may be:
   - planners
   - administrators
   - cost controllers
   - materials planners
   - purchasing, progress and expediting
   - contract administration.

Notes and references

1. Section 16.2 contains ideas contributed by Debbie Carlton and Simon Bissel. Ms Carlton is Director of Diploma and Certificate Programmes at Henley Management College. Previously she worked as a civil engineer in the water industry and design consulting.
2. Ferns, D., 'Developments in programme management', paper presented to The Association of Project Managers' London Seminar on Programme Management, Association of Project Managers, 21 March 1991.
3. BS 4335, *Glossary of Terms used in Project Management*, British Standards Institute, 1987.
4. Turner, J. R., 'Company resource planning in the food processing industry', in *Proceedings of the 12th INTERNET International Expert Seminar* (ed. S. Dworatschek), INTERNET, 1988.
5. Section 16.3 incorporates material written by Richard Morreale. Mr Morreale is managing director of Life Cycle Management Systems, a company providing project management consultancy services to the IT industry.
6. Anon., *PROMPT*, Learmonth and Burchett Management Systems.

7. CCTA, *PRINCE*, NCC Blackwell, 1990.
8. Anon., *PRISM*, Hoskyns.
9. Anon., *Plan of Works*, Royal Institute of British Architects.
10. Derby, P., Stirling, D. and Turner, J. R., *The Contract Control Review Guide*, Coopers & Lybrand, 1986,
11. Archibald, R. D., *Managing High-Technology Programs and Projects*, Wiley, 1976.

17
Project management information systems

17.1 Introduction[1]

I have mentioned several times the possibility of using a computer-based project management information system (PMIS). I explained in Chapter 9 how they can help formulate the cost estimate, and gather cost information to calculate earned value and draw S-curves; in Chapter 10 how they can perform complex time and resource scheduling, and what-if analysis; in Chapter 11 how they can help analyse risk and formulate appropriate contingency plans; in Chapter 14 how they can generate work-to lists and turn-around documents, and help gather and analyse control data; and in Chapter 16 how they can help manage the data required by programme management and configuration management.

However, in earlier chapters, I avoided presenting the management of projects as a computer exercise. This was deliberate. The manager must understand and follow the principles of good project management, and the methods, tools and techniques described in this book. Only after mastering the approach, should managers use a computer system to perform some routine processes, to handle the vast quantities of data involved, or to simplify complex analyses. This is similar to the reasons why school pupils should master long division before using an electronic calculator. You cannot use the electronic aid effectively until you understand the process, and can question on a conceptual level the answers it gives. Unfortunately, there are people who view project management as a computer-based exercise: some who say that project management is solely critical path analysis on computers; and some for whom the computer models become more important than reality. There is considerable anecdotal evidence for this. There was a television programme about project management in 1988, which concentrated almost entirely on the use of a critical path analysis to plan and track two sporting events, the Winter Olympics in Canada in 1988 and a car rally. About the same time, advertisements appeared in national newspapers for one of the packages, a

389

market leader of PC-based systems at the time, which claimed that the package would turn someone with no previous experience into an expert project manager overnight. The following year, the manager of a £30 million IT project attending a project management course at Henley said that he had a room with three people who spent all day, every day, developing plans in the same package, and he got no useful information out. When used effectively, a PMIS is an invaluable and powerful tool, and with the design of these systems tending to be more user oriented, their use will grow. However, like all tools they have their limitations: in the hands of an expert, they are invaluable; in the hands of an inexperienced person, they are dangerous.

In this chapter, I shall describe the use of computer systems in project management. I shall describe the types of system available and their use, how to evaluate and implement systems, and the implications of the use of the systems. Some definitions will be presented in Section 17.2.

I shall occasionally refer to examples of PMIS software. The packages mentioned all have versions available on IBM compatible microcomputers. Some have versions on DEC VAX and other minicomputers. ARTEMIS™, the market leader in the mini and mainframe environments, has versions available for DEC VAX, Hewlett Packard Minis and IBM and DEC Mainframe units. Although several hundred systems are available, and many of them are useful in their place, I have only mentioned those of which I have first-hand experience.

17.2 Definitions and rationale

The first question to consider is why is there a need for a PMIS. Most organizations have an extensive range of computer-based information systems. One of the most common is a computerized accounts package, and it might be argued that these could be adapted to provide cost control for most projects. However, functionally oriented systems are not appropriate for the management of projects, because they have many unique requirements, including:

– integration across the organization
– the planning and control process
– fast response times.

Integration across the organization

The management of projects involves the integration of several parties from within and outside the parent organization (Chapter 4) and this requires effective communication across the functional hierarchy. Traditional management information systems are designed to support functional units within a hierarchical structure.[2] Typical systems include the materials system used by the manufacturing department, the pay-roll system used by the personnel department, or the accounts system used by the finance department. There are examples of companies trying to share information between departments by basing all the systems on a common database management system (DBMS), such as Oracle™. However, there is a need for a PMIS which crosses all functional boundaries to satisfy the project's information needs for data gathering and reporting. The PMIS will gather its own data, and generate its own reports, as well as provide information to and obtain it from the functional systems. The reports produced may be in a variety of formats for the different parties involved: summary reports for the owner, or detailed reports for operational staff or users. Traditional information systems are unable to integrate interdepartmental data or to satisfy this requirement for providing compatible reporting across project interfaces.

The planning and control process

Because projects are transient, the planning and control process evolves throughout the life cycle, whereas in the functionally oriented systems it usually assumes a steady state. The planning process starts during proposal and initiation at the integrative level, and the project model is developed during the subsequent stages down through the three levels, until it is brought together as an implementation plan at the bottom level (Figure 2.5). This implementation plan may consist of networks, bar charts, and work-to lists (Table 14.1). It may also consist of drawing registers, material lists, or configuration reports. When the project is underway, progress information is gathered and processed to control the project. This feedback cycle continues to the end of the project.

Fast response times

These feedback cycles are of short duration – a maximum of two weeks (Chapters 6 and 14) – reducing to daily or twice daily at critical times. Many of the traditional systems are designed for much longer reporting periods, and so the information gathered is not presented in a time that is of any use for controlling a project. The company accounting package, for instance, reports at the end of a monthly accounting period, and so is typically presenting financial data that are, on average, three weeks old. That is of no use to a project manager trying to control costs on a week by week basis. The data come long after the point at which corrective action can be taken. The situation is worse if the accounting package is collecting payment data, and not commitments, because invoices can be paid any time after the project is finished.

One problem of maintaining a separate PMIS, using its own source data to provide fast response times for control purposes, is that there may be a discrepancy in the out-turn figures between the PMIS and, say, the company's accounting package. A project manager with a large engineering contracting company in the petrochemical industry told me once that the discrepancy may be as much as 5 per cent. Where the systems are using different source data, or even where the same data are just being entered twice into different systems, discrepancies might be considered inevitable. It requires quite rigorous audit trails to prevent this happening. Alternatively, the data can first be entered into the PMIS, and then be passed to the other systems.

Definition of a project management information system

From this discussion we can derive the definition of an information system for use by project personnel. A PMIS is used for collecting data from across various functions, and analysing and presenting those data in a form suitable for all the parties involved in a project. The systems are used for planning and controlling projects, throughout the project management life cycle, providing timely control information. The systems are also used for recording historical data for estimating of future projects.

A PMIS that fulfils these requirements can be viewed as having two parts[2] (Figure 17.1): a planning system and a control system. The planning system converts data on the schedule, cost and performance into structured, timely and accurate information. The control system uses that

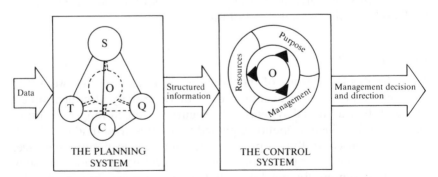

Figure 17.1 Model of a project management informations system

information to support management decisions and direction with respect to the project's organization and context (purpose, people involved and management procedures). The planning system manages the plan and control data relating to the five system objectives: scope, organization, quality, cost and time. The control system enables the manager to use the information generated to direct all elements of the project organization, including human resources, drawings, materials and finance. I shall explain how many of the packages available address only the planning system part of this model, and often only the time-related part of that.

17.3 Types of package

People talk about the PMISs currently available on the market as if they were all the same thing. They will compare two systems as radically different as Incontrol™ and Artemis™ as if they had comparable functionality. There are three types of package currently available on the market, and two types for which there is a need but which the software industry has yet to satisfy. They are, respectively:

- networking systems (including CPM and PERT)
- cost and resource management systems
- application generators
- capacity planning systems
- totally integrated, modular packages

Most of the available systems can be used as stand-alone packages, or as part of a distributed network over several locations, with a central head office corresponding with local sites.

Networking systems

Programmes to perform network analysis were the first computer-based systems developed. The critical path method (CPM) had been applied manually since the 1940s, but was first used on computer by duPont and Remington Rand in 1957.[3] The program evaluation and review technique (PERT) was developed jointly by the United States Navy Special Projects Office, Booz-Allen-Hamilton, and Lockheed Missile and Space Division.

The simplest systems are simply network analysis systems, CPA or CPM, which allow you to calculate early and late starts of the activities in the network, and to draw a network and bar chart. A package called Incontrol™, for example, costs about £50, and someone with very little project management experience can learn to use it in a few hours. The simplest PERT systems also include a field to record the planned or actual dates. Hence, at any point during the project, you can record the dates on which you are currently planning to start or finish each activity, or the dates on which you did, once these are in the past. This recording of planned and actual dates is often referred to as 'tracking the network'. In terms of the model in Figure 17.1, the CPA system without tracking is a planning system, and a PERT system with tracking is a planning and control system. Further functionality has been added to many PERT systems in response to the requirement that a PMIS should also provide planning and control of resources, costs and other things, and includes (Figure 17.2):

- data entry via the network, bar chart, WBS, spreadsheet or activity cards
- resource totals, shown as histograms or spreadsheets
- resource smoothing
- simple cost accumulation, with resource and material costs
- cost tracking
- nesting of networks and bar charts
- several calendars with individual holidays and a variety of working patterns
- report generation
- import/export to and from database management systems.

Three systems that I have found to be quite useful are Hoskyns' Project Manager Workbench™ (PMW™), Computer Associates' Super Project Expert™, and Welcome Software Technology's Open Plan™. The first of these I find very powerful as a planning tool for performing *what-if* analysis. It allows you to enter the bar chart and vary the timing and duration of the activities, while giving immediate indication of resource loadings, violation of resource constraints and logic. I found earlier versions to be slow and clumsy for tracking, although that has been improved in version 3.0, which allows data entry via timesheets. Super Project™ is much better for tracking, but the early versions would not allow you to violate resource and other constraints that you might sometimes want to treat as soft. (We shall return to Open Plan™ below.) With the exception of Open Plan™ (for reasons which we shall see shortly), many of the systems always appear to the user as little more than networking systems with limited, added functionality. People new to project management find them useful as an introduction. However, the functionality can very quickly become limiting, but the users will have invested so much time in developing plans in the system that it becomes impossible to migrate to some of the more powerful packages described below. Many of the systems, including the above three, allow data to be imported and exported to other data management systems, such as Lotus-123™ and dBase IV Plus™,

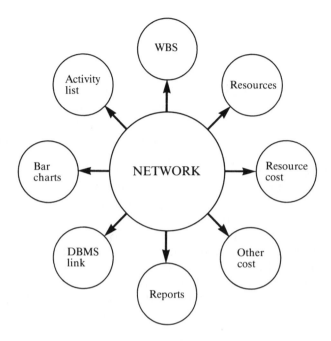

Figure 17.2   Model of a networking system with added functionality

and so additional functionality can be developed in those. In fact, Open Plan™ is written to run in dBase IV Plus™ (and other DMBSs). There are very few systems that support true PERT, with variable durations and Monte Carlo analysis. Open Plan™ has an add-on called Opera™ which allows that.

Cost and resource management systems

In Chapter 1 it was stated that the other fundamental methodology in project management is C/SPEC, based on the cost control cube. The several PMISs that apply this methodology are primarily cost scheduling and control packages, and provide a WBS, OBS and CBS, with cost data entered against elements of work at any level in all three breakdown structures. In the simplest systems, time schedule data must be calculated in a separate system, and entered by hand. However, many systems now have an attached networking system. Two systems I have experienced are Cascade™ by Mantix, which runs in Oracle™ on a minicomputer, and Cobra™ which is an add-on to Open Plan™.

Application generators

Many experienced project managers often want functionality beyond what the above systems supply. For example, they want material schedules, drawing schedules, and configuration management systems. To obtain this additional functionality they use a third type of system, known as an *application generator*. These systems combine a powerful DBMS, with project management functionality. You will often hear the DBMS referred to as a 'relational database', or 'fourth-generation language' (4GL). Oracle™ and dBase IV Plus™ are both DBMSs. (For information, the standard programming languages such as FORTRAN, Cobol, C and Basic are 3GLs; 5GLs include artificial intelligence and knowledge-based systems).

The users develop their own application in the DBMS, with the functionality they require, while the attached project management functionality provides the standard routines. These systems require advanced project management and computer skills before they can be used, and hence the reason why people start with the simpler systems described above. However, the functionality of the application generators is almost unlimited. The first system of this type was Artemis™, which was first developed by Metier in 1978. Other systems include Cresta™ from K&H Project Systems, Primavera™ and Panorama™. Artemis™ and Cresta™ come with their own proprietary DBMS, and so the user has another language to learn. The others use standard DMBSs such as Oracle™, BTrieve™, FoxBase™ and dBase IV Plus™. You will see that Cascade™ and Open Plan™ are effectively application generators. In fact, Open Plan™ breaks the syndrome described above, because the naive users can start using it as a packaged solution, but switch over to using it as an application generator as their skills grow.

All application generators allow data to be imported from and exported to other corporate systems. In fact this transfer becomes very easy if the systems are based in the same industry standard DBMS. It then is a simple matter to share input data. For instance, time-sheeting data can be shared between the PMIS, the pay-roll system, the personnel records system, and the company accounts. This eliminates the problem of discrepancies between the systems.

Capacity planning systems

There is some functionality which none of the systems provides. One requirement is the ability to share resources between concurrent projects. Some systems claim to provide multi-project scheduling. However, what they usually do is create a large network containing all the activities of all current projects. Within this mega-network, each project is assigned a priority. The project with highest priority takes all the resources it needs; the project with next highest priority takes what it needs from what is left; and the lowest priority projects have to make do with whatever is left over. The result is that the lowest priority projects receive only sporadic resourcing and effectively make no progress. The alternative is to make all the projects equal priority in the mega-network, but as yet there are no resource-smoothing algorithms that can share the resources between each of the projects in a sensible way, allowing each project to make uniform progress.

The solution to multi-project scheduling is to maintain what I call a *master project schedule*, or *rough-cut capacity planner*. This is analogous to a master production schedule (MPS) used in a manufacturing requirements planning system (MRPII). The master project schedule is a high-level plan in which each project is represented as a single activity, regardless of its size. (Some very small projects may be amalgamated into a single activity.) Each project is given a duration, a window and a resource loading within the overall resource constraints. Each project must then be managed within the resource profile to which it has been assigned (the resource profile also imposes start and finish dates). If a project cannot be managed within the imposed constraints, it must be returned to the master project schedule to negotiate more resources (Section 16.2).

Although no available systems formally supply this functionality, I have seen several organizations develop it for themselves using proprietary software. For instance, ICI maintained a master project schedule for maintenance projects on their Billingham site, a site with an annual maintenance budget of about £100 million. Each maintenance project, whether a two-month plant overhaul, or a week-long task force, or a minor capital project lasting weeks or months, was represented as a single activity, and resource were shared between projects at that level. Only day-to-day work was amalgamated into a series of week-long projects, consuming surplus resources. Each project was then planned individually, in their integrated maintenance system, called Merlin™, using the resources it had been assigned by the master project schedule. The actual package that ICI used for this purpose was a PC-based PERT system called Korkus™, supplied by K&H Computer Systems. I have seen the same thing done to good effect within the ship repair and electronic systems supply industries. I suggested to the company described in Example 3.5 that they develop a similar system to prioritize resources between their internal development projects.[4] The package I suggested they use for the master project schedule was not a PERT system, but dBase IV Plus™.

Totally integrated, modular packages

The other requirement missing from the PMIS market is a completely integrated, modular system, which provides all the functionality required by most projects, but requires no tailoring by the user. This would give the power of the application generators without the need to be expert in either project management or computer programming. In the manufacturing requirements planning systems market, there are several such systems available. In fact many companies use the adoption of such systems as a vehicle for implementing good manufacturing planning practice in their production facilities. The argument is that if your current practice does not match the functionality provided by any of the systems, then your practice is wrong since the systems represent best practice. (The same argument is slightly fallacious about PMISs, since they represent best project management practice in the IT industry, and not necessarily the engineering or other industries.) The closest to a modular approach in the PMIS market are the suite of programs sold by Welcome Software Technology (Open Plan™, Cobra™, Opera™, and others), and the system Cascade™, sold by Mantix. There are also a growing number of modules and standard applications written in Artemis™. Some of them are provided by the suppliers, and some by third party software houses.

If you require an integrated PMIS, with full functionality, you need to develop it yourself, using one of the application generators. The problem is that to do that you already need a high level of project management skill, and good programming expertise, which many organizations undertaking quite large projects do not have. They want to obtain a PMIS as a vehicle for implementing good project management practice! Also, developing the applications can require a large investment in terms of both cash and people's time. It cost ICI several million pounds to develop their system Merlin, but that was only a small percentage of their annual maintenance budget, and the system was very successful. I have seen other companies spending over a million pounds to buy the software and develop the applications, and the money has been totally wasted as the systems were a disaster. It is interesting to consider why project managers want individually tailored systems. People have said that every project is unique, and so project managers want a system tailored to their precise requirements (and to their bad practices as well). I also find this argument slightly fallacious, because every manufacturing facility is unique, but a limited range of MRPII packages seem to suffice for most requirements. Perhaps it says something about the psyche of project managers that each wants his or her own system.

Figure 17.3 shows the modules that might be contained within the

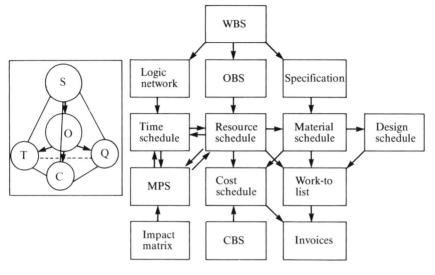

Figure 17.3 Modules contained in the planning systems of an integrated, modular PMIS

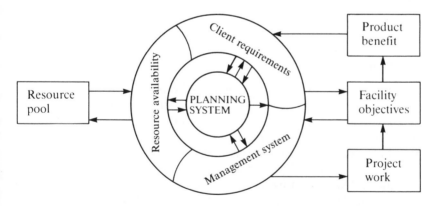

Figure 17.4 The fully integrated PMIS and its links to the context of projects

planning system of such an integrated system. Figure 17.4 shows how that planning system would actually sit within a control system which addresses the three elements of the context of projects (Figure 2.7 and Part Two). Two elements of the context, the client's requirements and the project strategy, are linked to the project-facility-purpose model (Figure 1.2). The third element, the parties involved, is linked to a resource pool.

Figure 17.5 shows data flows between the planning and control systems and the context.

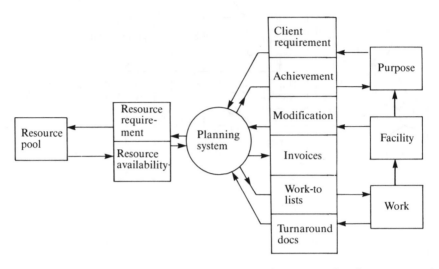

Figure 17.5   Data flows in a fully integrated PMIS, between planning system and control system, and between control system and context

Distributed networks

Many of the early packages were designed to be used as stand-alone systems, dedicated to a single project. However, the vast majority of projects now take place in a multi-project environment, and share resources with other projects (Chapter 21). They also take place within a parent organization, which has several current projects and wants to keep track of them all simultaneously to set priorities for resources depending on changing circumstances. Many organizations therefore want all projects managed through a single system, on a distributed network (Figure 17.6.).

At the centre is the master plan for all projects, which is housed on one of the systems based on a DBMS, and probably one of the application generators (or a modular system if one is ever developed). It will have all the project management functionality required by the organization, including the master project schedule. The system will also include the master plan for each project, and any corporate data, such as resource availability and the time-sheeting system. The hardware used may be a mainframe, but it is more likely to be a minicomputer, or one of the super micros (386 or 486 machine). The central system will almost certainly be

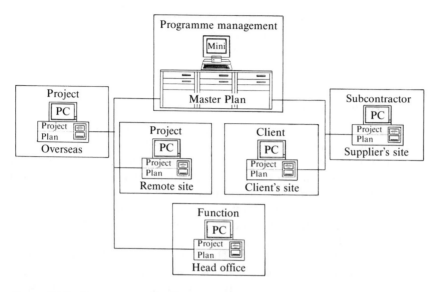

Figure 17.6   System on a distributed network for the multi-project environment

maintained by a Project Support Office (Section 16.6). The system will have password protection, so that only members of the PSO can change the functionality of the system, include new projects in the system, or revise project plans. All other people will be limited to interrogation only, or to interrogation and to input control data.

Each project area is linked to the central system via a PC. Areas in the same building may be linked via a local area network (LAN) and remote sites via telephone. Even sites overseas can be linked to the central system via the telephone network. The local PC may act as 'dumb terminal', and merely be used to interrogate the central system. Alternatively, it may maintain a separate version of the individual project plan used by the remote site. The local version of the plan may be maintained in a reduced version of the central package, or it may be maintained in a different package. One of the simpler PERT systems may have sufficient functionality for the local site. The local version is used for several purposes: to print work-to lists, to receive the input from turn-around documents, and to conduct what-if analyses. The local package transfers data to and from the central system regularly. If the connection is via a LAN, this may be done continuously, or it may be done on a fixed frequency ranging from every minute to once a week. At the regular interchange, changes to the master plan may be transferred to the remote site. Progress data can be sent from the remote site, but changes to the plan as a result of the what-if analysis can only be incorporated into the master plan with the authority of the PSO. This is because changes may have an impact on other projects, especially through the setting of priority for sharing resources.

17.4 Evaluating systems

When selecting a system, you need to draw up a list of requirements, and evaluate the available systems against the list. Figure 17.7 contains an evaluation for a company supplying process equipment to the chemical industry. In this evaluation, each requirement was weighted 1, 2 or 3 depending on its perceived importance to the selection. Each package was then awarded a mark from 0 to 3 against each requirement. A weighted average mark was calculated for each package. In this evaluation, the criteria chosen were loaded in favour of one of the application generators for the central system. However, even though PMW™ scored quite lowly for the central system, it was still the preferred package for the remote sites, because what-if analysis and simplicity of data entry were considered important to these sites. From this initial evaluation, a shortlist of packages was chosen for further evaluation. This was conducted against a more detailed list of requirements, based on a draft procedures manual. The more detailed list was weighted in favour of a system based on an industry standard DBMS, and so a system based on Oracle™ or dBase IV Plus™ was preferred.

Typical evaluation criteria for the shortlist included items detailed below.

Overall design

The primary purpose of a PMIS is to develop a numerical model of a project. All well-designed software should enable the user to do this, and to update the model readily. The package should be easy to use, 'user-friendly', but flexible enough to accommodate both the beginner and experienced users. It should come with standard screen formats to enable the novice to use the system with little training, but allow the experienced users to change the formats to suit their requirements.

Activity and project capacities

The maximum number of activities in a project, or the number of projects handled simultaneously, can be important. Some packages promise 32 000 activities but I doubt the need for such large numbers of activities

FEATURE	NEED	ARTEMIS PC MINI	PANORAMA PC MINI	PRIMAVERA	OPEN-PLAN AND SUITE	CRESTA	KERNEL	VISION	HORNET	PMW	CA- SUPER PROJECT	PLANTRAC
Relational database	High	Own 4GL / 3	Oracle / 3	Btrieve / 3	dBase IV / 3	Own 4GL / 2	OwnL 4GL / 2	Own 4GL / 2	Own / 2	Import/ / 1	Import/ / 2	Own / 2
Multi-projects	High	Nest Prog / 3	Nest Prog / 3	Nest Prog / 3	Nest Prog / 3	Nest Prog / 3	Nest Prog / 3	Nest Prog / 3	Nest Only / 3	Nest Only / 1	Nest Only / 1	High Only / 3
Two/Multi-tier work breakdown structure	High	Prog / 3	Yes / 3	Prog / 3	Prog / 3	Prog / 2	Prog / 3	Prog / 3	Nest / 3	Yes / 3	Yes / 3	Yes / 3
Matrix management structure	High	Prog / 3	Yes / 3	Prog / 3	Prog / 3	Prog / 2	Prog / 2	Prog / 3	Resource / 2	Resource / 2	Resource / 1	Resource / 2
Resource planning and control	High	High / 3	High / 3	High / 3	High / 3	High / 3	Medium / 2	High / 3	High / 3	T sheets / 2	Medium / 2	High / 3
Fast response user friendly changes	Low	Low with CSO / 1	Low / 1	Medium / 2	Medium / 2	Medium / 2	Low / 1	Medium / 2	Medium / 2	Medium / 2	High / 3	Medium / 2
Flexible reporting internal/client	Medium / 2	High (PSO) / 3	High (PSO) / 3	High (PSO) / 3	High (PSO) / 3	High (PSO) / 3	High (PSO) / 3	High (PSO) / 3	High (PSO) / 3	Low / 1	Medium / 2	Medium / 2
Full function purchasing/vendor files	High	Prog/ Link / 3	Prog/ Link / 3	Prog/ Link / 3	Prog/ Link / 3	Prog/ Link / 3	Prog/ Link / 3	Prog/ Link / 2	Prog/ Link / 2	No / 1	Link / 2	Link / 2
Full project monitoring and variance control	High	High/ Prog / 3	High/ Prog / 3	High/ Prog / 3	High/ Prog / 3	High/ Prog / 3	High/ Prog / 3	High/ Prog / 3	High/ Prog / 3	Low/ Given / 1	Medium/ Menus / 2	High / 3
Interface to CAD systems	Medium / 2	EMIS / 3	Prog / 3	Prog / 3	Prog / 3	Prog / 2	Tool Kit / 3	Prog / 2	Link / 2	Low / 1	Medium / 2	Medium / 2
Interface to manufacturing packages	High	EMIS / 3	Prog / 3	Prog / 3	Prog / 3	Prog / 2	Tool Kit / 3	Prog / 2	Medium / 2	Low / 1	Medium / 2	Medium / 2
Support client user base	High	High / 3	High / 3	High / 3	High / 3	High / 3	High / 3	High / 3	Medium / 2	Low / 1	Low / 1	Medium / 2
Password protection	High	Yes / 3	Yes / 3	Low / 1	Medium / 2	Medium / 2	Medium / 2	Low / 1	Medium / 2	No / 1	No / 1	Medium / 2
On-site operation and update	High	Yes / 3	Yes / 3	Yes / 3	Yes / 3	Yes / 3	Yes / 3	Yes / 3	Yes / 3	Yes / 3	Yes / 3	Medium / 2
SCORE		112	112	107	110	96	100	96	93	57	71	88

Key:	Prog	Programmable in the language
	Import	Import/export facility available to proprietary software
	T-sheets	Control data input via time sheets
	PSO	Project Support Office

Figure 17.7 Systems selection

in a network. If you have more than about 320 activities in your network it becomes very difficult to control. What is more important is the ability to nest networks, and many packages allow you to do that in one of two ways. In some packages you create a network, and then define it as an activity in a higher level network. You can transfer data between the low level and the master networks. When viewing the master network, you can view an activity corresponding to a low-level network either as a single activity or as a group of activities. PMW™ operates in this way, and it is very effective for rolling-wave planning. Some systems, for example Hornet 5000™, allow you to draw dependencies between the networks. (The dates in all other networks are fixed while your are interrogating the current network.) In other systems, you can define some activities as *hammock* activities. These are activities that summarize others, effectively at a lower level of work breakdown. When viewing the network, you can view all the activities or just the hammocks. This also facilitates rolling-wave planning, although the network can become very cumbersome. Hornet 5000™ also allows hammock activities, while other systems such as Super Project Expert™ and Cascade™ have formal work breakdown structures. I much prefer the former approach and try to avoid having more than about 20 activities in any network, although on one £400 million engineering project 100 activities were held in the master network. The application generators, by the very nature of the relational DBMSs, allow both approaches.

Input features

In most modern systems, data input, at least in beginner mode, is via standard screen formats. There are screens corresponding to activities, resources, calendars, dependencies, etc. When viewing the overall project, you view it as a network, bar chart, or work breakdown structure. Some systems display both a bar chart and resource histogram on the same screen, allowing you to view instantly the impact of a change of schedule on the resource loadings. This facilitates what-if analysis. In some systems you can only enter the activity or resource screens from the network or bar chart, and so as you move between activities, for example, you must always return to the project level. This makes tracking the project cumbersome. In others, you can leaf through activity or resource screens, and so easily update the project. In the more advanced systems, the users can design their own input screens to suit their requirements. In the application generators, and sometimes in the simpler systems, you can input data via a line editor, word processor or spreadsheet directly into the database. Most systems are menu driven in beginner mode, but allow the experienced user to move between functions using function keys, or the system's command language.

Output features and reports

Almost all modern systems will allow reports to be viewed on screen, or sent to an output device, such as a printer, plotter, or disk file. However, the form of these reports can vary. The simpler systems come with standard report formats, whereas the application generators allow you to produce an infinite variety of reports using the *standard query language* (SQL) of the DMBS. In between, many systems allow you to produce a series of customized reports from a (limited) range of options, although in some cases (such as Super Project Expert™) this limited range is so vast as to be virtually infinite. Even systems, such as PMW™, with a small range of reports allow you to export data to data management systems, such as Lotus-123™ or dBase IV Plus™, and in those systems you can create whatever reports you wish. The reports may be tables of data, or they may be pictorial (networks, bar charts, resource histograms or S-curves).

Network notation and processing

It is easier to write a program to perform precedence networking than activity-on-arrow, and therefore almost all systems provide the former. Many provide both, but they are usually written as precedence networks, with a conversion routine. The simpler systems usually allow only finish-to-start dependencies between activities, but the more advanced systems allow all four types of dependency. Almost all systems allow leads and lags on the dependencies, and so, even on those with finish-to-start dependencies only, it is possible to plan for overlap of activities.

Date formats

Some systems allow only three dates: early, late and planned/actual. Others allow the five suggested in Chapter 10: early, late, baseline, current plan and actual. Super Project Expert™, for instance, has the latter.

Resources

Simpler packages provide resource profiles only; the more advanced smooth resources automatically. A simple labour/equipment profile can be very useful, and may let the manager undertake resource smoothing by working interactively with the package (what people describe as 'handraulically'). Sometimes this gives the best result, because the resource smoothing algorithms cannot take account of constraints that managers can carry in their head. The algorithms follow rules rigidly, and sometimes produce nonsensical solutions. One particular rule that may be treated rigidly is the resource constraints, whereas this is in fact a soft constraint. You can have people working overtime, or have people changing resource type (Example 17.1). Most packages have a limit to the number of resources that can be used on a project, although this is usually not a constraint. Also, most packages only allow a uniform resource loading on an activity – although some do allow stepped profiles, and others triangular and normal profiles (see Figure 10.15).

In the research and development department of a food company, they had cooks, chemists and chemical engineers. The chemists were interchangeable with the other two resource types. Therefore if you had 10 of each, but needed 5, 10, and 15 respectively, you could have 5 cooks work as chemists, and 5 chemists work as chemical engineers. It is very difficult to represent that in a resource smoothing algorithm.

Example 17.1   Changing resource types

Calendars

If you are to relate the schedule to real dates, it is essential to have a calendar incorporating weekends, bank holidays and holidays. The simple systems have one calendar only; some allow a mixture of five-day and seven-day working for different resources; some allow you to mix the length of the working day; and some to define a calendar for each resource, with individual holidays for professional staff. There are even some which allow you to define country calendars, with different rest days: useful if you are working in Europe (Sunday), Israel (Saturday) and Saudi Arabia (Friday), but often an unnecessary complication.

Cost management

The level of sophistication of cost management is quite wide. The PERT systems, if they have cost management at all, only let you put a rate against each resource, and one other cost figure against each activity. The C/SPEC systems and application generators allow you to define lists of people and materials against each activity, and either a variable or fixed cost against each resource type. In this way you can develop extremely sophisticated cost control systems.

Risk analysis

There are a few systems which will allow you to perform true PERT, or Monte Carlo, analysis. However, these systems must be treated with extreme care, or the analysis takes over. You will spend an inordinate amount of time producing data of little value (Chapter 11).

Hardware requirements

Hardware configurations should be taken into account in evaluating systems. It is clearly sensible to select software that is compatible with equipment already used by the organization. Microcomputers are now used for a range of functions including word processing, data management, personal graphics, time management, and as a dumb terminal to access mini- and mainframe computers. On a remote project site a microcomputer can be a powerful personal productivity tool.

Size of project

Systems should be chosen which are consistent with the size of project within the organization. Mainframe systems are only really required if the annual project spend of the organization is above 100 million pounds per year; for an annual spend of tens of millions of pounds, then a networked system with a mini or super-micro at the centre will be sufficient; and under 10 million pounds per year, stand-alone micros may be adequate.

Supplier support and user base

The user will want back-up and support from the system throughout its life. The current number of sales and size of the user base can indicate the stability of the supplier.

17.5 Implementing systems

Figure 17.8 illustrates a procedure (project plan) for implementing a PMIS. There are essentially four major areas of work:

- diagnosis and business planning
- implementation of improvement projects

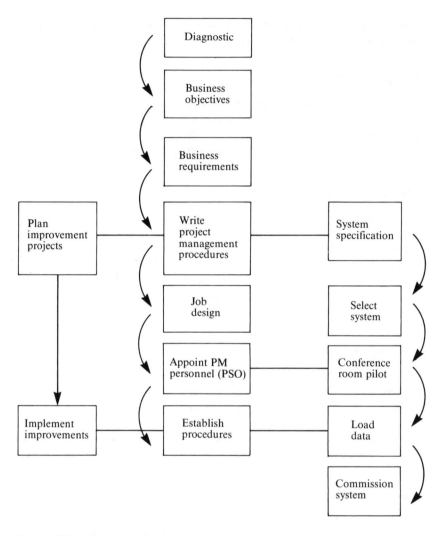

Figure 17.8   Procedure for implementing a PMIS

- implementation of best practice in project management
- selection and implementation of the system.

Diagnosis and business planning

Before you begin to select a system, you must decide its purpose and how it will be used. There are three steps to this process:

1. *Conduct a diagnostic audit*   This is the vital first step. You must know what you do now, and the strengths and weaknesses of that approach. There are two reasons. Implementing the system will be an opportunity for implementing good project management practice, so you must know where possible areas of improvement lie. However, at the other extreme, you may set yourself an ideal, which is unachievable. It is like asking the Irishman the way to Dublin station, and he says, 'I wouldn't start here!' Unfortunately, you do start here, and so you must know what your realistic target it. The diagnostic audit should be conducted against some definition of good practice, which may form the basis of a procedures manual later.
2. *Set business objectives*   Then, or in parallel, you should define what you want the system to achieve. I say in parallel because it might be worth while to define the ideal, before it is tempered by reality, but the final objectives must be set against the findings of the diagnostic.
3. *Write a statement of requirements*   The statement of requirements (SOR) is the strategy of how the system will be used, derived from the business objectives. It defines the major stages of managing projects, as outlined in Part Four. For each stage it defines the purpose and objectives of the stage, the inputs and outputs, and the major processes. The SOR is the document on which the other three areas' implementation are based.

Improvement projects

The diagnostic audit may have highlighted some major weaknesses in the practice of project management, and these can be eliminated through improvement projects. These must be planned and implemented like any other organizational development project, according to the principles of this book. The SOR will define the purpose and objectives of the improvement projects. There are three particular improvement projects:

- implementation of project management procedures
- selection and implementation of the PMIS
- training personnel in the procedures and system.

The first two of these are the other two areas of work. The third is common to both.

Project management procedures

I said above that the implementation of an information system can be an opportunity for improving the operation of the business, especially if a packaged solution which represents best practice is used. A PMIS need be no different. There are four steps to this process:

1. *Write a procedures manual* The procedures manual will be derived from the SOR, and will therefore presumably be based on the procedures followed in the diagnostic audit. (The structure of a manual was described in Section 16.4.)
2. *Establish the project management function* The procedures will imply certain project management roles to be fulfilled. These may be simply project managers, or it may include, project leaders, planners, project accountants and administrators. In the latter case it may be worth while to establish a Project Support Office (Section 16.6). Job descriptions should be written for all the roles.
3. *Obtain competent personnel* The jobs must then be filled. Similar jobs may already exist, with incumbents. They may be able to continue as they are, or they may require some training. Alternatively, it may be necessary to recruit and train new people.
4. *Implement the procedures* Implement first on a pilot project. This should be a project that has started, but is less than a third finished. The procedures should then be implemented on all new projects, and on those that have reached no more than a certain stage of completion. It is usually not worth while implementing them on projects that are more than two-thirds complete, or have less than six months to run (depending on the size of the projects).

Selecting and implementing the system

This is the *raison d'être* of the whole process, and yet the last thing to be considered. However, that is the right approach. You must make sure that a good project management practice has been defined and implemented before you rush into using a PMIS, otherwise its use will become an end in itself. The steps in selecting and implementing the system are:

1. *Design and selection* Working from the SOR, you develop a functional design, system design and detail design of the PMIS, as suggested in Part Four. You choose a shortlist of systems against the functional design, following an evaluation procedure as suggested in Section 17.4. You then do a thorough analysis of the shortlisted systems against the systems design. This analysis requires significant input from the vendors, and so out of fairness to them you should limit your shortlist to two, three, or at most four systems. With the supplier to the chemical industry mentioned above (Figure 17.7) we originally intended to limit the shortlist to three suppliers. However, we lost control and ended up having

a roadshow, with a team of three to five people visiting eight suppliers. A package is chosen, and bespoke work required to raise it to the requirements of the detailed design is fully defined and quantified.

2. *Conference room pilot* The system is tested on trial data, and the users familiarize themselves with it, making suggestions as to how it might be improved to meet their needs. You need to be careful, though, to make sure you do not make too many changes, thereby making the system too expensive or, worse still, unusable.

3. *Load the pilot project* The same pilot project as for implementation of the procedures should be used if possible.

4. *System implementation* The system will be implemented in parallel with the procedures. The same criteria for selecting projects on which to implement it should be used.

17.6 Assumptions and risks

I shall close this chapter by considering some of the assumptions and risks in using a PMIS. As previously stated, the major risks are that the system will be overly complicated for the need, that people will use a system only because they think that it is an essential part of project management even when it is not necessary, and that the system will take over from reality. What the system is saying will be given more credence than actual events. Even if all these are conquered, there are other issues.

Historical records

One use of these systems, which does not seem well publicized by software dealers, is to store historical data. Building up a library of past records may help in project auditing, but will certainly help the project manager when planning new projects. They can re-use data on previous, similar work packages, thus saving a lot of time in planning. (This has been one of the objectives of expert systems, but they have yet to find much acceptance by industry. They are very much a solution looking for a problem.)

Justifying the investment in the system

It is difficult to justify the investment in a PMIS. Because every project is unique, you cannot say that the project would have been less efficient if the system was not used. It is only if the organization is undertaking a number of projects that you can look to trends in improvement. A company in the food canning industry implemented a PMIS in their research and development department, and found that productivity of their R&D

staff increased by 6 per cent over two years.[4] Similarly, if a company knows that all its projects are three months late, and it expects an internal rate of return of 25 per cent on its projects, then late completion is costing that company 6 per cent of its spend on projects annually. If the organization could reduce the actual duration of its projects by one month, it could afford to invest 2 per cent of its annual project spend on a PMIS. The following simple formula could be a basis for justifying the cost of a PMIS. However, it is notoriously difficult to convince senior management, because the improvement can never be satisfactorily proved.

$$\text{Value} = \frac{\text{AIPD}}{12} \times \text{IRRT} \times \text{Spend}$$

where Value = the annual benefit from implementing a PMIS
AIPD = the average improvement in project duration, in months
IRRT = the threshold value of internal rate of return by which projects are assessed
Spend = the annual average spend on projects in the organization.

Proliferation of software

There has been phenomenal growth in the number of project management software packages available on the market. There are probably now in excess of 200. This has contributed to the confusion in the market. In addition, the prospective purchaser is not only presented with this vast range of packages, but is also faced with the unique range of features that each package offers. It has been suggested that a Pareto principle applies: 90 per cent of the users resort to only 10 per cent of the facilities offered by project management software; and only 10 per cent seem to make use of most functions.[5] But the reason for this may well be poor vendor support or inadequate training.

Inadequate support

Another factor hindering use of the systems is lack of training. In many organizations, information systems are the domain of the IT department. Microcomputers may be beginning to have some impact on their lives. However, their use in project management requires more than self-help, but the number of formal courses in the use of PMISs remains very limited. Furthermore, project managers who have learned how to use the systems may get very little training beyond their initial introduction, and so will not learn how to use the advanced features of the systems, as described above.

Information overload

Another concern is the amount of information generated by these packages. This is reminiscent of the problems of the early mainframe programs. However, effective use of the WBS should overcome this difficulty.

17.7 Summary

1. There are three requirements of a PMIS:
   - integration across the organization
   - the planning and control process
   - fast response times
2. There are two elements of a PMIS:
   - the planning system
   - the control system.
3. There are five potential types of system, although only three of these are available:
   - networking systems
   - cost and resource management systems
   - application generators
   - capacity planning systems
   - totally integrated modular packages.
4. To evaluate systems against your requirement, you decide on a number of criteria. Each criteria is weighted high, medium or low. You then judge each potential system against each criteria, and assign a score, from 0 to 3. You then sum the product of scores by weighting for each system, to come up with an overall score.
5. There are four major areas of work in implementing a system:
   - diagnosis and business planning
   - improvement projects
   - working practices and procedures
   - systems selection and implementation.
6. Diagnosis and business planning includes:
   - diagnostic audit
   - business objectives
   - statement of requirements.
7. Practices and procedures include:
   - procedures manual

- project management function
- competent personnel
- implementation.
8. Systems selection and implementation include:
 - design and selection
 - conference room pilot
 - pilot project
 - implementation.

Notes and references

1. Chapter 17 incorporates material written by Dr Padma Nathan. Dr Nathan is a senior lecturer at the Mara Institute of Technology in Malaysia. His doctoral research, undertaken at Henley Management College, was into the use of Project Management Planning and Control Systems.
2. Tuman, J. Jr, 'Development and implementation of project management systems', in *The Project Management Handbook* (eds D. I. Cleland and W. R. King), Van Nostrand Reinhold, 1988.
3. Bent, J. A. and Thumann, A. T., *Project Management for Engineering and Construction*, Fairmont Press, 1989.
4. Turner, J. R., 'Company resource planning in the food processing industry', in *Proceedings of the 12th INTERNET International Expert Seminar*, (ed. S. Dworatschek), INTERNET, 1988.
5. Webster, F., 'Vendor/user dialogue: PM186 at Montreal', *Project Management Journal*, **18** (3), 1987.

18
Project managers and their teams

18.1 Introduction[1]

I shall conclude this part about management procedures and systems by considering project managers and their teams. These are the mandatory elements of both the project organization and the management procedures and systems; without them, nothing will happen. I have to admit that, with the exception of Chapter 4, all other chapters of this book are fairly clinical in their approach. Even in Chapter 7, where I described the organization and spoke of 'human resources', one might think I was discussing androids rather than people. There are three reasons for this. First, to make progress it is necessary to describe an ideal approach. You may quickly recognize that, in any situation, the ideal is not fully achievable, and so must be adapted to suit the circumstances. (Remember the Irishman giving directions to Dublin station in Chapter 17?) However, the ideal of best practice always remains a guiding light. Secondly, the way in which the ideal must be adapted is different in every situation; no two projects are identical. I can therefore only describe the ideal, although it is hoped that by introducing a series of anecdotes I have shown how it was successful in some situations, but was unsuccessful in others. Thirdly, I am not an organizational psychologist or sociologist, but only a project manager. I cannot give advice beyond my specialism. It is better for you to read specialist books on situational management.[2,3,4]

However, this book would be incomplete without considering project managers and their team. If managers are to be able to deliver the project successfully, they must be able to manage the project team, and the individuals within that team. (This is the basis of an approach to management called *action-centred leadership*,[5] Figure 18.1.) Indeed, effective teams are the essence of successful project management.[6]

I shall define a project team, identify different levels, and explain the

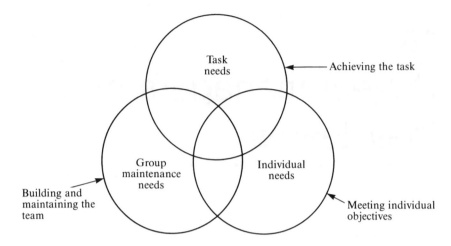

Figure 18.1   Action-centred leadership

processes of team formation and maintenance. I shall then identify how the manager can judge whether the team is performing effectively, and describe how to motivate the professionals working on a project team. My attention will then switch to project managers. I shall describe their leadership role, and consider what makes an effective project manager, explaining the leadership styles that can be adopted and the competencies required to fulfil the role.

18.2 Project teams, formation and maintenance

In forming the project team, the project manager brings together a group of people and develops within them a perceived identity, so that they can work together using a set of common values or norms to deliver the project's objectives. Handy[7] says this concept of perceived identity is critical to team formation; without it the group of people remain a collection of random individuals. What sets project teams apart is that a group of people, who may never have worked together before, have to come together quickly and effectively in order to achieve a task that no one has done before. The novelty, uniqueness, risk and transience are all inherent features of projects, as shown in Chapter 1. Because the team is novel, it has no perceived identity, *ab initio*, and no set of values or norms to work to. It takes time to develop the identity and norms, which delays achievement of the team's objective. Furthermore, because the objective is novel, and carries considerable risk, it takes time to define, and if the project is to be successful this must be done before the team begins work. In this section we shall discuss the levels of people who make up the project team and the process of team formation and maintenance.

Levels of the project team

In any context, there are three levels of groups[4] (Figure 18.2):

1. *The primary group*: the set of people who work face to face, and know everyone else in the group. On a project they are the immediate team, or task force, whether full time or seconded part time (Section 7.3).
2. *The secondary group*: larger than the primary group, consisting of people who interact with people in the primary group, and contribute directly to their work, but are not part of the task force. In a project environment, these are the functions or disciplines that contribute through the matrix organization. However, they must be treated as part of the larger project team to be effective.
3. *The tertiary group*: people who have influence over the members of the primary and secondary teams, or who are affected by the work of the project, but have no direct contribution to the work. Figure 18.2 shows the tertiary group split into three sections: those affected by the work of the project, the facility delivered, and the product of the facility, respectively. The first is the reference section, comprising people who have an effect on the members of the primary and secondary groups. They may be family and friends, peer groups, or professional bodies. The second section consists of people who live in the neighbourhood in which the facility is to be built (NIMBYs), or who will use or operate the facility after it is commissioned, or they may be people whose lives will be irreversibly changed (even made redundant) by the operation of the facility. The final section comprises the consumers, the people who will buy the product produced by the facility. (Sometimes they are the users, but often not.) The expectations of all the people in these sections must be managed if the project is to be successful, as they have a powerful ability to disrupt.

As an example, consider a team conducting an operation. The surgical team is the primary group. The secondary group is the department of the hospital within which it exists, and other departments such as Pathology and X-ray. The reference section consist of the College of Surgeons, other surgeons within the hospital, the medical ethics committee, and the hospital administration. The stakeholders and consumers are the patients and their families.

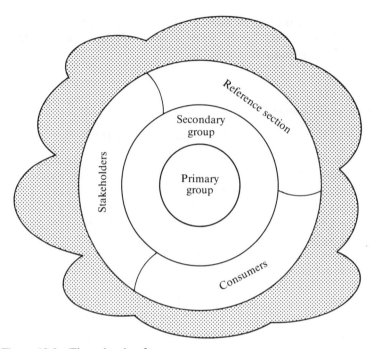

Figure 18.2 Three levels of groups

Formation and maintenance

The members of a team must identify themselves with the team, and develop a common set of values, or norms, before they can work together effectively as a group. The process of forming a team identity and a set of values takes time. Project teams typically go through five stages of formation called forming, storming, norming, performing and mourning (Figure 13.2).

During these five stages, the team's motivation and effectiveness goes through a cycle in which it first decreases, before increasing to reach a plateau, and then either increases or decreases towards the end. The manager's role is to structure the team formation processes in such a way that this plateau is reached as quickly as possible, the effectiveness at the plateau is as high as possible, and the effectiveness is maintained until the task is completed.

1. *Forming*: the team members come together with a sense of anticipation and commitment. Their motivation is high at being selected for the project, and their effectiveness moderate because they are unsure of each other.

2. *Storming*: as the team members begin to work together, they find that they have differences about the best way of achieving the project's objectives, perhaps even differences about its overall aims. They also find that they have different approaches to working on projects. These differences may cause argument, or even conflict, in the team, which causes both the motivation and the effectiveness of the team to fall.

3. *Norming*: hopefully some accommodation is achieved. The team members will begin to reach agreement over these various issues. This will be by a process of negotiation, compromise, and finding areas of commonality. As a result of this accommodation, the team begins to develop a sense of identity, and a set of norms or values. These form a basis on which the team members can work together, and effectiveness and motivation begin to increase again towards the plateau.

4. *Performing*: once performance reaches the plateau, the team can work together effectively for the duration of the project. The manager has a role of maintaining this plateau of performance. For instance, after the team has been together for too long, the members can begin to become complacent, and their effectiveness will fall. If this happens the manager may need to change the structure or composition of the team.

5. *Mourning*: as the team reaches the end of its task, one of two things can happen, as described in Chapter 15. Either the effectiveness can rise, as the members make one concerted effort to complete the task, or it can fall, as the team members regret the end of the task and the breaking up of the relationships they have formed. The latter will be the case if the future is uncertain. Again, it is the manager's role to ensure that the former rather than the latter happens.

These five stages of team formation mirror the four stages of the project life cycle, although all five can take place within a single project stage – see Figure 13.4(a). There are several group working techniques that the manager can use to shorten the forming, storming and norming stages, such as the application of the start-up processes described in Chapter 13, and, in particular, the use of start-up workshops.

Having formed the group, the manager's role is to ensure that it continues to operate at the plateau of effectiveness. Over the next two sections I shall describe the leadership role of the manager, and how to motivate a team of knowledge workers. First, the manager must be able to determine just how effective the team really is. On a simple level, this can be assessed by the way in which the team achieves its agreed targets, and by the way in which the individuals' and group's aspirations and motivational needs have been satisfied.[8] The team leader and the line management of the organization must ensure that both corporate and personal objectives are met. If only the corporate goal is met, then with time there will be an erosion of morale and effectiveness followed by staff attrition. Often, however, it is only possible to measure achievement of these objectives at the end of the project, by which time it is too late to take corrective action. Hence, we must also have measures by which to judge the cohesion and strength of a group during the project. Indicators of team effectiveness include[8]:

- *attendance*: low absenteeism, sickness, accident rates, work interruptions, and labour turnover
- *goal clarity*: individual targets are set, understood and achieved; the aims of the group are understood; each member of the team has a clear knowledge of the role of the group
- *high outputs*: high commitment to goal achievement, a search for real solutions, analytical, critical problem solving using all knowledge and skill, the search for widely tested and supported solutions
- *strong group cohesion*: openness and trust among members, sharing of ideas and knowledge, lively and constructive meetings, shared goal.

18.3 Motivating the project team[9]

How does the manager motivate the members of a team of professional, knowledge workers, to build and maintain their effectiveness and commitment to the project? In the project environment, without the functional hierarchies, distinctions of title, rank, symbols of power and status do not exist,[10] so many of the factors that are traditionally viewed as providing value to motivate professional staff are no longer available. In the project environment, managers must find new motivational factors that will be valued by their staff.

In this section I shall recall those features of the project environment that have a significant impact on the motivation of professional staff, and then describe the factors that are likely to be valued by knowledge workers in the project environment, and will therefore act as motivators. I also show how the effect of these varies throughout the project life cycle. The conclusion is that people are motivated by the development of their career, but, because they are no longer able to judge that development by their position in a hierarchy, they must measure it by their own growth and learning both within and through the organization. Money, however, remains a common yardstick by which individuals can measure that growth.

Impact of the project environment on motivation

There are three features of the project environment that have a significant impact on the motivation of personnel (Section 4.4):

MATRIX ORGANIZATION STRUCTURES

Within a matrix organization, people do not have the clear indicators of title, status and rank, as described. They also have reporting lines to two people, a short-term (project) boss, and a long-term (functional) boss. Although the project manager tries to motivate the individuals towards the project goals, they often give their primary loyalty to their functional manager. It is that manager who writes their annual appraisal, and has greatest influence over long-term career development. This is exacerbated if annual performance objectives are aligned with the functional hierarchy because projects are of shorter duration than the time scale over which they are set.

FLATTER ORGANIZATION STRUCTURES

With flatter hierarchies being adopted by project organizations, individuals have less opportunity for career advancement, as there are fewer levels to occupy. They spend longer on each level before progressing, which means they have fewer opportunities to measure progress against career milestones (disturbing for a project manager) and are less able to judge how their contribution is viewed by the organization. Words of encouragement are not enough, because individuals can only judge their perceived value by progression, which means promotion.[11] With decision-making processes by-passing the centre, individuals may also feel less able to influence their careers, as they no longer thave direct contact with senior managers making career decisions. They rely very much on their project managers or their functional managers to act on their behalf on career matters. This feeling of detachment can be heightened if the individuals do not entirely understand the direction or strategy of the company, or how their project contributes to it. Having no direct contact with the centre through their work, they will not have the opportunity regularly to question the reasons for strategic decisions, or to suggest alternatives. This can exacerbate all the previous problems if they perceive their manager as the cause of their isolation.

THE TRANSIENT NATURE OF PROJECTS

I showed above how the transient nature of projects means that an individual's annual performance objectives tend to be aligned with the functional rather than project responsibilities. Similarly, because projects only last a short time, they cannot satisfy an individual's long-term development needs and can only be stepping stones. It is the functional hierarchy that provides the focus for the individual's development, and if the individual is to be committed to projects, then those projects must be viewed as fulfilling the individual's development requirements. Furthermore, many people come to work for social reasons.[12] This can be lost in the project environment, and the impact of the second reduced, because people do not stay on a project long enough to develop long-term relationships. However, there are also people who relish the much larger number of contacts the project environment gives them. Such people are able to form new relationships very quickly.

The new motivational factors

A traditional view of motivation is Maslow's Hierarchy of Needs.[12] Maslow proposed that people have five essential needs (high levels first):

- achievement
- esteem
- belonging
- protection
- sustenance.

People are motivated initially by lower needs. However, as they satisfy one need, that reduces in importance and they become motivated by the next. As their needs move up the list the lower ones lose all effect. Many of the traditional views on motivation are not valid in the project environment. However, Maslow's hierarchy continues to provide a basis for motivational factors. Many people have now passed the point at which belonging is the primary need to be satisfied at work; they satisfy that through their leisure activities. They therefore look to satisfy their needs for esteem and achievement. This is especially true of knowledge workers, and leads to five new factors for effective motivation,[10] which I call the five Ps:

- purpose
- proactivity
- profit sharing

- progression
- professional recognition.

PURPOSE

People must believe in the importance of their work, and that it contributes to the development of the organization. It was shown in Section 4.4 that this sense of purpose, and the linking of the work of a project to the mission of the parent organization, can help overcome the uncertainty of the dual-reporting structures in a matrix organization.

PROACTIVITY

As career paths become less clear and predictable, and as senior managers become remote, people want to manage their own career development. Emphasizing the achievement of results, rather than fulfilling roles, and delegating professional integrity through results gives subordinates the opportunity to take responsibility for their own development. Furthermore, allowing people to choose their next project as a reward for good performance on the present one satisfies this need.

PROFIT SHARING

Allowing people to share in the entrepreneurial culture will encourage them to value it. Many organizations now encourage employees to solve their own problems, and to take the initiative to satisfy the customer's requirements, and are allowing employees to share in the rewards. The growing band of freelance workers also shows that many people are taking this initiative into their own hands.

PROGRESSION

As people near the top of Maslow's hierarchy, they become conscious of the need for self-fulfilment. They therefore value the opportunity to increase their learning experiences. Each new project is an opportunity to learn new skills, and thereby increase esteem and self-achievement. However, I said above that in the flatter organization structures, people may have fewer career milestones by which to measure their progression. The one yardstick they still have is money (or other status symbols such as company cars). These things remain important, not as motivators in their own right, but as measures of achievement.

PROFESSIONAL RECOGNITION

Another measure of achievement is professional recognition. Knowledge workers do not want the anonymity of the bureaucrat, but want to accumulate 'brownie points', to contribute to their esteem and achievement. I said above that, in the flatter hierarchies of project-based organizations, managers at the centre may not be in direct contact with professional employees. Line managers must therefore ensure that their subordinates receive due recognition.

Variation of the motivational factors with the life cycle

The efficacy of the 'five Ps' varies throughout the project life cycle (Table 18.1).

DEFINITION

During this stage, the project team try to determine what the project is about, so their focus on its purpose is high. They will try to determine how it can contribute to their development, and so the entrepreneurial spirit will be high. During definition, there will be some opportunity to demonstrate professional skill through problem solving.

Table 18.1   Variation of the motivational factors throughout a three-stage project management life cycle

Factor	Definition	Execution	Close-out
Purpose	High	Low	High
Proactivity	High	Medium	High
Profit sharing	High	Low	High
Progression	High	Low	High
Professionalism	Medium	Medium	High

EXECUTION

During this stage, the focus switches from the purpose of the project to the work done. The learning opportunities and chance of profit were set in the definition stage, and there is little chance to influence them during execution. However, through the use of responsibility charts,[13] people can be given responsibility for achieving milestones and some opportunity to demonstrate their professional skill.

CLOSE-OUT

During close-out all five factors come back into focus: the purpose becomes important again during commissioning; people deliver their results and receive their due reward, if the project has been profitable people complete their learning experience, and look foward to the next; they receive their professional recognition. During close-out, individuals can be given career counselling to help manage their careers. Individuals should be helped to define their development needs, plan how they are to be achieved, and to develop networks, internal and external to the organization, to be used in their career progression.

SUMMARY

The five factors have the least combined effect during the execution stage of the project. The manager must therefore look to make the maximum use of the two factors that do have some effect. (*Note*: Those factors that have a high ability to motivate, also have a high ability to demotivate if the appropraite action is not taken, or if the project goes badly wrong. If the project has been unsuccessful, then during the close-out stage there can be a rush to get off the project, with the result that work will be left undone.) Through all of this, if both the project manager and line manager understand the expectations and aspirations of the individuals in the team, and take proper account of them, then half the battle is won.

18.4 The role of the project manager

Our attention now switches from the project team to the project manager, whose main responsibility is to manage the team and its work *to deliver the promised results*. It is the leader's responsibility to create the climate for success.

Functions of management

In Section 2.3, I introduced five functions of management[14] (see Figure 2.1):

- planning the work to be done to achieve the defined objectives
- organizing the team of people to do the work
- implementing by assigning work to people
- controlling progress
- leading the team of people.

Parts Three and Four of this book provided a structured approach to the first four of these. Here, we shall focus on leading, the most abstract of the five functions. Leading involves:

– motivating and rewarding
– keeping perspective
– encouraging group decision making
– supervising and maintaining group behaviour
– ensuring that everyone gains.

MOTIVATING AND REWARDING

This ensure that all the members of the team know their work is appreciated and recognized, as described in the last section.

KEEPING PERSPECTIVE

This is important to keep team equilibrium and balance. Teams that have worked together for a long time often fall into the trap of becoming insular. This manifests itself in the team seeing other groups as inferior, being resistant to change or outside influences, attributing shortcomings to others and in other way setting themselves apart from the rest of the organization. Although a strong team spirit and pride is good, it can be counter-productive if it turns into vanity and aloofness as it can result in team alienation. It is the project manager's role to make sure that the team keeps its perspective.

ENCOURAGING GROUP DECISION MAKING

This means knowing when to draw on the decision-making skills of the group and when to make individual decisions. Research has shown that group decision making does not necessarily mirror that of the individual opinions in the group. For example, a strong leader may influence the group to make a high-risk decision to which individual members would not have agreed. Similarly, dissenting voices can either remain unheard or find themselves overruled or ignored.

SUPERVISING AND MAINTAINING GROUP BEHAVIOUR

This is an important leadership role. Groups can behave in a way that is uncharacteristic of the individuals in the group. Harnessing this potential is important for the leader. Well structured, positive teams can achieve more than any individual. The reverse is also true. Group behaviour can be destructive to the group and to those who depend on the group's work. Irrational group behaviour can take over from more moderate and modest individual acts.

ENSURING THAT EVERYONE GAINS

This is the essential factor in negotiating the contract through the planning process, as described throughout this book, and in motivating the team, as described in the last section.

18.5 The effective project manager

Finally, let us consider what makes an effective project manager. Handy[7] suggests that there are three possible criteria for effective leaders:

- *leadership traits*: effective managers have certain common traits
- *leadership styles*: effective managers adopt certain styles
- *a contingent approach*: effective managers adapt their styles to suit the circumstances.

Traits of effective project managers

Previously,[13] I proposed six traits of effective project managers:

- problem-solving ability and results orientation
- energy and initiative
- self-assured leader
- perspective
- communication
- negotiating ability.

For several years, I have conducted an exercise on courses whereby I ask delegates, individually and in teams, to select 6 traits from a list of 19. There is consistency in the answers, and the results agree with those listed above. Almost every team has four traits from the list, and many five or six. Handy,[7] in reporting research conducted in the United States into the traits of effective managers in general, says they have the first four of these traits. I recently conducted the exercise with a group of managers from Russia. The two teams returned with five traits from this list. The sixth in both cases was technical competence, which is never included by a team of British managers. On discussion, we decided that if the exercise were conducted with German or French managers, then it is likely that technical competence would appear on their list, but it is not something

valued by British managers. Conducting the exercise with course delegates has therefore reinforced my view of the six traits of effective project
managers.

Effective managers are usually of above-average intelligence, and are
able to solve complex problems by analysing the current situation and
recognizing patterns. Problem solving pervades project management.
The achievement of the project's purpose is a problem, as is the completion
of each stage of the life cycle. Chapter 2 presented a problem-solving
cycle (Figure 2.2) as both a view of the project management life cycle and
the management processes within each stage. Furthermore, the control
processes is also one of problem solving, planning recovery to overcome
variances from plan. Without a problem-solving ability a project manager
would be lost. This ability at problem solving should be coupled with
results orientation. The purpose is not to complete work for work's sake,
but to achieve the desired ends. The solution to the problems should
deliver the planned objectives and defined purpose, not necessarily complete the originally agreed work. *The end justifies the means* or *All's well that
ends well.*

ENERGY AND INITIATIVE

The project manager must also have the ability to continue working and
managing under considerable pressure and against considerable odds.
This requires the manager to be energetic and fit. This energy will be
coupled with initiative to see the need for action, and have the resolve to
take it. The Russian managers mentioned above said that this initiative
should extend to the management of one's own career as well as the task
at hand.

SELF-ASSURED LEADER

Managers must have the self-assurance to know what they are doing is
right. This does not mean they must be extrovert or brash; a manager can
be self-effacing while still self-assured. They must take action resolutely,
confident in their opinions and judgement. Sometimes it is better to take
action, based on incomplete information, being ready to modify the
action as new information comes to light, than to dither endlessly looking
for the perfect solution. Self-assured managers also delegate readily to
their project team, confident in the ability of the team's members, and

in their own ability to motivate the team. Sometimes, especially in the IT industry, good technologists are promoted into managerial positions, but are very reluctant to delegate because they believe, quite rightly, that they can do the work better than anyone else. They work themselves into an early grave, while their team members are idle and consequently demotivated.

PERSPECTIVE

Managers need to be able to look beyond the team, and to see how they fit into the organization as a whole. This need for perspective extends to the project work. The manager must be able to move freely through all three levels of the project hierarchy, and above as well, to understand the detail work of the project and how it will deliver the project's objectives, and to understand how the project's objectives will meet the needs of the parent organization. This ability is known as a *helicopter mind*.

COMMUNICATION

Similarly, managers must be able to communicate at all levels of the organization, from the managing director down to the janitor: they must be the ambassadors of the project, selling it to senior managers to win their support; they must be able to talk to their peers, functional managers and resource providers to win their cooperation; they must brief and motivate the team; and they must talk to the janitor, because the janitor often knows better than anyone how the project is progressing (see Example 18.1).

When I was a post-doctoral research fellow, I had an office in one half of a pair of semi-detached houses. We had offices in one house while the other was being renovated. The plan was: when the other was complete we would all move across into that house, while the one we were currently occupying was renovated. I was due to go the the United States for a month for a combined lecture trip and holiday. About a week before I was due to leave, the janitor, a retired Welsh miner called Frank, asked me when I was going to be away. From the 20th August to the 20th September I said. Frank said that we were due to move into the other house on the 14th September, so it might be worth while for me to put my books in a tea-chest before I left. I said that was a good idea, but decided to check it out first with the administrator of the Engineering Department. I spoke to his secretary, but she denied any knowledge of the move. So I next asked the builders, but they said they would not be finished until late October or early November. I locked my office door, and went off to the States. When I came back, I found that the door had been forced, and that the move had taken place on 14th September, the very day Frank had predicted. Of course, he had spoken to the University Estates people as they came to survey the work.

Example 18.1 Talking to the janitor

NEGOTIATING ABILITY

In Parts Two and Three the project plan was said to be a contract (Figure 2.6); it is in fact a contract between the project manager (showing what the manager and the team will deliver to the organization) and the project's sponsor (showing the support that person or group will give to enable the project manager to deliver the contracted results). Like all contracts this must be negotiated through bipartite discussions. The project manager relies on an ability to negotiate, because a project manager does not have as much direct line authority over resources as a functional manager. Project managers must win and maintain the commitment and cooperation of other people through their ability to negotiate and persuade.

Styles of effective project managers

Project managers can adopt four styles (Figure 18.3).

DEMOCRATIC

Democratic managers consult their team, and then decide the best course of action. Note that this style is different from the *laissez-faire* style below, which is almost anarchic, not democratic. This style may be appropriate during the feasibility and planning stages of a project, when you want to encourage people to contribute their ideas.

AUTOCRATIC

Autocratic managers dictate to the team what should be done and how. This style may be appropriate during the execution and close-out stages of a project, when the specification and design of the facility has been decided, real money is being spent, and so early completion of the project is required to achieve the revenue returns.

BUREAUCRATIC

Bureaucratic managers manage through rules and procedures. This style is usually only appropriate on a project with low risk, for which there is

	Democratic	Team	Bureaucratic	Team	Autocratic	Team	Laissez-faire	Team
Plan	PXD	CX	PXD	TX	PXD	I	Ad	XD
Organize	PXD	CX	PXD	TX	PXD	I	Ad	XD
Implement	P	Xd	PD	TX	PD	X	Ad	XD
Control	PD	Xd	PD	CX	PXD	C	Ad	XD

Figure 18.3   Different styles of project management

expected to be very little change, because a bureaucratic manager is unable to respond to change. This probably means it will only be appropriate during the close-out stages of a project.

LAISSEZ-FAIRE

Laissez-faire managers allow the team to manage themselves. They behave like all the other members of the team, and are there to advise if required. This style is appropriate during the early developmental or feasibility stages of a project, or on research projects.

TYPES TO BE AVOIDED

In addition, there are styles that should be avoided in project managers. I have already mentioned the technocrat, the person to whom the science is more important than the results, the means more important than the ends. This person searches for the ideal solution, rather than achieving an adequate solution that satisfies the customer's requirements, and is usually unable to delegate owing to a lack of faith in the project team's ability to achieve the perfect result. Taken to extreme, the bureaucrat can be ineffective as that person pedantically follows procedures, assured in the knowledge that the job has been done correctly, even if not effectively. A third is the salesperson, who is very good at selling the project, but not at delivering results. All three of these characteristics – technical ability, application of best practice, and the ambassadorial role – are strengths if applied in moderation, but they become weaknesses when applied to excess, and they become more important than delivering the results of the project.

Situational management

Many managers have a preferred style, but the effective manager is able to adapt that style, depending on the circumstances.

18.6 Summary

1. A project team is a group of people with a perceived identity, who collaborate according to a set of values or norms to achieve the project's objectives.
2. There are three levels of project team, primary, secondary and tertiary, and the tertiary group consists of three types:
   - reference groups
   - users and stakeholders
   - consumers.
3. There are five stages of team formation:
   - forming
   - storming
   - norming
   - performing
   - mourning.
4. The five Ps provide value to knowledge workers, and so can be used to motivate the team throughout the project life cycle. They are:
   - purpose
   - proactivity
   - profit sharing
   - progression
   - professional recognition.
5. The role of the manager is to plan, organize, implement, control and lead, and in leading must:
   - motivate and reward
   - keep perspective
   - encourage group decision making
   - supervise and maintain group behaviour
   - ensure that everyone gains.
6. The effective project manager has six traits:
   - intelligence
   - energy
   - self-assuredness
   - perspective
   - communication
   - persuasiveness.

7. The manager can also use one of four styles:
   - democratic
   - autocratic
   - bureaucratic
   - *laissez-faire.*

Notes and references

1. This chapter incorporates material written by Mahen Tampoe.
2. McGregor, D., *The Human Side of Enterprise*, Penguin, 1960.
3. Argyle, M., *The Social Psychology of Work*, Penguin, 1972.
4. Ribeaux, P. and Poppleton, S. E., *Psychology and Work*, Macmillan, 1978.
5. Adair, J., *Effective Leadership*, Pan, 1983.
6. Tampoe, M., 'Teams: the essence of successful project management', *International Journal of Project Management*, 1989.
7. Handy, C. B., *Understanding Organisations*, Penguin, 1982.
8. Walton, A., *The Nature of Management*, Financial Training Publications, 1984.
9. Section 18.3 incorporates material from a paper written jointly with Mahen Tampoe and Lynn Thurloway.
10. Kanter, R. M., 'The new managerial work', *Harvard Business Review*, November 1989.
11. Here lies our sovereign lord the King
    Whose promise none relies on;
    He never said a foolish thing,
    Nor ever did a wise one.
    The King's Epitaph (for Charles II, written before his death), John Wilmot, Earl of Rochester, 1647–1680.
12. Maslow, A. H., *Motivation and Personality*, Harper & Row, 1954.
13. Andersen, E. S., Grude, K. V., Haug, T. and Turner, J. R., *Goal Directed Project Management*, Kogan Page, 1987.
14. Fayol, H., *General and Industrial Management*, Pitman, 1949.

PART SIX
APPLICATIONS

19
Projects from the product life cycle

19.1 Introduction

The previous four parts described the processes of managing projects: Part Two identified the context of projects; Part Three described the management of the five system objectives; Part Four explained the management of the project life cycle and the execution of projects; and Part Five described management systems and procedures to support these processes. I shall complete this book by comparing the application of these processes to different types of projects. There is no agreement about how to classify projects, but I have found it useful to clasify them against three parameters:

- by the position of the project in the life cycle of the product produced by the facility, or in the strategic development of the parent organization
- by the type of industry or technology of the project or the parent organization
- by the size of the project.

Over this chapter and the next two, projects will be considered against each of these classifications in turn. The final chapter (Chapter 22) will consider a fourth type of project involving international collaboration and, in particular, will discuss how different cultural approaches can conflict during the project management life cycle. In this chapter, I shall describe the management of the product life cycle, and then consider two major sources of projects: new product development and technological development.

19.2 Managing the product life cycle

Several versions of the life cycle incorporate the project into a wider view of a life cycle of the product that the project produces. Wearne[1] proposed a model (Figure 19.1), which is essentially a life cycle of the facility, and is reminiscent of the problem-solving cycle shown in Figure 2.2. It starts with a survey of demand for the product produced by the facility. That part of the cycle on or within the circumference of the circle describes the life of the facility built by the project. The six steps, from study to commissioning, relate to the four stages of the life cycle used in Part Four, Figure 13.1. The next three steps extend the life beyond the project to use of the facility, its maintenance, and monitoring of its performance. Kelley[2] introduced a similar, though linear, model (shown in Figure 19.2). This is a life cycle for the investment programme, and differentiates between the control of the facility design and the project to build it.

Kerzner[3] proposed a model that addresses the life cycle of the product produced by the facility. It is the classic marketing view of a product life cycle[4] (Figure 19.3). This is the view of projects filling the planning gap, as shown in Figure 3.4(a), and draws very little distinction between the project and the product. Some people differentiate between the project and the product life cycle, saying the project is the period up to and including commercialization in Figure 19.3, and the product life is the period from introduction of the product until its decline.[5] The project period can last anything from three months in the electronics industry, to 10 years in the pharmaceutical industry, to 200 years for the Channel Tunnel.

Implied in Figures 19.1 to 19.3 is an assumption that the facility is an engineering plant that will fabricate a product (or perhaps provide a service through its operation, as with the Channel Tunnel). In this book, I have taken a wider view of projects and the facilities they deliver. As well as an engineering plant, the facility may be a computer system, a design, trained managers, a set of procedures. With this view, projects can occur at any step in the three models. From Wearne's model, there are projects to conduct a marketing survey, research and development projects, and maintenance projects. My first experience of industrial projects was on the maintenance of ammonia plants (see Example 5.1). From the marketing model, there are projects to launch the new product at 'market introduction', and to relaunch the product at 'deterioration' (Figure 19.4). Projects therefore occur throughout the product life cycle, or at any stage in the strategic development of organizations (see Section 3.2).

In this chapter, I shall examine two types of project arising directly from the product life cycle, which are common for many industries:

– new product development
– applied research and development.

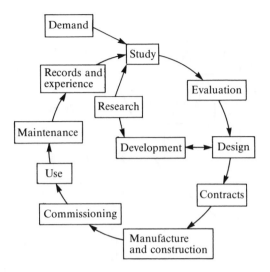

Figure 19.1   Wearne's life cycle for industrial projects

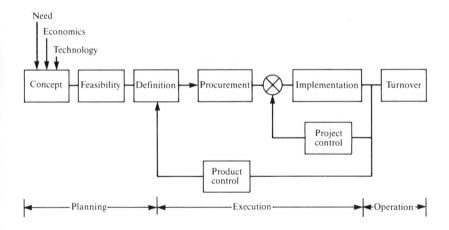

Figure 19.2   Kelley's model for the programme life cycle

Source: Reprinted with the permission of Lexington Books, an imprint of Macmillan, Inc., from *New Dimensions of Project Management* by Albert J. Kelley. Copyright © 1982 by Lexington Books.

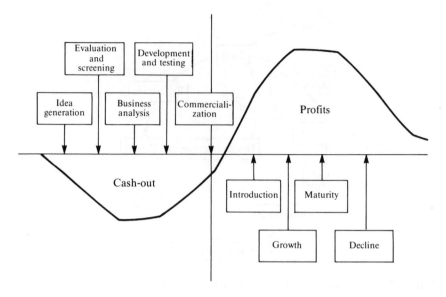

Figure 19.3 Classic marketing view of the life cycle of a product

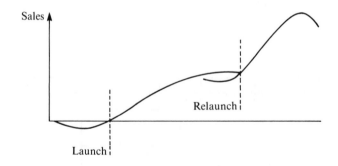

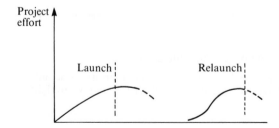

Figure 19.4 Product relaunch

19.3 New product development[6]

Let us start with new product development, which in turn can lead to many types of project, including:

- research and development
- product design
- prototyping
- facility design and construction
- product launch.

In this section, I shall describe how organizations create a culture for innovation, the types of organization they adopt for new product development, and how they plan and control the process.

Organization, people and culture

New product development has a key role to play in organizational competitiveness, yet is it one of the most difficult aspects of the company to manage. Organizations that choose in-house development must create a climate that favours innovation. Top management have a key role in this process, to encourage the establishment of a creative environment, which has three key components:

CLIMATE FOR INNOVATION

The innovative climate of an organization and its development policies are inseparable. Product development demands a flexible structure which encourages creativity, entrepreneurship and provides necessary conditions that favour development. However, there can be many pressures within an organization which act to hinder enterprise, and encourage bureaucratic policies and procedures that constrain change. Many of these were identified in Chapter 4.

INNOVATIVE ORGANIZATION

In order to harness innovation, organizations must be versatile and adaptable in their approach to their circumstances.[7] In essence, product development is at its best in organizations that encourage imagination and are organic in nature, rather than those with bureaucratic structures based on routine management processes.

Whether bureaucratic or organic, organizations consist of people, whose personalities and actions directly affect the success of projects and the overall performance of the business. Thus, organizations need to adopt structures that harness individual innovation. This will be reflected in recruitment and selection procedures, opportunities for development, removal of bureaucratic restraint, and rewards to innovators. It is not possible to prescribe the definitive organizational structure to achieve this; much depends on the company's response to its environment.

Product development organization

In a climate that welcomes creativity, the marketing function has two distinct roles:

1. *Routine, operational marketing tasks*, which demand a structure based on routine activities, planning, coordination of the marketing mix for products that form part of the existing product line.
2. *Novel projects* – activities requiring less defined structure. New product development projects operate in uncertain conditions, and though planned require freedom from routine organization.

In order to implement in-house product development, the first problem is to find the right organizational format. By nature, innovation is individualistic, requiring each company to develop its own working arrangements. There are several ways in which a business can organize itself for product development.

NEW PRODUCT COMMITTEES

These are senior committees meeting on a continual or ad-hoc basis, responsible for coordinating product development. Members are senior functional managers and executives from research, marketing, finance, production, engineering, etc. The principal responsibilities include reviewing and screening proposals, determining policy, planning and coordination. Often the committee is considered to be the coordinating function that ensures that the product maintains its momentum and controls the activities of the multi-functional team developing the product.

PRODUCT MANAGERS

Product managers may be given the responsibility for developing new products alongside their routine duties of managing existing product lines. There are several economies associated with this. In addition to monetary benefits, product managers may assume this responsibility as they are sympathetic to the customer requirements and considered to be in the best position to ensure synergy with the existing product portfolio. The disadvantages are, however, that the additional management time required may not be forthcoming, or the product managers cannot give this unique activity the specialized attention, resources and expertise required while maintaining responsibility for routine activities.

NEW PRODUCT MANAGERS

They are given overall responsibility for product development from planning to implementation. Often new product managers work alongside existing product managers but without their operational responsibility, and can thus turn their attention to the creative role and generate practical new product ideas. Although the establishment of a new product manager formalizes the product development role, there are strong links with existing product lines, leading to minor changes, rather than independent, novel or radical innovations.

NEW PRODUCT DEPARTMENTS

These are common in large organizations and take a high profile, working alongside new product managers in generating ideas, and evaluating their feasibility. In contrast to other methods, new product departments place the responsibility with a senior manager. The department provides the umbrella for coordination of various functions for continuous project management. It does not have responsibility for operational duties so may dedicate its efforts to producing quality new products. Sometimes a new product department may be situated within a larger department, such as planning, marketing, research and development, projects or engineering.

VENTURE TEAMS

These are composed of functional specialists who are working to a closely defined brief and are generally recruited on an *ad-hoc* basis for a short time. While located in the team, the individuals are removed from day-to-day activities. The team ideally would report to a non-operating executive.

TASK FORCES

These groups are organized on an *ad-hoc* basis. Members are seconded from operational duties for the duration of the project, or divide their time between routine activities and project work. The aim of task force management is to ensure continued support from the functions throughout the project. As the project reaches the latter stages, task forces may recruit more members with specialist skills to help manage the project.

PROJECT-BASED PRODUCT DEVELOPMENT

Product development involves individuals with specialist skills, from various functions and from managerial levels. The formation of project teams can be effective in solving problems and creating benefits which cannot be achieved in routine ways.[7] However, one particular structure may not be appropriate at all stages of the project. Just as the activity needs to be fluid and flexible, the perfect organization must also adapt to accommodate the different expertise needed throughout the project.

New product planning

The project teams have primary responsibility for the new product planning aspects of the market strategy. The nature of product development creates several planning problems, as projects range from modest expenditure to major investments, combined with indeterminate time constraints incompatible with routine reporting cycles. The diverse activities involved in new product programmes should move through a logical sequence of events. Though considered contrary to flexibility and creativity, development plans are necessary as they help determine critical components of the project. The sequence (project life cycle) suggested by Kotler[4] is often used to illustrate the new product planning process (Figure 19.5).

Plans should be used to enhance rather than hinder the development process. Management should not be limited by this logical progression. The sequence outlined is a guideline to help development, not constrain it. Idea generation, for example, does not always automatically occur as part of the formal planning sequence. Ideas may be initiated by users or employees during normal work (Figure 19.6). Similarly, product development does not always require radical change, and projects may be initiated to modify existing product lines (Figure 19.7). The project may also have several stages running simultaneously (Figure 19.8).

The planning process so far has not established links with business

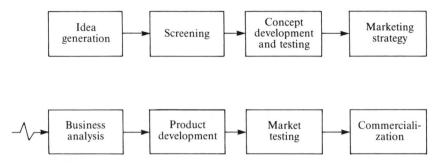

Figure 19.5   New product planning process (project management life cycle)

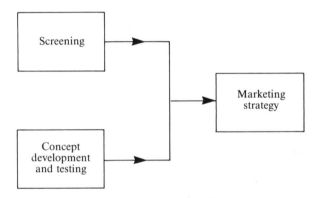

Figure 19.6   Revised sequence for ideas generated by users and employers

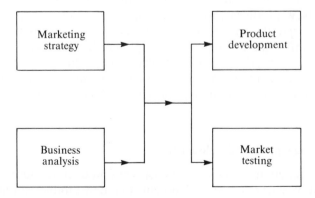

Figure 19.7   Revised sequence for products not requiring radical change

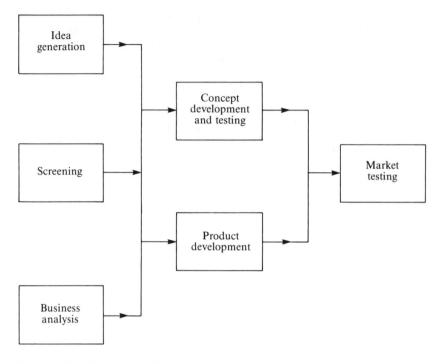

Figure 19.8   Sequence with several simultaneous stages

purpose or corporate strategy. Although not part of the routine of the company, project plans should be fully integrated into the strategic plans (Section 3.2). Product development should be complementary to existing products and meet the needs of the product portfolio against market demands. New products provide an important strategic capability for achieving corporate and business objectives.[8] Strategic issues should direct and influence the new product project in three ways: strategic focus, technical criteria, and market acceptance.[9] This leads to a revised product development planning process that combines strategic focus with the need to combine phases of new product development (Figure 19.9).

Controlling new product development

The control function is an important aspect of product development. The application of marketing control systems to a new product development process reduces the risk. Control processes should therefore be integrated

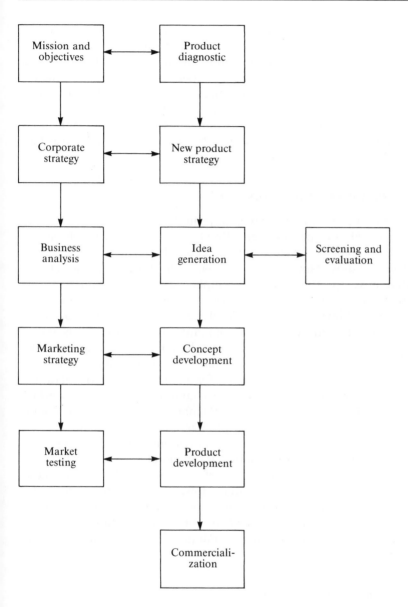

Figure 19.9   Revised planning sequence incorporating strategic focus

into all aspects of the plan and linked to critical components mentioned earlier. A continuous monitoring programme provides project teams with valuable information that may determine the successful completion and termination of projects. The key to any system is the extent to which it allows the manager to influence the success or otherwise of the outcome of the venture.[10] Several planning and control techniques may be used to monitor new product projects. Handscome[5] illustrates how these methods may be combined to monitor progress based on project objectives (see Figure 19.10).

19.4 Technological development[11]

Let us now turn to the management of projects in industrial and technological research and development, R&D. The discussion is relevant to process development as well as to product development. In this section, I shall focus on those aspects of project management within the R&D context that pose specific problems, emphasizing those features, while accepting that most of the principles of project management can be applied in the R&D environment. Well-recognized difficulties of building teams of collaborative scientists, of managing such specialists and of communicating with other functions in the corporation are discussed, together with more positive notes for management. I shall describe what project management means in practice for industrial R&D, so that (a) the non-R&D project manager can understand the requirements when liaising with R&D projects, and (b) R&D managers can put project management principles into the context of their work environment.

The difference between research and development should also be recognized. Different skills are required for exploratory research than for focused development. The definition of rigid time scale and cost constraints has less relevance in research. However, in the corporate world, research and development are often managed together as one unit, and so to outsiders appear to have similar management issues. In this section, I shall focus primarily on development, but indicate where generalizations can be made.

Project evaluation and selection

Project selection for research or development can be formal or informal, qualitative or quantitative. Rarely is it clear that a project *must* be undertaken, and even more rarely clear *why* that project should be done. There are several choices, and a lack of data allowing rational selection between them. This is one feature of R&D. Even with strong and clear

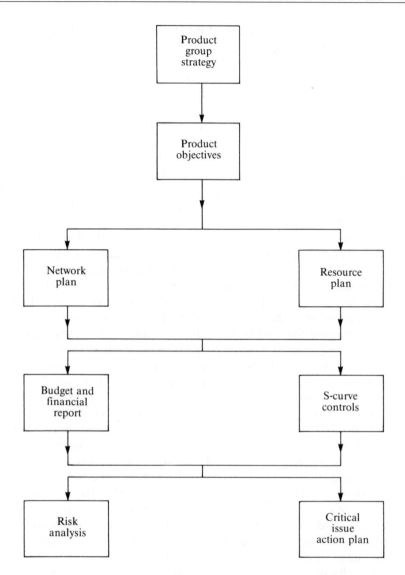

Figure 19.10 Schema for a hierarchy of plans for new product development

business objectives, the direction of R&D effort often carries a great deal of discretion. There is a lot of guesswork involved in evaluating options, and this may tempt decision makers to rely on *gut feel*, or do something because it seems interesting or exciting. Hence, there is always some uncertainty in R&D, both in selecting the 'right' projects and in evaluating the chances of success.

One criterion that is often handled badly for the business is the time scale. Often the development programme is slowed down, apparently to contain costs. This may have a disastrous effect on the ability of the company to compete in a rapidly changing market, where it is important to be first with a new product, or a swift second with a product modification. Speedy analysis of the risk issues at an early stage can allow more valid selection of major projects for fast tracking.

Important question for the effectiveness of R&D are: 'Where have the proposals come from? 'What is the push or pull?' Ideally, communications between marketing, sales, operations and development are close and open enough for productive cross-fertilization to occur, so that market pull and technology push are well balanced. Such open stimulations across functions must be a goal of the technology-based company. Ideas should also come from all levels within the organization, and this only happens if it is encouraged actively and openly, and if mental risk-taking is rewarded. There should be some formal or informal flexibility for preliminary evaluation of ideas from outside the formal project control system.

Project evaluation needs to be based on a strong awareness of business objectives and strategy (Section 3.2). A research or development team can only be effective in adding value if it knows where the business is going. This sounds obvious. Unfortunately in practice it is too common for the scientist or engineer to be blissfully unaware of whether or how their activity is contributing to the business. In addition, the industrial R&D organization should have a technology strategy. This should recognize the nature of enabling technologies that are currently the foundation of the business, and emerging technologies that will produce the opportunities or threats in the future. It should provide a consistent statement of how the organization will access the required skills; and how it will use these skills to achieve business results. Surprisingly few organizations have technology strategies, expressed in these terms, to guide project selection. The organization cannot afford to have a prescriptive strategy or approach that imposes blinkers on visionary or radical thinking. Flexibility is an important key, but the strategy should provide the framework on which all decision processes are initially considered. Any decision to break with established guidelines can then be seen for what it is and may indeed prompt reconsideration of the guidelines.

It is clear that some kind of formal evaluation procedure is desirable. This may use an equation in which key parameters are estimated. It should also allow a statement of coherence with, or divergence from, accepted objectives. Even when the decision to proceed with a project can be taken internally in R&D, it is wise to seek support from the operations and marketing functions wherever possible, even for a research project that is a long way from the marketplace. Research managers are often accused of being insular, and of marching to their own tune, not bothering to communicate with other functions. This works both ways: research managers can be exacerbated by the different languages spoken by functional managers. However, it is a powerful aid to the research manager to have support and understanding from those who will make or sell the product, once successfully developed.

Selection of the project manager

The project manager may or may not be a line manager in the organization. Many R&D organizations operate matrix management systems (see Sections 4.4 and 7.3). Multiple skills are often required for a technology development, and these skill requirements may cross disciplinary boundaries. It is common for physicists, electronics and systems engineers, and bio-technologists to work together on a project. The managers of these teams must be able to coordinate resources whose skills they appreciate but may not understand. They need to be as technically aware as possible, to have a strong sense of the true project objectives, and to have strong people management skills in order to be able to manage diverse individual objectives. In a radical matrix structure, the project manager may not be a line manager, and may have line managers as part of the team. This works well where it is an accepted part of the culture and where the project management line is key to operational success. It is difficult, though, to operate in a more formal, hierarchical organization.

An important feature of the leader in a research project, and to a lesser extent in a development project, is the ability to contribute creatively. Adventurous thinking is required from the team, and this may be reinforced or discouraged by the manager. The manager must be able to use networks of contacts, both internally in the company and externally, to access information and resources, and should have a strong ability to communicate at all levels within the company, and across functional boundaries. The promotion of the excellent scientist to a management position may be disastrous. Creative bench scientists may be lousy managers, so the organization sometimes loses brilliant doers, putting them in positions where they may actually do harm if they do not know how to motivate their team. The need to separate rank and role – allowing experienced scientists to continue to contribute to technical development while also developing their status and career – is still a problem in many organizations.

Project planning

R&D projects are difficult, if not impossible, to plan in detail. The very process of the project is to determine how to achieve the objectives. Therefore you can only plan at the integrative and strategic levels. The plan will use as its starting point schemes that have been produced during proposal and initiation. Ideally the project manager will have been involved in that process and will be familiar with the objectives and rationale. A milestone plan should be developed to indicate intermediate control points against intermediate deliverables. The planning process may involve some definition of time scales and costs to achieve the milestones. However, these may not be developed from any estimating process, but may just be constraints imposed by market conditions. If milestones are not achieved by a certain date and for a certain cost, the product will not be worth while. Some kind of critical path analysis may be desirable for large projects, which may also require the use of project planning software. Project managers learn which packages work best for them in which situations, and selections by different individuals for the same project might vary from a computer-based package, to the simple paper and pencil bar chart.

Whatever planning tool is used, and they all have strengths and weaknesses, an issue for effective management is how strictly deadlines and critical paths are treated. The wise handling of plans is perhaps the most demanding skill required of project managers. This may require them to:

– optimize motivation and productivity
– maintain momentum
– control waste
– prevent divergence

but it also may require them to allow divergence down a more promising path or accept delay where a promising route suffers an unexpected setback.

You may say that this is true of any project, but it is most critically needed in R&D, where components of the critical paths may simply not be physically possible to achieve, and other approaches may lead to new unpredictable possibilities. By its very nature, the uncertainty of R&D requires *more* of this skill than most other project types.

Access to information may be an issue for both planning and administration. Information systems are required to analyse previous work on similar systems, both inside and outside the company, and to assess the relevance of new ideas. Ideally project managers should have sophisticated sources of data at their disposal and should also access their networks of informal contacts. From the internal administrative viewpoint, they will also need some kind of management information system. This may use sophisticated software or manual paperwork or word-of-mouth. Working against this is an attitude that pervades the R&D environment: ALL paperwork and bureaucracy is a dreadful constraint of creativity.

The planning of the scope, time and cost is of course only part of the story. Selecting the project team members is another. In many R&D organizations this will be quite simple in that there may only be one person with each of the required skills. This assumes that an analysis of skills required has been done. Often, little consideration is given to this, which means that only the obvious sources of skills are considered. Project launch workshops (discussed in Chapter 13), overcome this, especially if people with a wide range of skills are invited, thereby introducing new views. For a large organization some kind of skills database may be needed. These are rarely well constructed, and rarely used by project managers who are more likely to ask for resources from people they have worked with before than from people they do not know. In a large organization a good relational database of skills can be invaluable for strategic skills analysis and rational skills sourcing. These should be well thought out, with key word connections underlying free text skill description, building on technical classifications relevant to the company's market focus.

The team should always include people who will take the product through to the next stages of development (production or marketing), even if they cannot contribute directly to the current technical issues. However, it is sometimes difficult to obtain their commitment. The manager must achieve that by involving them in the planning process.

Research and development scientists often work on several projects at a time. There is some experimental evidence[12] which suggests that most scientists and engineers are more productive when working on several projects, with peak effectiveness at about three projects. The rationale is that multiple contacts are more stimulating, and there is less risk of becoming stale or blinkered if tackling several issues. There are, of course, exceptions, and one meets individuals who give their best only in total dedication to one project at a time. Whether it is more appropriate to have a large self-sufficient project team or a core team who can call on additional resources as necessary depends on the organization structure and culture.

Building the project team and getting results

A technological R&D team includes people with diverse skills, working across disciplines and several projects. Industrial scientists are usually specialists, often with an academic research career behind them which they still use as the basis for their approach. They are often uncommunicative, preferring to explore ideas alone. This may be for fear of failure, a wish not to share success, or because the culture encourages this, or perhaps because of the kind of people they are. For whatever reasons, many project managers in R&D have trouble building coherent teams, and settle for a set of individuals working separately on the same problem. Lack of management skills in the leader exacerbates this. The extent of team working depends very much on the culture of the organization, departments and groups, and on personalities concerned. Standard management and people development skills are, of course, valid, although they may need targeted interpretation in this culture, as they would in any other (see Chapters 4 and 18). Administration and bureaucracy are almost universally seen as drains and dampeners of creativity. The imposition of unnecessary paperwork of any sort by the project manager may be the worst thing that could be done, in the eyes of the team!

Communication needs

Communication is a high priority, ensuring that new ideas are shared as early as possible. There is also a strong need for communication outside the team. Again, this is true of all project types, but in R&D it is often ignored. There is a danger that the technical team may not feel that it is necessary to communicate with others until a breakthrough is achieved, or the project is successfully completed. Communication is all important for continuity, validity and congruent relationships, and may be:

- upwards, with senior management
- outwards, with other functions who will take the successful development through production and sales
- sideways, with other R&D managers who may not even be involved.

R&D managers should see information sharing as an important part of their job. This is rarely taken seriously and is the cause of many unhappy endings to otherwise successful projects. The challenge of communicating across language and vocabulary barriers is often disabling, and the onus is really on project managers to put their ideas and results across in English, in a way that is understood by others outside their speciality.

Project review and follow-up

The project must be reviewed regularly, and progress judged against the plan and other initiatives. It follows from the comments made above that representatives of other functions should participate, as should senior managers or decision makers, and ideally also one or more scientists with different perspectives or backgrounds. One important requirement is that such review processes should not become unwieldy. Although it may be more efficient to hold a series of reviews of all projects in one day, better results are achieved if each is considered separately by fresh minds, unjaded by a series of apparently similar discussions.

When the project has been completed, and the product is moving from research into development and then to manufacture, it is important to have continuity. There should be representatives of the follow-up functions on the project team, and ideally the project manager will continue to be part of the team (if not managing it) in the next stage. The project manager is then the product champion, and so becomes more deeply committed to the programme.

Effectiveness vs efficiency

A theme running through this section is that there is often more concern about efficiency than effectiveness in the management of R&D. Effectiveness is doing the right things well; efficiency is doing what you have decided to do as quickly or for as little cost as possible. In order for industrial R&D to add maximum value to the business, it must be effective as well as efficient. Results and business success are not correlated with R&D spend in technology-based companies; nor are they correlated with the productivity (efficiency) unless the objectives are wise. They are correlated with effectiveness in the sense of flexible and top-quality thinking and appropriate actions. Since projects are the unit of operation for the R&D department, effective project management is the key to ensuring that R&D adds value (Chapter 1). You should demand flexibility and quality in approach, thinking, communication and practical experimentation. This means that the organization must have coherent and clear objectives that are shared with everyone (a clear mission). It must have a high skill intensity in its resources, and it must invest in their development through wise recruitment and training. The structure and systems of the organization must support innovation, and there should be formal and informal systems to encourage it. Lastly, very nebulous but very important, the culture must be congruent with objectives, standards and expectations, with the working environment supporting these. An attitude which says that we, the team, can win, and leadership which reinforces this expectation, can ensure success against all odds.

19.5 Summary

1. Projects can be classified in three ways:
   - by position in the project or product life cycle
   - by industry or technology
   - by size.
2. In addition to traditional projects to deliver and commission a facility, projects can conduct:
   - marketing surveys and product development
   - research and development
   - maintenance and decommissioning.
3. New product development can lead to many projects:
   - research and development
   - product design and prototyping
   - facility design and delivery
   - product launch.
4. New product development can be managed through:
   - new product committees
   - product managers
   - new product managers
   - new product departments
   - venture teams
   - task forces.
5. The stages of the product development life cycle include:
   - idea generation
   - screening
   - concept development and testing
   - marketing strategy
   - business analysis
   - product development
   - market testing
   - commercialization.
6. Selection of R&D projects should be against the corporate strategy, in particular a technology strategy that will recognize the enabling technologies of the future and how the company will exploit them.

7. Project managers should be chosen for their ability as leaders and communicators, and not for their technical expertise. Communications must be upwards, outwards, and sideways.
8. R&D projects cannot be planned in detail, so must be planned against key milestones (important intermediate deliverables), with time and cost constraints set by the market requirements. Skills types must be chosen systematically and creatively.
9. An organization must be effective in achieving its R&D objectives. There is no point in achieving nothing efficiently.

Notes and references

1. Wearne, S. H., *Principles of Engineering Organisation*, Edward Arnold, 1973.
2. Kelley, A. J., 'The new project environment', in *New Dimensions of Project Management*, Lexington Books, 1982.
3. Kerzner, H., *Project Management: A systems approach to planning, scheduling and controlling*, Van Nostrand Reinhold, 1984.
4. Kotler, P., *Marketing Management: Analysis, planning and control*, Prentice-Hall, 1988.
5. Handscome, R., *The Product Management Handbook*, McGraw-Hill, 1989.
6. Section 19.3 incorporates material written by Susan Foreman. Ms Foreman is an ESRC Teaching Fellow at Henley Management College. She specializes in marketing in the service industries.
7. Foxall, G., *Corporate Innovation, Marketing and Strategy*, Croom Helm, 1984.
8. Craven, D. W., *Strategic Marketing*, Irwin, 1985.
9. Buell, V. P., *Marketing Management: A strategic planning approach*, McGraw-Hill, 1968.
10. McDonald, M. H. B., *Marketing Plans: How to prepare them, how to use them*, Heinemann, 1984.
11. Section 19.4 incorporates material written by Gordon Edge and Janice Light. Professor Edge and Dr Light work for Scientific Generics, a technology-based consultancy. Many of the ideas expressed reflect their highly innovative and effective approach to the management of R&D projects. Professor Edge is also a visiting professor at Henley Management College.
12. Pelz, D. C. and Andrews, F. M., *Scientists in Organizations: Productive climates for research and development*, Institute for Social Research, 1976.

20
Projects from industries and sectors

20.1 Introduction

A second way of classifying projects is by the 'technology' used to 'build' the facility, or by the industry or sector in which the facility operates. It could be argued that technology and industry or sector are two separate classifications. However, they lead to very similar groupings of projects. I have also put the words 'technology' and 'build' in inverted commas to reinforce that I may not necessarily be talking about engineering or technology projects, but projects from all areas of human activity.

Considering first projects by sector, it is possible to produce a breakdown of all sectors of human activity (Figure 20.1). At the first level, two groupings of activity are leisure and work. At the second level, work can be broken into the public and private sectors. The public sector can be further divided in many ways. In the UK, by government departments is natural. In the private sector, there are two major groupings: producing industries and service industries, which can be divided as shown. The lists given in Figure 20.1 are by no means exhaustive, and there is considerable overlap. However, we can say that projects exist within all of these sectors.

Considering projects by 'technology', there are three major groupings of project:

- organizational change
- engineering
- information technology.

Projects may fall wholly within one of these groupings, or across two or all three of them. The CRMO Rationalization Project, which ran throughout much of this book, involved elements of all three. It is this second classification that is used as the basis of this chapter.

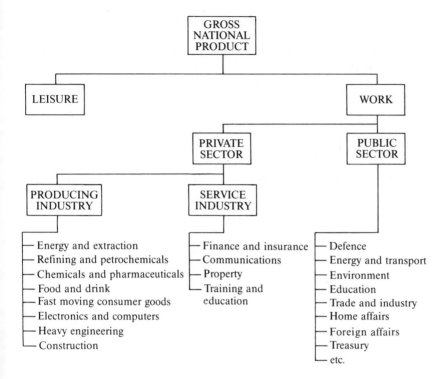

Figure 20.1   Sector breakdown structure of human activity

In this chapter, I shall consider three types of project: engineering design, engineering construction, and information technology. The first two of these illustrate the approach of a mature industry to the two major stages of a project, design and execution. The third illustrates the development of the life cycle in another mature industry. There is no section on organizational change, as that would repeat much of Chapter 4, especially Section 4.3.

20.2 Engineering design projects[1]

Engineering design involves the production of information to enable an engineering solution to be selected from a series of options and to allow one scheme to be manufactured or constructed. Information can be in the form of drawings, calculations, computer output, bills of quantities, specifications and fabrication or construction drawings. The target for good design managers is to produce the right amount of information, using the right people at the right time, to budget and to the client's satisfaction, while making a profit for their employers. This balance is not easy to achieve. Engineers are notorious for trying to satisfy the client's requirements, while forgetting the need of their own company to make a profit! The application of good project management procedures to the design process can help to ensure that the balance is achieved. It can also make the process more flexible and responsive to change, while allowing each facet of the design process to go ahead simply and efficiently within a framework of gentle control. Designers know what they are doing, why, when it is needed and what to do if the answer they come up with is not the one originally envisaged! In this section I shall consider:

– the problem of engineering design
– the design process
– the planning and control of engineering design.

A problem

While on paper the application of a project management system to the design process may seem to solve all ills, the reality is often very different. Project managers not only have to deal with the vagaries of their company's management structure but those of the client and fellow consultants as well. In a busy commercial environment, they rarely have exclusive use of all the experienced designers they require, and so must operate within a matrix management structure, in which they have to compete for the expertise they need. They also often have to deal with heavy pressure from the client to produce action and results. The need for careful planning before quantifiable results are produced is often not understood.

   Good engineering project managers should recognize the problems of working in the real world, and be able to tailor their management styles to suit the environments in which they work. Some projects may be large enough for a task force to be developed with a good working relationship, making communication and management much easier. Others may be multi-disciplinary, involving short-term input from many different parts of the company which have to be very highly controlled to ensure that the correct product is produced. Yet other projects may be small with very swift programmes that have to be fitted in between the longer running projects cutting across all other deadlines. A busy project manager will normally have to deal with various types of project all at the same time and all for different clients!

The design process

The engineering design process has four key stages (see Table 20.1) which apply for each work package within a project as well as for the project as a whole. On a civil engineering project, undertaken by a consultant for a client in the public or private sector, the stages can be further divided into work packages (Table 20.2). This describes a traditional approach to a construction project. Sometimes, on a private sector project, early stages are compressed for commercial reasons; or, on a public sector project, they are expanded due to the pressures of public accountability and inadequate finance. Design and construction can also overlap, compressing the latter part of these processes in an effort to bring a commercial project onto a 'fast track' programme to satisfy client demand for an earlier finish. Compression of the programme and overlapping and intermeshing of the stage deliverables will only succeed if adequate project management techniques are employed by the client and the client's consultant.

Table 20.1 Life cycle of engineering design projects

Stage	Activities
Definition	Appointment and problem definition
	Establishment of solution criteria
Feasibility	Evolution of alternative solutions
Option analysis	Analyses and evaluation of alternatives
Detailed design	Detailed design of selected solution
Construction	Production, fabrication or construction
	Facility construction

Planning and controlling engineering design

Prior to starting work on any of the stages listed above, the project manager should consider how the project will be planned and controlled. Examples 20.1 and 20.2 contain checklists for planning and control processes respectively produced by a firm of civil engineering design consultants. The design manager has to be as much a juggler of resources, costs and time as managers in any manufacturing or production process. In some ways the problem is more complex because the 'product' is unique and can change many times prior to completion. The manager must strike a balance between too much planning and not enough control and too much control and not enough planning, in all aspects of the design process.

Table 20.2 Work packages and deliverables of the design process

Work package	Deliverable
Definition stage	
1. Client's brief Fee agreement Establishment of consultant team	Letter of appointment
2. Desk study Problem definition	
3. Initial report Client approval to proceed	Project Definition Report approved
Feasibility stage	
4. Feasibility study and outline programme Initial consultations	
5. Feasibility report Concept and programme approval	Feasibility report approved
Option analysis	
6. Confirmation of alternatives and preliminary design	
7. Cost–benefit analysis	
8. Consultations: internal (client team) external (outside controlling bodies)	
9. Preliminary report Selection of favoured scheme Programme and cost confirmation	Solution confirmation by client
Detailed design	
10. Detailed design of approved scheme	
11. Statutory approvals Client/Budget approval	Scheme and budget approval
12. Tender preparation	
13. Contract release	Final scheme approval
Construction	
14. Construction supervision	
15. End of construction Commissioning	Client acceptance of product
16. Maintenance period Records and manuals	

PLANNING ENGINEERING DESIGN

P1   Examine the problem carefully with the client and if possible with the client's advisers. Establish what exactly the task is and agree a fee structure for the work covering various stages of design, taking note of the often highly variable nature of the initial design studies.

 The fee arrangement may also include a Collateral Warranty. This is now commonplace in the construction industry as a result of recent case law on the question of latent liabilities. This must also be recognized and dealt with as a milestone because the client frequently cannot get funding released for the project from the backers until the document is signed and completed. The time necessary to complete these procedures is often underestimated, which can cause delays.

P2   Establish the basis of a planning network, identifying key milestones to be achieved in design. Plan to do the detailed planning of each phase only when it is necessary, that is on a rolling wave basis.

P3   Confirm the work breakdown, and identify packages of design work. Seek the use of the appropriate work-package managers and teams from within your company. Select the right people for the right job, and match personalities to the nature of the task. A careful meticulous detailer cannot drive a high-pressured fast track project forward, but should be used to give support to the innovators and strong managers.

P4   Assess time and resource requirements for each phase of design work (at the appropriate time) using your own experience combined with that of the work-package managers.

P5   Check each stage of resource allocation against fee available prior to undertaking work. If fee is too small, re-evaluate the amount of design proposed and reduce, or delay applying resource or renegotiate fee arrangement. Aim to do the right amount of work at the right time.

P6   Using your simple master design plan as a basis, establish that available resource for each stage is sufficient to meet the programme. Introduce contingency allowances at a fairly high level in the plan so that you can control slippage. Try not to build contingency in at each level or else you will never create a workable programme.

P7   Establish, jointly with the department managers in your company, whether your use of their staff (particularly when the project is multi-disciplinary) is compatible with their other commitments and schedule resources accordingly. Tie this back to the basic network and evaluate any overall programme effect. As far as possible smooth out resource peaks to enable overall company staff planning to be easier and seek to adjust priorities to suit. A balance always has to be struck.

P8   Establish work packages, and if at all possible write down a brief for their managers as clearly and in as much detail as possible. This is often difficult to achieve but is very important because it establishes a firm criteria against which success can be measured in each design package. Ensure that this brief is a living document, and that it is continually referred to and updated by mutual agreement of the project manager and work-package manager as the design evolves.

P9   Establish the critical path from your network (which starts off at a high level of planning and is slowly filled in with relevant subnetworks). In theory, your critical path should be determined from the outset by the production of a stable network plan within which variations can take place. In practice, this may not be so easy to achieve as there are usually many unforeseeable events which erode your contingency and cause the path to shift. It is, however, always these key activities that dictate whether or not the project is completed on time.

Information and resource needed is the key to the well being of the whole project. It has been suggested that 80 per cent of design problems come from 20 per cent of the activities. However, an over-preoccupation with activities currently identified as critical can also backfire by reducing your awareness of other non-critical areas that can suddenly become critical. A balance has to be achieved and progress on each facet of the network must be regularly monitored and controlled.

Example 20.1 Planning the engineering design process

CONTROLLING ENGINEERING DESIGN

C1   Establish communication systems. Decide which level of designer should talk to which level in the client or consultant teams. Ensure that you are always in the picture as to progress. Ensure that work-package managers are aware of their responsibility to control communication. Only correctly considered information should be released to avoid incorrect action by outside bodies, which destroys confidence in the design team's abilities.

C2   Establish a design review procedure. Regular (fortnightly) design reviews should take place to ensure that the whole package is moving towards its target. An open forum in which work-package managers can discuss problems should be encouraged. People must not hide major problems but discuss them and seek help before they run out of control.

C3   Establish a design-checking procedure to interface the review process. Some projects need a full quality assurance (QA) system. This must be identified at the outset to ensure that a quality plan is written and implemented incorporating the project management systems identified. Some projects (e.g. bridges designed for the Department of Transport) have established checking procedures for each stage. These may include formal checks by other firms.

The checks and consequential alterations must be programmed at each stage of the design, and adequate resources and time allowed. If QA is required you must remember that this is only an aid to sound design office procedures and not a substitute. QA should only help formalize those procedures already being undertaken.

C4 Establish a regular system of internal meetings to interface the usual client/consultant design team meetings. These meetings may be held instead of or as well as design reviews, depending on the complexity of the job, and should bring together internal technical design issues as well as a review of external influences on the design. Following these reviews a short statement of progress, addressing key issues and problems, should be prepared for issue to client. Areas where information is required from others or where instruction is needed should be identified.

C5 As changes occur, ensure that the reasons are communicated, if appropriate, down to draughtsmen. There is nothing more demoralizing to a draughtsman than facets of the design being repeated when the reason is unclear. Although this may be tedious for the work-package managers, the project manager must encourage the team to keep communication lines open. One must always be conscious of the needs and desires of the individual as well as the objectives of the project, or neither will be achieved.

C6 Once design has begun, check expenditure against forecast costs and fee income, regularly. Often delays cause an increase in resources to recover the programme. Delays may require you to move staff from one project to another to avoid overloading one and under-resourcing another. While your plan and control systems should allow you to accommodate this, the financial side of your company must not be forgotten. Computerized monthly job cost summaries are out of date before you receive them, so ensure that you know what the projected cost effects are before they occur.

C7 Changes to the design brief are often made by the client as the design develops. This is a natural consequence of the design process and should be expected as the client begins to understand the impact of earlier decisions. While some change should be tolerated, major changes must be controlled, and additional fees sought before embarking on the additional work required. If the client is not aware of the financial implications of new decisions, then the client can have a change of mind without a second thought, which rapidly can cause your company to make a loss.

C8 Establish which outside bodies (stakeholders) must be consulted, and obtain their approval prior to commencing. These may be statutory bodies, environmental groups, planning authorities, etc. Time to obtain such approvals must be allocated and milestones recognized. You may also require discreet input from the consultant team at regular intervals and vice versa, depending on the product. You must identify and programme this flow of information as a strategic part of your design process.

Example 20.2 Controlling the engineering design process

20.3 Engineering construction projects[2]

Engineering construction is the construction of process or power generation plants. In this section, I shall describe how project management techniques are applied to engineering construction, and consider:

- the project management life cycle used in engineering construction
- how construction is planned, organized, implemented and controlled
- key issues for ensuring success.

The life cycle for construction projects

Table 20.3 shows how the four stages of the life cycle apply to engineering construction. The construction section of an engineering design company would have minor inputs at the conceptual design stage, have an advisory input into the detailed design and procurement stage, and lead the other two stages, during which the design and procurement activities will be reviewed and the plant built and commissioned. Traditionally there have been two problems with the management of the life cycle:

1. Construction are not involved in the early stages, so the initial design work is carried out without constructability reviews. Although this saves costs in the short term, the long-term costs, from rectification work and more expensive construction methods, far outweigh the cost of having construction people involved earlier.
2. During the construction and commissioning stages, the engineering and procurement man-hours have been expended, so it is often difficult to get head office support to solve problems as they occur in the field.

Table 20.3 The life cycle of engineering construction projects

Stage	Main activity
Germination	Conceptual design
Growth	Detailed design and procurement
Maturity	Construction
Death	Handover and close-out

With the trend towards fast track schedules, there is a growing realization that early construction involvement and continuing head office support are required if the projects are to meet their objectives.

Planning the construction stage

Initial overall planning is done during tender preparation before contract award. A preliminary schedule is included in the estimate. On contract award a detailed schedule is produced, linking engineering, procurement and construction stages. This is issued as the master schedule, and is the baseline for more detailed schedules (Section 14.3). From this document, the planner develops the construction schedule in sufficient detail to set milestones for individual subcontracts. On fully subcontracted projects, it is only necessary to highlight important milestones and interfaces with other subcontracts. A detailed, day-to-day schedule is produced by individual subcontractors. It is usual to establish payment milestones that encourage subcontractors to progress the project in accordance with the master schedule. The construction plan is linked to the overall project schedule, so the effects of any movement in front-end activities on the completion date can be seen, and timely corrective action taken. This linking also allows changes in construction activities to be fed back into the schedule to reflect different engineering and procurement requirements. In reality, it is necessary to build in some buffers to ensure that no one is working to the latest possible dates.

Organizing construction personnel

Having established the construction schedule, the manager then establishes the construction site. One of the key issues is mobilization of the staff in accordance with the schedule. A budget has usually been established for the staff at the estimate stages. The mobilization of staff becomes something of a juggling act between site requirements and the budget. Often the requirements have been underestimated, especially for the completion and handover activities, when prudence disappears in an effort to achieve completion on time. It is, however, important that personnel are mobilized in time to allow them to become familiar with the project. This is especially important during recessionary periods when companies are reluctant to retain staff, which means that most projects then have people who are new to the organization.

To have a successful project, all personnel should clearly understand their responsibilities, and work together as a team. The present trend is to keep the number of site staff to a minimum, with people carrying out multiple duties. It is then even more important that all personnel understand their responsibilities if duplication of effort or omissions are to be avoided. This is achieved by providing all personnel with clear job descriptions as they arrive on site, and by holding regular team meetings.

Before commencing work, all personnel (including subcontractors) undergo an induction period to familiarize them with site procedures and safety regulations. Weekly safety audits are carried out to ensure that site activities are being carried out in accordance with the procedures.

Implementing the construction stage

The construction stage consists of the following activities:

- site establishment
- producing specific site procedures
- prequalifying subcontractors
- compiling tender documents
- issuing tenders
- reviewing tender submissions and selecting subcontractors
- commencing work in accordance with the construction schedule
- controlling site activities
- handing over and closing-out project.

Usually a small team is established in head office to handle site preparation, including producing site procedures, developing requirements for temporary facilities, prequalifying subcontractors and awarding initial contracts. They also liaise with other departments to review the design and advise on construction requirements. This team also organizes initial site personnel, to coordinate initial civil work. It is usual for the team to move to site after the main mechanical subcontract has been awarded. This overlap with design activities reduces rework. Subsequent subcontracts (electrical, instrument, painting and insulation) are usually awarded directly from site. Weekly meetings are held on site with subcontractors to coordinate activities and address problems, both engineering and commercial. On fast track projects, it is common to hold afternoon coordination meetings daily with representatives of all subcontractors to make all parties aware of the next day's activities.

Construction control systems

It is very important to implement systems to maintain control of site activities. Traditionally these were manual systems, but gradually they are becoming more computerized, using information transferred from the engineering and procurement databases. As a minimum, systems are required to control the following activities:

- material receipt and issue
- engineering documentation

- subcontracts
- planning
- progress
- quality
- handover to client.

When developing systems, it is important to define exactly what is required, and to match requirements as closely as possible. There is a temptation to *computerize* a manual system, which may not be the best use of the technology. The reports produced should also be kept as simple as possible. In most cases a management level summary is all that is needed.

Making construction a success

There are three areas to be addressed to make construction a success:

GOOD PLANNING

All site activities should be planned. This includes the direct construction activities, and other work such as establishment of temporary facilities, recruitment and release of personnel and mobilization of vendor representatives. If the direct and indirect activities are planned and integrated, then their effect on the overall schedule will be seen.

GOOD COMMUNICATION

Having established a good plan, it is important that it is communicated to all parties, including people in the construction group, the client, the head office engineering and procurement staff, the subcontractors and the site suppliers. Most problems occurring on site are caused by poor communication, especially of revised plans.

GOOD TEAMWORK

It is necessary to establish good teamwork on construction projects. This should extend from the client to the workforce. Project schedules are now too tight to be successfully completed under the adversarial conditions that existed some years ago. This requires a change in culture, with projects being set up using task forces, and with client and main contractor personnel working together in one office. This builds an atmosphere of trust which assists in resolving problems at a later stage. Relations between main contractor and subcontractors are usually dictated by contractual terms and conditions, but it is being realized that these must allow a team approach to develop if the projects are to be successful.

20.4 Information technology projects[3]

As software becomes more complex managers have a greater need to understand its production. Numerous models of the software life cycle exist to illustrate this production, and many of the concepts are applicable to other areas of technology, and to R&D projects. The function of a life-cycle model is to determine the order in which software development should be undertaken, and to establish transition criteria to progress from one stage to the next. Transition criteria include completion criteria for the current stage, and choice and entry criteria for the next. More sophisticated models of software development life cycles have evolved because traditional models discouraged effective approaches to software development such as prototyping and software re-use. This section traces the evolution of the different models, and explains their strengths and weaknesses. The models described are:

- the code-and-fix model
- the stage-wise model
- the waterfall model
- the spiral model.

The code-and-fix model

The earliest model for software development had two, simple stages:

- *Stage 1*: write some code
- *Stage 2*: fix the problems in the code.

Code was written before requirements were fully defined, design done, and test and maintenance procedures described. The strength of this approach was its simplicity, but that is also the source of its weaknesses. There are three main difficulties:

1. *Maintainability* After a number of fixes the code becomes so poorly structured that subsequent fixes are very expensive. This reinforces the need for design prior to coding.
2. *User requirements* Often the software is a poor match to user's needs so it is either rejected or requires extensive redevelopment.
3. *Cost* Code is expensive to fix because of poor preparation for testing and modification. This highlights the need for these stages, as well as planning and preparation for them in early stages.

The stage-wise and waterfall models

Experience on large software systems as early as the mid-1950s led to the recognition of these problems, which resulted in the development of a stage-wise model. This stipulates that software should be developed in successive stages (Figure 20.2). Figure 2.2 shows another version. The waterfall model (Figures 20.3 and 20.4) is a refinement of the stage-wise model from the late 1960s. The major enhancement was that it recognized feedback loops between stages, but with a requirement to confine loops back to the previous stage only, to minimize the expensive rework resulting from feedback over several stages. I shall use the second waterfall model (Figure 20.4) to illustrate principles common to many of the life cycles, as it can be easily related to other models, although the specific stages and names vary between models.

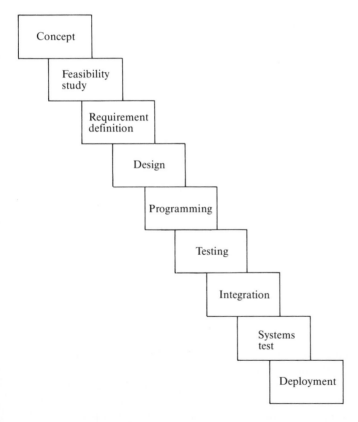

Figure 20.2   The stage-wise model

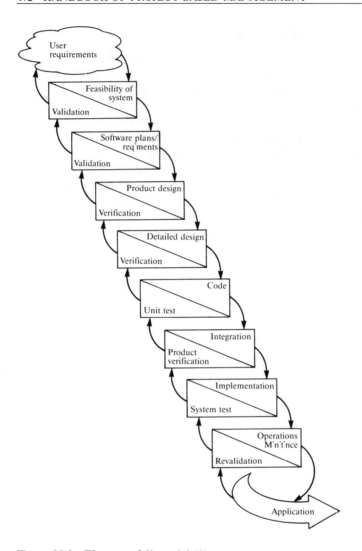

Figure 20.3 The waterfall model (1)

The waterfall model (2) is characterized by its V-shape. Down the left-hand side are stages which derive elements of the system, while up the right-hand side is the delivery of the elements to form the system (Table 20.4). Each stage is defined by its outputs, the deliverables, rather than its constituent activities. A tangible output is the only criterion of progress, the only thing that people can assess objectively. Only in this way can the 95 per cent complete syndrome be avoided. The products of each stage

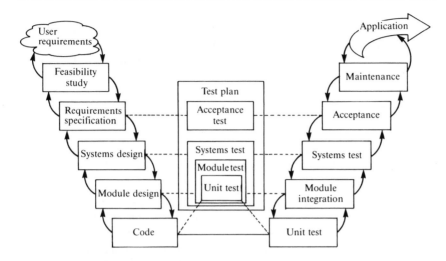

Figure 20.4   The waterfall model (2)

represent points along the development path where there is a clear change of emphasis, where one viewpoint of the design or emerging system is established, and is used as the basis for the next. As such, these intermediate products are natural milestones of the development progression and offer objective visibility of that progression.

To provide management control, the concepts of *baseline* and *configuration management* are introduced. The completion of a stage is determined by the satisfactory assessment of the quality of the intermediate products (or deliverables) of that stage. These deliverables then form the baseline for the work in the next stage. Thus the deliverables of the next stage can be verified against the previous baseline as part of configuration management and the quality assessment, before they become the new baseline. Each baseline is documented, and the quality assessment includes reviews of the intermediate products by developed personnel, other project and company experts, and usually customer and user personnel. This is similar to the concept of baseline introduced in Section 12.5. However, there the focus was primarily on baselining time and cost, whereas here it is on quality and scope. For these, you cannot baseline the whole project, only one stage at a time, as the definition of scope and quality evolve throughout the project. This evolution is controlled through configuration management (Section 16.3). It is the documentation and reviews which provide the tangible and objective milestones throughout the entire development process. The waterfall model shows how confidence in the project's progress is built on the successive baselines.

This simplistic description of the life cycle could imply that control of software development can only be achieved by rigorous control of the staging, so that no stage is considered complete until all prescribed docu-

Table 20.4 Stages of the software development life cycle

Stage	Description
Feasibility study	Production of verified/validated system architecture based on a design study, including allocation of tasks to staff and machines, milestone plan, responsibility chart, schedules of major activities, and outline quality plan
Requirements specification	Production of complete/validated specification of requirements (functional/non-functional) the system must satisfy. Produced in close liaison with the end user. Means of system acceptance also agreed with end user
Systems design	Production of complete/verified specification of overall architecture, control structure and data structure for the system. Production of draft user manuals, and training and test plans for integration
Module design	Production of detailed designs for each module, together with module test plans. This may actually consist of more than one level of design
Code	Module designs are converted into code units in the target language (such as C, Pascal and FORTRAN)
Unit test	Code units are tested by the programmer. Errors are corrected immediately by the programmer. Once complete, code units are frozen and pass to integration
Module integration (structural testing)	Component units of a module are integrated together, and tested as specified in module test plan. Errors detected are formally documented, and the affected area returns to a stage where the error was introduced
Systems test (functional testing)	Modules are integrated together to form the system, and tested against the system test plan. Errors detected are handled as for module testing
Acceptance test	Client formally witness the exercising of the system against agreed criteria for acceptance
Maintenance	Service life is often grossly underestimated. Software written in the 1960s is still being used. The cost of development can be small compared to maintenance, but the latter is given little consideration

ments have been completed to specified standards, and no stage can be started until all its input documents are complete (giving non-overlapping stages). Although the intended rigour of such an approach is commendable, it is unrealistic on a large development project. It is not intended that the life cycle should be interpreted in such a simplistic way.

The strengths of the waterfall model are that it overcomes the problems in the code-and-fix model. However, its great weakness is its emphasis on fully elaborated documentation as completion criteria for early stages. This is effective only for some specialist classes of software, such as compilers and operating systems. It does not work well for the majority of software – for example, user applications and especially those involving interactive interfaces. Document-driven standards have pushed many projects to write elaborate specifications of poorly understood user interfaces and decision support functions, and these have resulted in the design and development of large amounts of unusable code.

The spiral model

The spiral model[4] (Figure 20.5), which is still evolving, can accommodate all the previous models as special cases. The radial dimension represents the cumulative cost of undertaking the work to date. The angular dimension represents the progress of each cycle of the spiral. The model reflects the concept that each cycle involves a progression through a repeated sequence of steps for each portion of the product, and for each elaboration from overall concept document to coding of each individual program. The first stage is planned, then each loop of the spiral passes through four quadrants:

– determine objectives, alternatives and constraints
– evaluate alternatives, identify and resolve risks
– develop and verify the next level of product
– plan the next stage.

DETERMINE OBJECTIVES, ALTERNATIVES AND CONSTRAINTS

After planning and launching, each cycle begins with identification of:

– objectives of this portion of the product being set, including performance, functionality, ability to accommodate change, etc.
– alternative means of delivering this portion of the product, including alternative designs, re-use, or buying in
– the constraints imposed on final deliverable by the various alternatives, including cost, schedule, interfaces, etc.

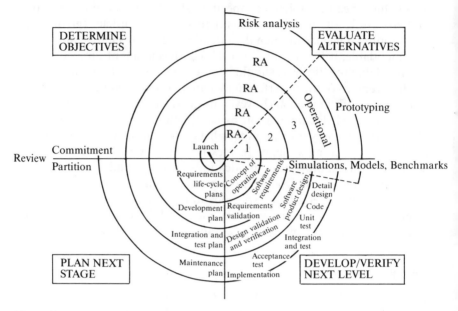

Figure 20.5 The spiral model

EVALUATE ALTERNATIVES, IDENTIFY AND RESOLVE RISKS

The next step is to evaluate the alternatives against the objectives and constraints. Frequently this process identifies areas of uncertainty that are significant sources of risk. If so, this stage should involve the formulation of a cost-effective strategy for resolving the sources of risk.

DEVELOP AND VERIFY THE NEXT LEVEL OF PRODUCT

Once the risks are evaluated, the next stage is determined by the relative importance of remaining risks. This risk-driven basis of the spiral model allows the model to accommodate any appropriate mixture of different approaches to software development, including specification-oriented, prototype-oriented, simulation-oriented, transformation-oriented, etc. The appropriate mixed strategy is chosen by considering the relative magnitude of the program risks, and the relative effectiveness of the various approaches to resolving risk.

PLAN THE NEXT STAGE

This completes the cycle. An important feature of the spiral model, as with others, is that each cycle is completed by a review involving the primary parties concerned with the product.

Management and the spiral model

There are four key points:

INITIATING AND TERMINATING THE SPIRAL

The spiral is initiated by the hypothesis that a particular operational objective can be improved by a software solution. The spiral evolves as a series of tests of this hypothesis. If at any time the hypothesis fails, the spiral is terminated. Otherwise it terminates with the installation of new or modified software.

FEATURES OF THE SPIRAL MODEL

The model has three essential features:

1. It fosters the development of specifications that need not be uniform, exhaustive or formal. They defer detailed elaboration of low-risk software elements, and avoid unnecessary breakages in their design until the high-risk elements of the design are stabilized. (This is rolling-wave design, and developing work breakdown to a lower level in areas of high risk at an earlier stage.)
2. It incorporates prototyping as a risk reduction option at any stage of development. In fact, prototyping and the re-use of risk analyses were previously used in going from detailed design to code.
3. It accommodates reworking or a return to earlier stages as more attractive alternatives are identified or as new risk issues need resolution.

EVALUATION

The main advantage of the spiral model is that its range of options accommodates the good features of existing software, while its risk-driven approach avoids many of their difficulties. Other advantages include:

- it focuses early attention on options re-using existing software
- it accommodates evolution, growth and changes of the product
- it provides a mechanism for incorporating software quality into product development

- it eliminates errors and unattractive alternatives early
- it identifies the required amount of each resource
- it uses the same approach for software development, software enhancement, or maintenance
- it provides a viable framework for integrated hardware and software system development.

However, the model is still evolving, and there are three areas that must be addressed before it can be called a mature, universal model:

1. *Matching to contract software* The model works well on internal development projects, but needs further work for contract software. Its adaptability makes it inappropriate for fixed price contracts.
2. *Relying on risk assessment expertise* The spiral model places a great deal of reliance on the ability of software developers to identify and manage sources of project risk.
3. *Need for further elaboration of the stages of the model* The steps of the model need further elaboration to ensure that all software developers are operating in a consistent manner. This includes detailed specification of deliverables and procedures, guidelines and checklists to identify the most likely sources of project risk, and techniques for the most effective resolution of risk.

RISK MANAGEMENT

Efforts to apply and refine the model have focused on creating a discipline of software risk management (Chapter 11). A top-ten list of software risk items[4] (Table 20.5) is one result of this activity. Another is the risk management approach discussed in Section 11.6.

The problems of real life

Unfortunately, the reality of software development is not quite as simplistic as these models might imply.

1. Exploratory work on subsequent stages, including costing, can be required before the current stage is complete – for example, design investigation is almost invariably required before it can be stated that the user requirement can be achieved within a realistic budget.
2. Problems encountered in later stages may require reworking of earlier stages – failure to recognize this leads to earlier documentation becoming inaccurate and misleading.
3. The users' requirement may not remain stable throughout a protracted

Table 20.5 A prioritized top-ten list of software risk items

Risk item	Risk management technique
Personnel shortfalls	Staff with top talent; team/morale building; cross training; pre-scheduling key people
Unrealistic schedules and budgets	Detailed/checked cost and duration estimates; design to cost; incremental development; re-use of software; requirements scrubbing
Developing wrong functionality	Organization/mission analysis; ops concept formulation; user surveys; prototyping; early user manuals
Developing wrong user interface	Task analysis; prototyping; scenarios; user profiles (functionality, style, workload)
Gold plating	Requirements scrubbing; prototyping; cost-benefit analysis; design to cost; value engineering
Continuing changes to requirements	High change threshold; information hiding; incremental development (defer changes to later increment)
Shortfalls in procured components	Benchmarking; inspection; expediting; reference checking; quality auditing; compatibility analysis
Shortfalls in subcontracted tasks	Reference checking; pre-award audits; fixed price contracts; competitive deign/prototyping; team building
Shortfalls in real-time performance	Simulation; benchmarking; modelling; prototyping; instrumentation; tuning
Straining the capabilities of computer science	Technical analysis; cost–benefit analysis; prototyping; reference checking

development process – it is then necessary to consider changed requirements and consequential changes in later stages.

Therefore, it is important that the life cycle is not rigidly imposed. In reality, there are no clearly defined breakpoints between the stages. Equally, all the stages are composed of several substages or packages of work. However, once this is recognized, it does not lead to the conclusion that the life-cycle model must be discarded, but it represents a valuable model of what is involved in the technical work of software development.

The biggest single problem in the software cycle is the communication across the boundary from one stage to the next. At each stage there can be a degradation of the definition of the users' requirements, as described in Section 8.2. Quality assurance (Section 8.3), and configuration management (Section 16.3), play a crucial role in managing this flow of information.

Resourcing the life cycle

I end this chapter with a cautionary note. Many of the names of stages in the life cycle are similar to resource types working in software development. This results in each type becoming primarily associated with a stage: systems analysts with design, programmers with coding. You will hear IT people referring to the work of each resource types as an 'activity', and then they confuse the 'activity' of the resource with the work of the stage. Resource types are then not assigned to the project until the work of the stage with which they are associated is about to begin. The result is that long lead items are ignored by earlier resource types, resources have no time to prepare before starting, and resources cannot complete their input within the time allotted. In reality, most resource types should work throughout the project. Where the work of one resource type overlaps with a stage, that defines a work package. Early work packages are in support of the design process, and in preparation for the stage in which the resource is primarily involved. Later work packages are in support of implementation.

20.5 Summary

1. Classifying projects by technology or by industry sector produces a similar classification. There are broadly three categories:
   - organizational change
   - engineering
   - information technology.
2. Engineering design projects have a four-stage life cycle. Each stage can be broken further into standard work packages. The stages are:
   - definition and appointment
   - feasibility
   - option analysis
   - detailed design.
3. Checklists are given for planning and controlling engineering design.
4. There are two key requirements for engineering construction:
   - involving construction management in the design process to achieve buildable designs
   - maintaining head-office support throughout the construction process, to solve problems as they occur.
5. There are four types of model of the life cycle for software development projects:
   - code-and-fix models
   - stage-wise models

– waterfall models
– spiral models.

6. Stages in all the models are identified not by the work done, but by the deliverables, or intermediate products, in which they result. The control process focuses on the quality of these deliverables.

7. Spiral models, which can incorporate any one of the other three as a special case, view the project as moving repeatedly through four quadrants:

– determine objectives, alternatives, constraints
– evaluate alternatives, and identify and resolve risks
– develop and verify the next level product
– plan the forthcoming stage.

Notes and references

1. Section 20.2 incorporates material written by Peter Brett Associates, engineering consultants. In particular, material was contributed by David Topping.
2. Section 20.3 incorporates material written by Steven Kirk. Mr Kirk is an internal project consultant to Brown & Root, a major international firm of design and construction engineers, and is chairman of the quality committee of the European Construction Institute.
3. Section 20.4 incorporates material written by Anne French. Ms French is acting head of department in Information Systems at the Farnborough College of Technology.
4. Boehm, B. W. 'A spiral model of software development and enhancement', *Computer*, May 61–72, The Institute of Electrical and Electronic Engineers, 1988.

21
Projects by size

21.1 Introduction

The third way of classifying projects is by their size. It is common to define three sizes of project: small to medium, large, and major. People put figures against projects in each category, sometimes by money spent, sometimes by number of people working at any time, sometimes by duration. However, the conclusion usually is that there is a huge overlap between the sizes, and it is dependent on industry. What is considered a large IT project is a small engineering project. The size of project has been found to be more a qualitative measure than a quantitative one. It is more dependent on the way the parties involved work together and collaborate on the project.

Classification of projects by size

SMALL TO MEDIUM-SIZED PROJECTS

These are undertaken by a single organization and share resources from a common pool. In these cases the primary team may be very small, consisting of the project manager and one or two others. The majority of people working on the project are in the secondary team, and they have less loyalty to the project. Even those assigned full time owe their primary loyalty to the organization, and can therefore be withdrawn at any time to be assigned to a project that has overtaken the original one in priority. The project manager may have responsibility for several projects; and it is quite common for organizations to give each project manager responsibility for one medium-sized project and several small projects. In these circumstances the organization has a continual need to assign priority for resources between projects: capacity planning is the main concern (Section 16.2). The main concern of the project manager is to obtain priority for the projects within the capacity plan, and to build the commitment of people who are working on several projects to their particular projects.

These are undertaken by a single organization and warrant a dedicated team of project resources for a significant period of time. This is in fact the classic project situation: a project manager with a large (though finite) team of people that can be assigned to the project's tasks in order to optimize the project's cost and duration. The main concern is to assign the team of people to the project's tasks so that events on the critical paths take place at the earliest possible time, while bulk work is used to fill the troughs in the resource demands, but takes place within the duration set by the critical paths. Large projects will have large primary teams and small secondary teams.

MAJOR PROJECTS

These are beyond the capacity of one organization. The mix of skills or financial risk is such that no organization has the resources or capacity to undertake them, so their execution requires organizations to collaborate in a partnership or joint venture. Note that on all projects, whether small, medium or large, the owner will procure skills and materials from contractors, subcontractors and suppliers. What distinguishes major projects is that the commitment of resources and financial risk is so great that no one organization can accept that burden as a sole owner, as the risk of failure is that the organization will surely collapse, and so the burden must be shared through a partnership arrangement. Traditionally, many major projects have been national infrastructure projects, and so one of the parties to the joint venture arrangement has been the government, perhaps in the form of a nationalized industry. During the 1970s and 1980s, the primary area of economic activity in the UK for major projects that did not involve the government was in North Sea oil field developments.[1] However, that has now changed. The approach known as Build–Own–Operate–(Transfer), BOO(T), of which the Channel Tunnel is the prime example, and the privatization of major public utilities, means that an increasing number of infrastructure projects must now be funded by the private sector, and will require organizations to share the risk.

Ratio of project activity by size

I said above that it is very difficult to put a definitive range of figures on each size of project, but with the above definitions we may say that a small project will be anything up to about £3 million, a medium-sized project up to about £30 million, a large project up to about £300 million, and a major project greater.

Major projects are the most visible. When they go wrong, the failure is public, and receives considerable media attention. There have been some disasters in the last 30 years.[1] There have also been some significant successes, such as Giotto (the spacecraft to Halley's comet), and the computerization of PAYE.[1] However, the total annual spend on all the major projects put together is not very great. You can identify what they are. The three primary ones in the UK in the early 1990s are the Sizewell Nuclear Power Station, the Trident Submarine and the Channel Tunnel. Adding any others that might be underway, the total spend is about £2 billion per year, less than 0.5 per cent of Gross National Product (GNP).

Large projects are the traditional type of project, and are therefore the type at which almost all the books and software on project management are aimed. By and large, both assume that each project has a dedicated pool of resources, and the main concern of the project manager is to determine and manage the duration of the project, and to schedule the activities so that the daily resource requirement stays within the capacity of the dedicated pool, which is the case only on large to major projects. To undertake a large project, a private company will need a capitalization of about £100 million or greater; that is, it will be within the top 100 companies in the country. Assuming each company starts one project per year, of average value of £100 million, and doubling the number to account for projects undertaken in the public sector, the total annual spend on large projects is about £20 billion, less than 5 per cent of GNP. Hence, the annual spend on large projects is 10 times that on major projects.

The total annual spend on projects in the UK may be 50 per cent of GNP, about £250 billion. It has just been shown that large and major projects account for less than 10 per cent of that, which means that small to medium-sized projects account for the rest, about £200 billion. Thus, the annual spend on small to medium-sized projects is 10 times that on large projects, and 100 times that on major projects. Furthermore, since larger projects tend to be more capital intensive, about 95 per cent of project personnel work on smaller projects. Yet they receive no media attention, and very few books or software packages are aimed at them. Some packages were intended for them, but as I said in Chapter 17, the main concerns of the manager in that environment are capacity planning and prioritizing, and no packages are available that have been written for that purpose.

Since large projects are the 'norm' (though they only account for 9 per cent of all projects), in this chapter I shall describe the two situations which deviate from that norm: multi-project management of small to medium-sized projects, and major projects, in particular joint ventures between collaborating organizations.

21.2 Multi-projects[2]

Small to medium-sized projects, by the definition above, occur in an environment where several projects compete for resources from a common, finite resource pool. This situation is called *multi-project management* and sometimes *programme management*. Some techniques for managing multi-projects within a programme of projects were described in Section 16.2. This section will consider:

– the problem of small to medium-sized projects (SMPs)
– the effect on the parent and project organizations
– the role of the project manager and programme manager (director of projects)

The problem of small to medium-sized projects

Within most organizations, there exists a large number of identifiable, smaller projects: some organizations' operations can be entirely based on SMPs. They can arise through:

– smaller companies, acting as subcontractors or suppliers to larger ones on several projects
– bespoke manufacturing companies (jobbing shops), making products for several customers
– mass production companies using project methods to introduce new products with reduced product life cycles (Chapter 19)
– engineering, management and other consultants scheduling expensive staff across several projects
– research institutions undertaking projects for several clients
– all organizations managing change, introducing new products or new technology, changing culture, or adopting total quality management.[3]

Often these projects, taken by themselves, would be less risky than large projects and could be managed effectively without the use of formal project management techniques. However, together in the multi-project environment, they can consume a considerable amount of management effort,[4] because of:

- poor selection processes
- poor management processes
- higher management overheads
- higher ratio of risk.

SELECTION

The primary reason for the failure of SMPs is they have inadequate priority for resources, alongside other projects and day-to-day operations. This is true for both organizations undertaking them as internal development projects and as contracts for external clients. Each project is small, and so the individual resource requirement does not appear to be much. However, when too many are taken on, there is insufficient resource to go round, with the result that no projects get completed[3] (Example 3.5). Programmes of projects are the vehicles by which organizations implement their strategy. Many organizations fail to achieve their strategy because they fail to manage the selection process.

MANAGEMENT

SMPs are often more complex than they first appear and yet only cursory attention is given to their planning. Reasons may be: the benefit is not as obvious as for larger projects; smaller organizations do not accept formal project management; project management software is focused on critical path analysis and time management, and this is not appropriate for managing a capacity problem. Also, because of their size, SMPs are often given to more junior managers, whereas the negotiating of priority requires more mature management skills.

OVERHEADS

The cost of management of SMPs can be a very large proportion of the total cost, which increase the pressure for inadequate management.

RISKS

On SMPs, risks are more essential than expected. Small to medium companies managing SMPs can be hit remarkably badly by small risks. In addition, project times are shorter giving higher risk, and making it harder to compensate for overruns. There is less opportunity to recover.

However, changes in the business environment have created a culture that needs to be more responsive to change, requiring more organizations to use multi-project management to manage their development pro-grammes. This requires companies undertaking SMPs to have criteria by which to judge the viability of new projects and to set priorities between them. There are techniques for appraising projects and assigning priorities. However, three steps that are cheap and within the control of both organizations and project teams are maintaining good records of past projects, ensuring that enough time is given to assessing project via-bility, and assigning priority to selected projects. Organizations who adopt multi-project management may be able to take on more business as a result of better planning, scheduling and resource allocation.

The effect on the parent and project organizations

The success of project management in any organization relies on having systems that are simple and flexible. The project management structure adopted depends to a certain extent on the relative importance of the projects to the organization and whether the organization's main busi-ness is multi-project management. Multi-project management creates a

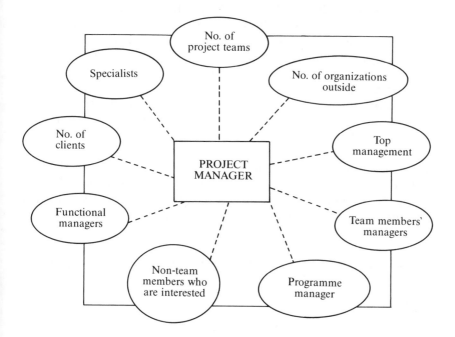

Figure 21.1   The project manager's lines of communication

large number of interfaces, all of which need managing. Because of the number of interfaces, multi-project management is really only workable when the projects are reasonably similar, whether technically or organizationally, or repetitive, because there is a limit to the amount of integration.

On any project, the project manager has to communicate with several groups (Figure 21.1); the communication needs across these interfaces in a multi-project environment are obviously greater. If multi-project management is to be successful, four groups must remain organizationally distinct:

- *programme management*: who define the requirements for projects, and set the boundaries between them
- *project management*: who perform the role of integration
- *project control*: who provide independent and accurate progress data
- *functional groups*: who carry out the tasks.

As organizations with large numbers of SMPs are more exposed to risk, a project matrix (Section 7.3) may be the preferred form of organizational structure, if integration and efficient scheduling, allocation and use of resources is to be achieved. The difference between the management of a single project and that of multi-projects is the latter need coordinating and therefore the project manager must be given sufficient authority to gain management attention at the right level. The reverse often happens; trainee project managers, who do not carry much weight within the parent organization, are put in charge of the smaller projects. The need to use a matrix structure creates a problem integrating multi-project management into traditional organizations with functional hierarchies. Although smaller businesses respond faster to change, they only tend to change organizational form as a last resort. Despite the fact that implementing multi-project management into a small to medium organization can be time consuming and costly, they must consider changing the way they operate if they want to manage smaller projects successfully. This may mean moving from a functional organizational structure.[5]

The role of the project manager and programme manager (director of projects)

THE PROJECT MANAGER

The main skills or emphasis of the project manager in a multi-project environment are different to the traditional environment of the larger project. The manager of smaller projects must:

- be a coordinator rather than a manager
- be able to set priorities between projects
- be impartial
- be more of a risk taker
- develop good, simple reporting systems and procedures
- have good client liaison
- deal with higher levels of management
- be more of a generalist than a specialist.

Appointing a project manager in a multi-project environment simplifies the management situation. Top management does not have time to achieve direct control, which means the project manager fulfils the role of coordinator. Also the functional manager's time can be minimized, as project managers can discuss the projects as a whole, and inter-project conflict and priorities are more readily resolved (and in a more independent manner), thus reducing friction between functional managers. In addition, the client feels that the project is important to the organization.

THE PROGRAMME MANAGER

The project manager must have adequate authority to manage the communication needs of SMPs. In some organizations, this is achieved by general managers appointing themselves as project managers, and appointing project coordinators for planning and communication. Another method of operation in large organizations is to appoint project leaders, several layers down the organization, and to appoint a manager or director of projects (sometimes called a programme manager or director – Section 16.2), a higher level, with responsibility for coordinating all projects. Information is passed up the organizational structure to where decisions are made. Both modes of operation illustrate that the role of the project manager and the way information is collected are different in the multi-project environment. The director of projects is responsible for:

- resolving project-related conflicts between senior managers
- directing and evaluating project management activity
- evaluating performance of functional managers and project leaders
- planning, proposing and implementing project management policy
- assuring project compliance with commitments and assessing project progress at major milestones.

This cannot be achieved unless the director of projects is in a fairly senior position. In most multi-project environments, it is also advisable for the programme manager (or director of projects) to appoint an individual who is solely responsible for collecting and analysing information on the individual projects. This may be the role of the Project Support Office (Section 16.6). A fast, simple and consistent mechanism is required if information is to be collected safely. The programme manager will constantly be changing the priorities of projects and the resource allocations, and therefore needs up-to-date information.

21.3 Joint ventures[6]

We shall now consider projects at the other end of the spectrum, i.e. those requiring collaboration between companies. A major project is one that is so complex or of such high risk that no organization can undertake it alone. In reality, most projects require several parties to collaborate in some way. No one organization has all the skills, technologies and services to undertake anything but the smallest of projects on its own. However, the relationship is usually as client and contractor. I shall consider here projects on which two organizations come together in some form of joint venture. There is a range of types of collaboration, from simple contracts to full merger. Joint ventures lie in the middle. The commercial aspects of these relationships are beyond the scope of this book. Here I shall describe the characteristic of joint ventures, why organizations enter into them, and how to manage them as projects to maximize success.

Characteristic of joint ventures

It is indicative of the complexity of joint ventures and the breadth of cooperative arrangements, that simple definitions are rarely attempted. When they are, they tend to reflect the writer's own interest. There are several types of strategic cooperative arrangement:

1. *Supply contract* is the simplest. A detailed specification of exactly what is required is drawn up, tendered for by a number of organizations, any one of which can meet the client's requirements, and once the contract is fulfilled all formal connection ceases.
2. *Vertical integration* is an arrangement in which a firm, recognizing the benefits of one supplier over all others, enters into a long-term arrangement. Marks and Spencer has this with many suppliers, and it is increasingly happening in manufacturing, in particular in the motor industry, where Just-In-Time, quality control and subcontracting of several inputs through a small number of coordinating suppliers is becoming the norm. A degree of managerial interrelationship becomes important, and strategic business decisions by both supplier and purchaser begin to be influenced by the contracts between them.

3. *Joint ventures* come next and follow from recognition that each party has something that the other needs, perhaps not of equal importance but of such significance that it is in both parties' interests to ensure longer term cooperation between them. This relationship will be central to the corporate strategy of each company and one of the most important ways of achieving the mission. The emphasis is on defining objectives for the business as a whole, rather than at the project or product level, which is dealt with by short- or long-term supply arrangements.
4. *Mergers* is where two companies become one, the ultimate cooperative arrangement, and may be entered into as a merger, or as the result of a successful joint venture. The decision to merge depends on the degree of common interest. Two companies with widely differing product portfolios may find that, in one particular area, the future lies in a joint venture, but that they have little common interest elsewhere. Where the majority of business sectors they both serve is common, a merger becomes viable. A takeover, friendly or otherwise, arises from the recognition of business fit by one or both parties, where the size and power of one is usually much greater than the other.

This range of collaborative arrangements suggests the essential features of joint ventures.

1. They require two or more autonomous parties to work together.
2. They rely heavily on mutual trust, understanding and assistance.
3. They have a complex managerial and technical structure that can be difficult to get right.
4. They should not be of indefinite length, but should be entered into to achieve a clearly identified business purpose.
5. They require each party to reveal its covert objectives, so any incompatibilities can be resolved at the formation stage.
6. They should be of significant importance within the corporate strategy of each party, and should be championed at senior executive level.

Business objectives served by joint ventures

There are many reasons for entering joint ventures. In the manufacturing and service industries a marketing view[7] gives the following objectives:

- to acquire new means of manufacture and distribution
- to penetrate and understand new markets
- to acquire new skills
- to achieve vertical integration of existing products
- to expand existing product lines
- to avoid cyclical or seasonal instability.

In the construction industry, joint ventures may be entered for more operational reasons,[8] such as:

- combining of resources or specialist skills
- sharing of loading requirements (optimizing resource scheduling)
- satisfying government requirements for local participation in international ventures
- sharing of risk
- increasing the likelihood of tender success
- acquiring political muscle.

Project management aspects of joint ventures

Joint ventures may be formed specifically to implement one project. However, joint ventures, whatever their purpose, should be treated as projects requiring all the attributes and skills normally associated with the management of change (Chapters 4 and 5), including:

- introducing change
- pitfalls
- communication
- human resource management
- structure
- decision making.

INTRODUCING CHANGE

It should be apparent by now that joint ventures institute change in the parties to the venture. This change arises from corporate decision making at the highest level, which means that the communication of the change and purpose of the venture should be dealt with in the same way as with other changes in corporate strategy, and all sponsors of the joint venture should attach sufficient importance to it at board level, and should ensure that adequate support and resources are allocated to enable the change to take place.

PITFALLS

Reasons why joint ventures fail may include[9]:

- the parties could not get along at executive level
- managers within the joint venture could not work together, or with the owners' or sponsors' managers

- the market disappeared, or benefits promised from or anticipated by one or more parties were not as expected
- owners could not get their people to deliver what had been promised to the joint venture
- partners reneged on their promises to deliver
- other reasons destroyed the partners' cooperative spirit.

COMMUNICATION

Successful joint ventures rely upon adequate communication across two interfaces:

1. *Across boundaries between the parties, at all levels where an interface exists*: recognizing interfaces is crucial, and enabling fruitful communication at each point is part of the project management of the venture. Taking conscious steps to limit the number of interfaces is a legitimate way of controlling the process; this may require the change of reporting paths within the parties.
2. *Through the functional structure of each party*: the existence, effects and benefits of the venture must be communicated from the outset. These should be monitored to ensure that the purpose is being assimilated and that the joint venture is being adequately served by individuals who may be allocated only part time to the venture. The purpose of the venture must be assimilated positively at the level of the individual, where performance, training and career progression reviews used in general and project management should apply.

HUMAN RESOURCE MANAGEMENT

Joint ventures offer an opportunity for changes in people management. Personnel are a resource, and joint ventures pool resources. This creates a more comprehensive resource pool, with more strength in some key skills, or offering the chance to reduce the total number of people employed, where the parties to the venture each employed more people than necessary. This reduces the number, but increases the quality and spread of knowledge and skills; indeed, especially in IT and other knowledge-based ventures, this may be a fundamental objective of the venture. This has implications for personnel management and training. Depending upon the depth of integration, the training programmes of each party can be rationalized to meet the needs of the venture, while still servicing those functions that are not affected by it. Where the venture leads to full integration through a merger, the training programmes and human resource planning should also fully integrate.

Personnel can play a key role in explaining the purpose of the joint venture to those people directly affected by its activities, and to those who remain within the parent companies. They must ensure that jealousy does not arise between those for whom the venture offers an opportunity for career advancement, and those whose work is unaffected by it. Conversely, those who join the venture must see a benefit, or at least no detriment, to their position. Activities of staff appraisal, such as career mapping, target setting, and performance review, need to be addressed for the joint venture personnel. It may be important that all those involved, from whichever party to the venture, are treated equally. This is bound to require changes in personnel procedures in one or more of the parties to the venture. This then begs the question: should the changes become company wide, to avoid any perceived inequality of treatment between *joint venture* and *original company* personnel within each party to the venture?

STRUCTURE

There are two broad categories of joint venture[9]:

1. **Integrated**   The parties agree their contributions to the project beforehand, then come together at all levels to achieve its purpose.
2. **Non-integrated**   The parties form a separate, semi-autonomous business entity to carry out the project, negotiating resources from the sponsor parties or purchasing them elsewhere as necessary.

The choices are either to maintain the existing structures of the parties more or less as they are, and allow joint venture to be carried out within them through close communication and cooperation of staff within the companies, or to create a new vehicle especially for the purposes of carrying out the joint venture. The benefits of the first approach are:

– speed of inception
– simplification of agreements
– minimizing the needs for transferring or hiring staff
– termination can be easier
– control by senior management is greater
– there is no danger of the joint venture competing with the original partners' businesses;

and of the second approach are:

– the purpose of the venture cannot get lost within the existing organization
– individuals recruited to the joint venture are totally aligned with and allocated to the venture

- the venture company can be given a broad degree of autonomy with its own set of objectives
- communication between the venture company and the parties that formed it is highly focused and restricted to executive level.

There may be difficulties in integrating two management structures.[10] Many international mergers fail to achieve effective management because systems are not truly merged: the original independent companies remain independent, even competitive. Would it not be better to leave the two companies independent, and achieve cooperation through better, more narrowly defined ventures? Conflict often arises in Japanese ventures with foreign partners and is the biggest reason for failure of those ventures.[10] Conflict occurred in a large number of partnerships formed in the 1960s to gain entry to Japan for Western technology. The terms were generally unfavourable to the Japanese who accepted them to gain the technology. When the oil crisis in the late 1970s resulted in large losses, there was great argument about who should bear them. Venture agreements that spelt out a profit-sharing mechanism failed to legislate for losses. The joint ventures terminated, largely to Japanese satisfaction, and they went their way having achieved their goal of amassing Western expertise. We know the story from then on. Three principle lessons to be learned are:

1. Successful agreements should be fair to both sides.
2. The agreement should take account of possible disasters like loss making, insolvency or takeover of one of the partners.
3. A time limit for the operation of the joint venture should be set, or at least a definition of the conditions under which it no longer becomes viable should be attempted.

The last item is difficult to achieve because a joint venture requires total commitment; any clause that appears to give one or other party a *let out* will weaken and undermine the agreement when problems arise.

DECISION TAKING

Decision taking is crucial, and must be regulated by clearly defined clauses in any agreements. This may be through shareholding structure, the issue of voting shares, or statements regarding who takes responsibility for certain decisions. However:

> majority voting seldom represents good business and seldom favours entrepreneurial decisions. Joint ventures tend to vote on critical matters in proportion to their equity holding. You can safely conclude that if a voting process is needed to decide critical matters, the joint venture has already failed.[10]

This might seem a little severe, but it alludes to the need not to allow a crisis to be reached where voting one party down is necessary to move forward. Concensus decision based on a common and thorough understanding and the will to accommodate make for much better joint venture decisions. Hence, the structured communication of situations and analysis using problem-solving techniques offer a project management approach that is preferable.

The future

Analysis of current affairs demonstrates the increasing use of joint ventures and other cooperative arrangements. This is due in no small part to the coming single European market as a result of continuing rationalization of European industry, and the desire of non-EC (particularly American, Scandinavian and Japanese) companies to take a stake in the market. These ventures will have far-reaching social, political and economic consequences on a world scale, as we move into the next century.

21.4 Summary

1. There are three categories of project by size:
   - *small to medium*: one owner, shared resources
   - *large*: one owner, dedicated resource pool
   - *major*: several owners, dedicated resource pool.
2. Because of their size, small to medium projects are often given inadequate management attention, and are assigned to more junior managers. However, the cumulative risk across a programme of projects can often be high. The effective management of the multi-project environment requires:
   - procedures for prioritizing projects in accordance with business objectives
   - clearly identified responsibilities for setting and reviewing the priority of projects
   - effective programme management systems
   - effective project management information systems.
3. There are four groups associated with programmes of projects who must remain distinct:
   - programme management
   - individual project management
   - project control
   - functional management.

4. The role of the project manager on small to medium projects is to:
   - be a coordinator rather than a manager
   - be able to set priorities between projects
   - be more of a risk taker
   - develop good, simple reporting systems and procedures
   - have good client liaison
   - deal with higher levels of management
   - be more of a generalist than a specialist.
5. The role of the programme director is to:
   - resolve project-related conflicts between senior managers
   - direct and evaluating project management activity
   - evaluate project performance of functional department managers and project leaders
   - plan, propose and implement project management policy and information systems
   - assure compliance with commitments and assess project progress at major milestones.
6. There are several types of collaborative arrangements including:
   - supply contract
   - vertical integration
   - joint ventures
   - mergers.
7. A marketing view gives the following reasons for entering a joint venture:
   - to acquire new means of manufacture and distribution
   - to penetrate and understand new markets
   - to acquire new skills
   - to achieve vertical integration of existing products
   - to expand existing product lines
   - to avoid cyclical or seasonal instability.
8. An operational view gives the following reasons:
   - combining of resources or specialist skills
   - sharing of loading requirements (optimizing resource scheduling)
   - satisfying government requirements for local participation in international ventures
   - sharing of risk
   - increasing the likelihood of tender success
   - acquiring political muscle.
9. The attributes required by the manager of a joint venture include:
   - introducing change
   - avoiding pitfalls
   - communication
   - human resource management

 - managing structure
 - taking decisions.

Notes and references

1. Morris, P. W. G. and Hough, G. H., *The Anatomy of Major Projects: A study of the reality of project management*, Wiley, 1987.
2. Section 21.2 incorporates material written by Debbie Carlton.
3. Turner, J. R., 'Company resource planning in the food processing industry', in *Proceedings of the 12th INTERNET International Expert Seminar* (ed. S. Dworatschek), INTERNET, 1988.
4. Dworatschek, S., 'The big problem of small projects', in *Proceedings of the 12th INTERNET International Expert Seminar* (ed. S. Dworatschek), INTERNET, 1988.
5. Gareis, R. (ed.), *The Handbook of Management by Projects*, Mohr, 1990.
6. Section 21.3 incorporates material written by David Topping.
7. Walmsley, J., *Handbook of International Joint Ventures*, Graham and Trotman, 1982.
8. Armitt, J. A., 'Joint ventures – formation and operation', in *Management of International Construction Projects*, Thomas Telford, 1984.
9. Harrigan, K., *Managing for Joint Venture Success*, Lexington, 1986.
10. Ohmae, K., *The Coming Shape of Global Competition*, Free Press, 1985.

22
International projects

22.1 Introduction[1]

This, final, chapter will consider a special kind of project – that involving collaboration between two countries – and discuss the cultural differences that can arise between the collaborating nations. In particular, we shall consider projects funded by foreign aid in developing nations. These projects seem to highlight the cultural differences and, as a result, have a high rate of failure, almost always being more costly, more time consuming and less profitable than originally envisaged[2] (Example 22.1). For 30 years, people have tried to find an answer to this problem, but projects have continued to fail, with an increasing opposition from both sides to further projects: the funding nations feel that the money given and the goodwill extended is misused and misinterpreted; the receiving countries feel that the money they so bitterly need demands intolerable adjustments to meet the terms and conditions set by donor country, which seriously conflicts with their own way of thinking, living and performing.

An example of an aid project of this kind is the Jamaica Maritime Training Institute Project, which has lasted for more than 13 years with Norwegian aid money. The project was originally planned for two to three years. However, as the project neared its original end date, local job opportunities for Jamaican staff were limited. Hence, they were concerned about their future, so had no desire to complete the project. This was also well understood by the local authorities. The prevailing prognosis, after 13 years of project work, is that at least another five to seven years of work are needed before the original goal, as it was formulated, can be reached. This does not even include the development of a counterpart staff professional enough to take over all necessary administrative and technical responsibilities!

Example 22.1 A foreign aid 'failure'

Recent research has indicated that the problem lies in creating a project strategy and setting the project in its context.[3,4] The donor and recipient countries may have:

- different objectives for the project arising from a different view of the recipient country's need
- different views of who the owner of the project is.

Different objectives

Projects are undertaken in developing nations for three conflicting reasons:

- as a vehicle for economic development
- to provide employment
- as a tool for management development.

At first sight, the first two may seem to be compatible; the first creates the second. However, the first requires project to provide good financial return for the investors, and that requires the right products to be produced at lowest cost, which often leads to the use of capital-intensive, high technology. However, for the recipient nation it may be socially, economically and culturally desirable to use labour-intensive processes to create employment for growing populations, to conserve foreign reserves, and to protect the cultural heritage. The project itself also provides employment, as described in Example 22.1, which works against its early, efficient completion. The need of developing nations to use projects as a vehicle for management development works against both the other objectives. Donor nations would like to use their own experienced managers, but Third World countries must use projects to develop efficient, wise management.[5]

Different view of the owner

The donor country views itself as sponsor, and primary decision taker; the recipient country view itself as owner, and the donor country as merely a funding agency. The donor country's desire to be primary decision taker may even be viewed as neo-colonialism. However, a greater problem arises through the cultural differences between the two countries, which may mean they take a radically different approach to managing projects. The donor nation often tries to impose its approach, because it has greater experience of project management, but that may not be appropriate in the cultural environment of the recipient nation, and indeed the recipient nation is best able to decide its own best interests. It also conflicts with the recipient nation's need to develop its own managers.

22.2 The problem of cultural fit

The different views of need and ownership just described create three problems of cultural fit on international projects:

– the problem of organization
– the problem of effectiveness versus efficiency
– the problem of close-out.

The problem of organization

It has previously been shown that certain organizational structures and planning procedures seem to support effective project management better than others, and certain information and communications systems seem to be more effective at achieving objectives that satisfy both the project and the parent organization.

Part Four described how a project is undertaken by managing four stages of the project management life cycle. Effective project management has all four stages under the control of one company or organization. This enables that company to set the basic rules for developing the right type of project organization, with particular emphasis on convincing all levels of management of the advantages of, and the necessities for, proper project management. The role of a project manager is far more than that of a middle manager in a traditional, functional organization, but this is seldom fully recognized by higher levels of management. Project managers find themselves under constant pressure not only to deliver results, but to deliver results that require extensive internal cooperation and high-level approval. Projects by nature demand change, and often senior management initially accept the importance of these changes, but when the execution of the project requires them to change their traditional roles, they refuse to cooperate because they find the new situation threatening.

This is particularly prevalent in developing countries. Too many projects have been initiated with the best of intentions from all parties involved, but have faltered because the project managers, or senior management, have not established a workable organization with adequate definition of responsibility combined with proper lines of communication. In environments where the participants have different values, different frames of references, different standards and cultural norms, and even different languages, these problems can quickly be magnified.

The problem of effectiveness versus efficiency

The importance of understanding cultural difference in performing projects in developing countries is well known, but the practical implications have not been widely recognized. The main reason is a problem of *measurement*. While money, goods and labour are readily measured, the change in cultural factors such as motivation, communication and leadership performance are more difficult to assess. However, without understanding how to develop metrics for the latter, the former is very difficult to influence. Since it is generally assumed that a sound society should be *effective* – that is, function according to its objectives – the purpose of administration must be to ensure that higher performance and effectiveness are obtained to achieve these objectives.

Effectiveness is the term used when describing private and public activities, but it is not easy to define (see Sections 1.2 and 19.4). Productivity is an easier parameter to observe, defined as the quantitative relation between outcome of production against input of resource. The output is either goods or services, specified in terms of quantity or measurable quality. The use of resources can be expressed as work, services, raw materials, equipment, plants and financial resources, measured in financial terms.

In the West, productivity is widely accepted as a central factor in fuelling economic growth, creating surpluses for increased living standards and combating inflation. However, productivity must be given a simple, commonly understood measurement if it is to be evaluated as a factor for economic growth; its measurement must be good enough to establish wage and income distribution policies, determine cost and price levels, and identify investment and training needs in particular sectors. The more complex an environment, as in development projects, the more difficult it is to attribute productivity measures to particular projects, as they can often mean different things to different people in different contexts.

Since high productivity can only exist in a supportive environment, project strategies in developing countries must ensure that the prevailing conditions for productive development exist. One shortcoming of the project teams of both the donor and recipient countries may be an inability to mobilize, allocate and manage financial, material and human resources against mutually acceptable productivity measures.[6] The West's models promote planned structural changes and procedural effectiveness. However, this can often lead to fatal misconceptions about what should constitute proper measures of project success in different cultures, and to a consistent failure to check whether local capacities match the requirements for project execution.

The problem of close-out

In developing countries it is often difficult to predict how the people working on the project will be employed after the project is completed. In organizations and cultures where projects are part of well-defined total strategies, this is less of a problem since the parent organization can usually cater for the released manpower from recently completed projects. However, this is not the case for development projects taking place in the Third World, where the end objective may in fact be unclear, and where the parent organization does not really exist within the country, but is imported from the funding country. In these situations, the staff are only employed for the duration of the project and there is no parent organization to return to on completion of the project. The problem is exacerbated if the economy of the country is weak and so there are only a limited number of job opportunities, which is generally the case in developing countries. Indeed, this is true even in Western countries at times of high unemployment.

22.3 Obtaining cultural fit

These cultural differences must be better understood if project performance in developing countries is to be improved in the future. Modern project management is a problem-solving tool developed in the West, and then adopted world wide. Since projects seem to fail so often in developing nations, it is natural to ask if this western technique is appropriate for controlling Third World development. The work of Hofstede[7] may provide an insight into the approach of different cultures to project management. He surveyed national differences in terms of four parameters:

- *power distance*: the extent to which the less powerful person in a society accepts inequality in power and considers it as normal
- *individualism*: the extent to which individuals primarily look after their own interest and the interest of their immediate family (husband, wife, children)
- *masculinity*: the extent to which the biological existence of two sexes is used to define different roles for men and women
- *uncertainty avoidance*: the extent to which people are nervous of situations they consider to be unstructured, unpredictable, or unclear, and the extent to which they try to avoid such situations by adopting strict codes of behaviour and a belief in absolute truths.

Cultural profile of countries

Hofstede surveyed 27 countries from 10 regions. Extracts of his findings are plotted in Figures 22.1 and 22.2. In these figures, the regions and countries are represented by the codes shown in Table 22.1.[7] In Figure 22.1, the obvious pattern is that the Third World countries tend to separate

Table 22.1   Regions and countries surveyed by Hofstede

Code	Region	Constituent countries (if relevant)
ARA	Arab countries	Egypt, Lebanon, Libya, Iraq, Kuwait, Saudi, UAE
DEN	Denmark	
EAF	East Africa	Kenya, Ethiopia, Zambia
FRA	France	
GBR	Great Britain	
GER	Germany	
ITA	Italy	
JAP	Japan	
MAL	Malaysia	
NET	Netherlands	
NOR	Norway	
PHI	Philippines	
SWE	Sweden	
THA	Thailand	
USA	United States	
WAF	West Africa	Nigeria, Ghana, Sierra Leone
YUG	Yugoslavia	

from the wealthy countries. The former are in the first quadrant, implying a greater respect for authority and society than in wealthy countries. In Figure 22.2, wealthy countries and Third World countries are found in all four quadrants of the diagram, meaning that 'masculinity/femininity' and 'uncertainty avoidance' are unrelated to national wealth.

Cultural 'profile' or project management

We can then consider what cultural approach is appropriate at different stages of a project. Jessen[3] surveyed 60 projects from three continents, and

Table 22.2   Preferred cultural approach, and assumed attitude scores, at each stage of the project management life cycle

Trait	Feasibility	Design	Execution	Close-out
Power distance	High (7.5)	Low (2.5)	Low (2.5)	High (7.5)
Individualism	High (7.5)	Medium (5.0)	Medium (5.0)	Low (2.5)
Masculinity	Medium (5.0)	Medium (5.0)	Medium (5.0)	Medium (5.0)
Uncertainty avoidance	Low (2.5)	Medium (5.0)	Medium (5.0)	High (7.5)

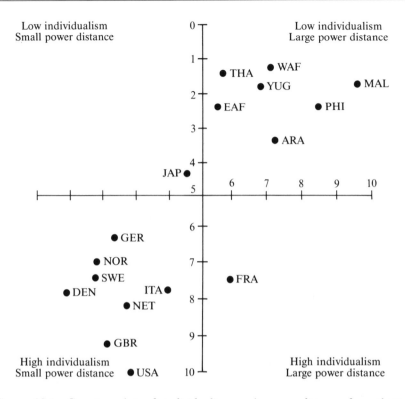

Figure 22.1 Country plot of *individualism* and *power distance* for selected countries, according to the cultural trait model
Source: Hofstede, 1984.

derived the conclusions shown in Table 22.2. He showed that attitude scores vary throughout the project management life cycle.

1. During initiation, *power distance* should be high, as this is when the manager must give priority to the requirements and direction of top management (or the client); *individualism* should also be high, as there is a need for creativity and innovative thinking during this stage; *uncertainty avoidance* should be low, as feasibility demands the ability to think in new directions and uncover new solutions, which often means risk, change and unpredictability.

2. During planning and execution the picture changes: *power distance* should be low, as the people who do the work should also be responsible for planning and executing it (Chapter 5). The main purpose of planning and execution is to ensure that the prescribed goals will be achieved,

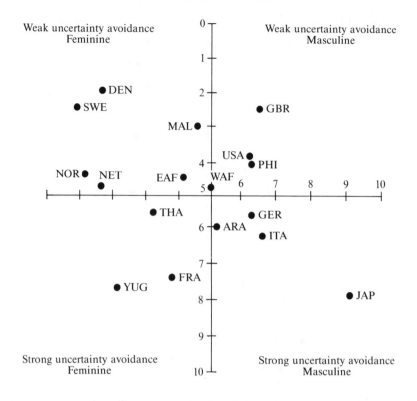

Figure 22.2 Country plot of *uncertainty avoidance* and *masculinity* for selected countries, according to the cultural trait model
Source: Hofstede, 1984.

and the project team are the best people to decide the method of achieving it.

3. During close-out attitudes should change again: *power distance* should be high, as evaluation of the work done and results obtained are the responsibility of top management, not only because they are able to evaluate the work objectively, but also because they are able to view the project in its wider context; *individualism* should be low for the same reason; *uncertainty avoidance* should be high, as the termination of the project needs to be a well-structured process (Chapter 15), ending with the achievement of the project's objectives and ensuing benefits. Furthermore, the project team may feel insecure about the future, and so the manager should aim to maximize their security.

Table 22.3 Country ranking of fitness for project management

Rank	Country	Region	Initiation Score	Planning Score	Execution Score	Termination Score	Total Score
1	Germany	N. Europe	6.10	2.17	2.17	2.49	12.93
2	Italy	S. Europe	5.56	3.86	3.86	2.43	15.71
3	France	S. Europe	5.10	4.80	4.80	3.61	18.31
4	USA	USA	5.23	5.03	5.03	4.28	19.57
5	Netherlands	N. Europe	5.89	4.66	4.66	4.44	19.65
6	Norway	Scandinavia	6.70	4.28	4.28	5.09	20.35
7	Gt Britain	N. Europe	5.45	5.12	5.12	5.26	20.95
8	Arab Countries	Middle East	5.48	5.11	5.11	6.49	22.19
9	East Africa	E. Africa	6.07	4.57	4.57	7.13	22.38
10	Sweden	Scandinavia	6.57	5.17	5.17	6.41	23.32
11	Denmark	Scandinavia	7.18	5.15	5.15	6.44	23.92
12	Japan	N. Asia	8.10	5.48	5.48	5.62	24.68
13	Thailand	S.E. Asia	7.43	5.16	5.16	7.43	25.18
14	West Africa	W. Africa	6.74	5.91	5.91	8.21	26.77
15	Philippines	S.E. Asia	5.59	6.80	6.80	8.73	27.92
16	Yugoslavia	E. Europe	8.17	6.58	6.58	7.67	29.00
17	Malaysia	S.E. Asia	6.07	7.93	7.93	10.04	31.97

Project management values and national cultures

Overlaying Table 22.2 onto Figures 22.1 and 22.2 provides some insight into why project management has varying success in different cultures (Figures 22.3 and 22.4). The results are summarized in Table 22.3, giving a ranking for each country's fitness for project management. The scores at each stage are obtained by taking the square root of the sum of the squares between the country score for each of the four parameters, and those recommended for that stage.

As expected, the table shows that project management is typically a Western approach to problem solving. It is probably also not surprising that Germany is top of the list; their very systematic industrial approach could well have been the model for the initial development of project management in the United States in the early 1950s. Arab countries and East Africa are, however, also in the upper half of the list, showing either an in-built ability in these cultures to use the project approach, or a very strong and perhaps forced implementation of project management in these countries by Western cultures, which may have directly affected their behaviour.

Most European countries fit into the accepted mould for project management, having the right structural tools for systematic planning, organizing

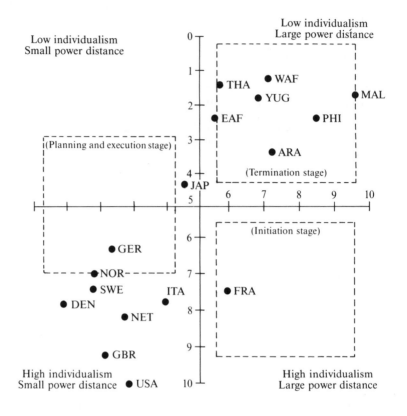

Figure 22.3 Country plot against Hofstede's cultural factors *power distance* and *individualism* against assumed preferred behavioural attitude scores within each project stage
Source: Hofstede, 1984.

and executing projects. They have self-confidence (high individualism) for taking on challenging tasks and doing them independently (low power distance), and accepting and fighting risks (low uncertainty avoidance). Their weakness occurs during start-up and termination, when it is necessary to ensure that the organization is doing the right projects, and ensuring that the completion of the project results in the required benefits.

Scandinavian countries, which often regard project management as typifying their cultures, score fairly lowly. They are well known for managing nearly everything through projects, with the result that organizations have far more projects than they have resources to handle, and large files of projects almost never terminated.

The United States, which invented the concept of project management

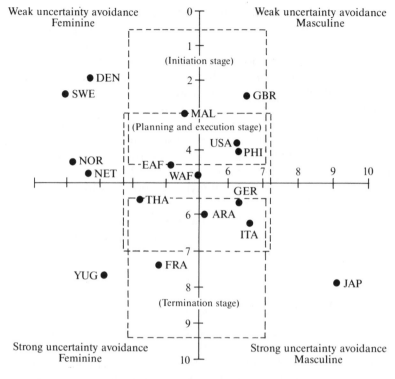

Figure 22.4 Country plot against Hofstede's cultural factors *uncertainty avoidance* and *masculinity* against assumed preferred behavioural attitude scores within each project stage
Source: Hofstede, 1984.

40 years ago, scores well in both diagrams, but their small power distance, and their high acceptance of risk, expressed as weak uncertainty avoidance, could result in weak project termination, implying unnecessary time and cost overruns.

Japan seems not to fit the project profile particularly well in any diagram, being too masculine, having too strong an uncertainty avoidance, and lacking a profile that triggers project initiation, planning and execution. As we know this has not prevented powerful industrial development in that country. It is probably also not so remarkable that the project approach is less used in Japan. Instead they prefer approaches such as production programming and quality circles which fit more with their cultural preferences, and are the backbones of their success.

Third World countries score fairly low on many of the described project management features, Indeed, these are the same factors for which they are often criticized by Western aid providers. However, they score fairly well on project initiation, and they have a good balance between femininity and masculinity. Furthermore, their balanced uncertainty avoidance is a great advantage during project planning and execution. Here their fit is much better than, for instance, the Scandinavian countries.

Finally, we can also look for a match in project performance between pairs of countries. This provides quite interesting comparisons. For instance, the USA and Great Britain get very high score values in Africa, the Middle East and South East Asia, and, surprisingly, the host country also acts as teaching agent with their greater ability at project initiation. It is also surprising that the Scandinavian countries, which in Hofstede's analysis came out with very much the same cultural profile, seem to behave quite differently when compared on the different project phases. Norway, for instance, performs very well at project planning and execution in East Africa, while Sweden seems to be much better off in the Middle East.

22.4 An attitude of mind

Hence, contrary to the common belief that the Western-oriented techniques of project management are just straightforward procedures that anyone can learn and implement, there are considerable cross-cultural problems in using the approach in non-Western countries. Usually, insufficient focus is given to the fact that project management is not just a technique; it is an attitude of mind. Project management originated in Western countries, and its popularity has been steadily growing, but the outcomes have not always been in line with the expectations, particularly in developing countries. Traditionally this has been explained as weakness in the local human resources, and the remedy being more training in the different mechanics of project execution, often in a Western setting. However, the reason for poor project performance may well be a weak understanding of local needs by Western countries, particularly needs beyond the project scope which are hard to articulate and define in Western terminology. Furthermore, many Western cultures are weak in both the project initiation and the project termination phases, due to their individualistic attitudes towards authority, risk and challenge, and quality of life. In summary, in spite of its increasing popularity and widespread appeal, the many pros and cons of the project approach should be given serious consideration before implementing it. In particularly, the following two issues should be addressed:

1. The project concept is based on a limited resource effort, laid out in a staged development. Each stage has its own distinguishing characteristics requiring a unique attitude; from the creative, strategy-oriented and holistic approach in the early stages, to the very formal, tightly controlled and administrative-oriented performance necessary towards the end of the project.
2. Even though the project approach originated in Western cultures, these cultures are not necessarily the best ones for staffing and directing all stages of a project's phases, particularly in developing countries. It could be quite educating for Western cultures to honour alternative approaches to problem solving and execution, particularly where other cultural attitudes in fact present the better project performance.

22.5 Summary

1. Projects in developing nations funded by foreign aid have a high rate of failure. The reason is probably a different cultural approach to project management by donor and recipient nations.
2. Developing nations undertake projects as a vehicle for economic development, and as a tool for management development. Donor and recipient nations give different weightings to these developments. Projects:
   - provide employment
   - ensure that skilled people are used effectively
   - drive an increase in productivity
   - train future managers.
3. There are three problems associated with cultural fit between donor and recipient nations, related to the project life cycle:
   - the donor government will view itself as the parent organization, and yet does not take a long-term view about continuing operations in the recipient nation
   - efficiency will be deemed more important than effectiveness in assessing success of the project, because the former is more readily measurable
   - the economy of the recipient nation may not be able to provide employment to project personnel on close-out.
4. The culture of countries has been measured in terms of four parameters:
   - power distance
   - individualism
   - masculinity
   - uncertainty avoidance.

5. These four parameters are of differing importance throughout the project life cycle. Comparing country profiles to the project profile reinforces the view that project management is a Western approach to problem solving. However, some recipient countries may be better suited to project initiation than donor countries, for the reason that the former cultures value greater certainty. There is also a better match between some pairs of countries than others.

Notes and references

1. The material in this chapter is adapted from a paper written by Dr Svein Arne Jessen for inclusion in the distance learning material at Henley Management College. The content is based on his analysis on projects in developing countries. Dr Jessen is an Associate Professor of Project Management at the Norwegian School of Management. He has previously worked as a consultant and manager on international aid projects which are his current areas of research.
2. Jessen, S.A. and Rist, R., *Jamaica Maritime Training Institute, Project Review 9 January–9 February 1988, Final Report*. NORINDECO A/S, 1988.
3. Jessen, S.A., 'Some reflections on project performance in developing countries', in *Proceedings of the 9th World Congress on Project Management* (ed. D. Gower), INTERNET, 1988.
4. Barley, S.R., 'Semiotics and the study of occupational and organizational cultures', *The Administrative Science Quarterly*, **28**, 1983.
5. Rodinelly, D.A., *Planning Development Projects*, PhD Thesis, Syracuse University, 1977.
6. Caiden, N. and Wildausky, A., *Planning and Budgeting in Poor Countries*, Wiley, 1974.
7. Hofstede, G., 'The cultural relativity of the quality of life concept', *Academy of Management Review*, **9** (3), 389–98, 1984.

Epilogue

In Chapter 5, I described pitfalls of project management, common management mistakes (as opposed to risks inherent in the work itself). From them, I derived five principles of good project management. I end by summarizing the five principles, and presenting the inverse of the pitfalls as profiles of success.

Principles of project management

The five principles of good project management are:

1. *Manage through structured work or product breakdown*   The objectives are:

   - to delegate responsibility
   - to define the scope
   - to isolate risk
   - to isolate changes.

2. *Focus on results*   Determine what to achieve, not how to achieve it, with the objective:

   - to control scope
   - to give a flexible, but robust plan (using rolling-wave planning).

3. *Balance objectives through the breakdown structure*   Provide a balance:

   - between areas of technology
   - between technology and culture (people, systems and organization).

4. *Negotiate a contract between the parties involved*   All project planning is a process of negotiation:

   - between the owner and contractor
   - between the project team members
   - through bipartite discussion
   - by trading benefits for contributions.

5. *Adopt clear and simple management reporting structures*   Use single-page reporting, nested through the breakdown structure, to give:

- visibility
- clarity
- commitment.

Profiles for success

The four profiles for success are:

1. *Foundation*

    - align the project with the business
    - gain the commitment of your boss and involved managers
    - create shared vision, a sense of mission.

2. *Planning*

    - use multiple levels, through a breakdown structure
    - use simple friendly tools, one sheet per level
    - encourage creativity, by delegating to experts through results
    - estimate realistically.

3. *Organizing and implementing*

    - negotiate resource availability
    - agree cooperation
    - define management responsibility
    - gain commitment of resource providers, through the shared mission
    - define channels of communication.

4. *Controlling*

    - integrate plans and reports
    - formalize the review process, through defined intervals, defined agenda, defined criteria, and controlled attendance
    - use your sources of authority as a project manager.

Subject index

Author and source index

Authors and their affiliations, books, journals and other sources

Proprietary methodologies, software and suppliers

Project index

Examples and companies

Types and industries

Fast moving consumer goods, 163, 459
Food, 47, 158, 366, 387, 406–414, 459, 498

Government, 37, 459

Information systems *or* technology, 25, 56, 83, 88, 94, 103–108, 127–132, 142, 160–163, 174–177, 182–196, 205, 291, 344, 367–370, 387, 398, 429
Infrastructure, 38, 77, 160, 189, 303, 354–355, 387, 459, 483–484
International, 71, 499–501

Leisure, 458–459

Management development (*see* Organizational development *and* Training)
Manufacturing, 3, 64, 160–177, 344, 358–360, 366
Mining, 459
Multi-disciplinary, 127–132

Nuclear, 77, 125, 242, 250

Location

Adriatic, 250
Africa, 510
Austria, 40

Baltics, 40
Benelux, 40, 110
Billingham, 250, 397
Birmingham, 83
Britain, 40, 57, 77, 242, 427, 504–510

Denmark, 300, 504–509
Dublin, 409

East Africa, 504–510
England, 57, 67
Egypt, 372, 504–509
Ethiopia, 504–509
Europe, 110, 406, 496, 508–510

Far East, 507–510
France, 40, 57–58, 77, 427, 504–509

Organizational development, 25, 88, 103, 108, 128–132, 160–166, 177, 187–195, 239, 344, 360–365, 409, 486, 500, 511

Petrochemical, 105, 186–194, 285, 392, 459
Power generation, 4, 10, 160, 459, 466
Process, 64, 459, 466
Product development, 360, 437–441

Research and development, 25, 103, 161–166, 190, 254, 431, 438–457, 470

Shipbuilding, 4–5, 11, 103, 113, 163, 290, 393
Service, 164, 457, 458–459, 492
Software development, 25–27, 213, 239, 275–276, 333, 344, 360, 387, 474–481
Space, 5, 354–360

Total quality, 23–24
Training, 4, 26–27, 108, 132, 187, 344, 360, 459

Geneva, 57
Germany, 40, 250, 427, 504–509
Ghana, 504–509

Hampshire, 57
Harpenden, 153
Holland, 110

Iberia, 40
Iraq, 504–509
Israel, 67, 406
Italy, 40, 173, 250, 504–509

Jamaica, 499, 512
Japan, 160–170, 495–496, 504–510

Kent, 55–58
Kenya, 504–509
Kuwait, 504–509

Lebanon, 504–509